tine

MESOPOTAMIA (IRAQ)
TRANSJORDAN

Weihaiwei

ARABIA

THE INDIAN EMPIRE

Trucial Coast

Kuria Muria

Aden

Sokotra

Laccadives

Andaman I

Hong Kong

BRITISH SOMALILAND

CEYLON

MALAYA

Singapore

N. BORNEO

BRUNEI

SARAWAK

E. AFRICAN PROT. (KENYA)

Maldives

Seychelles

NEW GUINEA

Gilbert Is

Baker I

ZANZIBAR

TANGANYIKA

Chagos

Solomon Is

Ellice Is

Phoenix I

Tokelau I

NYASALAND

Cocos or Keeling I

Christmas I

PAPUA

Santa Cruz

W. Samoa

Fiji Is.

Mauritius

AUSTRALIA

Tonga

ZILAND

TOLAND

A

Norfolk I

Lord Howe I

Kermadec I

NEW ZEALAND

Bounty I

The British Empire, as controlled from London

Auckland I.

Antipodes

Campbell I

Self-governing dominions of the British Empire

Macquarie I

Territories newly-won in the 1914–1918 war

45

# THE FALL OF THE BRITISH EMPIRE

*By the same author:*

George V, King and Emperor

# THE FALL OF
# THE BRITISH EMPIRE
## 1918 - 1968

by
COLIN CROSS

HODDER AND STOUGHTON

PRINTED IN GREAT BRITAIN FOR HODDER
AND STOUGHTON LIMITED, ST. PAUL'S HOUSE,
WARWICK LANE, LONDON, E.C.4 BY C. TINLING
AND CO. LIMITED, LIVERPOOL, LONDON AND
PRESCOT

For Michael, Harriet
and Stephen

The author is grateful to Mrs. Bambridge, Methuen and Co. Ltd. and the Macmillan Co. of Canada for permission to quote from verses by Rudyard Kipling: from 'Recessional' and 'Our Lady of the Snows' from *The Five Nations* and from 'The Widow of Windsor' and 'Mandalay' from *Barrack Room Ballads*.

# INTRODUCTION

In telling the history of the British Empire and Commonwealth from 1918 to 1966, the difficulty is to avoid also telling the history of the world. Empire and Commonwealth existed on every continent and were influenced by most things that went on in the world. Even so domestic a matter as American Prohibition had a deep impact upon a British colony, the Bahamas. So I have tried to keep to two fairly simple themes. The first is to describe how the British Empire actually functioned and the second is the sequence of events which led to its virtual disappearance. The histories of the component territories, including Great Britain herself, are relevant only in so far as they affected the Empire and Commonwealth as a whole. Thus the history of India between the wars was of crucial importance to the imperial idea and so I have tried to summarise it at some length. The domestic history of, for example, Australia in the same period was largely irrelevant to the main themes and so is left out. In the same way, the book gives a lopsided account of the Second World War. There is no attempt to retell the history of that war but merely an attempt to relate it to specific imperial considerations. Similarly the narrative is brought up to 1968 not to cover that year in detail but simply to record the final decision to abandon British power outside Europe and thus the very end of the imperial concept.

I have tried to be impartial and to leave it to the reader to decide what was good and what was bad in the old British Empire. The striking thing about it, in my view, is that it ever existed at all.

I would like to thank Miss Judith Bull for her great help in finding the illustrations and the publishers for much patience.

Colin Cross

# CONTENTS

# ILLUSTRATIONS

[1] *Daily Mirror*

[2] M. Sesai—Mansell Collection

[3] United Press International

[4] Massers', Malton

[5] Keystone Press Agency Ltd.

[6] *Radio Times*, Hulton Picture Library

[7] Fox Photos Ltd.

[8] The Associated Press Ltd.

[9] Royal Canadian Air Force

[10] Central Press Photos Ltd.

[11] Camera Press Ltd.

PART I

*High Noon*

# CHAPTER I

# Wider still and wider

EARLY on the morning of November 21, 1918, the light cruiser *Cardiff* steamed out of the Firth of Forth into a grey but clear dawn over the North Sea. About 20 miles out from Scotland she met a gigantic German armada—14 capital ships and 56 smaller vessels of war. Under the terms of the armistice concluded 10 days earlier, the Germans had come to surrender. *Cardiff* signalled to the German ships to form themselves into a single line. Then she led them towards the British coast. An American observer, Rear Admiral Hugh Rodman, afterwards recalled how the scene had reminded him of his old farm home in Kentucky where he had often seen a little child leading a herd of fearsome bullocks.

At May Island, at the mouth of the Firth of Forth, the convoy linked up with the full British Grand Fleet. The Germans must have found it an intimidating sight. The Grand Fleet was the mightiest force in the history of sea warfare. The Commander-in-Chief, Admiral Sir David Beatty, had 19 subordinate admirals flying their flags under him in 36 battleships, eight battlecruisers, 33 cruisers and over 100 destroyers. The white ensigns stretched seemingly endlessly into the morning mist. The only variety in the flags lay in a little squadron of six ships wearing the stars and stripes of the United States of America; few noticed their presence. Beatty marshalled his ships into two parallel straight lines, each six miles long. The Germans steamed between the British lines and then, at a steady 12 knots, the combined fleets cruised into the Firth, the British being ready at any moment to open fire. On arrival at the anchorage, Beatty signalled to the Germans: 'The German flag will be hauled down at sunset today, Thursday, and will not be hoisted again without permission.'

It looked like total and overwhelming victory at sea, the element which the British had traditionally regarded as their own. The vigorous and modern Imperial German Navy had represented the most serious apparent threat to the world-wide British Empire, dependent on its sea communications. Although naval rivalry between Britain and Germany had not been the actual cause of war in 1914, it had contributed towards a sense of antagonism between the two countries and had provided a context in which war was eagerly prosecuted.

The surrender at the Firth of Forth meant that Britain now faced no serious rival at sea. The British Empire could be considered safe from outside attack.

The war had brought gains, too, in the form of new imperial territories. In Africa, British and imperial troops had conquered South-West Africa, the territory which became Tanganyika and parts of Togoland and Cameroon. In the Middle East, Mesopotamia and Palestine had come under British rule. There was an idea of taking over Persia, too. In the Far East had been won German New Guinea and about a hundred Pacific islands. These newly-acquired territories were of an area totalling about 988,000 square miles—over eight times the area of Great Britain herself. The new population totalled about 13 million, varying from sophisticated Arabs in Bagdad to obscure African tribes which hardly realised that a war had been fought at all.

From London, the world's largest city, the British Government under the Welsh solicitor, Lloyd George, now controlled well over a quarter of the human race and over a quarter of the world's land surface. The British Empire contained 450 million souls, comprising representatives of practically every race and religion in the world. In terms of numbers, the predominant religion was Hinduism, next came Islam, the third was Christianity and the fourth various categories described in the contemporary *Whitaker's Almanack* as 'Polytheists and Idol worshippers.' The land area of 14 million square miles stretched to all five continents, the biggest slice being in Africa and the next biggest in North America. Throughout the English language was the leading medium of administration, the British Crown the symbol of sovereignty. The exact powers of the British Government varied from territory to territory but everywhere it included control of foreign affairs and, effectively, of defence. Among radical thinkers there was a tendency to describe the whole arrangement as the 'British Commonwealth of Nations,' a phrase which had been devised 30 years earlier by the Liberal Lord Rosebery, but in both official and common parlance the customary term was 'The British Empire.'

It was 'the empire on which the sun never sets.' At almost any hour there was some place in which the union jack was being hoisted at dawn. It was an empire which exceeded the most extravagant designs of Rome, of Genghis Khan or of Napoleon Bonaparte. In geographical extent of direct authority, it exceeded

'The unknown stared at us through his eyes'.
Mohandas Karamchand Gandhi

Mahomet Ali Jinnah, founder of Pakistan

anything achieved so far by the leading nuclear powers of the mid-20th century. Much of it was quite new —most of the African territories had been acquired within living memory in 1918 and the imperial concept itself had hardly existed before the 1890s —but there was an air of majestic permanence about it. School-children who in Britain learned the phrase about the sun never setting tended to regard it as a prophetic rather than a geographical statement. The British Empire, they were taught, was so powerful and so beneficent that it could be regarded as likely to last for ever. Past threats had principally come from rival European powers, France, Germany and Russia. Victory in the 1914–1918 war had eliminated these threats. France was an ally, Germany was beaten and Russia lay in chaos. There was a little anxiety that the wealthy United States, moving for the first time on to the world scene, might become 'top nation' but it could not be supposed that she would try to conquer the British Empire. A few specialists looked nervously towards Japan, the only country outside the European tradition to have built herself a world-power status, but Japan, too, had been a British ally in the war. With the cream of the Imperial German Navy safely in custody in the Firth of Forth, what further danger to the British Empire could possibly exist?

To express the national mood there was a great musician, Edward Elgar, and a great poet, Rudyard Kipling. Both produced work of enduring value. Many political establishments have been able to call upon hack composers and hack poets to extol their virtues. The British Empire, at its height, commanded artistic genius. Although neither had an appetite for the cruder forms of nationalism, Elgar and Kipling expressed the British instinct.

Elgar's melodic music—which 40 years later was to become a favourite in the Soviet Union—evokes the high noon of the British Empire: the wistful first symphony, the brilliant Cockaigne Overture, the grand Pomp and Circumstance marches. From the latter came a tune which in 1918 ranked as the second National Anthem—'Land of Hope and Glory.' It was commonly sung on public occasions and the words, by Arthur Christopher Benson, were regarded as appropriate to Britain's position.

'. . . Land of hope and glory, mother of the free.
How shall we extol thee, who are born of thee?
Wider still and wider shall thy bounds be set;
God who made thee mighty, make thee mightier yet . . .'

It should be observed that even in these apparently absurdly vainglorious words occurs 'mother of the free.' The British were proud of being free as well as of extending their political frontiers; the two things were not, in the last resort, compatible and the clash between them provides a key to many otherwise obscure aspects of imperial policy.

Kipling was the product of British India where he had been born and where as a young man he had worked as a journalist. He was the only 20th-century British poet who has so far become a household name. His works extol the glory of being British, but at the same time he warned his countrymen against undue arrogance, against forgetting the 'God of our fathers.' In his *Recessional*, which became a kind of national prayer, he warned how 'all our pomp of yesterday' might become 'one with Nineveh and Tyre.'

> 'If, drunk with sight of power, we loose
> Wild tongues that have not Thee in awe,
> Such boastings as the Gentiles use,
> Or lesser breeds without the Law—
> Lord God of Hosts, be with us yet,
> Lest we forget—lest we forget!'

At the head of this world system of authority stood a slight, bearded man about five feet six inches tall. In 1918 he was aged 53 and had been eight years on the throne. His title was 'George the Fifth, by the Grace of God of the United Kingdom of Great Britain and Ireland and of the British Dominions beyond the Seas King, Defender of the Faith, Emperor of India.' Grandson of the long-lived Queen Victoria, he was of largely German ancestry. He belonged to the House of Saxe-Cobourg-Gotha and there had been some doubt about what was his correct surname, some experts favouring 'Guelph,' some 'Wettin' and some 'Wipper.' It had not been a satisfactory form of nomenclature, especially in the antagonism felt towards Germans in the war, and in 1917 he had assumed the surname 'Windsor,' after his principal castle near London.

In most empires it had been usual for the ruling dynasty to have played a prominent role in conquest and political direction. This had not been so in the British Empire. The only monarch of the past perceptively to have affected imperial policy had been King George III and he had lost all the North American colonies save what is now Canada. Queen Victoria, the secluded, matriarchal personality whose memory in 1918 was still fresh, had presided over a vast expansion of British power but her actual influence over it had been of the slightest. (So, for that matter, had been the influence of most of the London politicians who had ruled the Empire in the Queen's name; most of the acts of expansion had taken place through local initiative rather than because of direction from the centre.) The monarchy was a symbol only of imperial power but as such it had gained in popularity. In 1918 when monarchies collapsed over much of Europe, the British crown was more secure than ever.

George V was a conscientious, fussy man. In his youth he had not expected to succeed to the throne and he had spent 15 years as a professional naval officer. The death of his elder brother had pitchforked him into the succession against his own inclinations. Although his thinking was narrow, he had a wider knowledge of and a deeper interest in the Empire than any of his predecessors. (His father, Edward VII, had regarded the Empire as such a bore that it was difficult to prevail upon him even to receive colonial governors when they were in London.) George V had sailed the oceans and seen for himself some of the most distant colonies. As Prince of Wales, he had inaugurated the new Commonwealth of Australia. He was the only British monarch who was ever crowned Emperor of India. This bizarre addition to Saxe-Cobourg-Gotha royal titles had been thought up by Prime Minister Disraeli for Queen Victoria in 1877. George V took himself seriously as Emperor and after his ordinary coronation in London had sailed off in 1911 to hold a 'Coronation Durbar' at Delhi. A crown had had to be specially manufactured for the occasion and then taken back to London, lest it fell into the hands of Indian insurgents. There had been a dreadful tangle over procedure: nobody could decide who should crown the Emperor and eventually he had emerged from his tent with the crown already on his head.

At his court at Buckingham Palace in London—from which he moved at fixed dates every year to his three other principal residences—George V maintained rigid standards of conduct. The uniforms, the robes, the parades, the ceremonies which symbolised British world power were his province and one he conducted with efficiency. His relations with his thrusting Prime Minister, Lloyd George, were bumpy. Lloyd George represented the aggressive, adventurous streak in British public life which had won the Empire. The King stood for the stability and somewhat pompous sense of honour with which the civil servants attempted to administer it. The combination in the British of two such opposite sets of characteristics, as exemplified in King and Prime Minister, is the explanation of 'pervidious Albion,' the widely held notion that the British were hypocrites. It was another facet of the contradication between 'mother of the free' and 'wider still and wider.' The King took the closest interest in imperial matters, especially in appointments to governorships, and tried to preserve British modes in the administration of the self-governing dominions. He could always be overridden by his ministers but in marginal cases his voice could be decisive. He had five sons, of whom one, a lifelong invalid, died in 1919. In the following years there were sporadic suggestions that the four remaining sons might be sent out as viceroys of the four major self-governing dominions, Canada, Australia, South Africa and New Zealand but both for personal and practical reasons the notion came to nothing. The young princes did, however, travel within the Empire on a scale so wide as to eclipse all their predecessors.

George V was 'King' in Britain, Ireland and all the dominion and colonial territories. In India he was commonly referred to as 'King-Emperor.' According to the uncodified British Constitution he had to accept the 'advice' of ministers who commanded a majority in the elected section of the legislature, the House of Commons. Such advice, tendered formally, was for practical purposes an instruction he had to obey. The British Empire contained many administrations and sets of ministers but only one set, that in London, had the right to tender binding 'advice' to the monarch; all the other administrations had to approach the King through British ministers. This applied even to the self-governing dominions, in spite of the fact that for practical purposes the London administration had no power over them.

The House of Commons was the forum in which the ministers won their reputations and the convention was that they were 'responsible' to the House for their official actions. The House of Commons was chosen by an entirely British electorate, with no representatives whatsoever of the Empire. Thus some 21 million electors in Great Britain had custody of the destinies of an empire of 450 millions. This, again, was bound to produce strains. Politicians making their way in public debate, free discussion and popular election were unlikely to have the attitudes of autocrats; their instinct would be to persuade rather than to command. Moreover, the opponents of British rule within the subject territories could always hope to find spokesmen to voice their view in the open British parliament. In 1918 the contradiction between a free parliament in London and autocracy overseas was latent rather than obvious. The landslide election victory of Lloyd George in that year was won in a campaign in which the Empire was hardly mentioned save for the special case of Ireland. The new Labour Party, which emerged in that election as the strongest opposition group, had a socialistic policy for home affairs but, beyond a generalised sympathy for underdogs everywhere, had no coherent doctrine on the Empire. Parliament customarily gave two days a year to debating India and one day to the colonies; otherwise, apart from questions to ministers and occasional items of imperial legislation, it devoted itself to domestic British affairs.

The two ministers who in 1918 were principally responsible for running the Empire were E. S. Montague, a 39-year-old Liberal who was Secretary of State for India, and Walter Long, 64-year-old leader of the squirearchal wing of the Conservative Party, who was Secretary of State for the Colonies (an office which included responsibility for the self-governing dominions). Both had reached their offices through the customary processes of party politics at Westminster and neither had first-hand experience of the territories for which they were responsible. Such direct experience was expected neither of them nor of their civil service staffs. Their departments were among the smallest in Whitehall; the India Office had 342 civil servants and the Colonial Office only 256;* all belonged to the Home Civil Service and expected to spend their entire working lives in London.

Of the two departments, the India Office, housed along one side of the Foreign Office quadrangle on the corner of Downing Street and Whitehall, was the more professional. It descended from the old East India Company, the privately-financed corporation which had originally acquired India for the British, and over the generations had built up settled customs of work. The officials, in constant contact with the labyrinthine Government of India with its bureaucracy of a million clerks, had to know what they were about. To advise the Secretary of State there was the India Council, a body of twelve men with long experience of India—nine were British and three were Indian. The office was divided into seven sections, corresponding to the departments of the Government of India, and each was headed by a secretary on a salary of £1,200 a year. The power of decision on major matters between the Secretary of State in London and the Viceroy in India varied according to the personalities involved; in the event of serious

* Figures for April 1, 1920.

dispute, the Viceroy could always appeal to the Cabinet over the head of the Secretary of State. The India Office did, however, maintain a continuous grip on the finances of India and over higher appointments in the Indian bureaucracy. It also, in 1918, still performed the functions of an Indian embassy in London but the following year a separate Indian High Commission was established. The first High Commissioner was an Englishman.

The Colonial Office occupied another side of the Foreign Office quadrangle and had three departments, each headed by an assistant under-secretary on a scale rising from £1,200 to £1,500 a year: they were the Dominions Department, which looked after the self-governing territories, the Crown Colonies Department which looked after everywhere else and the General Department which dealt with such matters common to the whole Empire as currency, posts and justice. The Secretary of State's assistant private secretary, Major Ralph Furse, advised on appointments to all the administrative posts in all the crown colonies. There was no settled system of competitive examination for colonial posts, as there was for the Home Civil Service and the Indian Civil Service; Major Furse interviewed candidates and the Secretary of State, without needing to refer to anyone else, appointed them to their jobs. In 1918 the Colonial Office was busier than it had been before the war but an amateurish, clublike atmosphere was still to be discerned in it. The handful of senior officials had worked there all their lives and knew each other well. They worked, before blazing coal fires in winter, on the affairs of remote territories which most of them had never seen, never expected to see and did not particularly want to see. Younger men, excited by the new imperial ideal, dubbed them 'the dinosaurs.' An unusually high proportion of them were bachelors and they had time to dabble in hobbies. One enjoyed studying trees, another etymology, another currency, another whaling. 'This,' wrote Sir Thomas Lloyd, a later Permanent Under-Secretary to the Colonial Office, 'was of great benefit to the Office in the days when life was simpler and the need for expert, whole-time Advisers had not made itself felt.'

The complete divorce between the bureaucrats in London and the administrators out in the field was a distinctive feature of the British imperial system. Save only for the India Council, no British overseas official, no matter how eminent, could ever expect an appointment in London. Almost never was a 'dinosaur' sent from his fireside to rule a colony. This was quite unlike the systems of other colonial powers, notably France, in which cross-postings were routine. The British system grew up by accident rather than by design. It had advantages in that it encouraged officials in the field to identify themselves with their territories and, indeed, to feel more emotional loyalty to the people under their sway than they did to the remote machine in Whitehall. At the same time, however, from the point of view of sheer imperial efficiency it was a weak system, reflecting more the governmental absence of mind in which the Empire had been acquired than the zestful ambitions of those who wanted to develop the British imperial estate and to make it a lasting institution.

Another department impinging closely upon the Empire was the Foreign Office which in 1918 was headed by Earl Curzon, a 67-year-old former Viceroy of India. The Foreign Office was directly responsible for administering Egypt and the Anglo–Egyptian Sudan and so had some of the aspect of a supplementary Colonial Office. In the previous generation it had been customary for the Foreign Office to administer territories new to British imperial sway. Then, when British rule had become established, they were passed on to the Colonial Office. The system had been administratively convenient to the British but not, perhaps, invariably entirely fair. There was a distinct difference between such an African potentate as the Sultan of Zanzibar or the Kabaka of Buganda negotiating, on theoretically equal terms, with Her Britannic Majesty through the Foreign Office and the same potentate appearing as a plainly subordinate ruler under the Colonial Office.

Besides its administrative responsibilities, the Foreign Office conducted the diplomacy of the entire Empire, self-governing dominions included. Britain had full rights within international law to sign treaties and to make peace and war on behalf of the whole complex. The self-governing dominions had acquired ill-defined rights of being consulted on foreign policy but they conducted virtually no diplomacy of their own. The nearest approach to the independent diplomatic representation of a dominion was the Canadian Minister in Washington, nominated by the Canadian Government, but even he worked as an integral part of the British Embassy. The Treaty of Versailles, which in 1919 formally ended the war with Germany, was signed by David Lloyd George specifically on behalf of the whole British Empire. Four of the self-governing dominions, Canada, Australia, South Africa and New Zealand, and the Indian Empire were also signatories, their names being grouped under the main 'British Empire' heading, but this was of emotional rather than legal significance. The Treaty would have been binding on them without their signatures.

Besides foreign policy, defence was primarily a matter for Great Britain. The professional head of the British Army was styled 'Chief of the Imperial General Staff.' The gigantic Royal Navy, which in 1919 possessed 63 battleships, was overwhelmingly controlled by and financed by Great Britain; it was built to a 'two power' standard which meant that it was supposed to be larger than the next two largest fleets in the world put together. The dominions had supplied a handful of ships towards the imperial navy and, if it had come to the point, would have been able to withdraw them from imperial service; in practice, though, these dominion ships came under the operational control of the British Admiralty. Dominion soldiers were in roughly the same position. Once committed by their governments to the theatres of war they became an integral part of the British forces, but the British had no power to force the dominion governments to provide them. Uniforms, training and methods of organisation of all the dominion forces were modelled upon those of Great Britain and much of the equipment was supplied by Britain. In 1919 the British Cabinet resolved to give up to a hundred aircraft free of charge to each of the dominions and to India to enable them to start air forces.

The defence relationship was imprecise and one that had grown up haphazardly rather than by design. It was clear that Britain had power to declare war on behalf of the whole Empire, as she had done in 1914. The declaration had been made by the King in London on the advice of his British ministers and it had been as binding upon Bombay and Brisbane as it had been on Birmingham. African tribesmen who had never seen a white man had been placed in a state of war with central European peasants who had never seen a black one. The Indian Army of 670,000 men, paid for by India but directed entirely by the British, was regarded as a normal instrument of British policy; detachments of it appeared even on the Western Front in Flanders and it was plentifully used in the Middle East against Turkey. The self-governing dominions, however, could be placed in a state of war but they could not be made to fight; their contributions to the war effort had been voluntary save in as far as South Africans and Australians found it necessary to fight German colonies contiguous to their own territory. The effect of dominion intervention was the growth in

London of a machinery of imperial consultation which, momentarily, gave the Empire the air of a unified whole. To supplement the system of occasional meetings of dominion leaders, Lloyd George opened his War Cabinet to such dominion prime ministers who happened to be in London and devised a body called the 'Imperial War Cabinet,' of British and dominion ministers, which held sessions in 1917 and 1918 as the supposed supreme directing body of the war. In fact, however, this turned out to be a false line of development; the main effect of the war was not to unify the Empire but to encourage the dominions to regard themselves as independent countries in their own right; their signing the Treaty of Versailles and joining the League of Nations was of more significance for their future than was the Imperial War Cabinet.

The peoples of the whole Empire, save for the inhabitants of certain 'protectorates,' were all 'British subjects' and enjoyed the rights of British citizenship. There were, in addition, many local citizenships, acquired by residence, and most of the overseas territories had regulations to control immigration. Great Britain, however, as the mother country, allowed entirely free entry by Empire citizens. It would, indeed, have appeared to be a contradiction in terms to have refused a 'British subject' entry to Britain. This had some odd consequences. An Indian, with no right to vote in India, could move to Britain and, after brief residence, qualify automatically as a voter for the imperial parliament. He could become a member of that parliament, as two Indians had done in the 1890s and one more was to do in the 1920s. Once in parliament, he was eligible to join the government and even, in theory, to become Secretary of State for India. In Britain his were all the rights of the free-born British subject and he had a vote and a voice in the affairs of the world-wide Empire. Yet the moment he returned home to India he forfeited the right to share in the ultimate direction of India. This illogical system only worked, of course, because the numbers of British subjects who came to Britain from India and the colonies were extremely small.

How far there was a racialist concept in the British Empire of 1918 is difficult to define. In most British people of the time there lay a deep-rooted belief that they were the best nationaity in the world. It was held that the particular mixture of English with Scots, Welsh and Irish had produced a 'race' peculiarly suitable for administering the affairs of other, less fortunate, peoples. It might be described as a 'master race' concept, modified to a greater or less extent by a desire to be of service. It could on occasion degenerate into hypocrisy. In Asia and Africa the British so nourished and strengthened the concept that many of the subject peoples came to believe in it, too. What counted was for someone of British stock to command in even the most trivial encounters an attitude of 'respect.' As Elspeth Huxley put it: 'Respect was the only protection available to Europeans who lived singly, or in scattered families, among thousands of Africans accustomed to constant warfare and armed with spears and poisoned arrows, but had themselves no barricades, and went about unarmed. This respect preserved them like an invisible coat of mail, or a form of magic, and seldom failed; but it had to be very carefully guarded. The least rent or puncture might, if not immediately checked and repaired, split the whole garment asunder and expose the wearer in all his human vulnerability. Kept intact, it was a thousand times stronger than all the guns and locks and metal in the world; challenged, it could be brushed aside like a spider's web.' One of the constant themes of the half century following 1918, when the British Empire collapsed, was to be the failing of 'respect.' Such catastrophes as the fall of Singapore had a little to do with the failure; the real truth, though, was that 'respect' was only the temporary by-product of an encounter between technologically advanced peoples and those less advanced and by its nature it could not last.

British racialism was not, strictly, a colour racialism. The British believed they were superior to other Europeans as well as to Asians and Africans. Kipling, possibly, expressed the attitude when he wrote of 'the Gentiles' and of 'lesser breeds without the law.' By 'Gentiles,' presumably, he meant Europeans outside the British chosen race. The 'lesser breeds' were the races actually subject to the British. There actually flourished a religious sect, the British Israelites, which believed that the British were the lost tribes of Israel and so called by God for high authority. Colour racialism flowed from this emotional kind of attitude rather than from such attempts at a scientific definition as was later to become characteristic of South Africa. As a working assumption, many British people assumed that a man's worth was likely to be in proportion to the whiteness of his skin; the praise Kipling's soldier gave to Gunga Din was that he was 'white, clear white, inside.' The British in the high days of Empire were entirely uninhibited at expressing their views on other races. 'The Chinaman,' said one writer, 'is not a desirable citizen. Economically, he is undesirable, for he can always undercut the white worker. Socially, he is undesirable, because, for all his good qualities, his outlook on life is so utterly different to that of our white civilisation that he brings a deep taint of degradation to the white people with whom he comes into contact.' The same writer gave advice on how to handle Africans: 'Be stern and prompt in punishment, but just, and you are all right. But you have to keep up a stern attitude, or there will be trouble.' He also, incidently, was fearful about the effects of the sun on white heads—'The man who takes too much whisky in Central Africa runs great perils. Step over the line just once in the matter of whisky, go out in the midday sun while the fumes of the spirit are in your head, and a funeral follows shortly after.'*

Whether the Empire was supposed to exist just for the enrichment and glorification of the British or whether it represented mainly a trusteeship on behalf of less fortunate peoples was none too clear. The Prince of Wales, calling upon his father, King George V, to open the 1924 British Empire Exhibition at Wembley, said: 'I hope, sir, that the result of this exhibition will be to impress vividly upon all the peoples of your Empire the advice that you have given them on more than one occasion, that they should be fully awake to their responsibilities as heirs to so glorious a heritage; that they should in no wise be slothful stewards, but that they should work unitedly and energetically to develop the resources of the Empire for the benefit of the British race, for the benefit of those other races which have accepted our guardianship over their destinies, and for the benefit of mankind generally.' The Prince's order of priorities—first the 'British race,' second the subject races and third mankind generally—aroused no particular comment. Indeed it was a platitude.

The 'British race' consisted of English, Scots and Welsh crowded together upon on an island of scenic beauty and temperate but variable climate. To them were attached the Irish as an influential but rebellious satellite. Except for the Irish, the British were an unusually united people with much intermarriage between the different strains of descent. Regional differences were relatively slight—the world's most elaborate railway system had during the past century helped to bind the British closely together. An Englishman's social 'class' counted for much more than his regional origin and the class system was a dynamic one with opportunities

* These quotations come from *The British Empire* by Sir Frank Fox, O.B.E., first published 1911, revised 1929.

for rising from one class to another. The two top classes, upper and upper-middle, formed a category of 'gentlemen' and 'ladies' who were still in 1918 regarded as being especially capable of carrying responsibility. The two lower classes, lower-middle and working, formed the majority of the population and by 1918 were becoming less and less willing to allow an automatic respect to their 'betters.'

It was largely members of the upper and upper-middle classes who administered the Empire.

The distinguishing mark of the upper class was its attachment to the land. Every head of an upper class family possessed a country estate which had belonged to his family for at least a generation. The estates were commonly safeguarded by 'entail' so that they passed intact in each generation to the eldest son. The topmost segment of the upper class possessed hereditary titles which, like the land, also passed to the eldest son. The titles included the five degrees of the peerage—duke, marquess, earl, viscount, baron—and the lesser hereditary rank of baronet. The peerages carried seats in the House of Lords and it was customary for between one third and one half of the Cabinet to be chosen from that House. In the past, peerages had been awarded in part merely as a recognition of the ownership of big estates but in 1918 the theory was that they should be given only as a reward for public service. (Lloyd George, to the anger of the King, muddied them by selling them in a blatant manner for cash down for political funds.) To obtain a peerage, or for an existing peer to obtain a step upwards in rank, was an event of the utmost significance for the individual concerned. It really mattered to get up to earl instead of being only a viscount.

In Empire administration, the peerage, especially the higher peerage, were allowed a distinct preference in appointments to senior posts. Of the 14 men who had been viceroys of India by 1918, 11 had been peers by inheritance. The 11th Earl of Elgin became Viceroy in 1862 and his son, the 12th Earl, became Viceroy in 1894. The 5th Marquess of Lansdowne was successively Governor-General of Canada and Viceroy of India. The reasoning was that men born to high title and substantial possessions brought a dispassionate attitude to the work of government and, too, that their high social standing gave them an edge over the rougher elements among the Empire pioneers.

The younger sons of the upper class had no rights in the family estates and they were expected either to marry an heiress and establish new landed lines of their own or to earn their livings. The more enterprising of this class of younger sons often found fulfilment in empire-building.

The upper-middle class, which was much bigger than the upper class, was characteristically urban. Its members included successful businessmen and industrialists, the higher civil servants and representatives of the older learned professions. In the wealthier reaches the members purchased country estates and merged with the upper class. Relations between the upper and upper-middle classes were generally easy. They could dine together and shared the common appellation of being 'gentlemen,' a subtle but definite term which referred in part to material possessions and in part to the practice of a detailed code of conduct and manners. To be a 'gentleman' was an essential qualification for employment in the administrative service of the Empire.

The unifying force between upper and upper-middle classes was a group of about 150 boys' boarding schools, known as 'public schools.' They were the places where 'gentlemen' were trained. Some were centuries old but most had been founded only two or three generations earlier. They had developed a common form of organisation, curriculum and attitude to life. The outstanding pioneer had been Thomas Arnold of Rugby but the system had not reached maturity until a generation after his death in 1842. In 1918 the system was at the full flood of vigour and in the 1920s new public schools were still being founded. In 1918 only one third of the Conservative members of parliament had received a public school education; by 1935 the proportion had reached two thirds. Moreover, public school aims and methods were being more and more widely imitated in the ordinary state schools. The public schools took boys at the age of 13 and kept them until 18, consciously attempting to mould them to a standard model. The headmasters were mostly clerics of the Church of England, although by 1918 laymen were getting more and more of the posts, and the boys learned in the school chapel a creed commonly described as 'muscular Christianity.' At its best, it was a creed which demanded personal honesty, a degree of austerity and a willingness to 'serve' those who had not been fortunate enough to acquire a public school education. Virtue, headmasters taught, was not to be acquired by passive contemplation of the mysteries of eternity but by vigorous action in the physical world. It was actually an American, Grantland Rice, who wrote the following lines but their spirit is that of the British public school as traditionally conceived:

'For when the One Great Scorer comes
To write against your name,
He marks—not that you won or lost—
But how you played the game.'

The main item on the public school curriculum was the study of the languages and literature of ancient Greece and Rome. Senior boys were expected to be able to compose verses of their own in these dead tongues, proficiency in the art being sufficient to win high university awards. It was held that close acquaintance-ship with these mainsprings of European civilisation was a sufficient academic qualification for a young man to enter the administrative service of India. By 1918 the dominance of Latin and Greek in the public schools was just beginning to wane but they still ranked ahead of mathematics, science, history and modern languages, these 'modern' subjects being regarded as the proper field of study only for the less able boys.

From the classical bias in British public school education it is possible to trace at least two characteristics in imperial adminis-tration. Firstly, it encouraged precision in the use of language, a thing not always found among the indigenous people of many of the tropical territories. The British administrator said what he meant and meant what he said. High importance was attached, especially in India, to written minutes and reports which, carefully filed, provided a detailed record of all that had been done. In any difficulty, it was easy to look up precedents and to follow them. Thus British administration came to possess at its best a virtue of consistency and continuity and at its worst an element of tactless-ness and inflexibility. The second influence of Latin and Greek was to foster a cult of the 'amateur' and the 'all-rounder.' The classics were regarded as a mental gymnastic which developed the intellect without cluttering it up with useful information. The classics man, with his trained mind, was presumed to be capable of tackling any problem which came his way. He might call upon a plumber or a geologist to give advice but so far as possible he worked by the light of reason alone. In the first stages of establishing a colonial administration, the 'all-rounder' had obvious virtues. He quickly acquired a little knowledge of every subject that concerned him; whether he was building a bridge, coping with an epidemic or trying a murder case, he could make an intelligent attempt. In the more advanced territories, especially India, the system by 1918 had developed countervailing disadvantages. The administrator tended to distrust experts and to treat them as inferiors; in self-defence he developed a mystique about his own functions and wrapped himself up in his 'respect.' In the worst instances, the 'all-rounder' acted as a brake upon development.

Apart from the Latin and the Greek, the principal activity in the public schools was the playing of games—cricket in the summer and, generally, rugby football in the winter. To most boys the games were more important than academic work and many of the more influential teachers took a similar attitude. The games were played not just for fun but for the definite purpose of training the character. Everyone had to play and to practice 'sportsmanship,' that is to keep within the unwritten as well as the written rules, to be courteous towards opponents and to avoid undue dejection in defeat. Importance was attached, too, to the 'team spirit,' that is the boy playing the game for the advantage of the whole team rather than for his own glory. The practice of 'sportsmanship' and 'team spirit' was commonly carried into adult life and formed, together with 'muscular Christianity,' the code by which many imperial administrators aspired to live. To them the 'One Great Scorer' was a reality.

The background was authoritarian and designed to produce a standard product rather than individuals. Corporal punishment, often severe, was the commonplace penalty for breaches of school rules or customs, for 'slackness' in work or games and for lapses from sexual continence. The thwack of cane upon trouser was as everyday a sound as that of bat upon ball. However much pain they felt, the boys were expected to keep a stiff upper lip and to avoid the display of distress. Much of the punishment was inflicted by the elder boys upon the younger, the theory being that one first learned to suffer and then to rule. This system had some slight influence upon British colonial administration in that corporal punishment was widely regarded as a suitable penalty even for political criminals among the subject peoples but it is not possible to deduce that it led to much actual sadism. What it certainly meant was that a boy of 18 regarded himself as equipped for under-taking the control of others; if he became an imperial adminis-trator, he took his own authority so much for granted that many of the subject peoples accepted it too. In this manner even the disci-pline of the public schools contributed towards the confidence-trick in which lay one of the secrets of the British Empire.

By 1918 the public schools had developed from mere educational institutions into bodies which claimed an absolute allegiance of their members. The boys, drawn from many parts of Britain and the Empire, felt, generally, far less loyalty to their home areas than they did to the schools. The totalitarian demands of the schools made a few boys intensely unhappy but most of them were moulded to the expected pattern. They acquired a sense of lifelong unity with their former schoolfellows. It was common for men to wear neckties in their old school colours. 'Nothing in life can sever the bond that unites us now,' runs the Eton Boating Song and this pledge was largely kept. Or as the fictional Captain Grimes put it in Evelyn Waugh's *Decline and Fall* first published in 1928: 'There's a blessed equity in the English social system that ensures the public school man against starvation. One goes through four or five years of perfect hell at an age when life is bound to be hell, anyway, and after that the social system never lets one down.'

That the Empire was run largely by old public school men—the classicists went to India and the athletes to the colonies—gave it an administrative code of manners which was the same in Sierra Leone as in Hong Kong.

To attend a public school in 1918 cost between £100 and £250 a year, which was about the same as the total wage of a manual working man. The overwhelming majority of the pupils were British but there was no colour bar and it was quite usual for wealthy Indians to send their sons to an English public school. Jawaharlal Nehru, first Prime Minister of independent India, was an old boy of Harrow. Only about one British boy in 40 attended a public school but from the public schools came practically all the higher civil servants, army officers and imperial administrators. There were, of course, many individual exceptions of men from other types of school who rose to high positions. No legal bar existed to prevent them. But they had a tough time on the way up and, once arrived, generally accepted the public school code of conduct and manners. How far public school education was regarded as 'normal' for the rulers can be seen, perhaps, in a line in autobiographical notes written by John Buchan, who as Lord Tweedsmuir served as Governor-General of Canada. Buchan had received an excellent education in a Glasgow day school. Yet he wrote: 'In the conventional sense, I never went to school at all.'

At the head of the British educational system stood the old universities of Oxford and Cambridge which recruited most of their students from public schools. Other universities had come into being in London and the provinces (and there were four old

Edward Wood, Baron Irwin (later Earl of Halifax) robed as Viceroy of India

British India. The Nehru household at Allahabad *c* 1885. Motilal Nehru with his wife Swarup Rani and their son Jawaharlal, future Prime Minister of the Republic of India

ones in Scotland) but Oxford and Cambridge had practically a monopoly of the public service.

The majority of the British population had very little to do with the Empire. A small proportion went out as emigrants to the colonies of white settlement but up to 1914 most British emigrants had gone not to the Empire but to the United States of America. The generality of the people were proud that there *was* a British Empire—its existence had hit the public consciousness a quarter of a century earlier during the jubilees of Queen Victoria—but it was not an institution that affected their daily lives. This, perhaps, was just as well for it meant that the Empire was irrelevant to much of the reality of British life and energies were free for things which in the long run were to matter more; compared, say, with Spain and ancient Rome, the British Empire did not adulterate the basic character, nor even the basic economy, of the imperial people. It was not until 40 years later when, for the first time, substantial numbers of immigrants from the old imperial territories arrived in Britain that any serious impact was made at all upon British domestic affairs.*

But for all the national self-confidence, for all the jubilation over the defeat of Germany, for all the satisfaction at the addition of new territories to the Empire, Britain was in 1918 a nation in mourning. There lay dead on the battlefields 680,000 young men, about one tenth of the male population of military age. The death rate had been particularly heavy among young officers from the public schools, the destined future leaders of Britain and the Empire. Every town and village was making plans for a war memorial. In public school chapels, the teachers of 'muscular Christianity' wept in front of their boys as the casualty lists were read out. In Whitehall, administrative centre of the Empire, was to rise a blank, white cenotaph as the national memorial. For a generation it was customary for passers-by to raise their hats to it. Once a year, in the grey November days, there was a two minutes' silence in memory of the dead and the bearded King-Emperor laid his wreath to symbolise the national mourning.

The massacre had taken place for reasons connected with European politics and most of the killing had been in Europe. The British had made their great sacrifice not for the Empire but for Europe.

While it is difficult to point precisely to cause and effect, the loss

---

* Apart, of course, from the economic impact; obviously the economic links between Europe and the rest of the world were important.

of 680,000 prime young men of the imperial race must have exerted an influence. In British domestic politics, certainly, there existed in the following two decades a lassitude which made a dull contrast with the buccaneering of the Victorian and Edwardian periods. This lassitude existed, too, in some aspects of imperial affairs. There was a tendency to take the Empire for granted, to luxuriate in the sense of grandeur it provided, to administer it rather than to develop it. Platitudes took the place of clear analysis. Nothing ever seems so normal as the world in which one grows up and by the inter-war period the dominant section of the population had known about the Empire since childhood and so mistook it for a normal, permanent thing. Changes there were in the British Empire, especially in India, but these came more from the initiatives of the colonial peoples themselves and rarely from the enterprise of Great Britain.

The British had become a nation filled with dreams and illusions. The surrender of the German High Seas Fleet was the fulfilment of a 20-year-old ambition but it had not truly represented victory at sea. The Royal Navy had won no victory in a major fleet action since Trafalgar in 1805; the German navy had surrendered because their country had been beaten on land—beaten because the entry of the United States into the war at a late stage had tipped the balance against it.

# CHAPTER 2

# The brightest jewel

'MR. GANDHI, you have made my task easy in one way by pleading guilty to the charge,' said C. N. Broomfield, District and Sessions Judge of Ahmedabab, India, on March 18, 1922.

'Nevertheless, what remains, namely, the determination of a just sentence, is perhaps as difficult a proposition as a judge in this country could have to face. The law is no respecter of persons. Nevertheless, it will be impossible to ignore the fact that you are in a different category from any person I have ever tried or am likely to have to try. It would be impossible to ignore the fact that, in the eyes of millions of your countrymen, you are a great patriot and a great leader. Even those who differ from you in politics look upon you as a man of high ideals and of noble and of even saintly life.

'I have to deal with you in one character only. It is not my duty and I do not propose to judge you in any other character. It is my duty to judge you as a man subject to the law, who by his own admission has broken that law and committed what to the ordinary man must appear to be grave offences against the state. I do not forget that you have consistently preached against violence and that you have on many occasions, as I am willing to believe, done much to prevent violence. But having regard to the nature of your political teaching and the nature of many of those to whom it was addressed, how you could have continued to believe that violence would not be the inevitable consequence, it passes my capacity to understand.

'There are probably few people in India who do not sincerely regret that you should have made it impossible for any government to leave you at liberty. But it is so. I am trying to balance what is due to you against what appears to me to be necessary in the interests of the public, and I propose in passing sentence to follow the precedent of a case in many respects similar to this case that was decided some twelve years ago, I mean the case against Bal Gangadhar Tilak under the same section. The sentence that was passed on him as it finally stood was a sentence of simple imprisonment for six years.

'You will not consider it unreasonable, I think, that you should be classed with Mr. Tilak, that is a sentence of two years' simple imprisonment on each count of the charge; six years in all, which I feel it my duty to pass upon you. And I should like to say in doing so that, if the course of events in India should make it possible for the Government to reduce the period and release you, no one will be better pleased than I.'

The judge, C. N. Broomfield, was aged 38 and had served 14 years in the Indian Civil Service. For a moment he became the voice of the British Raj in India against one of the strangest and most powerful personalities of world history. Mohandas Karam-chand Gandhi, commonly given the honorific title of 'Mahatma,' was aged 52. According to the Hindu religion in which he had been born it was possible for man to amass such a store of merit in his life as to become an equal of the lesser gods. For millions in India Gandhi was an almost divine being. 'The unknown stared at us through his eyes,' wrote his young aide Jawaharlal Nehru. This extraordinary prophet-politician had set himself in 1920 to drive the British out of India. Within 27 years he and his followers were to win total victory. For Broomfield the apparition of such a person in the dock of his provincial courtroom must have been bewildering. If even Nehru could not understand Gandhi how could he, an Englishman six thousand miles from home? Yet with the skill characteristic of his service, the young Broomfield turned his hand to the task and produced a judgement which stands to epitomise the better qualities of British rule in India.

The current cliché about India was that she provided the brightest jewel in the imperial crown. Her population of 315 million was three fourths of the entire population of the British Empire. In population she ranked after China as the second biggest country in the world. Her civilisation was a thousand years or more older than that of Great Britain. In 1918 she lay under the absolute rule of the British Government in London, a source of endless pride to the British and a key factor in the formulation of British foreign policy.

The British conquest of India began from Calcutta in the late 18th century, the primary urge being a lust for profit by employees of the East India Company, a trading concern chartered by the British Crown which had acquired some of the characteristics of a government. The company and its shareholders never made much money out of India but in the early period many of its officials on the spot gained vast personal fortunes for themselves. Defeating the superior forces of local Indian potentates, they laid

Bengal waste and returned home to Britain with the purchasing power of the modern multi-millionaire. It is arguable that the capital they brought home to Britain was the decisive factor in starting the industrial revolution which made their country the richest and most powerful in the world. The British Government stepped in to curb the excesses of the company's employees and in the first half of the 19th century the professed aim of the East India Company was to provide fair government of those sections of India it had conquered and to prosecute trade with the Indian. But some irresistible impulse in the British on the spot led them to conquer more and more territory until the whole sub-continent lay under their control. This was against the wishes of London, the cost of the military operations throwing the East India Company into debt. However, there was no electric telegraph and it took two years by sailing ship to transmit an order from London to India and to get a reply and the local officials acted largely on their own initiative.

The process of conquest had its own momentum. When a province had been conquered, troops were enlisted from it to conquer another one. At this period there was no outstanding financial profit to be gained by further conquest. It was largely a sheer hunger for power, rationalised as a desire to introduce decent standards of administration. The British in this period worked vigorously to abolish the custom of 'suttee' by which a widow was expected to throw herself on her husband's funeral pyre to be burned alive. The verve of the British in India was, possibly, an aspect of that strange high tide of vitality in early 19th-century Britain which expressed itself at home in an exploding birthrate.

In 1857 the Indian Army mutinied. The rebels gained control of practically the whole of India. Had the Indians at that stage produced anything like a settled administration, supported by the loyalty of the mass of the people, the episode would surely have been the end of the British connection. Yet politically India remained a vacuum. Bit by bit and rapidly the British regained control. As each mutinous regiment was subdued, the rebellion in its area died away. This had little to do with the occasionally atrocious methods of retaliation the British employed—mutinous soldiers were on occasion shot out of guns—it was simply that the British had become the only force capable of ruling India. The princes of India were divided and quarrelling bitterly among themselves. Many preferred to treat with the British rather than with members of their own race. There was practically no Indian middle class. Most of the people were rural peasants, poor and ignorant, and so far as they thought about politics at all were liable to consider British administration a lesser evil than anything their own aristocracy could produce.

The result of the mutiny was to fasten British rule on India on a permanent basis. The Crown took over the government from the East India Company, the effective authority becoming a member of the British Cabinet, the Secretary of State for India. The Governor-General acquired by official usage, although not by legal enactment, the title of 'Viceroy of India' and conducted himself with increasing pomp and ceremonial. One of the most glittering prizes a political career in Britain could offer was to become Viceroy, the ruler of one sixth of the human race. His salary of between £20,000 and £25,000 a year was the highest of any British public official. Not since the days of the Roman Empire, when populations had in any case been much smaller, had such a proconsulship lain in the gift of a government.

The principal medium of administration became the Indian Civil Service, recruited by competitive examination of young graduates from British universities, mainly Oxford and Cambridge. The pay was generous and the Indian Civil Service attracted young men of high qualification. Some of the best exponents in Britain of writing Latin verses went out to administer India. It was a tiny service of only about a thousand men but it held a grip on every aspect of government. Under it worked a bureaucracy of about a million locally-recruited public officials but the local men rarely achieved real authority. In theory it was possible for an Indian to join the Indian Civil Service and a handful actually had done so; there was no racial bar. But the competitive entry examination was held in London and an Indian candidate had to gather £100 to pay his fare and living costs. Moreover, he was unlikely to do well in the examination unless he had spent years in Britain at public school and university which alone could provide suitable preparation; this would cost £2,000, a sum beyond the reach of 99 per cent of Indian families.

Customarily a man enrolled in the Indian Civil Service—became a 'Civilian'—at the age of 23 or 24. He would serve about five years as an assistant to an experienced Civilian and then, at around the age of 30, become a District Collector which meant being potentate of a district containing perhaps a hundred villages and townships. Alternatively he might enter the judicial branch of the government; about a third of the posts of judges were reserved for Civilians. Others of the judges were barristers from England and many were Indians. The judiciary was the only public service in which Indians commonly reached high posts but the chief justices of the high courts were always British.

The Collector—the title recalled the simpler methods of the East India Company—was the key official on whom the whole administrative machine depended. He ran everything within his district— the revenue, the police, petty justice, health, roads, famine relief. He would have about half a million people subject to him. He was generally aged between 30 and 45. He travelled widely within his district being treated with obsequious respect both by the Indian authorities and by the local Europeans. British India was possibly the only community which has ever existed in which civil servants were the social superiors of everyone else.

About half the Civilians, worn out by their labours and by the climate, would retire on a generous pension in their early 40s. They rarely remained in India. Their custom was to return home to England and set up house as independent gentlemen, whole communities of them clustering together in such places as Cheltenham. Many did not live to taste the pleasures of Cheltenham; they fell victim to local disease and died in India. Their tombstones still stand in the undergrowth of cemeteries in the cool Indian hill stations whence they had gone in search of recuperation.

The abler and healthier Civilians would take a long home leave at about the age of 40 and then return to their labour for another ten or fifteen years. It was men in this category who filled the high posts in the Viceroy's immediate circle. They became members of the Viceroy's Council or would take charge of departments as secretaries of the Government of India. The official capital of India in 1918 was still Calcutta, the Bengal city which had been the scene of the first British penetration into India. But Calcutta was hot, crowded and subject to wearying humidity and for about eight months every year the entire Supreme Government of India moved to the hill station of Simla in the far north, where the climate suited British tastes. Aloof in the Himalayan foothills, the senior Civilians directed the destinies of the Indian millions in the plains below. It was like running Britain from a capital in the highlands of Scotland or the United States from the Rocky Mountains.

Simla was the true heart of British India. Until almost the last moment of the British Raj, Simla social life continued as during the reign of Queen Victoria. There were elaborate tables of precedence and code of manners. The Viceroy and Vicereine in their Scottish-baronial style palace would sit down to dinner with 200 guests. As they arrived to greet their guests, the band would play *God Save the King*. Women would curtsey to them. During the meal, which consisted of indifferent food served with immense ceremony, the band would play light music, perhaps Gilbert and Sullivan. Strangers found the Simla Civilians proud and pompous. They whirled up and down the steep streets in rickshaws each pulled by four coollies, acknowledging the salaams of Indians and the salutes of Europeans with awesome gravity. Their faces were set and serious, their shoulders bowed as though an Empire rested upon them. As indeed it did.

During the 1920s work was proceeding on building a new imperial capital at Delhi, the capital of the old Moghul emperors. To the designs of Edward Lutyens, spacious colonnades, beautiful buildings in yellow stone and wide roads with fine vistas were being created to make a capital worthy of the British Raj. Lutyens's aim, he wrote, was 'to express within the limit of the medium and of the powers of its users, the ideal and fact of British rule in India, of which New Delhi must ever be the monument.' Delhi has a cool winter season and a stiflingly hot summer in which temperatures can reach 120 degrees. The British intended to use the capital only in the winter so the offices and official residences were designed to attract the maximum sunlight, a fact which has not earned them the gratitude of their Indian successors who use them all the year round.

If there was one single British institution which set its mark on the Indian Civil Service it was Balliol College, Oxford. In 1920 there were 62 Civilians in India on salaries of 30,000 rupees (about £3,000) a year and higher. They were the senior men, the leaders of administration. All were British. Their ages ranged from 38 to 61, all but seven of them being in the 45–55 age group. At least 53 of them had attended English public boarding schools. All had university degrees, 38 from Oxford, 22 from Cambridge, three from London and one from Glasgow. (Two of the Oxford total had previously taken Glasgow degrees.) Balliol provided 11 of the 62; no other Oxford or Cambridge college provided more than three. Balliol was the college which in the second half of the 19th century under the leadership of Benjamin Jowett had combined academic learning with a contact with the outside world in a manner which was new to the hitherto cloistered traditions of British university scholarship.

How efficient were the Civilians? It was fashionable in the days of their power to call attention to their negative virtues. Unlike their East India Company predecessors of the 18th century, they were incorrupt. Against the whole tradition of Indian public administration, no Civilian ever took a bribe or private perquisite; he had a high salary and a good pension—his rates were about 50 per cent higher than those of civil servants at home in Britain—but the idea of making a fortune in India never entered his head. He hated injustice, by which he meant treatment of a man other than according to the law. He would go to meticulous, sometimes absurd, lengths to try to enforce laws which he regarded as the embodiment of excellence. In the narrow sense of day-to-day efficiency in running an office he was often very good. He saw that letters were answered on time, that adequate records were kept, that accurate reports were sent on high to the provincial governments and to Simla. The terms of his contract required him to place 24 hours a day at the disposal of the Government and often he did indeed work extraordinarily long hours. As a bureaucracy, the Civilians were among the most efficient in the history of the world, a feat the more notable because they were working in a land the ways of which were so alien to their upbringing.

The common complaint against the Supreme Government was that it was remote from the Indian masses both physically and mentally. From the mountains would come elaborate decrees which too often took insufficient account of the lives of the people. The younger Civilians in the field as Collectors were often the first to protest; there was often a healthy tension between the younger and older members of the Indian Civil Service. But the local men had their own deficiencies. Devoted to their own districts, they often thought little of the general needs of India as a whole. To the interests of the peasants of his own district the Collector was usually devoted. His contact with the Indian educated class came largely through the clerks on his own staff who in the classical period of British administration had been utterly subservient to the imperial power and, indeed, one of its strongest buttresses. Social contact between Civilians and Indians hardly existed at all; by the 1920s there were forced attempts at tea parties and the like but both sides generally found such contacts artificial and uncongenial.

The British preferred to retreat to their clubs which, to the very last, were commonly reserved for Europeans only.

The weakness of the Indian Civil Service was that in the customary sense of the word it was not a civil service at all. It performed the work which in most countries fell to politicians rather than to administrators. The whole initiation of policy lay in its hands and a bureaucracy, by its nature, is unlikely to produce many new ideas. Its bias will lie towards the maintenance of the existing order. In the late 19th century the Civilians *had* possessed a definite objective. This was gradually to 'Westernise' India, to mould it into as faithful a dominion of the Crown as Kent. Britain had railways and with energy the Civilians constructed for India the best railway system of Asia, a system which ran steadily at a profit to the relief of the revenue. By 1918, however, this assumption that India could be Europeanised had largely died away and the Civilians had little positive to put in its place. In such a negative problem as organising the transport of food so as to prevent a famine they could be superb. For the essentially political task of reforming the land system and persuading the peasants to adopt more advanced agricultural methods they were ill-equipped. In economic matters they were always weak. Time and again they failed to establish a workable exchange value for the rupee.

Yet the Civilians can only reasonably be judged in the standard of time and place. The best available comparison is that between India and China. During the period of British rule, India enjoyed law and order, settled government and freedom from outside invasion. The Chinese largely kept their independence but enjoyed few of the benefits of strong, settled administration. By any material standard the Indian peasant under British rule was better off than his Chinese equivalent under a local war lord. The ultimate result in India, a liberal but backward republic, may be regarded by many as preferable to the totalitarian and chaotic autocracy which assumed control of China.

Whatever the rights and wrongs of the system it was undoubtedly an unnatural one. It was simply not in accordance with the ordinary run of human affairs that men should travel from a smallish island off north-west Europe to administer a subcontinent 6,000 miles away. The system could not be expected to last.

One small but possibly significant symptom of impermanence was the decline after 1918 in recruitment to the Indian Civil Service. The India Office could not attract the recruits it wanted.

This was not due to the casualties in the 1914–1918 war for the decline continued right through the 1920s. It had been traditional for Britain to send of her best to India. Indeed some claimed that the British had impoverished their own public service for the sake of India. This was an exaggeration for the 30 or 40 young men who annually went out to the Indian Civil Service were but a minor fraction of the ablest of their generation. But up to 1914 entry to the Indian Civil Service had been regarded as one of the higher honours a young British graduate could win. To be an Indian Civilian offered a life both financially comfortable and honourable, a life spiced with exotic adventure, a life affording opportunity to taste the delight of power over human beings. Now, quite suddenly, the young men stopped coming forward and every year the position got worse.

Between 1924 and 1935 the India Office wanted 339 British recruits. It got only 256 and this was after standards had been allowed to fall. By the 1930s the weakened Indian Civil Service was under severe pressure from the locally-recruited Indians in the government departments. At the actual technical work of government the British officials on occasion found themselves inferior to the Indians, who had themselves been selected by severe competitive examination. The balance of power changed. The Indian officials were no longer the subservient clerks of the past. They had been infected by nationalist teaching and by the end of the 1930s many of them were as eager as Gandhi and Nehru to see the British depart. To some limited extent this had come about through deliberate policies of 'Indianisation' by the Simla Government but in the main it was an unplanned process. As late as 1939 the India Office was still recruiting British Civilians with the expectation that they would be essential to the working of the Indian Government for at least a further generation.

There were several reasons why after 1918 the Indian Civil Service failed to get the recruits it wanted. The Colonial Service was expanding and although it offered lower salaries some saw in it a more attractive career than in India. There was a rather greater tendency than before 1914 for British graduates to take posts in industry and commerce. The Montagu-Chelmsford reforms of 1918 produced Indian ministers in charge of some aspects of provincial administration; the civil servants under them were to act as advisers and clerks rather than as originators of policy. This was a role less attractive to the ambitious type of man than the old omnipotence of the Indian Civilian. Many retired Civilians—the 'pension wallahs' living in England—fulminated against the changes and warned young men not to give their lives to a land which was going to the dogs. Moreover, the reforms and the growth of Indian nationalism suggested that the days of the Indian Civil Service might be numbered and that it would no longer provide a life's career.

A subtle and unprovable deduction that could be drawn from the lack of recruits is that it demonstrated an early sign of the slackening in the British imperial spirit. The slogans of Empire still were chanted, often more loudly than ever. But many able young Englishmen voted silently against it; they voted with their feet by declining to go to India. At the time the shortage of recruits appeared to be a mere administrative inconvenience. In retrospect it might be considered as a symptom of the manner in which over the next 40 years British aspirations tended to retreat before nationalist advance.

The other great service in India which attracted young British men was the army.

In fact there were two armies in India.

First, there was the British army in India, about 40 battalions of the British regular army with supporting troops to a total of over 50,000 men. While in India they came under the Commander-in-Chief of India and they were paid for from Indian revenues. But they were entirely British in composition and were posted to India as part of a routine tour of duty for the British army. Customarily a unit served six or seven years in India and then returned home. The more advanced weapons in India, including practically all the artillery, were in the hands of these British units. Not since the mutiny had the Indians been allowed to handle big guns.

Second, there was the Indian army, a separate entity with a peacetime strength of some 200,000 men. The ranks of company commander and above were held almost exclusively by British officers holding the King's Commission. A second category of officers—'Viceroy's Commissioned Officers'—commanded platoons; these were all Indians promoted from the ranks. Unlike the Indian Civil Service, the Indian army until the very end of British rule attracted a plentiful supply of young British officers to lead it. This was largely for economic reasons. Junior officers in British fighting regiments were paid so little that they required private means or allowances from their families in order to live. In the Indian army the pay was much higher, starting at about £500 a year, and a young officer could live on it in comfort. The Indian army had the pick of Sandhurst. Between the wars there was some attempt to Indianise the Indian army officer corps but Indian recruits were few in numbers. The peasant Indians who formed the rank and file were considered unsuitable for commissions and the middle classes, largely for nationalist reasons, were uninterested. During the Second World War, immediately before Indian independence, 30,000 young men straight from British public schools had to be sent out to India to become officers in the war-time expansion of the Indian army.

The Indian army officers enjoyed their work and were efficient managers of their men. Among both officers and men there was a strong hereditary element, fathers and sons serving for generations in the same regiment. One of the more urgent danger signals to the British Raj in the 1930s was an occasional refusal of Indian troops to tackle nationalist demonstrators; up to that moment the entire loyalty of the Indian army had for 80 years been devoted to the British Crown. Each regiment of the Indian army had its local recruiting ground among a segment of the population: Sikh, Madrasi, Mahratta, Jat, Punjabi and so on. The best fighting troops of all were reckoned to be the Gurkhas, recruited from the semi-independent frontier kingdom of Nepal. Most of the Indian army was disposed with a view to defending the frontiers against external enemies. The Indian regiments in the interior were generally stationed well away from their home areas. The main responsibility for internal security rested with the all-British units which were dotted all over India.

Although relatively to the size of the country the Indian army was a small force, it had formed a useful adjunct to British strategic power. In the 1914–1918 war Indian troops had played an important role in the capture of Palestine and Mesopotamia (Iraq) and had served in France. The common complaint of nationalist politicians was that Indian troops were used, at Indian expense, to extend the British Empire. When in action in large units, the Indians were generally brigaded two Indian battalions with one British battalion; such a mixed unit almost always had a British commander. Only three Indian officers commanded brigades during the 1939–1945 war and this was at a time when the Indian army was two million strong.

In the early 1920s the young recruits from Britain for the Indian Civil Service, the Indian army and the British business houses in India still started their careers in the manner of the

19th century. The air routes to India were in the pioneering stage and the customary way out was by sea. The passage from London to Calcutta took four weeks and cost between £40 and £50 first class and between £30 and £40 second class. It was possible to knock a week off the voyage and to escape the rough seas of the Bay of Biscay by travelling by train across Europe and catching the ship at Marseilles or Brindisi. This land route cost more but gave an opportunity for a group of friends to hold a jollification in Paris.

Before setting out for the first time a young man would seek advice from old India hands. Among other things he was told that he should buy his tropical linen suits in India, where they were cheaper than in London. He was told to buy for himself a strong deck chair for the sea voyage; he would sell it again on reaching Calcutta. Above all, he was warned of the necessity of buying a good sun helmet in London before setting out. 'The midday sun of India is dangerous and it is advisable to wear a cork or felt helmet,' warned *Murray's Guide to India*, 1920 edition. 'A sun hat should have a brim that will protect the temples and back of the neck, at top of the spine, and is well-ventilated all round [sic]. Many London hatters have a large choice of sun-hats and helmets, for ladies as well as men; and travellers should be careful to wear such head protection whenever they are exposed to the sun during the voyage.'

It was, in fact, a common belief, supported by medical opinion, that it was dangerous to allow the rays of the Indian sun to strike the unprotected head. The belief collapsed when American troops appeared in India during the 1939–1945 war and went about in ordinary headgear without suffering ill-effects. The sun helmet, the solar topee, which had been the very symbol of the British in India, suddenly became a museum piece.

The voyage to India was a part of British folklore. From the moment of setting foot in the ship, probably a P and O liner, the young man had entered his new life. Practically all the passengers were destined for long service in India, many of them being old hands setting back after home leave. There were Civilians, soldiers, missionaries and traders who thought of themselves in a mystic sense as actually being 'India.' The phrase 'Indian opinion' was still at this period used to describe the views of the British in India. The views of the actual Indians were 'native opinion.' The conversation on the ships had a special flavour. The passengers, especially the older ones, felt that they had dedicated their lives to the service of India. To them India was more real than Britain herself. Jet air travel has placed Calcutta but a day away from London. It is possible to walk in Hyde Park one morning and in the Maiden the next. In the 1920s, though, the voyage was slow enough to give the passengers a sense of gradual transition towards the mysteries of the East.

Around the Bay of Biscay the passengers would point to the sites of the sea battles which had made the Royal Navy supreme. On a clear day they could, with luck, see the Atlantic waves crashing against Cape Trafalgar. The first stop would be the rock fortress of Gibraltar, shaped like a lion, guarding the narrow entrance to the Mediterranean. For a few hours the passengers would slip ashore. Military regulations prevented them sketching or taking photographs but they could look at the Gibraltar monkeys climbing over the rocks. The legend was that so long as the monkeys stayed in Gibraltar so would the British. In the worst part of the 1939–1945 war the monkeys began to die off; the fact was reported to the Prime Minister in London, Winston Churchill, and he ordered a fresh supply to be procured from Africa.

The next call would be at the island of Malta in the centre of the Mediterranean. Perhaps the Mediterranean Fleet would be lying there in Valetta Grand Harbour, the white ensigns fluttering in the sun. The passengers would see half a dozen battleships with swarms of attendant destroyers, all painted a special pale grey to match the Mediterranean, the crews in crisp white uniforms.

Then came Port Said, at the entrance to the Suez Canal, with its smelly, wicked streets and Arab traders bargaining furiously over the curios they were trying to sell. This was the beginning of the East and still the passengers were under the British flag. Until 1922 Egypt was a British Protectorate and even after it had won technical independence the British garrison remained and the British continued to control foreign relations. At the regulation five knots, the ship proceeded through the hundred miles of the Suez Canal, the empty desert stretching away to each side. Now the passengers in their deckchairs wore their sun helmets. From the Canal the ship sailed into the torrid sterility of the Red Sea. The sun burned down and the shores on either side appeared absolutely barren. The most comfortable cabins for the Red Sea were the outer ones on the port side and the P and O charged extra for them; the reverse held on the return voyage. 'Port out, starboard home,' abbreviated to P.O.S.H., passed into the language.

The Red Sea and the coast of Arabia marked the beginning of the sphere of the Government of India. In order to safeguard the route, Indian forces in the 19th century had seized British Somaliland on the African coast, the islands off Arabia and the colony of Aden. India had also established protectorates over the Arab sheikhdoms on the coast of southern and west Arabia. This had been mainly with a view to suppressing piracy but in the 1920s it was beginning to be realised that these parched lands with pauper populations contained some of the richest oil deposits on earth. In the 1920s the whole area was still under the Simla administration, political officers of the Government of India running British Somaliland, Aden and the islands and 'advising' the rulers of the sheikhdoms.

The ship stopped at Aden, one of the busiest bunkering ports of the world. Vessels of a dozen nations would lie there under the union jack fluttering at the Resident's House on Steamer Point. The passengers threw pennies into the harbour and watched Adenese boys diving after them; the Aden administration was trying to stop the practice—too many boys were being eaten by sharks. There might be an hour or two in which passengers could stretch their legs on shore. Aden Colony was an extinct volcano and they could tour the residential quarter, Crater, so-called because it was actually built in the crater. They could look at the giant salt pans. But the climate would be too hot and too humid for much walking. Traditionally Aden had been used as a 'punishment station,' the garrison consisting of troops who had misbehaved themselves elsewhere.

The voyage ended in the bustle of Bombay or Calcutta. It was such a contrast to the emptiness of Arabia to see the endless crowds of India. The newcomer, advised by the older hands, would engage a travelling servant at a pay of between 25 and 35 rupees (about £3) a month and buy himself a roll of bedding. Both were essential for any kind of travel by a European in India. Unless he had already done so, he would stock up his medicine chest. Quinine, of course, was essential. He would buy, too, a big box of Cockle's Pills, the recognised specific against stomach disorders. Dysentry was the constant hazard to which everyone was subject. Some British people suffered every day of their service in India from more or less mild diarrhoea. Cockle's Pills were a classic treatment.

Then he would set off by train for his final destination, perhaps in the heart of India. The journey might take him a further week.

Gandhi's India. At the age of 59, the aristocratic lawyer Motilal Nehru changed habits of a
lifetime. He ceased to wear European dress, slept on his bedroom floor so as to prepare himself
for prison. Here, with his wife, he addresses a women's nationalist meeting

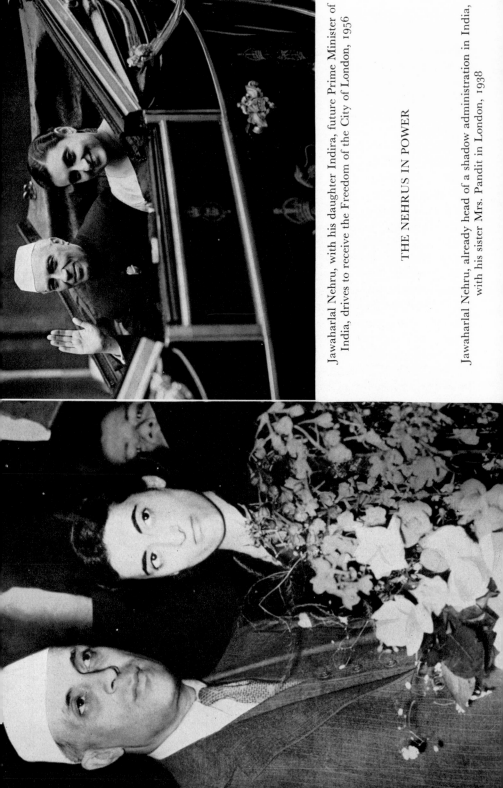

THE NEHRUS IN POWER

Jawaharlal Nehru, with his daughter Indira, future Prime Minister of India, drives to receive the Freedom of the City of London, 1956

Jawaharlal Nehru, already head of a shadow administration in India, with his sister Mrs. Pandit in London, 1938

Indian trains ran to time but they were very slow, even the expresses rarely reaching beyond 20 miles an hour. There were elaborate blinds on the windows by which the passenger could regulate the amount of sun and draught that entered his compartment. By night he would make sure his window was locked. The train ran so slowly that a thief could leap on board and rifle his belongings. Working on the railway as drivers, stationmasters and ticket clerks he would find members of the saddest community in India, the Eurasians. They were the descendants of unions between the early British arrivals in India and local Indian women, their features ranging in appearance from pure British to pure Indian. They spoke English in sing-song, almost Welsh, accent. They bore British names and referred to the England they had never seen as 'home.' Pure British and high caste Indians alike tended to scorn them. After about 1850 lasting unions between British and Indians had become rare and the Eurasian community had married within its own ranks and become self-propagating. They disliked being called 'Eurasian' and described themselves as 'Anglo–Indian' but in the 1920s the term 'Anglo–Indian' in common parlance still meant someone of pure British blood living in India. They were a Christian community and they all had elementary educations but, unlike the middle class Indians, they rarely sought higher education. The British looked after them to the extent of reserving jobs for them on the railways and in the customs service and in the 1920s they were loyal supporters of the British Raj which had given them birth. By the 1939–1945 war, however, under enlightened leadership they were beginning to think of coming to terms with Indian nationalism.

As the train journey proceeded, the passenger would telegraph ahead to order meals at railway refreshment rooms. The cuisine was adequate but monotonous. Each refreshment room had its own meal which it served to every European. One station served tomato soup, chicken curry and tinned pears for luncheon and dinner every day for a certain 30 years. For the last stage of the journey the passenger might have to leave the train and cover perhaps a hundred miles by horse, or by the cars and motor buses which were just coming into use. Food at this stage posed a problem. He might carry his own tinned provisions or he might rely on buying eggs, poultry and milk from the villages he passed. In no circumstances might he use Indian plates or cups; he was an outcaste and if he used an Indian eating or drinking vessel he would pollute it and it would have to be destroyed. His long

D

journey would make him begin to realise both the vastness of India and the swarming numbers of its people. About three fourths of the 700,000 villages of India were remote from any railway or main road. At the height of the British Raj it was possible for an Indian villager to live his whole life without ever seeing a white man.

Then finally he would reach his station or his regiment. He would be greeted with handshakes and shown the bungalow that would be his home—'bungalow' was one of the Hindi words which had passed into the English language. The British bungalows were customarily arranged in a 'cantonment' outside an Indian town. The bungalow for a young, single man would be sparsely furnished and might be in a rickety condition—he would peer anxiously at holes in the walls lest they admit poisonous snakes. He might be told tales of the cantonment ghost, the wraith of some British woman killed in the mutiny. To look after his sitting room and bedroom he would have a house servant. His gulkskhana—bath-room—would be the province of a low caste or outcaste man who was an hereditary 'sweeper.' Save in the most advanced canton-ments there was no main drainage and bathwater would run out of the gulkskhana through a hole in the wall, the sweeper clearing up the mess. This hole had a horrid reputation for admitting snakes. The furnishing was completed by the 'thunder box,' a wooden structure on four legs containing a porcelain 'top hat.' Having used the thunder box, the resident would shout for the sweeper who would clean out the 'top hat' over a fire he kept burning all day for that purpose. For the raw newcomer the ultimate fear was of finding a snake inside his 'top hat.'

Work would start almost at once, probably in an office piled with papers and files. Electric fans were coming into use but it was still common to find the old-fashioned 'punkah,' a swinging cloth to agitate the air, worked by a 'punkah wallah,' a servant who sat all day pulling the string. Office hours started at seven or eight in the morning, there was a break at noon for 'tiffin' (luncheon) and, unless there was something special to be done, work would finish at three or four in the afternoon. For the man with a little money there might be an opportunity for a game of polo. The Prince of Wales after his visit of 1921 described India as one vast polo ground where it was possible to get a game at any time. There was always the 'club' to go to, or for the army officer, the mess. The little British community would organise dances with a gramo-phone and amateur theatricals. There was much evening entertaining. It was a hierarchical society, the Civilians and their wives ranking first, then the army officers and finally the businessmen. The Simla Government issued an elaborate warrant of precedence with 63 ranks—the Viceroy at the top and a superintendent of a telegraph workshop at the bottom. It included military as well as civil ranks, the Archdeacon of Calcutta ranking immediately below a brigadier and immediately above the Tea Controller for India. If the cantonment was a substantial one there would be an Anglican or Church of Scotland chaplain, his salary, to the annoyance of Hindu and Moslem nationalists, paid out of the revenues of India. The prime function of the chaplain was to minister to the British community but often he also acted as a missionary to the Indians; the remaining colour bars in church were rapidly being eliminated in the 1920s and a chaplain customarily had less difficulty in getting Indians and Europeans to attend the same service than in getting Indian converts of different castes to sit together.

It was a stiflingly narrow way of life with 'shop' almost the only subject of conversation. In particular the women, relieved by their servants of domestic chores, became easily bored and, as a kind of sport, conducted feuds with each other. A stranger could find the feuds most virulent but they were largely artificial and devised to pass the time. If a baby caught dysentery, the mother's worst enemy would be the first at the door to offer assistance. The men had their work. The Civilian had to get to know his district, the army officer his men. There were languages to master. He would have had some instruction before leaving Britain but there remained an infinity to learn. First, probably, he would tackle Hindustani, the bastard patois in which a man could make himself roughly understood anywhere in India. Then the serious man would apply himself to one or more of the 14 major languages and 600 minor languages and dialects of India so that he could really talk to his people. In official India, hard work was the fashionable way of life.

The young Civilian between the wars started on a salary of £540 (equivalent in 1968 values to about £1,600) rising by annual increments of £45. At the age of about 30, when he got a substantial appointment, he went up to a scale rising from £1,300 to £2,385. Every competent official could rely on reaching this maximum and after 23 years' service he was entitled to a £1,000-a-year pension. For every year's work in India he earned two and a half months' leave on full pay or five months on half pay. If he wished, he could save up his leaves so that he could take a really long break in Britain—the maximum he could save was 28 months. During his initial 23 years' service he was entitled to four free first class passages home to Britain for himself and his wife; if he wished he could travel second class and so increase his number of trips home.

These were lavish terms of employment, the best offered to any officials under the British Crown. The cost of living in India was cheap and it was possible to save money. The daily toast by some was to raise a glass towards the setting sun and pronounce the formula: 'Another day off the calendar and another 50 rupees in the bank.' The high pay and the physical power which the young officer or official wielded helped give them a high opinion of their own abilities. Together with this went an invincible belief in the destiny of the British. Back in 1883 when the Ilbert Bill had proposed to make British residents in India subject to Indian magistrates, Seton Kerr, former Foreign Secretary of India, voiced the opinions of his countrymen when he declared that the Bill outraged 'the cherished conviction which was shared by every Englishman in India, from the highest to the lowest, by the planter's assistant in his lowly bungalow and by the editor in the full light of the Presidency town—from those to a Chief Commissioner in charge of a province and to the Viceroy on his throne—the conviction in every man that he belongs to a race whom God has destined to govern and subdue.'

It was no longer considered apt in the 1920s to express such sentiments so explicitly but they remained at the heart of many a British official's thinking. How else could he, indeed, in the last resort justify his own authority? 'The Chinese are said to be great believers in "face," ' wrote Jawaharlal Nehru, 'yet I doubt if any among them are so passionately attached to "face" as the British in India. For the latter it is not only individual, racial and national prestige; it is also intimately connected with their rule and vested interests.'

It was customary, especially in the army, for the new British recruit to India to be a bachelor. But he would rapidly feel the need for the companionship of a wife and as he saved money from his pay he became able to afford marriage. Little solace was to be found with Indian women. Affairs between the British and Indian girls did take place but they were furtive and unmentionable. Caste Hindus disliked them even more than the British. The only recognised sexual relationship between British and Indians was that of private soldiers in British regiments—who led the most miserable lives—with low-class Indian prostitutes. During the hot season young officers and officials might find a little fun up in the hill stations, whence married British women with their children retired for months on end while their husbands toiled on in the plains below. The women outnumbered the men in the hill stations and the recognised possibility existed of one of them taking a fancy to a young man. Such affairs were discreet, the couple addressing each other by their surnames again in the morning.

For purposes of marriage a young man might think of a girl friend in England to whom he wrote and who for years had been saving herself for him. Out she came by the P & O half-afraid of her new life and of the man she had not seen for so long. Such was her mental state that she might be seduced on board or even, in extreme cases, marry someone else; such events were part of the folklore of the voyage to India. Another method of finding a wife was to take a leave in the cool season and visit Calcutta where every year arrived whole cargoes of young spinsters from England in search of husbands. For a fee, a Calcutta matron would sponsor a girl in 'society' so that she could meet suitable young men. Such arrangements were made through newspaper advertisements. But the great lure in Calcutta was the Eurasian girls, who were so exceptionally spirited and beautiful that a man might fall hopelessly in love with one, yet knowing that if he married her his career would be hindered or even ruined. If all else failed, the young man in India would take a home leave in Britain where his condition and prospects readily attracted matrimonial interest.

Back in the cantonment the young married couple set up a household with cook, house servants, gardeners and sweeper. They would entertain their neighbours until they were sick of the sight of them; and then continue to entertain them. Babies were entrusted to an 'ayah' or woman servant. An ayah—the best kind came from Madras—was more expensive and more temperamental than the other servants, who were all male. An anxious mother, especially as standards of hygiene in the 1920s were advancing so fast, would worry constantly about her child's ayah. Then when the child was seven would come the great parting, the father swallowing hard on the lump in his throat. The child would go to England for education, if a boy to the customary career of preparatory school and public school. He might not see his parents again for three or four years; he would spend his school holidays with cousins or an aunt. 'Goodbye, old man,' said a father to a son whom he would never get to know again. Then he threw himself back into his work, back to the service of India.

Such was the classical character of British rule over this strange sub-continent.

For two generations it had worked. The pioneer of the Indian National Congress, Gopal Krishna Gokhale, wrote of 'the inscrutable wisdom of Providence' which had brought the British to India. The bizarre institution of British rule had somehow come to be regarded as being as normal a part of the Indian scene as the River Ganges. In their hearts many British administrators thought it should go on for ever. Even the most far-thinking in 1918 reckoned that British rule would see out the 20th century.

India was so vast and so variegated in population that it was indeed difficult to see what could efficiently replace the framework of British rule. It could be argued that Indians were no more a single race than were Europeans. There were, firstly, religious differences. Three fourths of the population were Hindus of one kind or another and one fourth were Moslem. Hinduism is a subtle, adaptable religion based on the theory of the transmigration of souls. A man who behaved badly might be reborn as a beetle in his next life. It contains a strongly pacific element which has made many Hindus adverse to warfare; this is one reason why India has been subject to so many foreign conquests. Around Hinduism cluster many legends of the gods, especially of the Lord Krishna, but there is little dogma and it is difficult for the outsider to distinguish between what is regarded as fact and what as parable. As an offshoot of Hinduism existed the caste system. This was and is a real factor in Indian life. A man was born into a definite station from which no exertion of his own could raise him. Strict members of the priestly caste, the Brahmans, were polluted if they had physical contact with lower castes. This applied in particular to eating; a strict Brahman had his food prepared by a Brahman cook and would not eat in the presence of anyone of another caste, a fact which contributed towards social awkwardness with the British. If a Brahman travelled to Europe he would, if he followed the strict code, undergo ceremonies of purification on his return home. Jawaharlal Nehru was a Brahman and although he explicitly renounced his caste privileges and, indeed, professed agnosticism, he was ready to admit that his Brahmanical origin had given him a peculiarly fastidious outlook on life. It also gave him extra authority in his political work.

Under the Brahmans existed a hierarchy of several hundred castes and sub-castes, each based on some hereditary trade or occupation. At the very bottom of the social scale stood some 50 million 'outcastes,' people who belonged to no caste at all. The life of the outcastes often appeared miserable indeed. They clustered in huts on the outskirts of each village, forbidden to use the ordinary village drinking water and scratching a living by performing the most menial tasks. In some cases they were expected to hide if they saw a high caste man approaching lest they pollute his eyes. In Kerala in Southern India it was customary for an outcaste or man of low caste to cover his mouth with his hand when talking to a man of higher caste, a courtesy which was extended also to the British. Both the British and reform-minded Hindus found the system intolerable and it had broken down almost altogether in the big cities. Yet there were religious consolations. An outcaste who lived a moral life could look forward to the possibility of becoming a Brahman in his next incarnation. The British, according to the strict rules, were outcastes but in practice they formed a special caste of their own and it is possible to trace in the hierarchical nature of British society in India definite Hindu influences.

As an offshoot of the Hindus existed the Sikhs who flourished in the Punjab, where stood their religious capital, Amritsar. In 1921 they numbered over 4 million and were increasing rapidly—they were more successful than even the Christians at winning converts. Doctrinally it might be said that they stand in roughly the same relation to orthodox Hinduism as do Protestant Christians to Roman Catholics. In appearance Sikh men are easy to identify because they all are required to wear beards and to have uncut hair coiled under a turban. The Sikhs repudiated caste and preached vigorous doctrines of self-help, self-defence and the necessity for positive good deeds. They did well in business and in the 1920s were acquiring almost a monopoly of knowledge in India of the mechanics of the motor car. They made excellent soldiers and Sikh regiments were among the most efficient in the Indian army. At the same time their vigorous outlook made some of them the most awkward opponents of British rule. The 'non-violence' preached by Gandhi had no automatic appeal to the Sikhs as it had to orthodox Hindus and such terrorist movements as existed against British rule were often Sikh in origin.

Another sub-division of Hinduism was the Jains, who numbered just over a million in 1921. They were a thoughtful, educated group who sought to purge Hinduism from superstition and their influence was wider than their numbers would suggest. The Nehrus had been a Jain family.

The second great religion of India was Islam, which in 1921 commanded over 77 million adherents, or nearly a quarter of the population. Originally the Moslem faith had come to India through Persian and Arab conquest but intermarriage and conversions over the generations had rendered most of the Moslems racially indistinguishable from the Indian population at large. Because they had originally come as conquerors and because they considered their monotheism to be a higher form of faith than Hinduism, they had traditionally considered themselves a superior people. Yet unlike the Hindus they had produced little in the way of an educated middle class. By the 1920s they were educationally and financially backward. Their main areas of strength were Kashmir, the North-West Frontier Province, East Bengal and the Punjab but they were to be found in substantial numbers in almost every part of India. Like the Sikhs they adopted a militant attitude towards the defence of their religion and so the Punjab was a noted centre of religious disorder.

Strain between Hindus and Moslems had existed for generations. Apart from historical antipathies and jealousies there were all kinds of day-to-day causes of conflict. The Hindus regard the cow as a sacred animal; one of the characteristics of India is the way in which cows wander all over the place, even in city streets, commanding the respect of the people. In some areas the Hindus actually gaoled people who killed cows. The Moslems, forbidden by their religion to touch pork, are beef eaters. The Moslems like to have an atmosphere of peace for their sunset prayers in the mosque. Yet sunset is a time when the Hindus like to make a loud noise by banging the temple gongs. Moslem fast days tend to clash with days of Hindu noisy jubilation.

Nobody in 1918 supposed that such incidental difficulties would lead to the partition of India into two separate countries which would actually go to war with each other. The leaders of Indian nationalism were professedly anti-sectarian and the National Congress included Moslem as well as Hindu leaders. The British, too, treated India as a single unit, district boundaries taking no account of religious characteristics. There was, however, some bias in the British towards the Moslems. This was largely instinctive. To a British administrator of Anglican upbringing the Moslem faith was more comprehensible than what was often dismissed as the 'paganism' of Hinduism. The Moslems, too, formed the backbone of the Indian army and as a largely peasant community were more willing than middle class Hindus to adopt an attitude of respect towards the British. The decisive political step taken by the British had come in the Morley-Minto reforms of 1909 which had introduced for the first time, on a most limited scale, the principle of election to the legislative councils. In response to Moslem pressure, the British had created special constituencies for Moslem voters. Although politics within the constitutional framework played little part in subsequent developments in India, it could be reckoned that Morley and Minto had sown the very first seed of Pakistan. Under a system of communal election it inevitably became necessary for candidates to appeal to their own religious group rather than to the population at large. Moslem candidates, in particular, had to make the most of their ability to defend Moslem interests. The social division between the two communities tended to become a political one.

The religions of India included also some 6 million Christians, who tended to be pro-British but exerted as a community little power, and the tiny but influential sect of 300,000 fire-worshipping Parsees centred on Bombay. The Parsees during the 19th century had been an important bridge between the Indians and the British. They were of Persian origin and, as their distinctive feature, neither buried nor cremated their dead; instead deceased Parsees were placed on high towers in Bombay—the 'towers of silence'—and plucked to pieces by vultures. More readily than any other Indian community, Parsees adapted themselves to European ways and made much money in business. They were the wealthiest religious community in India. All three Indians elected to the British House of Commons were Parsees. By the 1920s, however, the Parsees were dwindling in relative importance.

There were other divisive forces in India besides religion.

An obvious one was the differences between the racial groups, symbolised by the 14 different major languages of India. A Tamil-speaking Madrasi was as different from an Urdu-speaking Punjabi as an Englishman from an Italian. There was also some colour difference, the inhabitants of southern India tending to be darker than those in the north. To some extent, too, the members of the higher castes tended to be lighter in colour than those of the lower. In practice, however, racial differences had little political importance. The Indian sub-continent was a racial melting pot and had absorbed many waves of conquerors. It was sometimes claimed that the British were the only conquerors who had managed to avoid absorption; this was certainly true in relation to the tiny numbers of British actually ruling India but these British were vastly outnumbered by the Eurasians of mixed blood. Huge and mixed as India was, she had a rigid geographical unity. To the north she was cut off by the Himalaya Mountains, to the south by the sea, to the west by a desert and to the east by the vast marsh-lands of the Ganges delta. Any doubts about her unity had been settled by a century of British rule. In 1918 the exception to this essential unity was Burma, which still formed part of the Indian Empire. In race, their Buddhist religion and language the 8 million Burmese were distinct from the Indians and their country lay outside the natural boundaries of India. They had been conquered for no very clear reason by the Indian army in the 19th century and incorporated automatically within the sphere of the Simla Government. But both the Government and the Indian nationalists—as well as the Burmese themselves—regarded Burma as a separate country. In 1936 the British separated her from India altogether.

Socially the division of India into language groups counted less than the widening gap between Indians who lived in towns and those who lived in villages, the village-dwellers numbering over two thirds of the whole population. The towns included not only such great cities as Calcutta and Bombay which were larger than Manchester or Detroit but dozens of smaller places with popu-lations numbered in hundreds of thousands. With their schools and vigorous vernacular newspapers, their partial abandoning of caste distinctions, their tendency to develop manufacturing industry, the towns were producing a form of life which was both Indian and characteristically 20th century. Many townsfolk kept their roots in the countryside. It was common for them to be smaller land-owners and it was nothing out of the way for an ordinary clerk in a commercial or government office to travel once a year to his ancestral village to collect the rent due to him. The villagers resented the system rather less than Western-minded social reformers thought they ought to. The British, who were adept at dealing with princes and peasants, found the urban middle class a puzzle. The villagers continued a way of life which in substance had changed little for centuries, although they could thank the British administration for certain irrigation schemes. The narrow-ness of the Indian peasant's way of life was, in a negative sense, a factor tending towards the unity of India. A peasant had no particular feeling of being a Bengali or a Punjabi. His life was bounded by his own village and questions of caste and religion were more important to him than questions of provincial loyalty. A village 50 miles from his home might be as strange to him as one 1,000 miles away. What would really upset him was any suggestion that his religion was threatened.

Towns and villages alike were experiencing in common a rapid growth in population, a growth which between the world wars was running at over 10 per cent a decade. The 1921 census showed a population of 318 million, that of 1931 showed 352 million, that of 1941 showed 400 million. This could be accounted for in part by improved public health measures and in part by success in overcoming famines.

Yet another division of India was a fundamental political one, that between what was strictly 'British India' and the areas of India ruled by semi-sovereign Princes under British suzerainty.

The India of the Princes included nearly half the land area and about a quarter of the population. There was no continuous boundary between British territory and the princely states, the states being dotted all over the place as islands of semi-independent territory. The state boundaries were arbitrary lines drawn upon a map and had no relation to racial, religious or geographical factors. Most of the ruling families had acquired their lands in the warfare which had raged in India in the 18th and early 19th centuries. They had sided with the British, accepted British suzerainty and had their jurisdictions defined by the British. Altogether there were some 600 ruling Princes; they included in their ranks some of the richest men in the world, a state's revenue often being regarded as the private income of its ruler.

At the top of the scale stood His Exalted Highness Rustom-i-Dowran, Arastu-i-Zaman, Lieutenant-General Muzaffar-ul-Mulk Walmamalik, Nawab Sir Mir Osman Ali Khan Bahadur Fateh Jung Sipah Salar, Faithful Ally of the British Government, Nizamud-Doula, Nizam-ul-Mulk Asaf Jah, Grand Commander of the Most Exalted Order of the Star of India, Knight Grand Cross of the Most Excellent Order of the British Empire. In 1918 he was aged 32 and had ruled for seven years as Nizam of Hyderabad, a state the size of Italy and with a population of 14 million. He had his own university, railway system, coinage and army. His capital, Hyderabad, with its population of 400,000 and many historic buildings, ranked among the great cities of the world. He was entitled to a salute of 21 guns. He died, a recluse with the world revolutionised around him, in 1967. At the other extreme stood the Siem of Nongliwai who ruled 213 people on a hillside in Assam and was just a glorified farmer, entitled to no salute at all.

Large and small alike, the Princes were subject to the British. They were allowed no contact with a foreign country nor, officially, with each other save through the Simla Government and the British Foreign Office. Their authority in internal affairs was absolute save that if they became too grossly corrupt, inefficient or unco-operative they were liable to be deposed by the Viceroy. Their work was supervised by the Indian Political Service, recruited from the Indian Civil Service and the Indian army, and each Indian state, or in the case of the smaller ones each group of states, had its British Resident who kept an eye on what was happening, 'advised' the Ruler and dispatched reports to the Viceroy. The quality varied widely. The Maharajah of Mysore, ruling 6 million, was reckoned to be a model of enlightenment; he devoted himself to his people, gave them a constitution and introduced an iron and steel works. Another notable figure was the Ruler of Bikaner, who had set up two of the best hospitals in India for his 900,000 people and who had represented India in the Imperial War Cabinet and was to be one of her delegates to the League of Nations. At the other extreme were Princes who treated their states just as sources of personal income, gambling away their peasants' taxes on the tables of Monte Carlo. In 1923 the heir to the State of Jammu and Kashmir got involved in one of the biggest blackmail conspiracies ever known. He was entertaining a girl in his suite at the Savoy Hotel, London, when a man called Hobbs burst in and claimed to be the girl's husband. The Prince, fearing that his succession to the throne was in danger, paid Hobbs £300,000 to keep quiet. Later Hobbs quarrelled with his associates in the conspiracy and the story of the blackmail came out. The Prince had to give evidence in court, his identity disguised as 'Mr. A.' In 1925 he was allowed to become Maharajah of Kashmir, where he placed a tax on windows.

The common charge against the British was that they ran their Empire on a basis of 'divide and rule.' This was plainly true in the case of the Indian Princes. The 19th-century theory had been that the existence of semi-independent potentates bound to the British Crown was a support for British rule in India. If there were serious trouble they would come to Britain's assistance.

The British took pains to flatter and conciliate the Princes—not by giving them money, of which most of them had no need, but by the more economical method of loading them with titles, decorations and honorary ranks in the army. There was an elaborate code of military salutes. The King-Emperor present in person—this only happened once—was entitled to 60 guns. The Viceroy of India was entitled to 31. The ruling Princes were on a scale running from 21 for the heads of the largest states down to three for petty sheikhs in the Persian Gulf. A Prince who had pleased the British would be given extra guns as a 'personal salute.'

In truth, however, by the 1920s the Princes were ceasing to be a bastion of British power. Their people were generally more backward than in British India but nationalist ideas were beginning to spread and the intelligentsia regarded the Princes as tools of the British rather than as national leaders. When it came to constitution-making the Princes were a nuisance. It was impossible to provide a rational framework for India without incorporating the states and yet the British felt bound by old treaties to maintain the Princes in power. There was an attempt to run a 'Chamber of Princes,' a kind of official debating society in which it was hoped that the Princes would form common and progressive policies, but the leading characteristic of the Chamber was acrimony. What became more and more obvious was that, so far from the Princes being a support for British power, the British had become the prop of princely power. This became absolutely clear when on independence in 1947, the states nearly all collapsed, the Maharajah of Jammu and Kashmir as the final act of his prerogative handing his Moslem subjects to India rather than to Pakistan.

Such was the complex, quarrelsome India in which M. K. Gandhi in 1920 launched his non-violent programme of boycott, passive resistance and non-co-operation. His object was to eject the British from India.

Gandhi's instrument was the Indian National Congress which, for most of its history, had been a mild, middle-class body content to regard dominion status for India as a distant objective to be achieved by stages. The actual founders of the Congress had been two Englishmen, retired civil servants. The Congress was not in any sense a representative or parliamentary body. It was a political party. But anyone could join on payment of a subscription of a few pence a year and in 1920 it included representatives of every shade of native Indian opinion. Hindus predominated but there were also Moslem members, including at this stage the Bombay lawyer Mahomet Ali Jinnah, the future founder of Pakistan. The two outstanding Congress leaders of the pre-1914 period had both died prematurely, the moderate G. K. Gokhale in 1915 and the extremist B. G. Tilak in 1920. Gokhale had struggled against Tilak and in 1908 had carried a resolution to the effect that the Congress sought to win dominion status 'by constitutional means.' This remained Congress policy until 1920.

The 1914–1918 war had accelerated the growth of Indian nationalism. Many Indians, even those opposed to the British, had tended to regard Great Britain as being overwhelmingly the most powerful nation on earth. The proposition that Asians could defeat Europeans had been shown in the Russo–Japanese War of 1904–05 but most Indians thought only of the British. That Britain had failed to win the war quickly and, indeed, fell into grave military difficulties, had a profound psychological influence. Perhaps, after all, Britain was not invincible. More consciously, they saw Britain declaring as one of her war aims the freeing of European nationalities from alien rule. Why should India, too, not be freed from alien rule? Then the Indian nationalists were irritated by the way in which the Indian army, at India's expense, was being used to extend the British Empire in the Middle East. The campaign to conquer Mesopotamia (Iraq) had been grossly mismanaged with thousands of troops, nearly all Indians, dying of disease. In the early stages of the war Indians had flocked to volunteer for the army but, as the fighting went on, they became less willing to join up and what amounted to press gang methods to get soldiers were employed in the Punjab. The activities of the recruiting agents, together with other dislocations of war, had turned the always volatile Punjab into a condition of unrest and near-rebellion.

A subsidiary factor was that in fighting the Sultan of Turkey the British were also fighting the Moslem Calif, the Commander of the Faithful, and indeed stripping him of his empire. Moslem opinion in India was agitated at the way Moslem Indian troops in Mesopotamia, Palestine and Syria were being made to fight against the nominal head of their religion. The Moslem League, which had hitherto tended to be pro-British, changed sides and in 1916 signed the 'Lucknow Pact' to join forces with Congress. For a moment Hindu and Moslem nationalists were united against Britain.

The Secretary of State for India was Edwin Montagu, a young and radical Liberal. Confronted by disorder in India, he decided to break with the past and give what amounted to a revolutionary pledge. He laid it down for the very first time that Britain's ultimate aim in India was to allow the Indians to run their own internal affairs.

'The policy of His Majesty's Government,' he told the House of Commons on August 20, 1917, 'is that of the increasing association of Indians in every branch of the administration, and the gradual development of self-governing institutions, with a view to the progressive realisation of responsible government in India as an integral part of the Empire.'

In retrospect the words appear cautious enough but no British minister had ever promised so much before. They set a new and definite objective for the British Raj, that of training Indians for self-government in such a manner that when it was eventually achieved they would be willing to work voluntarily within the imperial system.

The Viceroy, Lord Chelmsford, was a shadowy figure, a member of an old military family. His only previous public post of importance had been the figurehead one of Governor of New South Wales. Why he had been selected as Viceroy, a job which ordinarily went to a politician of Cabinet status, remains obscure. In administration he was weak and hesitant but in policy he was in full accord with Montagu. Although few realised it, he was a man of radical temperament. Indeed to the general astonishment he turned up in 1924 as a minister in the first Labour Government in Britain.

Together Chelmsford and Montagu worked out the first stage of associating Indians with the Indian Government.

The basic principle was that of 'dyarchy'—double government.

Each Indian province was to have what amounted to two governments. The British Governor and his officials were to retain charge of finance, police, justice, and labour matters. The remaining functions of government—education, health, agriculture, public works and so on were to be transferred in each province to a council of ministers responsible to an elected legislature.

In the Supreme Government, that of the Viceroy, there was to be no dyarchy, but the Viceroy's executive council of seven was to include three Indian members. In addition there was for the first time to be a central legislature, with a majority of elected members.

The scheme was hedged around with safeguards. Viceroy and provincial governors were given powers to override legislatures and ministerial councils whenever they felt it necessary in the public interest. The franchise qualifications, based on income and education, were stringent. Out of a population of over 300 million only five million were qualified to vote for the provincial legislatures and only one million for the central legislature. The principle of separate representation for Moslems was widely extended.

The aim, obviously, was to enlist the Indian middle class as partners of the British Raj. If they proved good partners they would be admitted to further privileges later on—the scheme provided for a review after it had been going for 10 years.

Whatever chance the scheme had of being accepted by Indian nationalist opinion was wrecked by three factors—delay in bringing it into force, cruel and clumsy measures by the Government of India in suppressing disorder and, above all, the apparition of Gandhi.

'He was like a powerful current of fresh air that made us stretch ourselves and take deep breaths; like a beam of light that pierced the darkness and removed the scales from our eyes; like a whirlwind that upset many things, but most of all the working of people's minds,' wrote Jawaharlal Nehru of Gandhi. 'He did not descend from the top; he seemed to emerge from the millions of India, speaking their language and incessantly drawing attention to them and their appalling condition.'

Gandhi in 1918 was aged 49 and had lived most of his adult life outside India. He had qualified as a barrister at the Inner Temple, London, and had gone to practice among the Indian immigrants in Natal, South Africa. He had led a protest movement of the South African Indians against the treatment they were receiving from the government. During both the Boer War and the 1914–1918 war he had organised ambulance corps.

He was a thin, short man with bowed shoulders and thick spectacles, the kind of man who trots rather than walks. Ideas poured from his lips and to talk to he could be the most fascinating person in the world. To the most abstract and elaborate ethical principles he married a precise, lawyer's mind and subtle skill at political tactics.

More than any other single individual, Gandhi was responsible for the fall of the British Empire.

In his earlier years he had got on quite well with the British. He had been a nationalist but of the moderate, gradualist type. He had been able to see virtues as well as drawbacks in British rule.

His conversion to outright opposition to the British was as much religious as political. He had always been a high-minded man seeking to do good. Then in middle life he turned himself into a religious prophet. He abandoned European dress and wore the simplest clothes, often only a loincloth. He restricted his diet to what was within the means of the poorest of the poor, which meant in practice that he lived off dates and goats' milk which he secreted in his loincloth. He renounced sex, on occasion going so far to test his fortitude as sleeping beside beautiful young women without touching them. Above all he dedicated himself to the service of the poor and identified himself with them. The poor, he held, possessed virtues which had been lost in the materialism of the 20th century. He was not particularly interested in socialistic schemes for improving their condition. What really mattered was for everyone, especially the rich, to love and learn from the poor. So far from advocating the industrialisation of India as a means of abolishing poverty, he held that the simple life was the best life. He wanted industry to revert to the basis of a family workshop. In particular he advocated the hand-spinning of cotton as both an economic doctrine and a moral duty. He himself spun cotton by hand every day and he prevailed upon his followers to do the same. One of the odder features of the Gandhi era was the way in which plump, prosperous lawyers, traders and lecturers, members of Congress, would sit down at their spinning wheels to produce their day's quota of thread. They were hypnotised by the little man. The flag of the Republic of India today bears a spinning wheel as a lasting memento of those days.

Politically, Gandhi solved a dilemma which had agitated Indian nationalists for a generation. Should they adopt constitutional methods of opposition to the British, confining themselves to speeches of protest, or should they attempt violent rebellion? Both methods appeared futile.

Gandhi cut through the knot by proclaiming the principle of unconstitutional but non-violent opposition. Nationalists should be prepared to break the law, to boycott British organisations, to resign posts in the British administration, to hinder the working of government in any way possible but they should stick to strictly non-violent measures. In no circumstances should they physically hurt anyone. If they were struck by a policeman's lathi they should, if not turn the other cheek, just stand patiently and await the next blow.

Tactically it was a brilliant idea. The British had ample troops and weapons to smash any attempt at armed rebellion. They could have cowed the people and hanged the leaders and India's last

E

condition would have been worse than her first. But against non-violent resistance the British were powerless. The offenders were even willing to go to gaol. They automatically pleaded guilty to whatever they were charged with and choked up the prison administration. There was just no answer the British could devise.

The difficulty on Gandhi's side was to make sure that the policy was properly carried out. He was making superhuman demands of his followers, asking them to suppress their natural instincts. He could only do so by preaching non-violence not just as a political method but also as a religious ethic. To him truth and non-violence were the same thing and he even used the words interchangeably. Nor did he preach his doctrine just in relation to India. He applied it to the entire human race, believing that love and non-violence provided the solution to all problems. On one of his releases from prison he began a letter to the Viceroy 'Dear Friend.' Such was the magnetism of his personality that he convinced millions of Indians not only to accept his doctrines but also to carry them out. There were, of course, occasional failures when some of his followers did turn to violence and he himself could be awkward, sometimes capricious, to deal with. But, on the whole, he prevailed. He hypnotised the Indians and he mystified the British who, as Judge Broomfield put it, could reflect only: 'You are in a different category from any person I have ever tried or am likely to have to try.'

One secret of Gandhi's success was that he turned the Congress from a group of middle class intellectuals into a mass movement. He enlisted the masses of the Indian peasantry on the Congress side.

He started doing this in 1917. His method was simple. Equipped with staff and loincloth he just walked from village to village, appearing less as a politician than as a Hindu holy man. His speeches, delivered generally in Hindustani, were short and colloquial. The people would flock to hear him, on occasion as many as ten thousand crowding around him in the open air in a remote district. They knew he was a famous, powerful man, a learned man, and they were fascinated to see him dressed as the poorest outcaste. There was magnetism in his eyes, eloquence in the gestures of his hands.

Exactly what Gandhi's long-term political objective was at that stage is far from clear. He avoided precise definition. Indeed he afterwards claimed that he had still intended to work with the British. It was, he claimed, the Rowlatt Acts of 1918 which finally turned him against Britain. These were panic measures introduced by Chelmsford's administration in face of disorder in the Punjab and elsewhere to short-circuit the ordinary processes of justice. In the event they were never used and their net effect was just further to stir up nationalist militancy.

Then, the following year, came the worst atrocity in the history of the British Empire, indeed the only full-scale atrocity ever committed in the Empire by the British in the 20th century. It was the Amritsar massacre of July, 1919.

Amritsar, the Sikh holy city in the Punjab, had long been a centre of disorder and anti-government demonstrations. On July 19 a crowd of several thousand people gathered illegally in Jallianwala Bagh, a square in the middle of the city. They were unarmed. Brigadier-General A. E. Dyer arrived with a British battalion and, giving no preliminary warning, ordered his men to open fire with rifle and machine gun on the crowds. There was no means of escape from the square save by clambering over a wall, which many members of the crowd attempted to do. Dyer ordered his men to fire at the wall. The shooting continued for ten minutes and then, the troops running short of ammunition, Dyer ordered them to withdraw. He made no provision for looking after the wounded.

The casualties were 379 killed and over 1,200 wounded.

Subsequently Dyer ordered public floggings in Amritsar and made Indians crawl on their hands and knees through certain streets where his orders against public meetings had been disobeyed.

Defending his actions to an official inquiry, Dyer made it plain that the reason for his conducting the massacre was not to disperse the crowd, which could have been done with just a few shots, but to give the Punjabis an object lesson. 'It was no longer,' he told the inquiry, 'a question of merely dispersing the crowd, but one of producing a sufficient moral effect from a military point of view not only on those who were present, but more especially throughout the Punjab.'

Dyer was relieved of his command and told he could expect no further military employment.

Justifying Dyer's dismissal to the British House of Commons, Winston Churchill, Secretary for War, said: 'Frightfulness is the inflicting of great slaughter or massacre upon a particular crowd of people, with the intention of affecting not merely the rest of the crowd, but the whole district or the whole country. We cannot admit this doctrine in any form. . . . Governments who have seized power by violence or usurpation have often resorted to terrorism in their desperate efforts to keep what they have stolen; but the august and venerable structure of the British Empire, where lawful authority descends from hand to hand and generation after generation, does not need such aid. Such ideas are absolutely foreign to the British way of doing things. . . . Our reign in India or anywhere else has never stood on the basis of physical force alone, and it would be fatal to the British Empire if we were to try to base ourselves solely upon it.'

Churchill's condemnation of the Amritsar massacre had been rendered necessary because of a wave of sentiment within Britain and among the British in India in favour of Dyer. It was held that his firmness had prevented revolution in the Punjab. The House of Lords actually passed a motion of support for this officer.

But there was an even stronger wave of resentment the other way among the Indian nationalists. That British soldiers should kill in cold blood 379 unarmed civilians undermined in their eyes the whole moral basis of British rule in India. The British appeared not as lawgivers but as murderers.

The change was symbolised in the attitude of one man, the lawyer Motilal Nehru of Allahabad.

Aged 58 in 1919, Motilal Nehru was a fastidious Brahman of Kashmiri origin. To his family fortune he had added a considerable income as one of the most successful lawyers in India. He had habitually worn European clothes and had furnished his mansion, Anand Bhavan at Allahabad, in European style. For his children he had engaged English governesses and he had sent his only son, Jawaharlal, to England to be educated at Harrow and Trinity College, Cambridge. He himself enjoyed visiting England, where he appeared in cases before the Judicial Committee of the Privy Council and he would go on to take holidays in France, Germany and Switzerland. Jawaharlal was so anglicised that he appeared even to think in English. It was rumoured of the two Nehrus, father and son, that they habitually sent their linen to be laundered in Paris. The story was untrue but the fact that it could spread was an indication of the way others regarded them.

After Amritsar, old Motilal Nehru gave up his quasi-British way of life and turned Indian nationalist. He changed habits of a lifetime by wearing Indian instead of European clothes. Egged on by his eager son, Jawaharlal, who became secretary of the National Congress, he moved to the extreme position of demanding political independence for India. Among both British and Indians his prestige was immense and the fact that the British raj could no longer hold the allegiance of such a man was evidence of how far it had decayed.

There remained, however, doubts and divisions within the Congress. Should the aim be to fight for complete independence for India or only for self-rule within the British Empire? Gandhi settled upon a compromise. At his behest the Congress in 1920 adopted a resolution in favour of 'swaraj'—freedom. What exactly this implied was to be left to the judgement of individual members and to the course of events. 'If the British connection is for the advancement of India, we do not want to destroy it. But if it is inconsistent with our national self-respect, then it is our duty to destroy it,' Gandhi told the Congress. 'There is room in this resolution for both, those who believe that by retaining the British connection we can purify ourselves and purify the British people, and those who have no such belief.'

He went on to insist that the Congress should take vigorous measures to implement swaraj.

'I want you,' he said, 'to accompany the carrying of this resolution with a faith and a resolution which nothing on earth can move, that you are intent upon getting "swaraj" at the earliest possible moment, and that you are intent upon getting "swaraj" by means that is legitimate, that is honourable, and by means that is non-violent, that is peaceful. You have resolved upon this thing that so far as we can see today we cannot give battle to this Government by means of steel, but we can give battle by exercising what is often called soul force.'

So began Gandhi's first movement of non-violent civil disobedience. It had an effect which astonished the British administration. Several thousand teachers in government schools and clerks in government offices resigned their posts. Some Indians refused to pay taxes. There was a boycott of the new election machinery, only one third of the electorate voting in the 1921 elections. There were planned breaches of restrictions on public meetings, boycotts of British goods in the shops.

Chelmsford, the Viceroy, tried to hit back by claiming that non-co-operation would lead not to swaraj but to anarchy. He was particularly worried at Gandhi's appeal to young people and to the peasants.

'Of these two latest developments,' he said in a formal statement in November, 1920, 'the most immoral is undoubtedly the mischievous attack which has been made on the youth of the country who are to be sacrificed to the exigencies of a political campaign; it matters not to the leaders of the movement if the foundations of home life are sapped and children set against their parents and teachers, provided their own ends are attained.

'The appeal to the illiterate and the ignorant is also fraught with very grave danger—it has already resulted in at least one deplorable crime—and it is certain that the restless activity of the leaders who wander from one city to another stirring up excitement among the masses by inflammatory speeches and by the reiteration of false statements despite constant contradiction may at any moment result in serious outbreaks of disorder.'

As a result of the swaraj resolution and the adoption of civil disobedience, some of the more senior and experienced Indian nationalists quit the Congress. They set themselves up as the Liberal Party with the object of winning self-government only by constitutional means. The aim was to carry on the principles of the pre-war Congress and they argued that the Montagu–Chelmsford reforms provided a better framework for constitutional agitation than had ever existed before. But the Liberal Party had no Gandi and throughout its existence failed to attract mass support.

Another moderate group was the 'Swaraj Party' with Motilal Nehru as its principal leader. The swarajists retained their membership of congress but they stood for election to the new legislatures, arguing that they could be used for propaganda.

Between them, the Liberals and the swarajists controlled the legislatures and the new provincial ministries. They were far less co-operative than the Government of India would have liked. Year after year these supposed moderates threw out the Budget in the Indian central legislature and taxes had to be imposed by special order of the Viceroy.

But the main Congress leadership, with Gandhi as the fount of policy and Jawaharlal Nehru advancing towards the position of chief organiser, had captured Hindu India. The British remained, possessed of all the coercive powers of government. They gaoled Gandhi and thousands of his followers, but in the last analysis, they had for ever lost the initiative.

India was in the position of a runaway lorry with inadequate brakes. The British could slow her up a little but the harder they applied the brakes the quicker the linings burned away.

# CHAPTER 3

# The dark continent

AFTER India, the second great category of the British Empire was the colonies and protectorates which in 1918 numbered 47. This total includes the territories which had been conquered in the 1914–1918 war but excludes the five self-governing dominions. Each of the 47 had its own separate government with its own budget and taxation system, its own local laws and its own local system of administration; many of the 47 also had subordinate governments under them, notably in Malaya, Nigeria and the Pacific islands. British colonies were dotted over all six continents of the globe and contained representatives of almost every section of the human race. No two colonies were alike and no one man really knew them all. A Greek shopkeeper in Cyprus had nothing in common with a Borneo headhunter save that they both dwelled under the union jack and were subject to a governor sent out from London. Each colony had its own history and had joined the Empire for its own local reasons. Legally they all lay under the absolute control of Whitehall and the British parliament; this applied even to colonies which possessed their own elected legislatures. If a local parliament proved refractory it could be, and sometimes was, abolished.

According to principles current by the mid-20th century it was an unsuitable method of government. Indeed the very word 'colonialism' has acquired sinister connotations. So varied and so scattered were the territories that it was difficult to set about improving the condition of the people and such improvement was needed, practically all the colonies being poor and undeveloped. In London, the Colonial Secretary and his handful of officials could not possibly grasp what so many different places needed. At the same time the local officials in each colony were circumscribed in the initiatives they could take. Such indigenous leaders of the colonial peoples as existed in 1918 gave more time to squabbling with the officials than to regarding fundamental economic problems. It was a system which in the long run was bound to prove ineffective.

Yet, at the same time, British administration nearly everywhere was more efficient than what had gone before; it had outstanding characteristics of order and incorruptability. According to their lights and within the limits of the power allowed them, many and indeed most of the British officials did conscientiously dedicate their lives to their work. Pay in the colonial service was low—much lower than in India—and the only satisfaction was to try to do the job well.

British rule rested primarily upon consent. It would have required an army of millions to hold down the colonies by force. As had been shown by the Boer War of 1899-1902 and was to be shown by risings in Cyprus and Kenya in the 1950s, even a local rebellion in a small territory could, if it were well organised, cause the gravest embarrassment to Whitehall. The British army in the 1920s consisted of just over 200,000 regular soldiers, of whom 50,000 were stationed in India. Each colonial governor had the title of 'Commander-in-Chief' but the majority of colonies had no permanent British garrison. Where garrisons did exist they were generally at a strength of a single battalion, about 700; sometimes battalions were split between several colonies— when civil disturbances broke out in Cyprus in 1931 there was only a single company of British troops on the spot to deal with them. The essential reserve power lay, of course, in the Royal Navy which had 50 cruisers patrolling the oceans and providing armed force within reach of almost every colony. The very anchoring of a British warship in a colonial harbour was commonly sufficient to quell trouble. But the Royal Navy by its nature was incapable of putting down serious, organised rebellion and the security of the colonial empire lay in the fact that such rebellion was of the rarest occurrence. Most of the colonial peoples were too inefficient to run such a thing and, anyway, there existed a genuine willingness among many of them to accept British sovereignty. Also—and this was part of the confidence trick of the British Empire—the imperial system had an air of irresistible power. What could one little colony do against the power which ruled a quarter of the world? Even the leaders of the 300 million Indians felt physically helpless against the British Empire. The corollary, of course, was that once one or two territories had had the nerve to demonstrate that the Emperor had no clothes, the system rapidly collapsed.

By far the largest section of the colonial empire was in Africa. Most of it had been acquired within living memory and so it can be reckoned that the British had far less experience in dealing

with Africans than they had with Indians; in 1918 it was customary to write off the African peoples as being hopelessly backward
and to describe them as 'children' or even as 'savages.' African
society was, in rough terms, tribal rather than national. Of the
total colonial population of 72 million, 53 million lived in the 17
colonies of British Africa. Nigeria, alone, had nearly half the
population of the colonial empire; she had over a hundred tribes.
The British Empire was easily the greatest power on the African
continent and it was possible to travel from Cape Town to Cairo
without ever leaving the protection of the union jack. Few made
such a journey; the lines of communication in Africa followed the
old slavery routes and ran inland from the coast rather than across
the continent. The Africans, technologically backward and inept
at self-defence, had for centuries existed as a raw reserve of
manpower on which other countries drew. The British had once
taken a leading part in the slave trade; later, under pressure of
the humanitarian strain which, as always, contrasted so oddly
with the more ruthless aspects of imperialism, they had played the
leading part in suppressing it.

In 1918 British policy for the administration of Africa was raw,
new and by no means settled in its objectives. Indeed it is impossible to trace any occasion before 1960 on which a British Government surveyed its whole African responsibilities and prepared a
comprehensive programme for the future. (And that programme
was a simple one of getting rid of them.) Among the colonial
administrators themselves the prevailing doctrine was that of
'Arcadianism,' by which Africans were to be sheltered from too
much contact with the outside world; traditional tribal institutions should continue under the paternal care of British district
officers. The leading exponent of the theory, Sir Frederick Lugard,
was still in 1918 Governor-General of Nigeria. Lugard, who had
started life as an army officer in India, had both pioneered British
penetration into west and east Africa and inaugurated the settled
system of government. So far as British African administration
worked to settled principles, it was Lugard's principles. Lugard
had worked them out for himself without being influenced by
what the Colonial Office thought in London.

In his *The Dual Mandate in Tropical Africa*, published in 1922,
Lugard spelled out the principle that the African colonies should
be exploited both for the benefit of the occupying power and of the
local people. Both colonisers and natives had their rights. His
words convey calm self-assurance.

'The tropics are the heritage of mankind and neither on the one hand has the suzerain power a right to their exclusive exploitation, nor on the other hand have the races which inhabit them a right to deny their bounties to those that need them. . . . The merchant, the miner and the manufacturer do not enter the tropics on sufferance or employ their technical skill, their energy, and their capital as interlopers or as "greedy capitalists," but in fulfilment of the mandate of civilisation.'

As with so much else in the British Empire, the British entanglement in Africa had resulted partly from the great central entanglement in India. Africa lay on the way to India and whether the route were around the Cape or through the Suez Canal it was regarded as essential to prevent hostile European powers establishing bases there. This was as much a rationalisation as an operative cause, but pushful British pioneers on the spot could always claim London support by using the argument of communications with India. The most obvious chain of conquest on these lines had been that in east Africa. To protect the Suez Canal it was regarded as essential to control Egypt. To control Egypt it was necessary to control the hinterland, Sudan. To control Sudan and the source of the Nile, on which Egypt depended, it was necessary to control Uganda. To control Uganda it was necessary to have a railway running from the east coast. To control the railway it was necessary to control Kenya, the territory which the railway crossed.

Moreover, much of the development and exploitation of the east African territories had not been British at all but Indian; the vast majority of new settlers had been enterprising Indians, bringing with them trade and minor industries. The Indian influence upon eastern Africa in the first half of the 20th century was at least as great as the British influence.

The desire to protect communications to India, however logical it may appear in its remote consequences, was not, however, the prime reason for British penetration into Africa. The true driving force was the same as that which had taken the French, the Germans and the Belgians into Africa during the late 19th century. The explorers had gone first with the pure zest for discovery characteristic of the scientific spirit of Europe. Then had come the missionaries to try to convert the people to Christianity and, finally, the traders. Once missions and trade had been established the demand arose for settled government upon European lines and the territories were annexed. To 19th-century Africans, white men had been objects of awe. They were so pale that they looked like ghosts. Resistance to white rule had been sporadic and, on the whole, weak—white men had guns and the more primitive Africans had not. When they had signed treaties, African chiefs had rarely understood the principles on which Europeans would interpret them; the concepts of national sovereignty or the ownership of land were alien to them. Moreover, it would be false to categorise the European incursion into Africa as merely a combination of material greed with fanatical religious fervour; the Europeans also brought tangible benefits which the Africans recognised and adopted as their own. The process of the Europeans taking over Africa was accelerated by the rivalry between the Europeans themselves—thus the British acquired Kenya for the negative purpose of preventing the Germans getting it. The definitive partition of Africa, along frontiers which still substantially persist, took place at Berlin in 1890; white politicians, some of whom had possibly never seen an African, drew lines on a map to split up the continent into spheres of influence among the British, the French, the Germans, the Portuguese, the Spanish and the Italians.

What above all else had counted was that Africa was a political vacuum into which the boisterous greed of Europe was bound to penetrate.

The British African territories can be divided into four groups: those which had been acquired by penetration from the north, those from the east, those from the west and those from the south.

In the north the mightiest incursion of the British Empire had been to establish a protectorate over Egypt but, for present purposes, it is convenient to deal with Egypt in the following chapter as a part of the Middle East rather than of Africa.

Below Egypt lay Sudan which had its own special place in the British system. In theory, Sudan in 1918 was a 'condominion' of Great Britain and Egypt, the flags of the two countries flying side by side on public buildings. In practice, though, the administration was entirely British and the Egyptians, to their annoyance, were allowed only a formal role. For the next four decades it was to be a constant aim of Egyptian policy to incorporate Sudan into Egypt but the British eventually managed to establish it as an independent state on its own. The Nile—its White and Blue branches converging at the capital, Khartoum—was the principal highway of a country which was otherwise largely desert in the north and jungle in the south. British officials cruised down the

Nile in steamers to take up their work. The country was about the size of France and Spain combined and in 1918 was thought to have only three and a half million people; in fact the population was really much larger—the first proper census in the 1930s put it at nine million. The people were part Arab and part Negro and in the black hinterland had been devastated by generations of slave-trading. In 1918, probably, a little slavery still persisted but it had been a constant occupation of the British to put it down.

Because of its special status, Sudan came not under the Colonial Office but the Foreign Office. It had its own little service of about 140 men from Britain; there were only about half a dozen recruits a year and the service had a club-like quality and its own 'Sudan spirit.' Originally it had consisted mainly of former army officers but by the 1920s the recruits were mainly young civilians. Resignation or dismissal were almost unknown and the members of the service reckoned to devote their whole working lives to this territory of which the outside world knew nothing. On camel or horse, by canoe, or, even, on foot, the district commissioners toured the sprawling expanses of the country, dealing with everything from murder to the preparation of maps. 'Boys, fresh from Cambridge and Oxford, and away from home for the first time, were put in complete charge of a district that might be twice the size of England,' wrote a Sudanese, M. A. Nigumi, in his *A Great Trusteeship* (1957). At the top stood the Governor-General who resided at The Palace, Khartoum, and combined the job with that of Sirdar (Commander-in-Chief) of the Egyptian army. The Governor-General in 1918 was Major-General Sir Lee Stack who was aged 50 and had transferred from the British to the Egyptian army in 1899. His assassination by Egyptian nationalists in 1924 was to cause the British to take a yet firmer grip on the Sudan.

The Sudanese Moslem intelligentsia, which formed the leading group of the population, were generally pro-Egyptian and, as a counterbalance, the British brought on the more backward people in the south and encouraged Christian mission work. In terms of efficient administration carried out in difficult conditions, Sudan was a model of the British Empire at its best but, because of Egypt, it did not join the Commonwealth on attaining independence.

Going clockwise around the map, the next group of territories were those which had resulted from penetration from the east. There were six of them—British Somaliland, Zanzibar, the East

African Protectorate (in 1920 renamed Kenya), Uganda, Tanganyika and Nyasaland.

If the map of Africa is likened to the head of a man looking eastwards, the tip of the nose is formed by Somalia, a coastal strip bordering the Red Sea and the Indian Ocean. In 1918 most of it belonged to Italy and the French, too, had a little bit. The British share had an area twice the size of England but only 300,000 people. The only reason for being there was to prevent French or Italians interfering with ships to India; indeed the original occupation had been carried out by the British government of India. The outsider finds it one of the most dispiriting places on earth—hot, humid and diseased, the inhabitants migrating with their skinny cattle around huge deserts in search of water. Despite the hardship of their lives, the people, tough and of the Moslem religion, were antagonistic to alien occupation and for 20 years under a leader the British called the 'Mad Mullah' had conducted sporadic warfare to try to get out of the British Empire. 'I like war but you do not,' he wrote to the King's representative. 'The country is a jungle and that is no use to you. If you want wood and stone you can get them in plenty. There are also many antheaps. The sun is very hot.' For considerable periods the British retreated to the coast leaving the rebels in control of the interior; as the Mullah had pointed out, the territory was uninviting for them and had it not been for considerations of prestige and the route to India they would have pulled out altogether. Eventually in 1920 a new force was formed which, aided by six airplanes sent out from Britain, finally defeated the rebellion. The Mullah fled to Ethiopia where he almost immediately died of influenza. It had been a wearisome business and the British imperial spirit in Somaliland had worn thin; the best that could be hoped for was to keep the administration on an even keel and to beware of more mad mullahs. (It may be observed that the 'Mad Mullah,' Mahomed bin Abdillah Hassab, was an ambitious Moslem holy man of sound sanity and considerable enterprise; that the British should stigmatise him as 'mad' for rejecting their rule forms an interesting pointer to the attitudes of 1918.)

The British administration was headed in 1918 by G. F. Archer, who had been appointed four years earlier at the unusually early age of 32. He had previously served in Kenya and had conducted a trigonometrical survey of East Africa. His salary and allowances of £1,800 a year put him among the lowest paid of British governors; from his capital, Berbera, he controlled just six district commissioners. Yarns about the camel corps, which had been formed to fight the 'Mad Mullah,' had brought the territory quite prominently to British public attention but it was difficult to get anyone actually to work there. It was the end of the line in the colonial service. In the Second World War it was to be the only British African territory to fall to outside conquest.

The fruitful area for British penetration into East Africa lay further south in the wide lands clustered around Mount Kilimanjaro, which, although it was on the equator, had snow on its peak. They were Kenya, Uganda and German East Africa which the British renamed Tanganyika.

The gateway for these territories was the Arab sultanate of Zanzibar, an island lying 20 miles off the coast. In the past it had been a centre of the slave trade but now it lay under British 'protection' and the principal industry was the cultivation of cloves. Nearly all the cloves in the world came from Zanzibar and travellers could smell them for miles before they reached the island. From Zanzibar had set off the 19th-century explorers— Livingstone, Stanley, Burton, Speke, Rebmann, Krapf—who had first related to Europeans the marvels of Africa. The Zanzibaris had already known it well—they had been exploring Africa to get slaves centuries before the Europeans came. In 1918 it was an historic but decaying place with crowded streets and back alleys where every vice was satisfied. People of every kind jostled against each other, pimps against missionaries, Germans against Armenians, freed slaves against millionaire traders. Slavery had been legal up to 1897 but the Church of England had built a cathedral on the site of the former slave market. By African standards it was a crowded country: the main island, Zanzibar, had 115,000 people on its 640 square miles and the satellite island, Pemba, had 83,000 people on 380 square miles. The leading influence was Arab but over the generations there had been copulation between the Arabs and their African slaves and much of the population was of mixed blood. The freed slaves and their descendants formed a growing segment of the population which within half a century was to overthrow Arab supremacy.

The Sultan, His Highness Seyyid Khalifa bin Harub, K.C.M.G., K.B.E., was a wealthy but largely powerless figure. Real authority rested with the British Resident, Major F. B. Pearce, who was subordinate to the Governor of Kenya. No decree of the Sultan was legal unless Major Pearce countersigned it and the majority of the Sultan's council was British. Major

Pearce drew £1,800 a year in salary and allowances and headed quite a sophisticated administration, all the key posts of which were in British hands. In all but name, Zanzibar was a British colony.

On the East African mainland the key territory, from the point of view of British penetration, was Uganda. The explorers Burton and Speke had thrilled the 19th-century British public with the news that the source of the River Nile lay in Uganda; they had named the huge lake from which it flowed Lake Victoria after the Queen. The actual source lay in the Uganda kingdom of Buganda, which under its sovereign the Kabaka, was among the most sophisticated black African societies. Missionaries of various kinds followed the explorers and competed for the Kabaka's ear and actual religious wars broke out, reproducing in tropical Africa the conflicts of 17th-century Europe. At one point the Kabaka himself conducted a mass slaughter of Christians, many of whom displayed remarkable loyalty to the faith to which they had been so newly converted. Then came traders, who demanded political stability. Conditions were unsettled and the fear existed at the back of the British mind that the Germans or French might get control and, in some unexplained way, tamper with the source of the Nile and so wreck Egypt and the route to India. The man on the spot was Lugard, then aged 30, who was working as agent for the Imperial East Africa Company, a commercial concern chartered by the British Crown. Using Sudanese and Indian troops, Lugard built up a chain of fortified posts between Buganda and the coast; when the company shareholders complained that this brought them no cash dividends he sailed home to England and aroused public opinion by arguing how crucial it was to British interests for the source of the Nile to be within the Empire. The Government then acted directly and forced treaties on the Kabaka and the lesser Uganda chiefs by which they accepted British 'protection.' Later the Kabaka rebelled and was exiled to St. Helena where, in 1918, he was still living. The reigning Kabaka, Daudi Chwa, had replaced him when a baby of one; in 1918 he was aged 21 and was firmly under British control—although his relaxed attitude towards monogamy was to cause perplexity to the Archbishop of Canterbury when it came to deciding who was his legitimate heir.

As African countries went, Uganda was a prosperous, fertile place. Vegetation blazed violet, blue and yellow around the blue waters of Lake Victoria. Bananas grew as if they were weeds. By 1918 there had been established on British initiative a flourishing cotton industry which, in entirely African ownership, made Uganda one of the richer lands in the continent. The country was about the same size as Italy with a population in 1918 of three million; Buganda was about a third of the whole. The flaw in what was otherwise a paradisical land was the tsetse fly which, breeding upon Lake Victoria, set off epidemics of incurable sleeping sickness.

The Governor, Sir Robert Coryndon, a South African, lived in the British-built administrative capital of Entebbe on the shore of Lake Victoria. He drew £4,000 a year salary and expenses. Entebbe was a trim, bureaucratic place with the officials' bungalows set in colourful gardens. There was a golf course. From Entebbe set off the peripatetic officials on tours of hundreds of miles across their domains; the country had never been properly surveyed and nobody in 1918 knew for sure where all the boundaries were and exactly how many people there were. For local journeys the officials pedalled on bicycles along the narrow jungle paths. Sir Robert himself had a motor car, there being a road just wide enough for him to use it to travel in state to the Buganda capital, Kampala, 24 miles from Entebbe. His chauffeur, one Baron Romanelli, earned £250 a year plus £15 for uniform, and was regarded as important enough to be listed among the senior officials in the Colonial Office list. For longer journeys the only method of getting along was to walk. An official would set off with a train of 50 porters, each carrying a bundle on his head, forming a self-contained expedition which could be away and out of touch for weeks on end. A collapsible flagpole was carried to display the union jack at each stopping place but, despite the cartoon jokes of a later generation, it was not customary to dress for dinner.

Entebbe was an entirely British creation, the population being only about 10,000. Kampala, the Buganda capital, was the real metropolis; it had 50,000 people, the Kabaka's palace and the Anglican and Roman Catholic cathedrals glowering at each other from adjacent hills. By 1918, however, the old antagonisms between the two faiths had largely died away and the missionaries were a powerful force, controlling all the education in the territory. By 1918 about half the African children were getting elementary schooling.

Although Uganda straggled the equator, most of it stood at an altitude of 3,000 or 4,000 feet and so the climate was not excessively uncongenial to Europeans. But there was no European settlement. The European population in 1918 numbered only one thousand, practically all of them officials and missionaries and their families. There were about 5,000 Indians, mainly small traders. In the early years of the century there had been some talk of encouraging Europeans to acquire land and form a settled population but this had come to nothing. Uganda was remote from the sea routes; Kenya, next door, had much better access to Europe and had an even better land and climate. No pioneering European leader had arisen to set an example to others. Moreover, Uganda had strong African authorities who would have been capable of vigorous resistance to alienation of the land. In 1915 Andrew Bonar Law, as Colonial Secretary, had definitively laid it down that Uganda was to remain an African country and so it was to continue for the remainder of the period of British administration. Uganda politics were to have their own complications and conflicts but there was to be no settler problem.

In contrast to the racial unity of Uganda stood the territory which lay between it and the sea. In 1918 this land was still called the East African Protectorate but in 1920 it was renamed Kenya. It was of 248,000 square miles with a population of 2,500,000. Over the following generation it was to be a place of enterprise and conflict, one of the cockpits of Empire, and eventually it was to provide a formidable armed rebellion which was to be one of the causes of the downfall of the entire British colonial apparatus.

Kenya had owed its very existence as a British colony to Uganda. In the early days of British penetration to the source of the Nile, the pioneers had crossed Kenya without really noticing it. It had been regarded as an empty, desolate land, with dangerous lions capable of rushing about at the speed of racehorses. The African population had appeared to be small, primitive and scattered—there had been nothing to compare with the sophisticated Kingdom of Buganda.

No sooner had Uganda been established under British rule than the need appeared to link it up with the east coast; Uganda officials in the early days had been allowed six months' extra home leave because the only way they could get to and from their posts was by walking the 800 miles to the coast. So had been built the wonderful Uganda railway which in 1918 still counted as the greatest constructive achievement of the British in Africa. It ran across desert and jungle, zig-zagged down the slopes of the Rift Valley and provided scheduled services in what only a few years earlier had been regarded as savage, unknown territory. Although it was called the Uganda railway it was really the Kenya railway. The

F

end of it only just touched Uganda and it was Kenya, the land the railway crossed, which was revolutionised by it.

At about the same time as the construction of the railway, a swashbuckling young British peer, Lord Delamere, had been exploring the territory—he had entered from Somalia in the north. Delamere had looked at the Kenya highlands, through which the railway passed, had fallen in love with them and decided to make his life among them. To many Englishmen these highlands rank among the most beautiful land on earth, providing an irresistible combination of the best of the English countryside with the warmth and luxuriance of Africa. 'When I first saw this country,' a Kenya settler told Winston Churchill in 1907, 'I fell in love with it. I had seen all the best of Australia. I had prospered in New Zealand. I knew South Africa. I thought at last I had struck "God's own country." ' When Delamere had first seen the Kenya highlands they had been covered with myriads of coloured butterflies and, apart from small and scattered villages of the Kikuyu tribe, they had appeared to be empty of people. In fact the Kikuyu, to whom they belonged, had been suffering from a prolonged typhoid epidemic which, temporarily, had reduced their numbers below the normal level.

Delamere had set about farming the dreamland. Strange diseases had struck his crops and herds and he had lost his family fortune. He had borrowed another fortune and lost that too. Then, in conditions of the utmost privation, he had borrowed yet more money and tried again and this time he had succeeded. By 1918 he had become a wealthy landowner, others had followed his example and the highlands he loved had been marked off as the 'White Highlands' in which only Europeans were allowed to farm. With Delamere as their leader, the settlers dreamed of Kenya becoming a white dominion, another Australia or New Zealand. The British administration, while never finally abdicating its responsibilities to the indigenous African population, had supported white settlement: apart from anything else, it had been a way of making the Uganda railway pay its way.

In the years after 1918 more and more British settlers rattled in on the railway to follow Delamere's example. They got off the train at what had started as a railway construction camp, Nairobi. In 1918 Nairobi was developing into the wildest and most enterprising town in Africa. It was full of contrasts. Lions still sometimes stalked the streets at night while, indoors at the bar of the Norfolk Hotel, slick speculators sold off tracts of land the size

of English counties. Newcomers were promised that a modicum
of supervision of such land would yield an automatic fortune. (The
British had coolly proclaimed the Kenya highlands to be 'crown
land'; the speculators and settlers were allowed long leases of it at
low rents.) Save for those with the amplest capital, farming virgin
land in Kenya was not so comfortable as the speculators made out
and many of the newcomers had to work very hard to keep their
heads above water. Their relaxation, once or twice a year, would
be to take two or three days' driving to Nairobi by bullock cart and
there to indulge in high jinks. The highest jinks were associated
with the Nairobi horse races which were held in a saturnalian
context. Farmers from the bush got drunk and rode whooping
through the town, a favourite midnight sport being to run rick-
shaw races. Delamere himself loved such full-blooded enjoyment.
He shot out the Nairobi street lamps with his revolver. Once, when
the manager of the Norfolk Hotel refused to serve any more drink,
Delamere locked him up in his refrigerator. The white man's sin in
Kenya was to run out of money; no 'poor whites' could be allowed
to detract from European prestige. Indigent white men were
arrested and put on the next ship to Bombay where they were put
out on the dockside and left.

This roistering society had a strain of corruption running
through it for it was based upon what the Africans regarded as the
theft of land. (That the settlers made good use of the land is
beside the point on the question of theft.) The corruption bobbed
to the surface in many kinds of ways. In 1918 there were still only
9,000 Europeans but, after the war, numbers rose steadily. The
popular way for the English aristocracy to get rid of a wild son was
to send him off to farm in Kenya. Pioneering new land was a
tough, heart-breaking task but the rich newcomer could buy
settled land and set himself up in feudal splendour with retinues
of servants and log fires flickering in the evenings. There were
packs of hounds, the settlers turning out in pink to the sound of the
huntsman's horn. Delamere had stocked the streams with trout
from Scotland. There was cricket and polo and incessant entertaining. Marital ties were weak and white Kenya was supposed to
have the world's highest divorce rate; the settlers attributed the
laxness of their sexual principles to the combination of hot sun and
thin air at the altitude at which they lived. Near the Kinangop
plateau, 7,000 feet above sea level, lay an area of rich pastureland
which in the 1920s became legendary as the 'Happy Valley.'
Everyone there was fabled to be very rich, very drunken and very

promiscuous, with wives being exchanged nightly. There was a cliché of a joke, endlessly retold: 'Are you married? Or do you live in Kenya?'

Kenya had a social structure which was unique in the Empire. In ordinary British colonies, as in India, the government officials formed the highest social rank. They set the style in manners and stood top in precedence. In Kenya, however, it was not smart to be an official. The qualification for entry to the best society was to be a landholder; officials were blackballed when they tried to join the leading club, the Muthaiga Country Club just outside Nairobi. This was not just because many of the settler landholders were of a higher social rank back at home in England but also for practical political reasons. The Colonial Office administrators, while abetting white settlement, still regarded Kenya as an African country rather than as a potential white dominion. In the legislature the officials, with an automatic majority, sat on the government front bench; Delamere and the other elected settler leaders sat on the other side of the chamber as a permanent opposition. Conflict between the settlers and the Colonial Office was the leading feature of Kenya politics almost until independence four decades later.

Churchill in 1907 had recorded: 'Every white man in Nairobi is a politician; and most of them are leaders of parties.' This was still so in 1918, the settlers throwing themselves into politics with the same zest as they did into farming, drink and sex. They argued passionately among themselves about points of detail but they practically all agreed that what Kenya needed was the replacement of Colonial Office rule by a white parliament with a white government responsible to it. The quasi-independence of Southern Rhodesia in 1923 with this kind of constitution was a model which white Kenya wanted to emulate.

The burning issue of the moment, in 1918, was whether or not the Kenya Indians should be allowed to hold land in the 'White Highlands' and to be represented in the legislature. (The question of such rights for Africans simply did not exist.)

The Indians, who in 1918 numbered 35,000, had at least as much claim as the whites to have pioneered the new Kenya. They had come originally to build the railway and had stayed to develop the commercial life of the country. Practically the whole of the retail and wholesale trade was in Indian hands and they provided, too, most of the skilled workers—plumbers, electricians, clerks, railwaymen. Although Kenya in its existing form could not have continued without them, their position held long-term dangers. They were at once slighted by the Europeans and resented by the Africans: they and not the whites provided the first barrier to the advancement of Africans who had acquired a little education. An African could readily become a plumber's mate but if he attempted to go on to become a plumber he might find himself against a colour bar. The more enthusiastic of the Indian leaders regarded Kenya as an Indian rather than a British colony and actually campaigned for its administration to be transferred from the Colonial Office to the Government of India.

The British settlers, under Delamere's leadership, resisted Indian claims. Delamere argued that the British, as members of the imperial race, were alone fitted to rule. If pressed, white settlers would go on to argue that if concessions were made to Indians there would be no logical barrier against Africans, too, being admitted to government and then all would be lost. During the early 1920s, against a background of white agitation, Indian boycotts and the earliest stirrings of African political consciousness, the colonial administration struggled to find an acceptable way of ruling Kenya. At one stage the white settlers planned to seize the administration and declare independence as a self-governing dominion; they went so far as to select the country house, with good fishing, to which the Governor was to be conveyed and held in confinement. Whitehall got into a dreadful panic when, through an error in communication, it momentarily appeared that the coup d'état had actually taken place. Had it happened, though, it is difficult to doubt that the British Government would have felt strong enough to deal with it more firmly than it did when the same thing actually happened in Southern Rhodesia a generation later. But, despite all the upsets and agitations, the pattern of the Kenya constitution was set in 1919 and remained unchanged between the wars. Executive power lay with the Governor who usually allowed two settlers to sit with his senior officials among the eight members of his executive council. The legislature consisted of 11 elected Europeans, two (later five) elected Indians and 17 members nominated by the Governor. Two of the nominated members were white missionaries appointed to represent African interests. No actual African became a member of the legislature until 1944.

Moreover, despite the apparent dominance of white interests in day-to-day administration, the Colonial Office itself did not, in the final analysis, lose sight of the fact that Kenya was predominantly an African country. The Devonshire declaration of 1923, by a Conservative Colonial Secretary, and the Passfield declaration of 1931, produced by a Labour one, both stressed that the overriding consideration in British policy must be the welfare of the Africans. The latter Colonial Secretary, Passfield, used to declare that he could not sleep at nights for worrying about Kenya.

The newly-appointed Governor in 1918 was Major-General Sir Edward Northey, who had spent most of his career as a soldier in southern Africa. His salary and allowances of £5,500 a year made him one of the best-paid colonial governors and he headed the most sophisticated administrative machine in East Africa. He had 40 district commissioners and about a thousand other white staff ranging from his Colonial Secretary* on £1,800 a year down to three Gaolers, Third Grade, on £200.

In the service of the Nairobi municipality as a water inspector there worked a young African of the Kikuyu tribe. His name was Kamau wa Ngengi and in 1918 he was aged 27. He had been brought up in a tribal background but Church of Scotland missionaries had given him an elementary education and he had read widely on his own. He had gifts of persuasion and an instinctive understanding of the workings of human nature. In his own mind he was trying to reconcile his tribal background, of which he was proud, with the challenge of European innovation. He went about his duties an unusually sturdy man for a Kikuyu. He had deep-set, shrewd eyes in a narrow, bearded face. He habitually wore a beaded belt, called in the Kikuyu language 'mucibi was kinyata' and from this he derived a new name for himself: Jomo Kenyatta.

The Kikuyu were at once the most advanced African tribe in Kenya and the one most exposed to white influence. In the 1920s they formed the first African political groups, the East African Association and the Kikuyu Central Organisation, the aims being land reform and African representation in the legislature. The young Kenyatta joined them and rapidly became the leading personality; he had the special gift, rare among African politicians, of being able to appeal equally to the traditionalists among his people and to the younger, educated elements. While faithful to his own Kikuyu—he wrote a book about them of lasting anthropological value—he could also rally the other tribes. In the 1920s

---

* A Colonial Secretary in a colony was head of the bureaucracy and, normally, deputy to the Governor. The title should not be confused with that of Secretary of State for the Colonies in London, who, also, was often called 'Colonial Secretary.'

he and his followers counted for little in practical politics but the day was to come when the name of Nairobi's main thoroughfare was to be changed from Delamere Avenue to Kenyatta Avenue. The whites regarded him at first as a joke, then as the devil incarnate and, ultimately, as 'the old man,' an object of respect and of some affection. In his lifetime Kenyatta was to see the birth, the rise and the fall of a complete culture, that of white Kenya.

To the south of Uganda and Kenya lies Tanganyika, a country of 365,000 square miles, more than four times the size of Great Britain. In 1918 it was newly conquered from Germany—the actual fighting had continued for two weeks after the armistice in Europe. Four years later the territory was formally mandated to Great Britain under the nominal supervision of the League of Nations. It was a 'Class B' mandate which envisaged colonial rule continuing for an indefinite period. The principal requirements were that Britain should report annually to the League and should 'promote the material and moral well-being and the social progress of the inhabitants.' In practice Tanganyika was administered on the same principles as any other British colony. Nobody in 1918 appeared to think it odd that the government in Tanganyika should change because of warlike convulsions 3,000 miles away in Europe.

Most of the German settlers had quit because of the war and the population of four million was almost entirely African. A few British, Greek and Indian farmers came in and, later, some Germans returned but there was no settler community with an influence comparable with the one in Kenya. In 1918 there were only 2,000 Europeans. The Germans had tried to break down the African tribal system and had ruled through officials called 'akidas' who were Arabs or sophisticated Africans from the coast and had no connection with traditional authorities. The British changed this and, on their usual principles, sought to build up the prestige of tribal chiefs and use them as government agents. The aim, as the Governor, Sir Donald Cameron, put it in 1925, was 'to develop the native on lines which will not Westernise him and turn him into a bad imitation of a European.' The tribes were weaker and less sophisticated than those of Uganda, there being nothing like the Kingdom of Buganda, and so the policy meant the buttressing of minor rural potentates. Educated Africans were allowed no share in administration save as junior clerks. In the 1920s a legislative assembly was set up but it consisted entirely of

Europeans and Indians appointed by the Governor; it was explained that it was impossible to appoint an African member because none of the available candidates—that is the chiefs—could speak English. Not until 1945 did the first African reach the Tanganyika legislature.

In 1918 the Provisional Administrator was Sir Horace Byatt, a professional colonial official. After taking his classical degree at Oxford he had joined the administration in Northern Rhodesia and then had gone on to work, successively, in Somaliland, Gibraltar and Malta. In 1920 he was confirmed as Governor of Tanganyika with salary and allowances of £5,000 a year. The more vigorous implementation of the 'indirect rule' policy came with the appointment of his successor, Cameron from Lugard's Nigeria, in 1925.

The new British administration took over the former German capital of Dar-es-Salaam, an ancient port with a landlocked harbour three miles long which had once figured prominently in the slave trade. It was quite a pleasant place. The Kaiserhof Hotel, next to the Lutheran church, had a broad terrace overlooking the sea; one could sit there in the cool of an early evening watching the Arab dhows scudding along the trade winds from Zanzibar. Further along the sea front there was also the Dar-es-Salaam Club. Tanganyika, like Uganda but not Kenya, counted as a tropical area and the officials habitually wore a kind of uniform of white shirt, white shorts, white stockings and sun helmet. A man would push his pipe down his stocking. Looking crisp and cool, the officials talked endless shop, addressing each other by their surnames. Grave and incorruptible, they were living and working according to the pure doctrine of 'arcadianism.'

In 1921 Chief Burito Nyerere of the Zanaki tribe in Northern Tanganyika had a son whom he named Julius. Despite his aristocratic parentage Julius Nyerere did not go to school until he was aged twelve. He grew up a practising Roman Catholic and became a teacher. At the age of 41 he was to move into the white residence of the British governors as the first President of Tanganyika and that would be the end of the reign of the men in short trousers.

The four east African territories of Zanzibar, Uganda, Kenya and Tanganyika formed a natural geographical and political unit and from the beginning of British rule there existed the distant ideal of joining them into a single state. The League of Nations'

mandate for Tanganyika—largely drafted by the British themselves—specifically provided for the possibility of the territory
being linked with its neighbours. The Kenya white settlers thought
of themselves as leading and dominating the whole. These vast
territories, the size of Western Europe, would become another
dominion on the scale of South Africa; the hope of achieving it
was thought of as an epic upon the scale of the 19th-century
conquest of the American west. From the settler point of view, the
main doubt was whether or not the climate was suited for a
permanent white population. The thin air of the 'Happy Valley'
had already produced results unconsonant with the more austere
of European traditions. What further damage, in the long run,
might be wrought by the equatorial sun and high altitudes upon
the white man's characteristics? The possibility was widely canvassed of damage being done to the actual genes and so to the
imperial race itself. This kind of problem customarily aroused
more attention than the possibility of resistance by Africans.
Winston Churchill, who examined the problem in 1907, came
ponderously to the conclusion that it would take two or three
generations to prove whether or not Europeans could safely bring
up their families on the equator. 'Till that is proved,' he wrote,
' "the white man's country" will remain a white man's dream.'

The deepest point of British penetration into Africa from the east
was the little protectorate of Nyasaland, a narrow country some
600 miles long and 100 miles wide running along the shore of
Lake Nyasa between Tanganyika and Northern Rhodesia. It had
become British almost entirely through the initiative of Scottish
missionaries and the Africans still customarily spoke English with
a Scottish accent. The main town was called Blantyre after David
Livingstone's home in Scotland. It was a poor but quite contented
country. Historically and administratively its links were with the
east but its newer, economic links were more with the Rhodesias
and South Africa. The more ambitious of the younger Nyasas,
having learned in mission school to read and write and to recite
'The Lor-r-r-d is my shepherd,' customarily migrated southwards
to look for work. Hastings Banda walked to South Africa at the
age of 13 and did not come home again for 33 years. He was
typical of Nyasaland exiles in that he did not lose touch with his
native country; when he did eventually return it was to lead it to
independence.

That Nyasaland should ever become independent was not
conceivable in 1918. It was a matter for desultory discussion

whether it should link up eventually with east Africa or with the Rhodesias but its population of one million was too poor and too small ever to stand on its own. The Governor, Sir George Smith, ran a tidy club-like bureaucracy in the administrative capital, Zomba. He was aged 60 and the job was a form of reward after his 41 years' service in various colonies; he drew £3,000 a year in salary and allowances and ruled mainly through 25 district residents who got between £400 and £700 a year.

British penetration into Africa from the south had been based upon sovereignty over South Africa, with its settled white population and self-governing institutions. Beyond noting this fact, it is sufficient to postpone consideration of the Union of South Africa itself until Chapter Six, which deals with the dominions.

In 1918 the Governor-General of South Africa, Earl Buxton, had a dual responsibility. He was the constitutional head of the Union, acting upon the advice of his ministers, and he was also High Commissioner supervising, without ministerial advice, the other British territories in the area—Basutoland, Swaziland, Bechuanaland, Southern Rhodesia and Northern Rhodesia. For this work (which does not appear to have occupied a great deal of time) he got an extra £3,000 a year added to his salary as Governor-General.

The first three of these territories were appendages of South Africa and, indeed, the first two were actually surrounded by South African soil. All had considerable land areas but were sparsely populated. It was vaguely supposed that at some time in the future the ruling chiefs would agree to being incorporated politically into South Africa, of which for currency, customs and communications purposes they were already a part; the more enterprising of the population customarily entered South Africa to work. Meanwhile nobody took much notice of them; they were treated with a lassitude which was unique even by the most relaxed standards of normal colonial administration. Each came under a Resident Commissioner on between £1,000 and £1,500 a year; in the case of Bechuanaland even the word 'resident' was a misnomer—the territory was administered from Mafeking on South African soil.

In terms of population, the biggest of these territories was Basutoland which contained in an area of 11,700 square miles half a million people, the broken remnants of tribes which in the 19th century had resisted European incursion into southern Africa. There had been a grave alcohol problem with the danger of the people drinking themselves to death but this, by 1918, had been largely overcome. The country was still, however, badly infected by leprosy—although it was reckoned to be a good convalescence centre for Europeans getting better from malaria. It was divided into seven districts, each ruled over by an hereditary chief drawn from a single royal family descended from the 19th-century Chief Moshesh.

Swaziland had an area of 6,700 square miles and a population of about 114,000. The Paramount Chief or King was a little boy called Sobhuza; during his minority his grandmother, Labotsibeni, was acting as Regent; the Swazis called her 'Cow Elephant.' The land was both fertile and accessible to European centres and there was some tendency for European farmers to move in—the British in 1909 had declared two thirds of the land to be the property of the Crown and capable of being sold to non-Swazis.

Bechuanaland, the country with its capital outside its own territory, had 275,000 square miles—about the size of France—but it was practically all desert and supported only 200,000 people. The leading personality was Tshedeki Khama, proud Chief of the Bangamwato tribe, which numbered about half the population. In his own territory Tshedeki was virtually an absolute ruler until, in 1933, he had the temerity to convict a white man of rape and sentence him to be flogged. The news of this shook the Empire and Royal Marines entered Serowe, Tshedeki's capital, and forced him to abdicate. Later, after giving a formal apology, he was restored to power. The episode illustrated the crucial importance of the 'prestige' and 'respect' upon which British rule partly depended. No white man, whatever he had done, could be flogged by a black one. The Colonial Secretary of the time was no crusted Tory but a railway trade union leader, J. H. Thomas, who had risen to power through the Labour Party. The strategic importance of Bechuanaland was that it lay between South Africa and Southern Rhodesia and carried the railway which linked the two countries.

The remaining responsibilities of the Governor-General of South Africa, in his capacity of British High Commissioner, was the huge central African territory administered by the British South Africa Company and named Rhodesia after the company's founder. Northern and Southern Rhodesia stretched over 430,000 square miles, which was about four times the size of Great Britain, and in 1918 was regarded as a most promising area for white settlement.

Rhodes, a diamond-mining millionaire and Cape politician, had been a man of genius tinged with madness. He had believed that the Anglo-Saxon race, with the possible assistance of the Germans, was fitted to rule the entire globe. His dream in the 1890s had been to strike northwards and to bring all central Africa under British settlement. This was partly for sheer love of conquest and partly with a view to commercial profit—he raised capital for his ventures by promising huge dividends from the mineral wealth that would be discovered; in fact during his life-time the British South Africa Company had made no money at all. Under Rhodes's direction the pioneer columns had trekked up from South Africa and by a mixture of bribery, deceit and brute force (the story is a discreditable one) had won control. He had named the capital Fort Salisbury after the British Prime Minister, the Marquess of Salisbury, as a means of attracting London support for his enterprise. For his own burial he had selected a site in the Matapos mountains near Bulawayo, the commercial capital of Southern Rhodesia. It is a grim place called the 'World's View.' In his lifetime Rhodes had clambered up there over the hot rocks to gaze over the vista of blue-grey plains which he had hoped would bear his name through the ages to come. Rhodesia, made by Rhodes and called after Rhodes—no millionaire ever had a bolder ambition. In 1918 he lay buried on the mountain, the lizards crawling over a massive stone lacking any cross or religious symbol. 'A haunted, sinister, pagan place,' wrote a British High Commissioner, Lord Alport.

The two Rhodesias in 1918 lay under the administration of the British South Africa Company, which had its head office at 2 London Wall Buildings, London, E.C.2, and a board of directors appointed in the ordinary way by shareholders. On the spot there were company-appointed administrators with, for Southern Rhodesia, an advisory council elected by the white settlers. An Imperial Resident Commissioner, appointed by the Governor-General of South Africa, represented the British Colonial Office.

Southern Rhodesia consisted of the former African kingdoms of Mashonaland and Matabeleland. For its 149,000 square miles it had, it was estimated in 1918, only 845,000 African inhabitants. They lived in scattered groups and it was possible to travel 20 or 30 miles across country without meeting a single person. In fact the population was probably larger than the Europeans thought but it did appear beyond doubt that there was plenty of room for new settlement and by 1918 some 30,000 immigrants had arrived, mostly from South Africa. Any notion that the scattered, primitive Africans could ever claim the country would have been regarded as ridiculous; it was nearly 30 years since the last serious trouble. They were of no more importance than the American Red Indians or the Australian aborigines. The only substantial issue was whether Southern Rhodesia should become a part of South Africa or go ahead on its own. The Rhodesia settlers had the same kind of ambitions as those in Kenya but they were a duller lot, possessing little of the fey strain of the white Kenyans. Rhodesia compared with Kenya was said to be like a sergeants' mess compared with an officers' mess.

Northern Rhodesia, which ran northwards from the Victoria Falls and the River Zambezi, was twice the size of Southern Rhodesia. It included the Kingdom of Barotseland, the ruler of which, the Litunga, was approached by his subjects crawling on hands and knees, plus half a dozen other major tribal groups. Although the Company ruled the territory, the major European influence was that of the missionaries; David Livingstone, the most famous of them, had died there half a century earlier and the capital, Livingstone, was called after him. (In 1935 the capital was to be moved to the more central town of Lusaka.) In 1918 the European population numbered only 2,000 compared with an estimated 980,000 Africans. The land and climate were suited to European settlement but it was a long way up from South Africa and the Company preferred to develop Southern Rhodesia first. This, to some extent, was a miscalculation for really Northern Rhodesia was the richer of the two territories.

In 1918 there lived in Chinsali in Northern Rhodesia an ordained Church of Scotland minister named Kaunda. He was a Nyasa who, after mission training in his own country, had gone to take the message to another country. He married the first African woman schoolteacher in Northern Rhodesia and, in 1924, they were to have a son they called Kenneth. Within 40 years that boy was to wipe the very name of Rhodes off the map of his country and lead it to independence as Zambia.

Neither the settlers nor the Colonial Office regarded Company rule as a satisfactory system. The charter giving it political power was due to run out in 1923 and nobody, not even the Company itself, wanted to renew it. (The expiry of the charter did not extinguish the Company's rights to land and minerals.) Winston Churchill, during a brief period as Colonial Secretary, decided in 1922 that Northern Rhodesia should become an ordinary colony and that Southern Rhodesia should become a province of South Africa. The Southern Rhodesian whites were predominantly of South African origin and Southern Rhodesian institutions, notably the law, followed South African models. Thus a junction between Southern Rhodesia and the Union would have been not illogical.

There was nobody to oppose the Northern Rhodesia part of the plan and, accordingly, the territory in 1924 was inaugurated on the ordinary colonial model with a governor appointed from London. In Southern Rhodesia, however, the whites were allowed a plebiscite and, to the general surprise, they refused by a small margin to join South Africa. The reasons for the plebiscite going the wrong way are difficult to disentangle. It had something to do with the volatility which is characteristic of politics among white settler minorities. It had something to do, too, with a dreamlike but intense Rhodesian nationalism; within months of their arrival new immigrants would proclaim that they were 'Rhodesian' as if they and their families had lived there for generations. Then, too, there was the consideration that the Boer element in South Africa was anti-British and therefore uncongenial. Whatever the cause, the plebiscite was one of the decisive events in southern African history. Had it gone the other way, the issue of Southern Rhodesian independence under minority government would not have arisen in the 1960s. And, further, the predominantly British Southern Rhodesian vote might well have been sufficient to keep the South African Boer Nationalists out of power in the late 1940s and so the history of South Africa would have been different, too.

In any event, the only thing left was for Churchill's successor as Colonial Secretary, the Duke of Devonshire, to make Southern Rhodesia, too, a colony. It was, however, a colony of a unique kind. Real power went to a settler government responsible to a settler legislature and the Governor was a ceremonial figurehead as in a self-governing dominion. The Southern Rhodesian Prime Minister was allowed to attend Imperial Conferences with the dominion Prime Ministers; the legislature also controlled its own police and army. The British Government retained a theoretical veto over legislation affecting Africans but this was never used and, indeed, it would have been difficult to enforce. It was quite unlike Kenya where the settlers were never allowed control over their own police and defence. The constitution was fraught with inherent weaknesses which at the time were not evident, it being assumed that a continuing relationship between little Southern

Rhodesia and the great British Empire was of benefit to both sides. Nor did the 1923 constitution represent a handing-over of power by the British Government; the Colonial Office had never, save as a remote supervising body, exercised effective power in Rhodesia. The transfer of true power was from the British South Africa Company to the Southern Rhodesian settlers; so the flaws lay not so much in the 1923 arrangements as in the older method of allowing commercial companies to assume political power in extending the British Empire. The man who accepted power was Sir Charles Coghlan, a flamboyant South African lawyer who became Southern Rhodesia's first Prime Minister; he believed fervently in the British Empire and in white settlement and so set a pattern which was to persist for decades after his generation.

The division between 'white' Southern Rhodesia and 'black' Northern Rhodesia did not work out so well as had been expected. Between the wars Southern Rhodesia had a difficult time economically, her mineral wealth not living up to the hopes of the early prospectors. Her mainstay became the cultivation of tobacco which, in 1918, was only just emerging from the experimental stage. The settler government, anxious to encourage white immigration, inaugurated a Land Apportionment Act which reserved half the land in the colony for white settlers. The greater part of it remained empty, the settlers not arriving in the desired numbers. By 1939 the white Southern Rhodesian population was still only 60,000. Northern Rhodesia, on the other hand, turned out to be richer than anyone had expected because of its huge copper deposits on the border with the Belgian Congo. Mineral rights, which Rhodes and the British South Africa Company had acquired, or claimed to acquire, for a few rifles or trinkets turned out to be worth incalculable millions of pounds. In the 1930s came a white immigration, principally from South Africa, to run the mines and these new arrivals wanted and expected self-government on the Southern Rhodesian model.

The man who was to emerge as leader of the Northern Rhodesian whites and then, briefly, as white leader of both Rhodesias was in 1918 aged nine and halfway through his schooling. He was the 13th and youngest child in a family which kept a 'poor white' boarding house in Salisbury. His father was, by origin, a Lithuanian Jew and his mother was South African. His name was Roland Welensky but people already called him 'Roy.' He was to leave school at 14 and become a boxing champion and an engine driver before entering politics by way of railway trade unionism. Every step in his career was a fight—he had been born to fewer hereditary advantages than, say, Kenneth Kaunda the minister's son. He liked to describe himself as '50 per cent Polish, 50 per cent Jewish and 100 per cent British' and by one of the stranger turns of destiny he, remote from the British ruling class, was in the 1950s to become the guardian of the last-ditch dream of a British dominion covering all Central Africa. Welensky refused, in the last resort, to commit treason against the British Crown. The leader who was actually to do so, Ian Smith, born in 1919 in Southern Rhodesia, was of a more obviously conventional type. His family was South African but he was to have a secondary and university education which would appear to make him fit more readily than Welensky into the British pattern.

In the three areas of Africa so far considered—the north, the east and the south—the power of the British Empire in 1918 was paramount. The interests of other European powers were small or weak. In west Africa, however, the British were a relatively small colonial power; they had one big country, Nigeria, and three smaller ones, the Gold Coast, Sierra Leone and Gambia. In terms of acreage they were outstripped by France, Belgium and Portugal. Nevertheless, Nigeria was easily the biggest single colony in the British Empire and, economically, the west African colonies were among the most profitable imperial possessions.

The original British connection with west Africa had been the slave trade, first in operating it and then in suppressing it. This had involved occupation of small points on the coast with no requirement to strike inland—indigenous African authorities themselves had found it profitable to look after the actual supply of slaves. Other trade had developed alongside slavery and west Africa had been thought of in terms of 'coasts' supplying specialised products: the Pepper Coast, the Ivory Coast, the Gold Coast, the Slave Coast. By the 1860s the slave trade had been eliminated and there had been some talk of the British abandoning their fortified coastal bases. Then, in the usual combination of late 19th-century circumstances—promotion of trade, support for missionaries, rivalry with other European powers, joy in conquest —the British had struck inland and established complete colonial administrations. They were hot, humid, unhealthy areas commonly referred to as 'the white man's grave'; ravaged by dysentery and malaria, the pioneering British suffered a higher death rate than in any other colonial region. Thus there was no west African equivalent of the white settlers in southern and eastern Africa; an

'The mandate of civilisation'. Lord Lugard (centre), pioneer of British colonial administration in Africa, visiting London Zoo with a party of African chiefs, *c* 1925

'You cannot make a republic of the British Commonwealth of Nations'. Jan Christian Smuts of South Africa

Englishman went out to do a job and hoped to live to come home when it was finished. By 1918 the health position was improving; the annual death rate among British officials—men in the prime of life—was only 16.5 per 1,000 compared with 27.3 in 1904. Even so, colonial administrators in west Africa got special high rates of pay and long leave to compensate for the climate and the risk of death; the starting rate for a newcomer in west Africa was £500 a year compared with only £300 in east Africa.

Despite financial inducements, the administrative services were often undermanned by the British and this gave opportunities for local Africans. (There were no Indians, either, to compete with the Africans.) By 1918 the middle-class Africans of the west, who at the coast had traditions of contact with Europe going back 350 years, were among the most sophisticated and literate on the continent. While nobody in 1918 foresaw anything but the indefinite continuance of colonial administration, there already existed African teachers, doctors and lawyers. The tendency at this stage was for the educated Africans to identify themselves more with the British than with the rural African masses.

The colonising powers, France, Belgium, Portugal and Britain, had little contact with each other in the field and developed their territories on different lines. Africans from the various colonies rarely met each other and, when they did, required interpreters to translate between English, French and Portuguese. The French tended to regard their colonies as extensions of Metropolitan France and between the wars developed the system of their being represented in the National Assembly at Paris. This, alone, was alien to British political principles. Then the French believed that their culture was capable, in the long run, of being assimilated by members of other races and that 'advanced' Africans could be turned into Frenchmen. Although French rule was autocratic and sometimes harsh, few Frenchmen shared the characteristically British preoccupation with skin colour and there was a good deal of sexual mixing. The dividing line, for the French, was that between the 'civilised' and the 'uncivilised'; few Frenchmen shared the British fascination with tribal life and the 'noble savage.' The Belgians in the Congo acted according to plain commercial principles, regarding their colony as an estate to be developed for the benefit of the homeland. Right up to the moment of independence, 40 years later, no inhabitant of the Congo, African or Belgian, was allowed any political rights. Belgian rule was efficient and provided the best elementary education system

G

of any colony but this was run for commercial rather than political reasons. The Portuguese in Angola were autocratic and sluggish. So far as they had a policy, it was an antique version of that of the French. They had no colour consciousness at all and actual marriage between Portuguese and Africans was not out of the way. The British in 1918 rather despised the Portuguese.

The distinctive British principle was that of 'indirect rule,' district commissioners supervising traditional tribal authorities. It was exemplified above all in the huge colony of Nigeria with its 16 million people scattered over 335,000 square miles. The colony was as big as Britain, France and Belgium put together but the European population, which included all the administrators, totalled in 1918 only just over 2,000. As a sheer administrative triumph, Nigeria ranked as the most significant British work in Africa. The man largely responsible, Frederick Lugard, still reigned in his Governor-General's palace on the steaming island-capital of Lagos. He drew salary and allowances of £8,250 a year, the highest of any colonial governor. Under him ran a bureau-cratic machine that was the marvel of the Empire. He had two lieutenant-governors on £3,000 a year to look after the northern and central provinces. Below them was a hierarchy of 400 residents, district officers and cadet district officers who on salaries ranging from £500 to £1,680 actually supervised the tribal authorities. Their very names evoke British Africa—C. Hornby-Porter, Captain H. L. Norton-Traill, H. Cadman, F. Ferguson, Lieut-Col W. R. R. Ffrench, F. S. Williams-Thomas, all listed at Lagos in order of seniority. To advise him Lugard had a Nigeria Council consisting of 22 senior officials, seven non-official Euro-peans and six African rulers. Nigeria was the heartland of British colonialism, a training ground and a model for lesser colonies. Lugard was hailed as the greatest of colonial governors; scholars produced whole tomes analysing and describing his work.

Half a century later it was possible for an able young scholar to write a short historical book about western Africa without even mentioning Lugard's name. (*The New States of West Africa* by Ken Post, 1964.) Indeed it could be argued that Lugard's aim of developing tribal government, and creating it where it did not previously exist, was no more than an historical side-track. Against all Lugard's intentions, Nigeria was soon to turn to be ruled not by aristocrats but by brash, educated politicians and army officers. Such a development was just what Lugard was trying to avoid.

About a hundred miles up the coast from west Nigeria lay the richest and most sophisticated of Britain's African colonies. For historical reasons, it was called the Gold Coast but it was not really a coast at all. It was a rectangular country with one of its short sides on the sea and the River Volta flowing down the middle. The area was 78,000 square miles, about the same as Great Britain, and there were 2,000,000 inhabitants in 1918, only 1,500 of them European. About half the people lived in the coastal belt and the remainder in the old tribal areas to the north, including the former Ashanti kingdom, which the British had finally subdued only 17 years earlier after the most bitter fighting. The coast possessed proportionately the biggest middle class of black Africa, including traders, peasant farmers and, by 1918, professional men. The legislature of 20 members included six African members nominated by the government—three of them tribal chiefs and three from the coastal middle class. English was ousting African tongues as the territory's main language. If anyone in 1918 had thought about self-government for an African country, the obvious candidate for such a status would have been the Gold Coast. But nobody thought in such terms; as late as 1934 a British left-wing cartoonist, David Low, was portraying the inhabitants of the Gold Coast as a sort of nigger minstrels clasping spears.

The Gold Coast still exported gold but overshadowing it vastly in importance in 1918 was a far more valuable product, cocoa. The British at home possessed the sweetest tooth of any race and delighted to consume large and growing quantities of chocolate. They also liked to make cocoa into a drink. It nearly all came from the Gold Coast and the growing of it was mainly in African hands. This was quite unlike Kenya where coffee was a 'white' crop which Africans were forbidden by law to plant. Cultivation of Gold Coast cocoa had started in the late 19th century and in 1900 only £27,000 worth of it was exported. By 1918 this figure had jumped to £1,800,000 and, with the end of the wartime shipping shortage, it passed £10 million in 1920. By African standards the Gold Coast was a wealthy country and, between the wars, some of the middle class began to wonder whether British administration was enterprising enough in using the wealth to develop the country. Although it had such a thriving trade, the Gold Coast did not possess even a port; merchant ships lay out at sea off Accra and cargoes had to be ferried backwards and forwards by canoe. Certainly the British officials knew little of economics, distrusted business and had no incentive to take risks; such things lay outside their ways of thought. The Governor in 1918 was Sir Hugh Clifford, a 58-year-old expert on Malaya where he had spent most of his career. He had written a Malayan dictionary and a dozen other books about Malaya. The Gold Coast, where he had arrived as Governor in 1912, was his first African posting. He drew £6,000 a year salary and expenses and lived behind battlements in Christianborg Castle, Accra, which had been built by the Danes in the 17th century. For the Gold Coast people, the glowering castle with its rusty cannons stood as the symbol of British rule.

At Nkroful in the western Gold Coast there lived in 1918 a boy aged nine years, Francis Nkrumah. He was the son of a goldsmith and was receiving a middle-class education from Roman Catholic missionaries. Later he was to change his first name to Kwame. Within 40 years he was to take up residence in Christianborg Castle as the Osafegu or 'Redeemer' of his people and as a pioneer of a new, continent-wide African nationalism.

Up to the 1914–1918 war, Germany had possessed two colonies in west Africa—the Cameroons and Togoland. The British and the French had conquered them and, under League of Nations mandate, shared them between each other. The British got 31,000 square miles of the Cameroons with a population of 650,000 and 19,000 square miles of Togoland with a population of 18,000. They were tacked on to Nigeria and the Gold Coast respectively and, despite the mandate, became integral parts of the two colonies.

At the far west of Africa, on the tip of the sprawling French possessions, stood the two remaining British African colonies, Sierra Leone and Gambia.

Sierra Leone had started in the 18th century after slavery had been ruled by the courts to be illegal within the United Kingdom. Supported by charitable donations a shipload of indigent Africans from London, many of them former slaves, had come out to the territory and, by treaty with the local ruler, had acquired a peninsula 25 miles long and 12 miles broad. Later the territory had been used as a general depository for freed slaves, many of them rescued from slave ships on the high seas, and the capital had been called Freetown. The little territory had something in common with its neighbour Liberia, formed by freed slaves from the United States, but the British had retained a firm administrative grip, the territory having strategic importance. In 1918 the population of the Sierra Leone peninsula was about 75,000 and the main asset was the port, the best in West Africa.

During the 19th century the British had struck inland, as everywhere, and had set up a protectorate over the indigenous tribes. Protectorate and colony together in 1918 had an area of 31,000 square miles and a population of 1,400,000.

Freetown had an air of decay and of having seen better days, as indeed it had for by 1918 its strategic value had declined. The climate was dreadful; in the 19th century the administration had almost vanished as governors and officials had kept dying. For three months of the year the territory is plagued by a hot, dry wind, as from an oven, bearing fine Sahara sand. When that wind dies down there come thunderstorms and tornadoes to mark the start of the rainy season which lasts the remaining nine months of the year. With a rainfall of around 130 inches annually, Freetown is one of the wettest places on earth. In 1917 there were ten deaths among the 1,090 Europeans, nearly all of them men in their prime. The Governor, R. J. Wilkinson, had arrived there in 1916, aged 52, after 27 years in Malaya where he had been, at various times, inspector of schools, land revenue collector and postmaster general. He had never worked in Africa before. This all-rounder drew £4,000 a year, which was about double what he had been getting in Malaya and, besides being Governor, he had the honorific title of Vice-Admiral; despite such advantages he must at times have longed for the road to Mandalay.

Gambia was an even tinier colony and also one of historic importance in the British Empire. The British connection with it dated back to Queen Elizabeth I. It had an area of 310 square miles and a population in 1918 of about 150,000. Really it was just a strip of land on either side of the estuary of the River Gambia, with the capital, Bathtown, on a sandbank in the middle. The Governor in 1918 was Sir Edward Cameron who had spent most of his career in the West Indies. He was aged 58 and drew £3,250 in salary and allowances.

Such was the Africa of which the British Empire in 1918 ruled two thirds. It was still an unknown and largely unsurveyed continent, its indigenous inhabitants regarded as picturesque savages. The union jack flew at the Cape of Good Hope and over Cairo, over the steaming harbour of Sierra Leone and over the cool Kenya highlands. District officers with lines of porters picked their way through jungles to parley with tribal chiefs, perhaps returning trembling with malaria and borne on a litter. It was inconceivable that within a generation such a thing could become a cliché of humorous cartoons. The men who thought deeply about

Africa were those who wanted to build new white dominions in the east and the centre to match that which already existed in the south. It could make a white man's head spin to consider what might be achieved.

Yet it nearly all had been won in one generation and it was to be lost in the next. In 1918 it was high noon for the British in Africa.

CHAPTER 4

# Palm and pine

ALTHOUGH the African territories comprised well over half the British colonial Empire (that is excluding India) they rarely in 1918 and the years between the wars rose to the forefront of British Government thinking. Colonial Office responsibilities extended over four other continents—America, Europe, Asia and Australasia—and the area which posed the most difficulties was the Middle East where three of them joined together.

The most numerous people at this world crossroads were the Arabs, a proud race who a millenium earlier had themselves been an expanding, imperial power. An Arab had founded the Moslem religion which now spread all the way from Morocco in the west to Borneo in the east and was winning multitudes of new converts in Africa. Arab mathematicians had provided much of the groundwork which had rendered possible the science and technology of Europe. Arab traders had known Africa while to Europeans it was still *terra incognita*. The British never subdued the Arabs as they did for a while the Indians and the Africans. The Arabs failed to fit the imperial formula—it was difficult to decide, even, whether they should be counted as civilised or just as 'natives.' Pro-British Arabs regarded themselves as allies rather than as subjects. The Arabs with which British pioneers and officials generally felt most at ease were the rural Bedouin who wandered through the deserts with their tents and camels. They could be counted as 'tribes' and so fitted into a colonial formula. Unfortunately, though, power among the Arabs lay in the cities and not among the Bedouin.

The British had gone into the Middle East ostensibly because of India and, indeed, the original incursions had been from the Indian side. During the 19th century the Government of India had established protectorates on the coasts of Arabia and the Persian Gulf with the idea of protecting the sea routes. Inland the Government of India had long feared invasion from Russia and had sought to get the interjacent countries of Afghanistan and Persia under British–Indian influence—the Government of India had at times conducted an almost independent foreign policy.

British diplomats and consuls in Afghanistan and Persia were commonly drawn from the Indian Political Service. (The body which directed the Indian princely states.) During the 1914–1918 war the Indian Army had occupied Persia and used it as a base from which to conquer (with some difficulty) the Turkish province of Mesopotamia. Curzon as Foreign Secretary seriously considered in 1918 the possibility of annexing Persia outright to the Empire.

Apart, however, from the occupation of Egypt and the island of Cyprus, British policy in the Middle East before 1914 had been to avoid excessive entanglement in local political affairs. The aim had been to prop up the decaying Turkish Empire as the most economical method of protecting the route to India. The British had developed a half-respectful, half-patronising attitude to 'brother Turk' and had regarded him as a good fellow. But brilliant German diplomacy in 1914 had brought Turkey into the war against Britain and by the use of British and Indian forces, supported by Arab irregulars, the British had conquered Palestine, Syria and Mesopotamia. The capture of such historic cities as Jerusalem and Bagdad had served as a useful propaganda counterpoise for setbacks in Europe. The Arabs, with British support, had established a new Kingdom of Saudi Arabia.

By 1918, too, a new factor was appearing in the Middle East, that of oil. The Royal Navy was converting from coal to oil and the internal combustion engine was on the way to becoming the basis of land transport. Great Britain herself had no indigenous oil resources and so it became an imperial interest to prevent Middle East oil wells falling into hostile hands. The Mesopotamian campaign had been planned partly with a view to oil and Curzon's proposed annexation of Persia had some connection with the British-controlled oil industry there. At this stage, however, oil was a subsidiary rather than a decisive factor in British policy. The major expansion of Middle East oil production was not to come until after the Second World War.

The central entanglement in the Middle East, that in Egypt, had come largely because of the Suez Canal. Although the canal had been a French project upon Egyptian soil, its main customers from the start had been British, in 1918 about two thirds. It was, as the cliché went, the 'lifeline of the Empire.' Accordingly, after disturbances in Egypt, the British had moved in and established control. In 1918 Egypt was ruled, approximately, on the lines of an Indian princely state. She had her own Sultan but her defence and foreign policy were entirely British-controlled and the key posts in her internal administration were filled by British officials. The most powerful man in Egypt was the British High Commissioner; he was responsible to the Foreign Office and not the Colonial Office but his functions were more those of a Governor than of a diplomatic representative. Customarily the post went to a leading general and in 1918 Field Marshal Viscount Allenby, conqueror of Palestine, was appointed to it on a salary of £7,600 a year.

Although the reigning dynasty in Egypt was of Albanian origin and the higher social classes were mostly Turkish, the mass of the 12 or 13 million people of Egypt were Arab. They lived in teeming cities and, subject to extortionate landlords, along the narrow belt of agricultural land on either side of the Nile. With 363,000 square miles, Egypt was over four times the size of Great Britain. Cairo, the capital, was an ancient and cosmopolitan city. There and in the port of Alexandria lived a busy foreign population— 57,000 Greeks, 40,000 Italians, 24,000 British (not counting troops), 21,000 French, 4,000 Russians and 25,000 of various other non-Egyptian nationalities. If they committed crimes or conducted lawsuits, such expatriates went before a special consular court separate from the Egyptian legal system. On Gezhira Island in the Nile at Cairo the British had laid out an elaborate club complete with racecourse and cricket pitch.

Relations between the British and the Egyptians were the worst in the whole Empire. The two sides, as peoples, seemed to dislike each other and to find difficulty in detecting virtue in each other. The Egyptians regarded the British as invaders who had moved in by force; the best revenge was to plunder the soldiers as much as possible. The British, on their side, regarded the Egyptians as lazy and corrupt, ungrateful for schemes for their benefit. The Egyptians became actual objects of hatred among many of the British soldiers—about a quarter of a million had served there during the war—in a manner which happened nowhere else in the British Empire. Egypt, from beginning to end, was an imperial weakness. In 1890 the explorer H. M. Stanley wrote: 'Only a Carlyle in his maturest period, as when he drew in lurid colours the agonies of the terrible French Revolution, can do justice to the long catalogue of disasters which has followed the connection of England with Egypt.'

Anti-British feeling among the Egyptians exploded in 1919 into serious rioting in Cairo and Alexandria. The British at first tried to hold firm and Allenby issued an uncompromising statement of intentions: 'The policy of Great Britain in Egypt is to preserve the autonomy of that country under British protection, and to develop the system of self-government under an Egyptian ruler. The object of Great Britain is to defend Egypt against all external danger and interference by any foreign power, and at the same time to establish a constitutional system wherein—under British guidance so far as may be necessary—the Sultan and his Ministers and the elected members of the people may, in their several spheres, and in an increasing degree, co-operate in the management of Egyptian affairs.'

This statement, with the implication that the most the Egyptians could hope for was to 'co-operate' in running their own country led to further trouble and so the British made one of their first imperial surrenders. By treaty in 1922 they formally recognised Egypt as an independent country and the Sultan became King Fuad I. It was a precarious form of independence with the British High Commissioner and garrison remaining in Egypt and asserting continued control over foreign policy. The unfortunate King was torn between the British, who had the effective power to depose him, and a singularly corrupt set of nationalist politicians. The British themselves were sensitive about the surrender—it smacked of loss of 'respect'—and signs of further weakness in Egypt would spark off sharp reactions from Buckingham Palace downwards. Amid storm after storm, the British garrison in Egypt hung on for another 34 years. Then hardly had the last soldiers left in 1956 than they were back again with guns firing as if Gladstone were still alive. There was something masochistic in the British attitude to Egypt. They disliked the place but could not leave it alone. The rationalisation, always, was the 'lifeline of the Empire' but the emotion aroused was warmer than political or commercial considerations would appear to justify.

For all the difficulties it presented, Egypt in 1918 was at least recognised internationally as British territory. The position over the newly-conquered territories of Syria, Palestine and Iraq was fraught with complications which sprang largely from conflicting promises. The Arabs who had fought for the British against the Turks had the impression that they were to be allowed sovereign independence. At the same time the British had promised their allies, the French, a share in the conquests and, for good measure, had promised to allow Jews from Europe to set up a 'national home' in Palestine. In terms of honour, the conflicting pledges are difficult to justify. They can be explained only in terms of the inevitable stresses of war. After much haggling, the French got Syria (with which they had maintained a connection since the crusades) and its Christian border region, Lebanon. The British got Mesopotamia and Palestine. The Arabs got independence only in Saudi Arabia, which none of the Europeans wanted. The French and British shares were 'Class A' mandates under the League of Nations, which meant that the occupying powers undertook to guide the territories towards early self-government. (They were thus unlike the 'Class B' mandates of Africa in which there was no mention of self-government.)

In Mesopotamia (Iraq), British rule failed to get off the ground. It was an ancient, formerly prosperous country lying between the rivers Tigris and Euphrates and it contained the ruins of Babylon. The population was some three million people in 143,000 square miles. In the remote past, when there had been a proper irrigation system, there had been many more people and the capital, the *Arabian Nights* city of Bagdad, had ranked as a major centre of world civilisation. The British Chief Commissioner, Major-General Sir Percy Cox of the Indian army, set up his administration in Bagdad and tried to reproduce the Indian system. Most of his officials were from India and they brought with them the procedures and attitudes which had served them there. It did not work. Arabs were not Indians and within months there were serious disorders and a formidable threat of rebellion.

Fearful of spending too much money on running the country, the British hit on an ingenious solution. To hand there was the princely Feisal from Saudi Arabia. He had fought with the British against the Turks and reigned briefly as King of Syria until the French ejected him. The British introduced Feisal as King of Mesopotamia and, after a plebiscite, handed over internal authority to him. Thus in a single act they discharged the debt of honour to Feisal and put Mesopotamia on a workable footing. This neat scheme had much to do with a woman, Gertrude Bell who, aged 50 in 1918, had carried into reality the fashionable fantasies of western women of getting to know romantic Arab sheikhs. After being one of the earliest Oxford 'bluestockings,' Miss Bell had through years of travel acquired an expert knowledge of the Middle East and especially of Bedouin tribes. She had joined the government service at Cairo in 1914 and, after the conquest, had moved up to Bagdad, through which she habitually rode side-saddle and wearing a bowler hat. Such was her intelligence and authority that her influence counted for more than that of the men officials. It was written of her:

'From Trebizon to Tripolis
She rolls the Pashas flat,
And tells them what to think of this
And what to think of that.'

Once she had got Feisal installed, she became his confidante and adviser. (Though she said she would never make anyone a King again—it was 'too exhausting.') She promoted archaeology and, on her death in 1926, was buried in Bagdad with military honours and Arabs mourning her as a true 'daughter of the desert.' Miss Bell's arrangements worked. The British continued to exert a strong influence over Iraq—by mandate to 1930 and afterwards by treaty—and until the royal family was deposed in 1958 it remained a satellite of the British middle eastern empire.

In the neighbouring land of Palestine there was no Miss Bell and no easy solution. The territory became one of the leading disasters of British imperial history. Superficially it had appeared to be a wonderful conquest. To the glittering array of British possessions there was added Jerusalem, the Holy City of three world religions. The colonial official reached his apotheosis when the appointment 'District Commissioner, Jerusalem, £600 × £50 × £800' appeared in the Colonial Office List. 'There is no promotion after Jerusalem,' wrote one official, Sir Ronald Storrs. It was the seat of Pontius Pilate—and just as uncomfortable as he had found it. Britain experienced only storm and hatred in Palestine. She made such enemies there as to weaken her power in the Middle East and her prestige across the world. In acquiring Palestine, the British Empire acquired some of the seeds of its own destruction.

Palestine in 1918 did not really exist as a separate country; it was just three administrative divisions of Turkish Syria, totalling together some 13,000 square miles. The principal element in the population was 515,000 Moslem Arabs, mostly primitive agriculturists, who tilled land belonging to absentee proprietors. By Middle Eastern standards, Palestine was quite an advanced area with a relatively high degree of education but the land was producing far below the potential that could be made available by introduction of scientific skills and new capital. In addition to the Moslem Arabs, the population also included 62,000 Christians (mostly Arabs) and some 65,000 Jews. Thus it was predominantly an Arab country and had been so for many centuries; had it not also been a Holy Land it would have remained at peace save, possibly, for an orthodox anti-imperial struggle.

In 1918 the world contained two principal Jewish communities, one in Eastern Europe and one in the Arab countries. There were also Jews in the United States and Western Europe but they were there mostly as a result of recent emigration from Eastern Europe, where in the 19th century they had suffered severe persecution. How far the European Jews were true blood descendants of the Jews who inhabited Palestine in biblical times is a matter for dispute. At various periods the dispersed Jews had taken in new members by conversion and by marriage. European Jews looked and behaved like Europeans and Middle East Jews looked and behaved like Arabs. Distinctive Jewish culture had its roots in the Old Testament but it had flowered in the ghettos of Russia and Poland, as had some of the secondary characteristics of the Jewish religion. The Jewish vernacular language, Yiddish, had developed entirely in Europe. At the same time, however, religious Jews had consistently over the generations looked to Palestine as the cradle of their community and the land which had been set apart for them by God; every Jewish family at the Seder festival spoke the ritual formula 'next year in Jerusalem.' Devout Jews on reaching old age travelled to Palestine to die there—during the 19th century a whole new suburb had grown up outside the walled city of Jerusalem to accommodate them. In addition, there had always been a small Jewish community native to Palestine. Relations with the Arabs had generally been good and, despite the religious attachment to Palestine, it had occurred to few European Jews before the 20th century that they should try en masse to take over the country.

For generations the Jews had been a civilising element in Europe, benefitting the countries in which they had settled. Yet, at the same time, because they had refused to adopt the Christian faith they had frequently been objects of persecution—because they were different they were treated as scapegoats when things went wrong. During the later 19th century this tendency had developed viciously in Russia and Russian Poland, heartlands of European Jewry. Under pressure of brutal pogroms, Jews had migrated westwards in hundreds of thousands and in such countries as Germany, Great Britain and the United States had found opportunities for leading proper lives. Nevertheless some of the younger and more energetic Jews had decided their people could never be really safe so long as they lacked a country to call their own. The country which naturally occurred to them was Palestine, which figured so prominently in the history of their religion. Under the leadership of the Jewish–Hungarian journalist Theodore Herzl, there had sprung up in the 1890s the Zionist Movement which sought to promote Jewish settlement in the Holy Land. The more extreme Zionists already thought in terms of turning Palestine into a sovereign state, with Jews from all over the world streaming home to become citizens of it but, at this stage, most Jews doubted both the practicability and the desirability of such an objective. Apart from anything else, the Turkish Empire stood as an obvious obstacle. (In 1913, David Ben-Gurion, future Prime Minister of Israel, was thinking that there might one day be a Turkish parliament with himself in it as a Palestine representative; he went specially to Constantinople to study Turkish institutions and qualify as a lawyer.)

The spectacle of this gifted people looking for a land of their own attracted the attention of British politicians. Could not the Jews, with their international influence, be brought into alliance with the British Empire? In the 1900s the Colonial Secretary, Joseph Chamberlain, had offered land in the newly acquired terri-tories of East Africa for a Jewish national home. The Zionists had seriously considered accepting the offer and, had they done so, would presumably have become a self-governing unit within the Empire. What their future would have been against African nationalism two generations later must be a matter for conjecture. From the Zionist point of view, however, the difficulty was that the notion of a national home attracted only a minority of Jews and unless it were linked with Palestine, with its religious asso-ciations, it could never hope to win general support. Against Herzl's own wishes, Chamberlain's offer was turned down and the Zionists began to collect money in Europe and the United States to buy land in Palestine and set up pioneer communities of Jewish settlers, who came mostly from Russia and Poland. David Ben-Gurion arrived a penniless immigrant from Plonsk, Poland, in 1906. Two years later was started the first Jewish town, Tel Aviv, as a suburb of Jaffa. The scientist Chaim Weizmann, who in 1918 ranked as the world's leading Zionist and was to become the first president of Israel, came from another Polish town, Pinsk; in 1918 he was a naturalised British subject.

In the early 20th century such movement from Europe to underdeveloped countries of the Middle East was in accord with common tendencies. Settlers from Britain had done the same thing in three continents and the Jews, unlike many of the British, paid a fair price for the land they acquired. A Pole from Plonsk had as much right to settle in Palestine as a Welshman from Pontypool to settle in Cape Province. The Jew was the more fervent settler; he was going to what he thought of as the land of his remote ancestors, land which his religion taught him had been allocated to his people by actual divine provision. 'I will give to you and to your seed after you the land of your abode, the land of Canaan, for an everlasting possession' (Genesis, XVII 8). What could be more definite?

During this early Zionist period, relations between Jews and Arabs had generally been friendly. Arabs lacked the anti-Semitism characteristic of some European countries and thought the arrival of Jews was good business, sending up the value of land. The notion that handfuls of immigrants from Russia and Poland could take over the country hardly occurred to the Arabs before 1917. The Jews, on their side, lacked a proper policy towards the Arabs and this was a crucial weakness of Zionism. No leader made a proper study. There existed in a muddled way the idea that the Arabs were a wandering people who, properly compensated, would move happily to neighbouring lands. For Arabs who remained, Jewish enterprise would transform the standard of living for the better. The Jews had suffered too much at the hands of others to wish to maltreat a minority in their own country. It was the sincere hope of the Zionists to build a land which would stand before the world as the model of enlightened government. Then the idea that the Arabs could themselves become nationalists, could themselves yearn to become a nation-state, had hardly existed before 1914. British and Zionists alike instinctively regarded them as 'natives' who should defer to a race more technologically advanced. Weizmann had to go out of his way to warn that the Palestinian Arabs were a vigorous, civilised people. 'Palestine is not Rhodesia,' he told the 14th Zionist Congress at Vienna in 1925.

The British conquered Palestine in 1917, Allenby entering Jerusalem on Christmas Day on foot. They immediately undertook to sponsor Jewish settlement. This was done in the press of war and, as the cabinet records show, the argument was advanced that it would win Jewish support in Europe for the war against Germany. Another idea—in which there would appear to be at least a shred of truth—was that the Prime Minister, Lloyd George, gave the undertaking as a reward to Weizmann for his scientific services in developing warlike explosives. At any rate, Palestine seemed to be a conquered territory lying at the disposal of the victors. The Foreign Secretary, Arthur Balfour, who had long admired the Jews, set out the policy in November 1917 in what became known as the Balfour Declaration. 'His Majesty's Government view with favour the establishment in Palestine of a national home for the Jewish people, and will use their best endeavours to facilitate the achievement of this object, it being clearly understood that nothing shall be done which may prejudice the civil and religious rights of the existing non-Jewish communities in Palestine.' Oddly enough, the only Jew in high office in Britain, E. S. Montagu, the young Secretary of State for India, was an anti-Zionist and so hated the declaration that he circulated a memorandum accusing his cabinet colleagues of 'anti-Semitism.'

The Balfour Declaration was a disastrous document, the words 'national home' being capable of no precise political meaning. Palestine was in one sense a 'national home' for the Jews already, thousands having emigrated there. If, however, 'national home' meant, as the Zionist enthusiasts wanted, the Jews setting up a sovereign state in Palestine this was incompatible with Arab aspirations. No matter how abundantly a Jewish majority respected Arab civil and religious rights, nothing could alter the fact that the Palestinian Arabs would lie under the rule of people they regarded as Poles and Russians. To enforce the declaration Britain had to offend either the Zionists or the Arabs—or, as it turned out, both. The cool way in which a British administration undertook such a burden was an expression of the limitless self-confidence the British felt in imperial matters in 1917. Palestine was a small, newly-conquered territory which could be treated how London chose. (Actually, though, the British did a little later try to get the mandate transferred to the U.S.A.)

In the very early stages the experiment did work reasonably well. British occupation of Palestine was confirmed by a League of Nations mandate which specifically recognised 'the historical connection of the Jewish people with Palestine and the ground for reconstituting their national home in that country.' Lloyd George chose as the British High Commissioner to rule the country the British–Jewish politician, Herbert Samuel. Aged 48 in 1918, Samuel was a leading personality in the British Liberal Party and had served in the cabinet. His outlook was a British one but he had shown general support for Zionist aspirations. A thrill ran around world Jewry when in 1920 he arrived in Jerusalem to take

'Rule Britannia!' British Battleships steaming into Valetta Grand Harbour, Malta, 1935

## PRIDE AND FALL

The surrender of Singapore, 1942. British officers carry the white flag and union jack side by side. Striding out of the picture on the far right is Lieutenant-General A. E. Percival, Commander of the 100,000 strong Singapore garrison

Independence almost by stealth. Aung San, who played off Japanese and British against each other to win control of Burma

up his office. On his first Sabbath he attended the Grand Syna-
gogue in formal state and read from Isaiah: 'Comfort ye, comfort
ye my people, saith your God. Speak ye comfortably to Jerusalem,
and cry unto her that her warfare is accomplished.' Even though
it was taking place under the union jack, it was like a miracle to see
a Jew ruling again in Jerusalem. Samuel established Hebrew, the
religious tongue which the Zionists were adapting for vernacular
use, as an official language to rank equally with English and
Arabic. Samuel's primary allegiance, however, was not to Zionism
but to Great Britain and to the dismay of Jewish immigrants he
showed that he was at least as eager to support Arab interests as
their own. His purpose was to lay the foundations of a sound
British-style administration, not to create a Jewish state.

At first only about 8,000 Jews a year actually came to settle in
Palestine. This was fewer than before the Balfour Declaration and,
indeed, more Jews were moving from Europe to the United States
than were moving to the 'national home.' Those that did come,
though, were the most fanatical Zionists. Unlike British settlers in
Kenya and Southern Rhodesia, they had no wish to lord it over
the established population and to engage local labourers to work
their agriculture. They wanted to build a self-sufficient Jewish
nation with Jews doing every kind of job. The pattern was that
they would buy land, often from an absentee proprietor living in
Lebanon, eject the existing Arab tenants and set up a communal
Jewish agricultural settlement. To Arab peasants this looked like
aggression and from 1920 onwards there developed a dreary
pattern of attack and counter-attack between the two communities. The Jewish Agency co-ordinated the Jewish settlers and
became almost a shadow-government. However, the pace of
Jewish immigration was so gradual that optimistic British
administrators could look forward to stabilising the situation. At
an immigration rate of 8,000 a year it would be generations
before Arab predominance in Palestine was seriously imperilled.
(For 20 years the British had no settled policy on exactly how
many Jews *ought* to be allowed in.)

Then came two events which had nothing to do with either
Arabs or British. In 1924 the United States cut its Jewish immigration quota. At the same time the government of newly-
independent Poland began to place restrictions on Jews attending
universities and working in the public service. There was little
violence or physical persecution but many Polish Jews were reduced to despair. They had suffered under the pogroms of

Tsarist rule and now they were suffering under the new and supposedly enlightened Polish nation-state. What possible future could exist for them in Poland? And the United States was no longer easy to enter. In 1925 immigration into Palestine abruptly quadrupled to 34,000 Jews, of whom half were from Poland. Among such Poles existed a neurotic, violent element prepared to adopt any methods to overcome opposition to 'Eretz Israel.'

By now the early British enthusiasm for ruling Palestine was fading. It was turning into an unrewarding task which could bring Britain few obvious benefits. British administrators among themselves tried to justify their presence by dragging up the hoary argument of India. Palestine was a useful reserve post from which to guard Egypt, which in turn meant guarding the Suez Canal and so the route to the East. It was a tenuous line of reasoning which confused the issue and gave a handle for both Arab and Jewish attacks upon British 'imperialism.' Many British officials got on ill at a personal level with the Jews; a Polish Jew in Tel Aviv did not feel disposed to regard a British district commissioner with the 'respect' that was expected from colonial subjects. The Arabs could be fitted rather more easily into the category of 'natives' and, especially among junior British officials, there developed signs of pro-Arab bias.

The eastern section of Palestine, running from the left bank of the Jordan, was set up as the Arab Emirate of Transjordan under Abdullah, brother of the Feisal who ruled first over Syria and then over Iraq. Relations were happier than on the coastal side of Palestine. Under British guidance there developed an efficient little army, the Arab Legion, to police the Bedouin tribes. The population, about 100,000 in 1918, was scattered over 4,000 square miles of territory, largely desert. Keen Zionists wanted it in 'Eretz Israel' but there was no attempt at Jewish settlement. In 1918 there were only two known Jews living in Transjordan, and four years later, Churchill, as Colonial Secretary, specifically confirmed that the Balfour Declaration did not apply to it.

South of the great territories of Egypt, Iraq and Palestine, the British in 1918 possessed a medley of smaller Middle Eastern colonies and protectorates. They were all administered by the Government of India and had been acquired for the traditional purpose of protecting the route to India. Most of them in 1918 were little-known desert sheikhdoms, sparsely populated and containing few obvious natural resources. That under the desert sand might lie vast supplies of oil was hardly suspected.

The only such territory with continuous contact with the outside world was Aden Colony on the tip of the Arabian peninsula.
It had been the first new bit added to the British Empire in the
reign of Queen Victoria—an expedition had sailed from Bombay
to capture it for a coaling station. It consisted of 80 square miles of
black, barren rock. The main residential quarter was Crater. The
climate was vilely hot and humid, dysentery was prevalent and the
few water taps ran neither hot nor cold but invariably lukewarm.
It was the legendary burial place of the first murderer, Cain, and
salt tanks there were supposed to have been built by King
Solomon. The major asset was the huge natural harbour which
under British administration had developed into a major shipping
centre, a dozen or more vessels arriving every day. It was a place
for refuelling, for exchanging cargoes and for the sale of souvenirs
to passengers who swarmed ashore at Steamer Point. The population was some 5,000 scattered in white houses among the
blistering rocks; they were a mixed lot—Arabs, Indians, Somalis
and a handful of Europeans—and good opportunities existed for
profitable business. The richest merchant was a Frenchman,
Antonin Besse, who out of his millions eventually financed a new
college for Oxford—St. Anthony's. Administratively Aden came
under the Governor of Bombay who was represented on the spot by
the Political Resident, Major-General J. M. Stewart of the
Indian army, who drew £2,400 a year. He sweated under whizzing
fans in a handsome white house overlooking the harbour. 'Tell
Daddy we are all happy under British rule' read a placard displayed at Steamer Point when the Prince of Wales arrived on a
brief visit in 1921.

Behind and around Aden lay deserts of thousands of square
miles inhabited by scattered Arab tribes. To the east lay Yemen,
a former Turkish territory which had won independence in the
war. The Imam of Yemen, an ambitious and cruel despot,
claimed the whole of southern Arabia as his, including Aden itself.
He and the British competed for suzerainty over the tribes of the
interior and there were many minor wars. During the 1920s and
1930s the British pushed inland from Aden to establish protectorates over about 25 tribal sheikhdoms occupying a total of
some 112,000 square miles of land. The population totalled
something in the region of half a million. These baking stretches
of desert were the last new acquisition the British Empire ever
made.

On the south-eastern corner of Arabia lay the Sultanate of

Muscat and Oman ruled by the Taimur dynasty, which in the past had enjoyed wide dominions, including Zanzibar. The Sultan's flag was plain red; he issued no money of his own and the main currency was the Maria Theresa dollar, still specially minted in 18th-century form in Vienna. The British had been in treaty relations with the dynasty for 150 years but had not intervened in internal affairs. Technically it was not even a protectorate but the Political Agent, R. E. L. Wingate of the Indian Civil Service, controlled external relations. The territory had 82,000 square miles of land and a population of about half a million, much of which was in rebellion against the Sultan. It was a wild anarchic place and visitors were warned that they landed at the risk of their lives.

Up the eastern edge of Arabia, in the Persian Gulf, the Government of India controlled a further chain of territories.

Working from the south upwards, the first group was the 'Trucial Coast.' It consisted of eight turbulent little sheikhdoms which had once been infested with pirates who had sailed out to attack Indian shipping. The British had imposed a 'truce' in piracy from which the area had acquired its name. The population in 1918 was about 50,000 and the area about 32,000 square miles. The Political Resident, Lieutenant-Colonel A. P. Trevor of the Indian army, exercised a sketchy overall control. Also in Colonel Trevor's sphere came the Sheikhdom of Qatar, just north of the Trucial Coast, which had accepted British influence as recently as 1916. It was a little more settled than the Trucial sheikhdoms and had about 30,000 people living in 4,000 square miles.

North of Qatar lay the Bahrein archipelago which had six inhabited islands. It was the most prosperous place in the Persian Gulf. The islanders, numbering about 110,000, had a thousand boats engaged in a busy pearl-fishing industry. They bred famous white donkeys and ran a flourishing port. Their Sheikh, an absolute ruler, was 'advised' by the Political Agent, Major H. R. P. Dixon.

At the very top of the Persian Gulf lay Kuwait which, with a population of 50,000, occupied a key strategic position at the point where Arabia, Mesopotamia and Persia adjoined each other. It had long been under British influence but the Germans before 1914 had tried to infiltrate it and to use it as the terminus for a railway they had planned to build from Bagdad. The prospect of the railway had alarmed the Government of India—it thought, for reasons which are none too plain, that it might be used as an invasion route. Simla had sent a special mission to claim stronger control over the Sultan, who in 1918 was in receipt of an annual subsidy from India. The area of Kuwait was some 5,800 square miles.

Around this array of Arab sheikhdoms there flourished in the 1920s an aura of romance and mystery. The desert ruler, with his harem of wives, concubines, slave girls and page boys, was a fascinating man. The American film star Rudolph Valentino made himself an international idol by playing the role of a sheikh. An eccentric Oxford don, T. E. Lawrence, who had liaised with Arab levies in the war against the Turks, acquired the status of a legendary hero. Desert Arabs, with their codes of manners and hospitality—the guest tended to be offered the eye of the roasted sheep and if he was a European he was rarely sure whether to chew it or swallow it whole—attracted curiosity. Specialists called 'Arabists' devoted their lives to trying to understand them but rarely succeeded—it required more than a sheep's eye, a Bedouin head-dress or, even, a homosexual relationship to get properly to terms with them. Gertrude Bell probably came closer than most. When 'Arabists' returned home from their desert travels they could be sure of attracting audiences for magic lantern lectures. One reason why British administration failed in Palestine was that too much weight was allowed to 'Arabists.' Fascinated by what they thought of as the 'true Arabs' of the desert, the British took insufficient account of the urbanised middle-class Arabs among whom was to stir a more sophisticated nationalism than that of the sheikhs. Most Arabs were not sheikhs. As it turned out, the British policy of creating a Jewish national home in Palestine accelerated nationalism and wrecked any hope of the Arab countries becoming permanent satellites or allies of the British Empire.

Britain had become a power in the Middle East for the theoretical purpose of protecting the route to India, the Far East and Australasia. Between the wars, however, there arose a new mystique, that of oil. At first in Persia and Iraq, then in Bahrein and Kuwait and, ultimately, in the Trucial sheikhdoms were exploited vast oil deposits. There developed gradually and without challenge the notion in British foreign and colonial policy that the oil could flow safely only if held under British military and political control.

Westwards from Egypt were three British colonies, Cyprus, Malta and Gibraltar, whose role in imperial strategy was, it was taken, to protect the Mediterranean approach to Suez and so to

India. They were European, Christian territories, the only such in the entire colonial Empire.

Cyprus lay in the eastern Mediterranean just off the coast of Turkey. It had associations with the birth of ancient Greek civilisation but it had lain for centuries under Turkish rule. The British had acquired it more or less casually while mediating in a dispute between Turkey and Russia; there had been no immediate use for it but the feeling existed that it might be valuable as a base if ever Egypt got out of hand. It stood only 260 miles from the Canal. British rule, which in 1918 had existed for four decades, had been moderately progressive but remote from the sentiments of the people. Roads and a railway had been constructed, trade had been developed with Egypt and steps had been taken towards the eradication of malaria. There was quite a democratic constitution with a legislature of 12 elected members plus six officials. It was becoming common for retired officials from the British tropical colonies to settle in Cyprus, it providing a convenient compromise of hot sunshine with a European mode of life. In the administration the senior posts were all held by British officials but the Cypriots themselves filled most of the lower ranks. In the medical department, for example, the three 'first grade' doctors were British on a £500 to £600 salary scale; the three 'second grade' doctors were Cypriots on £300. The island's area of 3,500 square miles was similar to that of a couple of big English counties and the population was about 300,000 which, with the aid of doctors of various grades, was increasing rapidly. Four fifths of the people were Greek and one fifth Turkish.

The British High Commissioner (the title was soon to be changed to Governor) was Major Sir J. E. Clauson whose main career had been in Malaya. He drew £3,600 a year in salary and expenses and presided over an administrative staff which had a somewhat transitory character; it was normal for officials to be posted to Cyprus on a temporary basis to give them a rest between more arduous localities. The true leader of the island, or at least of the predominant Greek majority, was His Beatitude Cyril III, Archbishop of Cyprus. The independence of the Cypriot church from outside authority dated back 1,500 years and through centuries of alien rule the Archbishop had been the embodiment of Greek-Cypriot traditions. He bore, indeed, the additional title of 'Ethnarch' or national leader. Greek-Cypriots were Greek by language, culture and aspiration. Rich Cypriots customarily sent their sons to be educated not to Oxford or Cambridge but to

Athens. Cyprus, the Greeks thought, was just another Greek island which should, in justice, be reunited to the motherland. A plebiscite of the inhabitants at any time during British rule would, in all probability, have yielded a majority in favour of 'Enosis'—union with Greece. Indeed at one point during the 1914 war the British had offered to trade Cyprus to Greece in return for an alliance against the Central Powers of Europe. Apart from wartime exigencies, however, the British were simply not in the habit of relinquishing territory, especially territory on the route to India, and they generally treated 'Enosis' as if it were a kind of hobby of Greek-Cypriots and far too insignificant to affect the majesty of world-wide British rule. There was also the consideration of Turkey, near which Cyprus lay and which provided a substantial minority of the Cypriot population. Apart from the circumstances of the 1914 war, it was not a British habit to offend the Turks.

It was a strange reflection on the British educational system that Cypriot demands, even as far back as 1918, were taken so lightly. Reverence for the classical Greek language, for Greek literature and Greek philosophy was a cornerstone of the British educational system. In the public schools the boys were brought up to believe that no culture had ever been so enlightened as that of ancient Greece. Yet when in Cyprus the British encountered real Greeks no reverence was felt at all. It hardly entered the head of the average British official that the unshaven, gesticulating Greek-Cypriot spinning out the day in conversation in a Nicosia café was of the blood of Socrates. Even less did it occur to the British that the Greek-Cypriots would become capable of rising in such an armed revolt as would be one of the crucial factors in the ultimate fall of the British Empire.

A thousand miles to the west of Cyprus lay the island of Malta. This was nearly unique in that the inhabitants, in 1814, had actually asked to be taken under British rule. In 1918 the island contained 200,000 people, quick-witted and industrious, crammed into only 121 square miles of land. The soil was none too rich but every available inch was cultivated and there was a major income to be made, too, out of the British. Malta was only 58 miles from Italy and Italian as well as English was recognised as the official language. The Fascist Mussolini, when in power in Italy, was eager to get Malta into his dominions and, between the wars, there was some agitation on the island to this end. But it had nothing like the force of the Cypriot desire for union with

Greece. The Maltese were not really Italians—they were a mixture of Italian, Arab, Greek, Phoenician with a fair infusion of British seed. The Maltese had their own language which, under nationalist pressure, was developing from a patois into a regular form of speech. In religion the Maltese were fervently Roman Catholic and the Archbishop of Malta had the same kind of authority as his counterpart in Cyprus, with the difference that the Maltese Archbishop was a whole-hearted supporter of British rule. In 1918 the Archbishop of Malta had the distinction of being simul-taneously a Benedictine monk and a Knight Commander of the Order of the British Empire. (In the 1870s, when Rome was taken over by nationalist Italians, there had been a serious suggestion that the Pope himself should move to Malta and reconstitute the Holy See under British protection.)

British and Maltese had a bumpy relationship, at one moment detesting each other and at the next affirming eternal friendship. In 1918 things were going well and the British were on the point of introducing a dual system of government. For internal affairs there was to be a Maltese council of ministers responsible to an elected legislature. The Governor was to retain control over defence, foreign policy and external trade.

Life and business in Malta revolved around the battleships and cruisers of the Royal Navy. The British Mediterranean Fleet between the wars was always powerful and often the strongest single naval formation in the world. Malta Royal Dockyard gave work to 6,000 men and the island's retail trade depended upon British naval families. The plunging, narrow streets of the capital, Valetta, were thronged by day by anxious British housewives in cotton frocks bargaining with the Maltese shopkeepers; the pay of a petty officer was only 5s. 6d. a day and so the wives had to haggle carefully. At night the shoppers disappeared and the bars and brothels opened, the centre of the red-light district being an evil little quarter known for generations as 'The Gut.' About the worst term of abuse in the Royal Navy was for one man to liken another to 'a Maltese ponce.' When the Mediterranean Fleet arrived at Valetta Grand Harbour it seemed as if the whole population turned out in welcome, crowding the battlements. It was a stirring scene, an epitome of British world power. First into view came flotillas of destroyers streaking across to their own separate harbour of Sliema. Then, out of the heat haze on the horizon, loomed the battleships and cruisers, signal lamps flashing. They held perfect formation, the battleships in single line, each 500 yards from her neighbour. The ships were painted a special silvery grey against which stood out the white uniforms of thousands of ratings lining the decks. On the quarterdeck of each battleship stood a Royal Marine band crashing out 'Hearts of Oak' and 'Rule Britannia! Britannia rule the waves!' Perhaps there would be as many as six battleships, the most powerful fighting units the world had ever known. Among them might be the battlecruiser *Hood* which, with her displacement of 41,000 tons, was the biggest warship ever possessed by any navy. Women's handkerchiefs fluttered as, one by one, the ships passed through the entrance to Grand Harbour and moored at their buoys. Admiralty tugs steamed up at once and turned them around—at Malta the Royal Navy always anchored with bows facing the sea. To the accompaniment of bo'suns' pipes, the Commander-in-Chief, a full admiral at the climax of his career, stepped into his barge and sped over the bright blue water to pay ceremonial calls on shore. There followed a round of balls, regattas and parties attended by the 'fishing fleet' of girls from home in quest of naval husbands.

This fleet, with Malta as its principal base, made Britain a power in the Mediterranean and, it was supposed, covered the route to India, the Far East and Australia. Its existence was proof of British aspirations for continued world authority. By later standards, it was astonishingly cheap to run. The whole Royal Navy in the 1920s cost only about £100 million a year, of which the Mediterranean Fleet accounted for perhaps a quarter or a third. For considerably less than £1 a head a year from the home population, the British Empire dominated the Mediterranean.

Although in both size and population Malta was one of the smaller British colonies, her strategic position made her one of the most prominent. The Governor was invariably a famous army officer, a general or field marshal. (Curiously, never an admiral.) In 1918 the Governor was Field Marshal Lord Methuen who had won victories against the Boers in South Africa at the turn of the century. He lived in high state on a salary of £4,500 a year, plus £500 'table money,' plus army pay.

A thousand miles westwards from Malta lay the only British colony which was part of the actual mainland of Europe. It was the tiny peninsula of Gibraltar on the southern tip of Spain. In area it was less than two square miles but it had a good harbour and it commanded the narrow channel, only 20 miles wide, connecting the Atlantic to the Mediterranean. The British had conquered it from Spain as far back as 1704 and by 1918 the 20,000 inhabitants, of mixed British, Spanish and Maltese blood were happy with their political condition. The Gibraltarians made a good living out of the British garrison, the Royal Navy and merchant shipping. Spain, however, persistently insisted that Gibraltar was really Spanish territory and from time to time flared up with demands that the British should give it up. The Gibraltar question formed a minor but lasting complication in European diplomacy and it meant that Britain and Spain could never be really friendly. The Spaniards could do little to enforce their demands, their country being so decayed and anarchic as to be incapable of challenging the British Empire at its peak. Nevertheless the British took care to keep Gibraltar well-garrisoned. The Governor was always an active army officer who combined civil duties with those of direct military command. (All British governors had the formal title of 'Commander-in-Chief' but only in Gibraltar did this entail the working command of troops.) In 1918 the Governor was Lieutenant-General Sir Horace Smith-Dorrien who had commanded a corps during the bloody fighting in France. He drew £5,500 a year salary, covering both his civil and military roles, from the Colonial Office plus £500 'table allowance' from the army. The lion-shaped Rock of Gibraltar, honeycombed with fortifications and with monkeys scrambling over it, was one of the prime symbols of the British Empire.

Westwards from Gibraltar lay the Atlantic Ocean on which British maritime power had first asserted itself three centuries earlier. The original British Empire, the chain of colonies and islands on the east of North America, had been won by sea power. Spain and Portugal had pioneered the conquest of the Atlantic and the American continent but by 1918 their power was defunct and Britain was, for practical purposes, the only trans-atlantic colonial power. During the 19th century when the dynamism of British expansion had been absorbed by India and Africa, Whitehall had paid little attention (apart from the slavery question) to these older territories and by 1918 they had fallen, generally, into stagnation. The expanding United States of America had disliked European colonialism in its part of the world and, according to the 'Monroe Doctrine,' had declared it would regard further European incursion as an unfriendly act. The British had been content with this doctrine and, indeed, their naval power had given silent support to it. By 1918, however, the United States had emerged as a world power in its own right.

The mid-Atlantic island of St. Helena, a tiny tip of land projecting steeply upwards from the deep ocean bed, formed a particularly vivid example of obsolescence. Like so much else in the British Empire, St. Helena had originally been acquired on the rationalisation of securing the route to India. In the period before the opening of the Suez Canal it had provided a useful stopping place on the long voyage from Britain to India by way of South Africa. The British East India Company had annexed it as early as 1651. It had no aboriginal population but, over the centuries, settlers of mixed but mainly British blood had established an inbred little community. They had an odd way of life; St. Helena is only 47 miles square and stands in isolation in mid-Atlantic, 1,200 miles from Africa and 2,500 miles from South America. The British used it as a place of exile for notable political prisoners, the greatest having been Napoleon I, Emperor of the French. In 1918 the deposed Kabaka of Buganda was pining away there. Until the opening of the Suez Canal, St. Helena had been a prosperous place, its harbour under green mountain slopes crammed with world shipping. The Canal had killed its economy and by 1918 the port subsisted on a handful of stray tramp steamers and the Royal Mail liner from London which came once a month. The British had made grants from the imperial exchequer to set up a lace industry to give the people some livelihood but the population was rapidly declining. It stood at about 3,600 in 1918 and had gone down by 25 per cent over the previous quarter century. To be Governor of St. Helena was the humblest independent charge in the Colonial Service; the salary was only £775 a year, for which the incumbent also acted as chief justice. In 1918 the Governor was Major H. E. S. Cordeaux who had started his career in the Indian army and transferred to the Colonial Office after adventures against the 'Mad Mullah' in Somaliland. In 1920 he was promoted to the governorship of the Bahamas.

Some 760 miles north of St. Helena lay the even tinier colony of Ascension Island which was administered by the Admiralty as a kind of naval establishment. It was commanded by a major of the Royal Marines and had a population, mostly Royal Marines, of about 150. The area was 38 square miles. Apart from its potential utility as a military base it was noted mainly for its turtles which for five months every year heaved themselves out of the ocean to lay their eggs on the beaches. From Ascension Island the turtles

were taken to the heart of the Empire, to Guildhall in the City of
London, where they provided the turtle soup which was a
traditional dish at Lord Mayors' banquets.

The most isolated British possession of all was Tristan da Cunha
which lay 1,200 miles south of St. Helena in the widest and
loneliest part of the Atlantic. The British had occupied it to prevent
it being used as a base for the rescue of Napoleon I from St.
Helena. When the garrison had come to withdraw, three soldiers
had elected to stay behind and had sent home for wives. They
had called their chief settlement Edinburgh and, their numbers
reinforced by shipwrecked sailors, had built up an adequate
standard of living by cultivating the soil. In 1918 the population
was about one hundred. At intervals of a few years the British
would send expeditions from Cape Town to inspect them and to
offer to evacuate them to South Africa. They were impossible to
administer in any conventional sense and a Colonial Office document of 1922 described them in puzzled terms: 'The inhabitants
practically enjoy their possessions in common, and there is no
strong drink on the island, and no crime. It was at one time
proposed to give them laws and a regular government, but this
was found unnecessary for the above reasons, and they remain
under the moral rule of their oldest inhabitant.'

The main British possessions in the Atlantic lay among the
hundreds of islands off the eastern seaboard of continental
America—the Bahamas, the Bermudas, the West Indies and, down
in the far south off Argentina, the Falklands. Spanish, Portuguese
and British colonialists in their earliest and rawest stages had
virtually eliminated the aboriginal population from these islands
and most of the inhabitants were now descended from African
slaves who had been shipped over to work in the sugar plantations.
A secondary group in some of them were Indians from India who
had voluntarily come halfway round the world for the same
purpose. European settlers in the past had been mostly rich
plantation owners but by 1918 this aristocracy was but a shadow
of its ancient self. Among the mass of the people, the black-
skinned ones, practically all cultural links with Africa had long
been broken and British traditions, coloured with a little extra
vivacity, were dominant. They spoke English as their mother
tongue, learned about English kings at school and looked upon
Britain (although it seemed remote) as the 'mother country.'
They played with delight and skill the characteristically English
game of cricket. So far as the British Empire ever produced

assimilés—that is colonial people converted to the culture of the colonial power—it was in these islands.

Traditionally the economy of most of the islands had depended upon sugar; during the 18th century the planters had made great fortunes, bought seats in the House of Commons in London and exerted a definite influence upon imperial policy. By 1918, however, sugar was being produced more cheaply elsewhere and the islands lay in chronic depression. Over the previous two generations there had been a persistent fall in population. Some of the people had migrated to the United States and Latin America—though few had taken advantage of their right to go to Britain, which seemed too remote and too unwelcoming. The Colonial Office, busy digesting the new African colonies, had tended to take the islands for granted and had made little effort to alleviate the poverty which afflicted them. There did exist, however, a reasonable educational system and a high degree of literacy. The 1914–1918 war had brought a brief boom in sugar but by 1920 it had finished, prices in that year dropping from 20 to four cents a pound.

The most northerly group, the Bermudas, was a mass of some 300 coral islands 500 miles from the American coast. The total land area was only 19 square miles and the population, reckoned to be one third white and two thirds black, was only 21,000. Generous use of new artificial fertilisers was enabling a green vegetable crop to be produced for the American market but most of the people were still poor. By 1918 the congenial climate—hot but healthy—was attracting American tourists and the foundations were being laid for the territory to become a rich man's playground. Bermuda had the oldest parliament in the Empire (oldest, that is, after the one in London). It dated back to 1620 and was formed on the classic pattern of the pre-independence American colonies. It had 36 members elected on a very restricted franchise; only 1,413 of the 21,000 population were allowed to vote. Subject to the Governor's veto, this oligarchical assembly enjoyed full legislative power and control of taxation. Unlike the legislatures of the newer colonies, there was a separation of executive from legislative powers, none of the Governor's officials sitting as members of the legislature. The Governor in 1918 was General Sir James Willocks, who had just been given the job at the age of 60 as a reward for a lifetime's service in India. He drew £3,300 a year salary.

The next group, going southwards, was the Bahamas which had

been discovered by Christopher Columbus himself. The white sandy beach of San Salvador in the Bahamas had been the place at which Columbus had first stepped ashore on the New World. After Columbus, the Bahamas had undergone a raffish history and had been the haunt of such pirates as Kidd and Teach; for a period the pirates had actually ruled the place, electing their own governor. The piratical tradition continued and the territory, which lay only 50 miles from the United States, was a centre for smugglers. The people had enjoyed high prosperity from running the blockade during the American Civil War and in 1918 they were on the verge of a bigger boom still. The Volstead Act, prohibiting the sale of alcoholic liquor in the United States, turned the Bahamas into the centre of the bootlegging industry. During the 1920s fast launches from the Bahamas sped in continuous traffic over to Florida or New York laden with gin and whisky and earning millionaire profits for their owners. Sometimes they engaged in running gun battles with the United States customs. Washington strenuously protested against the Bahamas being used in this way but the British government stolidly insisted that it regarded liquor as a legitimate article of commerce. (The Bahamas administration did, however, collaborate with the Americans in trying to put down drug smuggling.) The annual value of Bahamian exports jumped from £300,000 to £2 million and the administration collected £500,000 a year revenue on drink imported into the territory for re-export to the United States; there was a serious proposal to erect a statue of Senator Volstead in the capital, Nassau, to go with those of Columbus and Queen Victoria. The bootlegging magnates—'the Bay Street boys' —became a leading force in the colony; they invested much of their profits in building up the tourist industry and so, when the Americans finally repealed Prohibition, a lasting benefit remained. Winston Churchill called the colony 'The Ganymede of the New World where Americans came to enjoy soft breezes and hard liquor.'

The Bahamas consisted of 20 inhabited islands and about a hundred uninhabited coral islets and rocks. The population of 55,000 was five sixths Negro and the rest white. The Governor's salary was only £2,100 a year but the post was regarded as an important one because of its contacts with Washington. In 1918 the Governor was Sir William Allardyce who was aged 57 and had spent most of his career as an administrator in the Pacific colonies. The constitution, like that of the Bermudas, ran on a

17th-century model with an elected legislature and division of powers. Anyone with a house worth £2 8s. a year was entitled to vote but a £200 qualification for membership of the House of Assembly kept things under white control.

Immediately south of the Bahamas lay the West Indies proper, the great islands of Jamaica, Barbados and Trinidad, together with the smaller Windward and Leeward groups, all sweltering under the Caribbean sun. Some other islands in the same area had thrown off colonial rule but their governments were ineffective and chaos was modified by spasmodic intervention from the United States. British administration could be accused of being negligent but at least it maintained a degree of settled administration and public order. Cuba and Haiti were not noticeably happier than, say, their neighbour Jamaica.

A mountainous island of 4,450 square miles, Jamaica had like St. Helena the distinction of having been added to the Empire while the mother country was a republic. It had been captured in 1655 under Oliver Cromwell and the head of the administration still bore the Cromwellian title 'Captain-General and Governor-in-chief.' For two centuries the island had also possessed an oligarchic 17th-century-style legislature on the same pattern as Bermuda and the Bahamas but in the turmoil following the abolition of slavery the members had in 1866 voluntarily surrendered their powers to the Colonial Office. In 1918 Jamaica had a constitution typical of the newer colonial fashion with a legislature consisting of six officials, ten nominated members and 14 elected ones. From Jamaica came the best rum and the best coffee in the world but the historic mainstay, sugar, was collapsing and the mass of the population lived in poverty. The development of a fruit industry, with bananas cultivated on a vast scale, was no adequate substitute for sugar. Of the 858,000 people 98 per cent were black or of mixed blood, practically everyone being able to look back to slave ancestors. But in 1918 political and most economic power still rested with the tiny white minority. The masses as yet had no effective leadership and few or none of the administrators sent out from London considered they would be capable of running their own affairs in the foreseeable future. But it was a Jamaican, Marcus Garvey, who, as President of the United Negro Improvement Association, was pioneering three revolutionary movements which by the middle of the century were to be crucial factors in the world—African nationalism, West Indian independence and civil rights for United States Negroes.

In 1918 Garvey was working in the United States but later he returned home to Jamaica and was gaoled when he accused the judiciary of corruption. The future Prime Minister of independent Jamaica, Alexander Bustamente, was aged 24 in 1918 and away serving as a soldier in the Spanish army in Morocco. Jamaica was populous enough to support quite a sophisticated administration but over the previous generation it had been weakened by frequent withdrawals of officials to serve the new African colonies. The 'Captain-General' ranked as the senior colonial official of the western hemisphere and drew £5,500 a year in salary and allowances. In 1918 the post was held by a professional, Sir Leslie Probyn, who was aged 62 and had spent half his career in the West Indies and half in Nigeria.

Subsidiary to the Jamaican administration were the Turks and Caicos Islands and the Cayman Islands, which between them had a population of about 11,000.

Along the eastern edge of the Caribbean Sea, where it met the Atlantic, ran a narrow chain of 30 islands stretching some 600 miles from north to south. Two of them in the middle, Guadeloupe and Martinique were French colonies, but all the others were British. The British ones were divided into two groups, the Leeward Islands and the Windward Islands, the names reflecting the northeast trade wind which had been vital for the British mariners who had pioneered colonisation 300 years earlier. The populations were small, scattered and poor but there was quite an elaborate constitutional structure, the little communities being linked in quasi-federal system. They were reckoned to be among the most loyal of British colonies.

The Leeward group included the Virgin Islands, Antigua, Dominica and the oldest of the British West Indian possessions, St. Christopher (usually called St. Kitts). The total land area was some 704 square miles and the population 131,000. The Governor, who got £3,250 a year including travelling allowance, was Sir Edward Merewether, a 60-year-old veteran of the Malayan service. In the Windward group the main islands were St. Lucia, St. Vincent and Grenada and there was a total land area of 524 square miles and a population of 180,000; the Governor, who also drew £3,250 a year, was Sir George Haddon-Smith who had previously served 28 years in West Africa.

Geographically the two big islands of Barbados and Trinidad formed part of the Windward group but each had its special characteristics and was big enough to support its own separate administration.

Barbados, the most easterly of the Caribbean islands, is surrounded by dangerous coral reefs and its very existence had been unsuspected during the first century of European exploration. When the British had taken possession in 1605 it had been uninhabited. At first it had been granted to private proprietors on a semi-feudal basis but this had led to such disputes among rival claimants to the property that in 1662 King Charles II had established Crown government with a house of assembly elected by the leading settlers. During the 18th century the island, which is of 166 square miles, had developed a rich sugar industry worked by slaves imported from Africa. In 1918 the population, which had been sharply declining, was about 156,000, mostly the descendants of slaves. The 17th-century constitution still subsisted and less than one per cent of the population had the right to vote. The Governor in 1918 was Lieutenant-Colonel Sir Charles O'Brien, who had just arrived aged 59 for his first service in the West Indies. His previous career had been in the army and in the administrative services of southern and western Africa. He drew £2,500 a year.

Unlike Barbados, which found cause for pride in its unbroken British tradition, the island of Trinidad had figured largely in wars among the Spanish, the French, the Dutch and the British and it had not passed finally under British sovereignty until 1802. In 1918 the Spanish and French tongues were still in common use and the name of the capital, Port of Spain, was a standing reminder of the past. Unlike the older British West Indian colonies it had never possessed an elected assembly and in 1918 legislative power rested with a council appointed by the Governor. The most obvious effect of British control had been the immigration of substantial numbers of Indians from India who in 1918 numbered 180,000, nearly a third of the population. Indians from India had also settled in others of the West Indian islands but Trinidad was the only one where they were a substantial force. Trinidad had formerly depended upon sugar but by 1918 her oil was becoming increasingly important. She was also exploiting a huge asphalt lake, 114 acres in extent. She attracted outside capital more readily than did the other West Indian islands and did, indeed, provide the traditional dream of the British upper-middle class—a safe ten per cent return. The area of Trinidad and the satellite island of Tobago was some 2,000 square miles and the population in 1918 was some 362,000. The Governor, who drew the unusually

I

high salary of £5,000 a year, was 58-year-old Sir John Chancellor, an army engineer who had risen to influence through staff work with the Committee of Imperial Defence. His only colonial appointments had been in the rank of Governor.

Superficially the West Indian islands appeared to have much in common with each other and already by 1918 there was some talk among the British of trying to weld them into a single political unit. The people were mostly of the same African descent, shared the same English language and the Christian religion. To join them altogether looked like a tidy solution. The people themselves, however, took far less interest in unity. Each island had its own local customs and knew little of the lives of its neighbours—the main lines of communication ran direct to Britain and America, not between the islands. Between the two most populous islands, Jamaica and Trinidad, lay 1,400 miles of sea and few travelled from one to the other. In total area, including sea, the British West Indies were about a third the size of the U.S.A. but most of the area *was* sea and it could take weeks to traverse it. Unity was a matter for vague discussion after dinner by forward-looking officials, not any definite proposal that was being made. Apart from a shadowy primacy exercised by the Captain-General of Jamaica, there was no single British authority for the area other than the Colonial Office in London. And the Secretary of State and his senior officials had their hands too full of matters in other parts of the world to spare time for the West Indies. Indeed it was an inherent weakness of the whole colonial system that the territories were so diverse and scattered that it was impossible for the handful of officials at decision-making level in London to know about them all. If Jamaica reached the Secretary of State's desk it might be pushed off again just because some crisis had arisen in, say, Hong Kong.

On the actual American mainland Britain had two colonies, British Honduras and British Guiana. There had been moments during the 19th century, following the collapse of Spanish and Portuguese power, when it had seemed possible that the British Empire might expand much further. In particular there had been massive British intervention on the economic level into Argentina, where the complete railway system was British-owned. Whenever the Argentine government fell into disorder, there had been suggestions of establishing a British protectorate. The immovable obstacle to such designs was the British strategic decision to accept the Monroe doctrine of the U.S.A. Although in this period Britain had been a far stronger military force in the Americas than the U.S.A., one of the underlying principles was to avoid a quarrel with that country; in expanding the Empire the British, generally, had come into conflict only with weak and archaic countries.

British Honduras was a strip of coast in Central America, next to Guatemala, to which British pioneers had gone in the 17th century to cut timber. In 1918 mahogany and cedar were still the mainstays of the colony's primitive little economy. The land area, which included huge swamps, was 8,600 square miles, much of it still unexplored. The 45,000 inhabitants were a mixed lot, mainly American Indians and Negroes plus about 600 Europeans and white Americans from the U.S.A. The Governor, Sir Eyre Hutson, drew £2,000 a year; he was aged 54 and had spent most of his career as a West Indian administrator. One of the minor problems of British policy was spasmodic claims by Guatemala to British Honduras.

On the north-east coast of Brazil lay the much more substantial colony of British Guiana, 8,500 square miles in area. In the early days of European exploration of the Americas, it had been a key area, believed to contain the riches of the fabulous El Dorado. British, French, Spanish and Dutch had jostled each other for control. Now it was parcelled out in three sections, British Guiana, Dutch Guiana and French Guiana, the French using their share (which included the notorious 'Devil's Island') as a convict settlement. The British had acquired their part as a by-product of the Napoleonic wars and had imported massive numbers of Indians from India who, by 1918, numbered a quarter of the population. They had come in as indentured labourers to work the sugar plantations and, on the expiry of their articles, had set up as free workers and developed a rice-growing industry. As in Trinidad, the status of the Indians was generally lower than that of the Negroes, who formed almost all the rest of the population, but the Indians—influenced by news of what Gandhi was doing at home in India—were politically the more lively and they also had a higher birth rate. Altogether in 1918 there were some 300,000 people living in the colony which, with its rotting wooden buildings, exuded an air of decay. The constitution dated back to earlier Dutch occupation and had as its centrepiece the 200-year-old Court of Policy, partly nominated by the Governor and partly elected on a restricted franchise; a handful of the richer and better educated black people played a small part in public life but the Indians, at this stage, were allowed no voice at all. The

Governor, Sir William Collett, aged 62, had served in the Pacific, Cyprus, and British Honduras. He drew £4,500 a year.

Off the far south coast of South America lay what in sheer area was the most scattered and extensive colonial administrative area of all—the Falkland Islands and their dependencies. They covered 3,500,000 square miles, including sea, and stretched in theory to the south pole. (The interior of the continent of Antarctica was reckoned to be the common property of the countries which had established footholds on the coast.) The Falkland Islands themselves supported a prosperous little population of 3,400, mostly sheep farmers of Scottish descent. The Falklands had originally been settled from Argentina, which still laid claim to them, but when the British had taken over in 1832 they had been uninhabited. The climate was chilly but exceptionally healthy, the perpetual westerly gales sweeping away disease germs. There was a miniature but complete colonial administration with the Governor, W. D. Young, settled in the capital, Stanley, on £1,800 a year. He must have felt the cold for he was aged 60 and had spent his whole preceding career in the West Indies. Young's writ ran also among the largely uninhabited dependent territories—South Georgia, South Orkney, South Sandwich, South Shetland and Graham Land. Visited by explorers and by whaling vessels they were subject to snow, ice and gales and were among the most inhospitable places known to man.

The final great division of the British colonial empire, after Africa, the Middle East and the Americas, lay in the Far East and the Pacific. Much of it had grown out of the central entanglement with India but it represented, too, expansionism by the settler-controlled dominions of Australia and New Zealand and 19th-century dreams of bringing China itself into the British orbit.

The Indian Ocean itself was practically a British lake, nearly every scrap of land within it having been snapped up to prevent hostile European powers establishing bases.

The most southerly of the Indian Ocean colonies was Mauritius, which the British had conquered from France during the Napoleonic wars with a joint expedition from South Africa and India. In 1918 the legal system was still based upon the Code Napoleon and French settlers were the leading social group. Some of the French families were descended from the pre-revolutionary nobility and those who were not customarily followed aristocratic manners. In Mauritius there subsisted the ghost of Bourbon France. The French sugar planters lived elegant lives and although their families had for generations been Mauritian it was still common for them to send their children to France for university education. Their racecourse, the Champ de Mars at Port Louis, was claimed to be the most beautiful in the world. By 1918, however, French supremacy was being undermined by massive immigration from India, the Indians already numbering two thirds of the 370,000 population. The French, supported by Africans, still staffed most of the public administration and provided the elected members of the legislature. All save the very top public offices were filled by local recruitment and the English and French languages had equal status. The Governor was Sir Hesketh Bell, a cosmopolitan man who had been educated in France, had acquired early colonial experience in the West Indies and become an expert on the Gold Coast. He was aged 53 and drew £4,000 a year.

A thousand miles to the north of Mauritius lay the Seychelles, a sheltered group of about a hundred islands. They were a great place for tortoises, some of which grew to a huge size. The Governor maintained tortoise pens in the grounds of his residence with 60 specimens on display. The population, mixed British, French, Indian and original Seychelloise was 24,000 and the land area about 156 square miles. Few people knew much about the Seychelles but those that did regarded it as a paradise. It had an equable climate, coral shores and colourful vegetation. The Governor had formerly been a Liberal member of the British House of Commons and was called Sir Eustace Twistleton-Wykeham-Fiennes. He drew £2,500 a year. In Parliament, Twistleton-Wykeham-Fiennes had won no outstanding fame but in the Seychelles he was lord of a paradise and of the tortoises. The paradise was a handy place for keeping political prisoners. In 1918 the King of Bunyoro, Uganda, was living there, a sad figure in a frock coat. Later the Archbishop Makarios III of Cyprus was to be exiled there.

The major island of the Indian Ocean was Ceylon, the pear-shaped appendage to India, about the size of Belgium. It was a place of ancient culture, dating back to the fifth century BC and was an important centre of the Buddhist religion. During the 17th century the Dutch had settled on the coast and the British had taken over from them during the Napoleonic wars. Independent kings of Ceylon had reigned in the interior with their capital at Kandy, until the British in 1815 conquered them and established a full colonial administration. Although at the nearest point Ceylon was only 27 miles from India, it was by race, religion and language entirely separate. The economy depended upon tea, which during the 19th century had become the British national drink, and rubber plantations which were developing in scale. The population of 4,500,000 made it one of the most important colonies and the capital Colombo, with 250,000 inhabitants, was one of the metropolises of the Empire.

Ceylon had its own Civil Service recruited on the model of the Indian Civil Service but with rather more scope for local people. In 1918 the top posts were still held entirely by Englishmen but by the 1920s as many as a third of the 'cadet' grade—new entrants from the universities—were Ceylonese. The British got on better with educated Ceylonese than they did with educated Indians and the gradual development of self-government proceeded with remarkably little friction. In 1920 a new constitution established a legislature with half the members elected, although on a restricted franchise. The Governor in 1918, Brigadier-General Sir William Manning, was not a product of the Ceylon Civil Service; he had spent most of his career in the Indian army and had devoted years to trying to eliminate the 'Mad Mullah' in Somaliland. He was aged 55 and drew £6,500 a year. A sort of feudal dependency of Ceylon was the Maldive Archipalego, made up of 17 groups of islets, with a population of about 70,000. The people, who were Moslems, lived by fishing and were ruled by their own Sultan. It was an isolated place and its main communication with the outside world was an annual embassy sent by the Sultan across 400 miles of sea to 'pay tribute' to the British.

Other Indian Ocean islands—the Adamans, the Nicobars and the Lacadives—were administered as an integral part of India.

Around the eastern end of the Indian Ocean, where it met the China Sea, lay a giant group of territories of strategic and commercial value and containing large populations. In 1918 these were parcelled out among four colonial powers:— the United States had the Philippines, the Dutch had Sumatra, Java and most of Borneo, the French had Viet Nam, Laos and Cambodia and the British had Malaya, North Borneo and two bits of China itself, Hong Kong and Weihaiwei. The only independent country in the area was Siam (Thailand) which had kept free from European control because of the ability of its ruling dynasty and because British and French would not tolerate each other annexing it.

The bastion of British power at this world crossroads was the island of Singapore, only 217 square miles in area but the principal business centre of South-East Asia. It lies just south of the Malayan peninsula. Until a century earlier it had been inhabited by only a handful of fishermen but Sir Stamford Raffles of the East India Company had appreciated its potentialities and leased it from the Sultan of Johore, ruler of the neighbouring mainland. By 1918 it had grown into a wonderful port, with 50 different shipping lines using it, and in British imperial mystique it ranked second only to the Suez Canal itself. In 1918 the population—mixed Malayan, Indian and Chinese—was approaching half a million, men outnumbering women by two to one. The sexual disparity was a proof of the pioneering nature of the settlers, especially of the Chinese. It had become common for energetic Chinese men to migrate to Singapore in the hope of making their fortunes; they did not send home for wives until they had made their way. Some in fact did make fortunes; Singapore had grown under British leadership but largely by Chinese enterprise and work.

Between the wars the British embarked on the fortification of Singapore. The aim was to make it the Gibraltar of the Far East, a lasting bastion of British power. Hitherto the main naval base for the Far East had been Trincomalee, Ceylon; the move eastwards indicated how as late as the 1920s the British were still instinctively thinking in terms of the Empire as an expanding force, the frontiers still being pushed out. Another factor in the Singapore plans was the power of Britain's wartime ally, Japan. Already Japan had thrust herself into the forefront of world naval powers and she obviously wanted to become the leading influence in the Far East. The Singapore base commanded the maritime approaches to both India and the self-governing dominions of Australia and New Zealand—the Australians were particularly eager supporters of it. Year by year the British built up the fortifications, setting great guns in concrete to shatter an attacking fleet.

North of Singapore lay the Malayan peninsula which by 1918 was all British, although much of it only recently so. The long-established British section was the Straits Settlements, which consisted of Singapore itself, the island of Penang and the mainland territory of Malacca. The rest of the peninsula consisted of princely states ruled by sultans and rajahs subject to British suzerainty. Four of these states had been long under British influence and their rulers had become figureheads, real power resting with British officials. These states formed a federation, its bureaucracy run entirely by the British. The remaining five states of the peninsula had nominally been subject to Siam (Thailand) until 1909 when they had formally accepted British overlordship. These states retained more independence than the 'federated' ones, their rulers having about as much power as Indian ruling princes. Each federated state had a British 'Resident' who was the *de facto* administrative head. Each unfederated state had only a British 'Adviser,' formal control—and a measure of real control—rema-n ing with the ruler. The peninsula had a natural racial and geographic unity and the British aim was to weld it into a single colony. The people had their own distinctive culture and were pacific in outlook. They showed no burning desire to develop their own country and the most enterprising people in Malaya were immigrants who were pouring in from India and China. The total population of Straits Settlements and Malaya was about 2,300,000 and the area 46,000 square miles.

There were the soundest economic reasons for British expansion in Malaya and the arrival of the immigrants. It had become the world's leading producer of rubber. Cultivation of rubber had been a British idea; the Marquess of Salisbury as Secretary for India in the 1870s had conceived the idea of transplanting South American rubber seeds to the Far East and in Malaya the soil had proved to be suitable. British planters, employing largely Indian and Chinese labour, had made fortunes by hacking rubber plantations out of the jungles which covered most of the peninsula. By 1918 the capital value of the industry was reckoned to be £150 million and Malaya was providing half the world's rubber. It was the most spectacular economic success of British imperialism.

Ruling over this thriving community in 1918 was 64-year-old Sir Arthur Young, who had worked in Cyprus and the West Indies before transferring to the Malayan service in 1906; he had been promoted to Governor in 1906. His responsibilities were the widest of any colonial governor, extending to most British interests in South-East Asia. He was Governor of the Straits Settlements, High Commissioner in charge of the Malayan princely states, British Agent for North Borneo and British Agent for Sarawak. He drew salary and allowances totalling £7,000 a year for his different functions and had under him a complete Civil Service on the Indian model; new recruits, who came from British universities, were called 'Eastern Cadets.' Malaya had formed a reservoir of trained colonial administrators from which officials were drawn for the new African territories.

The population of Malaya, including Singapore, in 1918 was 2,400,000 in an area of some 47,000 square miles.

Administratively attached to the Straits Settlements were Christmas Island and the Cocos or Keeling Islands. They lay between Australia and the Dutch East Indies (Indonesia) and were of 120 square miles, altogether, and had a population of about 2,000. Christmas Island contained phosphates of lime and everyone who lived there, save the District Officer, was dependent upon the Christmas Island Phosphate Company.

Four hundred miles east of Malaya, but still under Sir Arthur Young's jurisdiction at Singapore, lay the British part of the great island of Borneo. The Dutch had most of Borneo but the British held the northern coastal area, about a quarter of the whole. It was reckoned to be a dangerous territory. The less sophisticated of the local inhabitants enjoyed head-hunting, successful practitioners tying shrunken human heads to their belts. Anthropologists were interested in the 'long houses,' each containing a whole tribe of people. Some tribes, fearful of head-hunters and wild beasts, lived in homes built on stilts over lakes. The British at home remembered 'the wild man of Borneo' who had been exhibited in a cage at 19th-century fairgrounds.

The British had penetrated Borneo through the Sultan of Brunei, a Moslem ruler whose ancestors had carved out a kingdom on the north coast five centuries earlier. During the 19th century the Sultan had leased most of his territory to the British North Borneo Company and to a British adventurer, James Brooke. In 1918 the Sultan had only 4,000 square miles left for himself, with a population of 25,000. He was 'advised' by a British Resident and held in disfavour by the Colonial Office because a combination of extravagance by his administration and sharp dealing by traders had placed his state in debt. The former Brunei territories of British North Borneo and Sarawak had become entirely separate.

Like Rhodesia, British North Borneo in 1918 was administered by a commercial chartered company; its headquarters were at 37 Threadneedle Street in the City of London. It did not carry on any actual trading but covered administrative costs and paid dividends on its shares out of taxes levied on the people and by the leasing of land and mineral rights. It had its own little Civil Service and an adventurous community of planters and mine operators; the hope which illuminated their lives was that of finding workable deposits of gold. The territory formed part of the British Empire but the governor was appointed by the British North Borneo Company, subject to Colonial Office veto. In 1918 he was A. C. Pearson who was aged 52 and had spent his entire career in the territory. The company paid him £2,500 a year. He ruled 220,000 people, 30,000 of them Chinese immigrants, and an area of 31,000 square miles.

The biggest territory of northern Borneo, Sarawak, was unique in the British Empire. Many pioneers in many parts of the world had founded new British colonies. Kitchener had conquered Sudan, Raffles had founded Singapore, Rhodes had got a huge chunk of Africa called after him. All these, though, had acted under the ultimate authority of the British Crown. Only one British pioneer, James Brooke of Sarawak, had carved out for himself his own independent country and achieved quasi-royal status. Brooke obtained his first territory by grant from the Sultan of Brunei and so extended it that by the middle of the 19th century Sarawak had become the major territory and Brunei itself only an enclave. Brooke had established himself as 'Rajah' and his son as 'Tuan Muda,' or heir apparent. For the first 40 years of this arrangement Sarawak had functioned as an independent state, although Brooke himself had remained a British subject. This had been against one of the canons of British imperial expansion by which new territory conquered by British subjects was supposed to come under the Crown. Although Sarawak was such a remote, little-known place, Brooke's assertion of independence could not be tolerated. The British had threatened to send a naval expedition to subdue the territory and, under this pressure, Brooke had accepted British 'protection.' In 1918 this arrangement continued; the 'White Rajah' ran Sarawak's internal affairs but Britain controlled such foreign relations as the territory had. Also the ruler was not to extend his dominion any farther without London's consent. From the standpoint of international law, Sarawak was on a par with an Indian princely state which happened to have a British instead of an indigenous hereditary ruler. The third 'White Rajah,' grandson of the original, had just acceded to the throne in 1918. He was His Highness Charles Vyner Brooke, aged 44. With the assistance of some 50 British officials, chosen by himself, he was the despotic ruler over 600,000 people and about 50,000 square miles of land. He had his own little army, the Sarawak Rangers, his own newspaper, *The Sarawak Gazette* and his own coal mines. The Brookes generally took their duties conscientiously and, while making more money than the ordinary colonial governor, did think of the interests of their people.

During the 19th century the ultimate dream of advanced British imperialism had been to round off the British Empire by including China within its sphere. Today the very possibility makes the mind boggle: 'Victoria, Queen of the United Kingdom, Empress of India, *Empress of China.*' There had never been a settled scheme towards this end but for decades it had been an occasional theme for after-dinner conversation among imaginative British officials. Troops for the conquest of China would, of course, have been Indian and, indeed, the Indian Empire under this scheme would have become just the advanced base for the movement into the even bigger empire of China. Such notions had come to nothing for a variety of reasons. Too many other countries had been interested in establishing footholds in China for British claims to be paramount as they had been during the conquest of India. Then the Chinese themselves, although their political institutions had been decaying and tending towards anarchy, had possessed such an inner self-confidence as would have rendered rule by 'foreign devils' a difficult undertaking. When Japan, eventually, tried to colonise China she found that it was easier to win military victories than to destroy the ultimate will to resist. Above all, it had simply not been the method of the British Empire to expand according to grand designs of conquest. New territories had been snapped up for local, pragmatic reasons and because they did not seriously resist—nobody had ever proclaimed in advance: 'We are going to conquer India.'

Nevertheless the intervention of Britain and other European powers in Chinese affairs had been one of the factors of the 19th century. The East India Company, indeed, made more money out of China than ever it did out of India. In such Chinese cities as Shanghai there were in 1918 whole areas marked out as European territory and administered by the European consuls. The Government of India had eliminated all but theoretical Chinese sovereignty over Tibet. British gunboats sailed up Chinese rivers. Also there were two actual British colonies on Chinese soil, Hong Kong and Weihaiwei.

Hong Kong had come to Britain in 1842 as a result of one of the less glorious episodes of imperial history—the Opium Wars to force China to allow trade in opium. In 1918 opium in Hong Kong was a government monopoly and provided a quarter of the public revenue. The island part of the colony was under full British sovereignty and the mainland section, Kowloon, was held on a lease due to expire in 1997. Under British administration the huge harbour, ten square miles in extent, had grown from just a fishermen's centre into a great international port, a centre of trade between China and the rest of the world. Chinese had flocked into Hong Kong by the hundred thousand and the population of about half a million was rapidly growing. Hong Kong was also the transit and classifying centre for Chinese who wanted to migrate to other British territories. It was a bustling place with a total area of about 35 square miles, the granite hills giving it an air reminiscent of Scotland. The Governor, Sir Francis May, drew £7,200 a year and presided over a sophisticated bureaucracy. He had a legislative council of 14 members, two of them Chinese and the rest British.

The other British Chinese territory was Weihaiwei, a coastal strip and adjoining islands lying over a thousand miles to the north of Hong Kong. It was in the sensitive area of Korea, Manchuria and Port Arthur which had long been the scene of warlike upheavals involving Russians, Japanese and Chinese and the British had acquired it in 1898 mainly as a naval base. It was reckoned to have one of the best climates in China and it contained a sanatorium popular in the Royal Navy. The ruler was the Civil Commissioner, Sir James Stewart Lockhart, who was aged 60 and had spent his whole career in the China service. He and Weihaiwei were regarded as almost inseparably linked; he had held his job for almost the entire period of British possession. China, however, wanted the territory back and had American and Japanese support; the British by the Washington Naval Treaty of 1920 agreed to go and they eventually left in 1928. Shortly afterwards the territory was overrun by the Japanese in their invasion of China. The population in 1918 was 150,000 Chinese plus varying numbers of Royal Navy officers and men. The area was 285 square miles.

The final section of the colonial empire, and the one most distant from London, was that in the Pacific Ocean. It consisted of hundreds of islands, the different groups separated by thousands of miles of sea. They lay mostly in the tropical parts of the south Pacific and their inhabitants, isolated from the rest of mankind, had built up over the generations a distinctive way of life. The Pacific breakers surged against their coral reefs under clear blue skies and they were full of light and colour. Early British explorers had regarded them as a paradise.

The centre of British administration in the Pacific was the Fiji group of islands, which were about 1,500 miles from Australia and about 6,000 miles from South America. Fiji consisted of eight major islands and about 200 subsidiary islets and rocks, the total land area being some 7,083 square miles. Under the impact of European settlement the local population had at first declined disastrously, the people dying of imported diseases. In one year, 1875, a quarter of the population of Fiji had died of measles. By 1918, however, numbers were rising again, the population having increased by 10,000 to 150,000 over the previous decade. Fifty years earlier it had been 200,000.

From Fiji the British officials travelled by steamer to the other British Pacific territories—the Gilbert and Ellice Islands, the British Solomon Islands, the New Hebrides, Tonga, the Phoenix group, Pitcairn and Nauru. These islands, scattered over eight million square miles of ocean, formed the Western Pacific High Commission with its headquarters at Fiji. The population was reckoned to total about 300,000 but nobody knew the exact figure. The most organised was Tonga which had its own monarchy, a new Queen, Salote, having just acceded to the throne at the age of 18. The Queen of Tonga was the only subordinate ruler in the entire British Empire to share the King-Emperor's appellation of 'Your Majesty;' all other princely rulers, the maharajahs of India and the most powerful chiefs of Africa, were allowed at most 'Your Exalted Highness.' In Tonga the young Queen presided over an administration staffed almost entirely by her own subjects; Methodist missionaries were at least as influential as official British advisers. Already in 1918 the 23,000 population was well on the way towards complete literacy. Constitutionally the most interesting of the Pacific territories was the New Hebrides which, with a population of 100,000, belonged jointly to Great Britain and France, each country appointing a Resident Commissioner of equal status. Pitcairn Island had 145 inhabitants, descendants of the crew of the *Bounty* who had mutinied against Captain Bligh in the 18th century. The mutineers had married women from another island, Otaheite, and set up a permanent community on Pitcairn. In 1918 they were ruled by a Chief Magistrate, F. Christian, who was descended from the mutineers' original leader. The British Solomon Islands were regarded as a savage place, with cannibalism still existing in 1918; the population of about 150,000 was being decimated by outbreaks of dysentery. The Gilbert and Ellice Islands were scattered, the scene of intensive missionary work; they included Ocean Island, the Union group, the Fanning and Washington Islands and Christmas Island, which last was to become the test ground for British nuclear weapons.

The chief British official in the Pacific was C. H. Rodwell, who drew £3,000 a year as Governor of Fiji and a further £1,000 as High Commissioner for the Western Pacific. He was aged 43 in 1918 and had just been appointed from South Africa, where he had served for 18 years on the staff of the Governor General. He was supported by his own little Civil Service, recruited from Britain. There were about two vacancies a year in the 'cadet' grade. The 'cadets,' new graduates from Oxford and Cambridge, spent three years learning about the islands before being appointed to responsible posts. Their life had its hardships but, also, its compensations. Many of the islands were beautiful. So too were the women and the sexual austerity characteristic of British colonial officials was not always upheld in the Pacific. (Although in Malaya it was reckoned that the best way to learn Chinese was to set up a Chinese mistress.) Some Pacific officials preferred to stick to one girl but harems were not unknown. One man in the Solomons practised monogamy with a lazy girl who lay on in his bed after he had got up in the morning. The Chinese houseman regularly ejected her by pulling up the sheets and smacking her bottom. Then the man went home on leave and married an English girl. He brought her out to the Solomons—and the joke was that on the first morning the houseman treated her as he had her predecessor.

So in 1918 the British colonial empire girdled the entire globe. It was an object of devotion to the officials who ran it. A magnetic urge drew hundreds of British people to strange lands, there to take control. The colonies, said a Conservative Colonial Secretary of the 1920s, Leo Amery, were 'deep-rooted in the instincts of the nation.' The instinct took them over the Atlantic, southwards to Africa and, above all, to the east. 'If you've 'eard the East a-callin', you won't ever 'eed aught else,' wrote Kipling in *Mandalay*. When planters, officials and soldiers returned to their homeland they still yearned for the distant places in which they had served—as did Kipling's soldier:

'If you've 'eard the East a-callin', you won't ever 'eed aught else.'

# CHAPTER 5

# His Excellency

ONE of the leading characteristics of the British colonial empire was its decentralisation. Power and initiative rested more with the officials on the spot than with London. The function of the Colonial Office—the staff of which belonged to the Home Civil Service and practically never visited the colonies—was to supervise finance, make appointments to senior jobs and to act as the channel of communication between the colonies and the home government. The regular and niggling interference was over finance. A Governor with powers of life and death might have to get permission from London to buy a bicycle for a court messenger. Save where some special matter arose, a rebellion or a new constitution, it was no part of the function of the Colonial Office to intervene in general administration. Indeed so scattered and so varied were the colonies that it would have been impossible for one minister to govern them all. Even the most devoted Colonial Secretary might have to think twice before he could remember the location of Togoland. One Colonial Secretary of the 19th century, asked about the Virgin Islands, replied he knew nothing about them but supposed they must be a long way from the Isle of Man. Until the advent of Joseph Chamberlain at the end of the 19th century, the Colonial Office had been regarded as an unimportant post. Palmerston, forming a new administration, found he could get nobody to be Colonial Secretary. So he said he would take the office himself, as well as being Prime Minister, and strode upstairs to look up 'the damned places' on the map.

Between the wars there was no difficulty in getting politicians to become Colonial Secretary. The post had among its perquisites the Secretary of State's private room, the biggest ministerial room in Whitehall. Lord Beaverbrook described it as 'thoroughly uncomfortable and most unsuited for business purposes. It was a place for a pompous man.' When the colonies were split off from the dominions, the room went to the Dominions Secretary, which office was regarded as more important than Colonial Secretary.

In the half century 1916–1966 there were 27 holders of the office of Colonial Secretary, so the average period of incumbency

was less than two years. Only two of the holders, Bonar Law
(1915–16) and Winston Churchill (1921–1922) ever went to the
top in politics. Only four holders, Leo Amery (1924–1929), Oliver
Stanley (1942–1945), Arthur Creech Jones (1946–1950) and
Alan Lennox-Boyd (1954–1959) could be counted as colonial
specialists. This latter, naturally, is a subjective judgement by
the author. Another such judgement is that, of the total of 27,
only a dozen could really be regarded as politicians of the first
rank.

The true linchpin of the colonial system was His Excellency the
local Governor who, in his territory, ranked immediately below
the deity. Everyone deferred to him. On formal occasions women,
including his own wife, curtseyed to him. In his own house, as in
everyone else's, a Governor went into dinner first and was served
with food before anybody else. He ranked superior to everyone
else who happened to be in his territory save only the monarch
himself. If the Secretary of State from London, or even the Prime
Minister himself, visited a colony he ranked in social precedence
below the Governor. The heir to the throne, the Prince of Wales,
also ranked below a Governor in his own colony. Most colonies
had their own local flags but the Governor himself flew the plain
union jack over his official residence. He was entitled to a 17-gun
salute from warships and land batteries. The Colonial Office
wrote to him in polite terms, treating him as a potentate to be
conciliated rather than as an employee. On ceremonial occasions
he wore a special uniform, white in the tropics and blue elsewhere,
with a vast cocked hat adorned with ostrich feathers.

The justification for the pomp, for the expenditure of £50 worth
of explosive for salutes, was that the Governor had to impress
ignorant native peoples by cutting a glamorous and awesome
figure. In truth, however, there was a little more to it than that.
By 1918 the more educated of the colonial peoples were beginning
to find the ceremonies pretentious and irritating. What kept the
pomp going was the taste of the British themselves, officials and
unofficials. 'It is the British and not the Orientals who care most
about these things, and for whom they must be maintained. . . . As
a race we ourselves possess most of the characteristics which we
ascribe to the peoples of the East,' wrote Sir Charles Johnston who
was Governor of Aden in the early 1960s.

Under the Governor the chief official was the Colonial Secretary. (This designation should not be confused with that of the
Colonial Secretary in London, properly called the Secretary of

State for the Colonies.) The Colonial Secretary of a colony acted as a kind of Prime Minister and supervised the bureaucracy. Between him and the Governor lay a gulf in status and authority. The Governor represented the King and held a commission signed by the King's own hand. The Colonial Secretary was just a very senior clerk. Customarily a Governor's salary was at least double that of his Colonial Secretary.

An examination of 34 Governors holding office in 1922 shows that the youngest was aged 42 and the oldest was 65. Most of them were in their 50s, the average age being 55. Of the 34, 19 were professional colonial administrators who had devoted their whole adult lives to the service; of these ten held governorships in areas where they had worked for many years and nine had been transferred from elsewhere—for example from Malaya to the West Indies. Of the remaining 15 Governors, those who might loosely be termed the non-professionals, seven had been army officers of long service, two had been members of the Home Civil Service, two had come from the Indian administration and one had been an elected politician in South Africa. There was no Governor who had been a career naval officer.*

The tendency between the wars was for the proportion of Governors who had been career officials to rise. It became exceptional—but not unknown—for 'non-professionals' to be chosen. Every recruit to the colonial administrative service could dream of eventually rising to the ineffable height of Governor; no other career could offer a prize of such prestige and power. At a rough estimate, perhaps one long-service official in every 20 attained the rank. It was regarded as a weakness in the service that officials who managed to get into the secretariats in the capitals had a better chance of becoming Governors than district officers who spent many years in the field and really knew the people. A successful official reached Colonial Secretary rank by his early 40s, after 20 years' service, and was then poised for promotion to Governor at the age of about 50. Indeed the alternative was often between promotion or retirement. A Governor generally served five years and was almost never re-appointed to the same territory. He might, however, get promoted to a further five-year term in a bigger territory. It was rare for anyone to serve more than two terms as a Governor.

Absent from the procedure was any suggestion of a political 'spoils' system. Appointments to colonial governorships represented

* Totals compiled from the Colonial Office List 1922.

K

patronage on a considerable scale and, potentially, they could have been used as rewards for political services. This almost never happened—the few British politicians who did become Governors did so on merit rather than as a reward. The only imperial post which did regularly go to a politician was that of Viceroy of India and it, of course, ranked in standing equally with that of membership of the Cabinet in London.

It can also be observed how the colonial system worked in a separate compartment from the elaborate Government of India. Despite shortages in staffing newly-acquired colonies, it was rare for an official to be transferred from India to a colony.

Governors' salaries in 1922 ranged between £775 in St. Helena to £8,250 a year in Nigeria, the average being £3,070. These figures include various special allowances. (In the Home Civil Service the highest official, the Permanent Secretary to the Treasury, drew £3,500; a Cabinet minister drew £5,000.) A colonial Governor also got free accommodation in his official residence, Government House, but out of his allowances he had to entertain guests and hold receptions on a scale suited to his dignity. Few Governors had much fortune of their own and they rarely saved money while in office. They never took bribes; indeed for any official to be detected in financial corruption was the worst disgrace that could befall him. The Colonial Regulations spelled out the rules very carefully: 'Governors, Lieutenant-Governors, and all other servants of the Crown in a Colony are prohibited during the continuance of their service in the Colony from receiving valuable presents (other than the ordinary gifts of personal friends), whether in the shape of money, goods, free passages or other personal benefits, and from giving such presents. This regulation applies not only to the officers themselves but to their families. It is not intended to apply to cases of remuneration for special services rendered and paid for with the consent of the Government. Money which has been subscribed with a view to marking personal approbation of an officer's conduct may be dedicated to objects of general utility and connected with the name of the person who has merited such proof of the general esteem. Presents from kings, chiefs or other members of the native population in or neighbouring to the Colony, which cannot be refused without giving offence, will be handed over to the Government. When presents are exchanged between Governors or other officers acting on behalf of the Colonial Government in ceremonial intercourse with native kings, chiefs or others, the presents received will be handed over to the Government and any return presents will be given at the Government expense.'

These rules were obeyed uniformly the world over, breaches of them being so rare as now not to be worth noticing. No British colonial administrator expected to make a personal fortune out of his work; he just looked forward to living to draw his pension. There existed no equivalent of the millionaire fortunes which the 18th-century employees of the East India Company had extorted from the populations under their control.

The acknowledgement for good service was not money but a decoration. By 1918 the British honours system was acquiring a Byzantinian complexity, with literally dozens of different kinds of honours, decorations and titles, all graded in complicated orders of precedence. The special order for the colonial administrators was The Most Distinguished Order of St. Michael and St. George. It was administered from the Colonial Office and the Permanent Under-Secretary of State was registrar. Unlike such orders as the Garter and the Bath which had a tenuous connection with medieval chivalry, the Order of St. Michael and St. George was modern. It had started in 1818 to reward various Maltese and Greeks who had helped the British in the Napoleonic wars and immediately was given also to British people who had served in the Mediterranean. Rapidly it became the standard reward for all overseas service, its size expanding to keep up with the growth of the Empire. In 1818 the limit had been fixed at only 44 members. By 1922 the original establishment had been enlarged six times and the limit had risen to 1,125 members. Two thirds of the places were reserved for colonial administrators and one third for diplomats. The King was Sovereign of the Order and the Prince of Wales was Grand Master.

Successful officials got into the order after 15 to 20 years' service and started in the lowest grade, that of Companion. The recipient added the letters 'C.M.G.' to his name but stayed a plain 'Mr.' The King gave him a fourteen-pointed cross to hang around his neck on a ribbon. Every Governor was, or soon became, at least a C.M.G., it being considered unsuitable for the occupant of such a post to have no decoration to wear on formal occasions. Most Governors, in fact, belonged to the next grade, that of 'Knight Commander,' which carried the title 'Sir' and a star worn on the left breast. The Governor of a substantial territory became K.C.M.G. either on his appointment or within his first year. The top grade, that of 'Knight Grand Cross' (G.C.M.G.), was reserved for the leading personalities of the service, often those who had ruled more than one colony. A Knight Grand Cross was allotted a stall in the Order's chapel in St. Paul's Cathedral, London, and hung a banner with his personal coat of arms over it. He was allowed a star and a gold collar and was entitled to wear a blue satin cloak, lined with scarlet silk and tied with cords of blue, red and gold. A chestnut of a joke was that C.M.G. stood for 'Call Me God.' K.C.M.G. 'Kindly Call Me God' and G.C.M.G. 'God Calls Me God.'

In its early days the Order had attracted little respect, it being regarded as a gaudy innovation. By the 1920s, however, men were proud to belong to it; it had become a kind of club of successful administrators. In precedence it ranked between the two Indian orders—the Star of India and the Order of the Indian Empire.

A new decoration, which despite its title was not connected with imperial administration, was The Most Excellent Order of the British Empire, founded by King George V in 1917. It rapidly became the biggest order of all and its original purpose had been to reward people who had served well in the war. The title of the order survives as the last remaining official use of the term 'British Empire.' Many colonial officials got into one or other of the five classes into which it was divided but they regarded it as inferior to their own St. Michael and St. George and they were greatly outnumbered by recipients from other spheres.

Every Governor enjoyed the additional title of 'Commander-in-Chief' which gave him supreme command of the local defence forces of his colony and, also, a degree of seniority over the commanding officer of any British garrison. His powers did not, however, extend over the Royal Navy which remained always subject to the Admiralty and its own Commanders-in-Chief. Naval captains were bidden to attach respect to the wishes of Governors and to fire off guns to salute them but actual orders could come only through naval channels.

The whole administrative service of every colony was responsible to the Governor and, technically, appointed by him. The Colonial Office in London chose who was to fill the higher posts but the actual documents of appointment were always signed by the local Governor. The custom was to allow the Governor unfettered discretion in filling jobs worth less than £300 a year; for higher posts the candidates were chosen by the Colonial Office, although the Governor exercised significant powers of recommendation and of veto. Until 1930, every colony, or regional group of colonies, had its own Civil Service with its own qualifications for recruitment and its own salary scales. Transfer from one colony to another happened only to the most senior officials. The career of a brilliant official might place him for his first 20 years in West Africa where he might go up the ladder to Assistant Colonial Secretary on £960 a year; his next promotion, to Colonial Secretary, might entail transfer to the West Indies. He would now be being closely watched as a candidate for one of the plum appointments. If all went well he would get a junior governorship, with a salary of about £2,500 and a knighthood, at around the age of 50; five years later he might rise to one of the highest governorships, Nigeria, Jamaica or Straits Settlements, before retiring to live on his pension at Cheltenham. Less outstanding officials would serve their careers as district commissioners, perhaps reaching provincial commissioner grade as the summit of their careers; they would not move out of their original territories. Generally an administrator who started in a cadet grade on £200 to £300 in his early 20s could rely on reaching £900 to £1,000 a year by the end of his career. This was well below the rates in India, where every I.C.S. recruit could rely on reaching at least £1,500.

In the very smallest colonies the Governor acted as Chief Justice as well as ruler but the general policy was to separate the two functions. Lower down in the judicial system it was commonplace in 1922 for district commissioners to exercise petty judicial functions as part of their routine duties but, between the wars, the tendency developed of appointing specialist magistrates, often legally qualified, for judicial work. The ordinary ladder of promotion in the judicial establishment was for a young British barrister to start as a magistrate or an assistant attorney general and rise to become a puisne judge and then, perhaps, a chief justice. The lawyers were transferred more freely between the territories than their administrative counterparts. The two functions, judicial and executive, were by no means formally separated. A judge was just as much a colonial official as any other and could be transferred or dismissed at the will of the Colonial Office. Also it was quite usual for a chief justice temporarily to take over the functions of Colonial Secretary or Governor, on an acting basis, if one of those officials happened to be absent. Unlike other senior officials, judges did not sit as members of colonial legislatures, it being reckoned that it was their work to enforce the law, not to make it. In practice, though not formally, the judges enjoyed a high degree of security of tenure, it being against the bias of British administrative traditions to penalise, or seem to penalise, a judge for making inconvenient decisions.

A colonial judge was generally on a salary scale of between £1,000 and £2,000 a year. He had no hope at all of getting into the judiciary at home in Britain or of achieving membership of the Empire's supreme court, the Judicial Committee of the Privy Council in London. The Judicial Committee was staffed by senior judges of the British domestic courts, plus a few representatives of India and the self-governing dominions. Such limited prospects did not attract the best British lawyers to the colonial judiciary and, on occasion, standards were less than adequate—there were tragi-comic legends of lazy judges drinking themselves to death in the remoter dependencies. The presence of an inefficient or grossly eccentric judge was one of the more awkward problems a Governor could encounter. In general, however, the colonial judiciary provided a settled framework of law and justice, often in difficult conditions.

In most colonies the basic legal system was the English common law with such modifications and additions as had been made by local legislation. The notable exception to this was Ceylon which ran on a basis of Roman–Dutch law. British Acts of Parliament were binding only if they specifically referred to the colonies. Many of the colonial criminal codes were based on that of India. In white settled territories, a white man often had a right of trial by jury for serious offences but the more normal colonial pattern was for a judge to adjudicate on his own. Every Governor had prerogatives of mercy exercised on his own discretion. The death penalty, by hanging, existed everywhere for murder but only in conditions of extreme civil disorder was it used for other offences. In the more primitive territories executions were sometimes carried out in public. This could lead to unexpected results. There was the tale of the district officer in Nigeria who wished to impress upon his people the wickedness of murder and so decided to conduct an execution in a remote village. The scaffold was carried in pieces for miles through the forest and eventually put together in the centre of the village. The people had never before seen such a thing and thronged around, full of interest. The official harangued them with a solemn speech about the wickedness of murder and severity of the penalty for it. Then the prisoner, with a burly African constable on each side of him, ascended the scaffold. The noose was fixed around his neck. The official gave a signal and the hangman pulled the lever. But the scaffold had been wrongly assembled so that the prisoner remained where he was and it was the two constables who abruptly disappeared down the trapdoors. The assembled population went into such howls of laughter as to destroy the solemnity of the occasion. Capital sentences were not excessively employed—and, of course, normally were executed inside prison. The characteristic form of punishment in a British colony was flogging, which was widely applied for offences of theft and violence, and sometimes, too, for political offences. In Africa, delinquents were commonly beaten with bamboo canes as if they were naughty boys at a British public school; the widespread use of such punishment reflected, possibly, the paternal attitude of officials towards their subjects.

The rapid expansion of the British Empire over the previous generation had caused serious staffing difficulties, many of the African administrations, in particular, having been improvised on a makeshift basis. The 1920s saw the system settle down. The colonial service could offer little of the prestige—or the pay—of the Indian service but it had its own attraction for the right kind of man. The district officer in the field in Africa enjoyed far more independence than the bureaucrat in India; intellectual qualifications counted for less than sheer instinct on how to handle people regarded as children. Then, too, the colonial service appeared to offer a stable career. Anybody could foresee the possibility of revolutionary changes in India but the African colonies were still at only the threshold of development as British countries; the colonial administrator reckoned that he was working on a structure that would take generations to complete.

In the years immediately after 1918 the new recruits to the colonial service were young ex-officers from the war. They were selected by interview in London. As the supply of ex-officers dried up, the recruits were drawn from Oxford and Cambridge. There was no particular stress on the class of degree required—what counted, especially for the African service, were 'personal qualities.' The explicit aim was to recruit men who had been educated at public schools—as late as 1937 a semi-official work on the Civil Service stated: 'The public school spirit is greatly valued in the colonial service, and it is a matter of conscious policy to ensure that the supplies of it shall be constantly replenished.' Lugard of Nigeria, an old boy of Rossall, explained in 1922 why public school qualities were important: 'The District Officer comes from a class which has made and maintained the British Empire. . . . His assets are usually a public school, and probably a university education, neither of which have provided him with an appreciable amount of positive knowledge especially adapted for his work. But they have produced an English gentleman with an almost passionate conception of fair play, of protection of the weak, and of "playing the game." They have taught him personal initiative and resource, and how to command and obey. There is no danger of such men falling a prey to that subtle moral deterioration which the exercise of power over inferior races produces in men of a different type and which finds expression in cruelty.'

During the 1920s the recruiting of such men proceeded at an accelerating pace. There were 173 new administrative recruits in 1922 and the number increased every year until 1928, when there were 527. After 1928, partly for reasons of economy and partly because the service had become adequately staffed, the rate of recruitment tended to decline until there was another big rise after 1945. The recruits of the 1920s became the lasting backbone of the colonial service. It was they who set their mark upon it and, to their surprise, the most successful of them who ultimately supervised its dismantlement.

The actual machinery of recruitment was, by British Civil Service standards, almost unbelievably casual. The colonial service lay in the personal patronage of the Secretary of State, who was advised on the matter by one of his private secretaries Major (later Sir) Ralph Furse. The Colonial Secretary in theory could get his butler made Governor of the Seychelles and his family solicitor Chief Justice of Jamaica without infringing any law or regulation. The only competitive examinations were for the 'Eastern Cadetships' for Ceylon, Malaya and Straits Settlements and for the Pacific service. Other appointments were by interview. Furse, under various designations, administered colonial recruitment over the staggering period of 38 years—from 1910 to 1948. His only absence was during his military service in the 1914 war when there was practically no recruitment anyway. At the end of his career in 1948 he still on occasion wore the same suit of brown West of England tweed in which he had arrived at the Colonial Office on his first day in 1910. He had been to Eton and to Balliol College, Oxford, where he had obtained a third-class degree in 'Greats.' In choosing staff he admitted to a weakness in sympathising with others who had got 'thirds.' His original ambition had been to enter the cavalry but this was closed to him because he suffered from deafness. So, at the age of 23, he had become through personal introduction Assistant Private Secretary (Appointments) to the Colonial Secretary. He was then paid £150 a year and it was meant to be a temporary position—his academic standing was not high enough for him to hope to become an established administrative civil servant. Furse loved his work; he stayed in the job and built up its influence until he was, for practical purposes, in supreme control of colonial appointments. His high days came after 1918 when, aided by a staff of assistants he chose himself, he recruited hundreds of new colonial administrators every year.

Furse attached high importance to the impression given by a candidate at an interview. Because of his deafness, Furse could not easily hear what the candidate was saying but his quick eyes took in personal mannerisms. In the 1920s Furse and his assistants worked together in a big room next to that of the Secretary of State. Their desks were far enough apart for them all to be able to conduct interviews at the same time; out of the corners of their eyes they looked at each other's candidates. Furse found this a sound arrangement. 'Interviewing boards normally sit on one side of a table, with their victim on the other,' he wrote. 'For instance, a man's face may not reveal that he is intensely nervous. But ,a twitching foot, or hands tightly clenched under the table, will tell you this, and you can make the necessary allowances and deductions.' So personal a system of recruitment was obviously open to abuse but Furse tried to prevent jobbery; he specially wrote in the regulations that anyone who canvassed a Member of Parliament would be disqualified. He also resisted pressure from his superiors. Winston Churchill, as Colonial Secretary, tried to appoint a friend to a colonial post. Furse looked into the man, decided he was unsuitable and told Churchill so. 'What is the use,' growled Churchill, 'of my being Secretary of State if I can't give a job to a friend?' His principal private secretary, Edward Marsh, who was also present, piped up in his squeaky voice: 'You should choose your friends better, Winston.' With a grunt, Churchill acquiesced. Furse believed in the virtues of the 'public school spirit' and within his terms of reference worked faithfully to get the best men and to encourage able schoolboys and undergraduates to look to the colonies for a career.

The informal system of appointment by the Secretary of State on Furse's advice lasted until 1930. Then in that year the administrations of most of the colonies were united into a new body, the Colonial Service, under the new charge of a new Colonial Office department, the Personnel Division. Furse became director of the new division. At the same time a Colonial Appointments Board was set up on the model of the Civil Service Commission which ran the Home Civil Service. For practical purposes Furse remained in charge. He was to appoint the new wave of colonial administrators after the Second World War as he did after the first. By the end of his career practically every administrator in the British colonies looked to him as progenitor of his career.

Furse himself travelled widely around the Empire to look at working conditions on the spot but this was unusual for Colonial Office staff, most of whom stayed permanently in London. The overseas staff, on their side, generally disliked the Colonial Office and would avoid having to visit it so far as they could. Certainly there was a difference in personality and outlook between the hard-bitten district officer of the old school from the tropics and the classically-educated bureaucrat in London. The only official link between the two groups was the Corona Club, which had been founded by Joseph Chamberlain. The function of the club was to hold an annual dinner in London for everyone available who had been connected with colonial administration. It was an all-male event, the Colonial Secretary presiding and making the only speech, and home and overseas men eyeing each other suspiciously over their drinks.

An entirely separate channel of recruitment for imperial service was the Crown Agents for the Colonies, who functioned as a kind of combined embassy in London for all the colonial administrations. The Crown Agents chose people for technical as opposed to administrative posts and looked more for actual qualification than for public school background. Such people as engineers, harbour-masters, telegraph operators and road surveyors were chosen through this source. They were commonly appointed on a contract for a specific number of years and at the end received a lump gratuity instead of a pension. In the 1920s Crown Agents' appointments, like those of the administrative services, were increasing in numbers, so reflecting the growing sophistication of colonial rule. There were 523 Crown Agents' appointments in 1922, rising to 1,299 in 1928.

Furse's young men did not realise it at the time but, in retrospect, the inter-war period can be seen as the classical age of British colonialism. The strains of acquiring new territory and suppressing rebellions were over. The newer strains of nationalism, of political campaigns directed against British rule, were hardly dreamed of. The colonial empire looked as if it were a permanent institution.

# CHAPTER 6

# Mistress in their own

ONE of the unexplained mysteries of social history is the explosion in the size of the population of Great Britain between 1750 and 1850. For generations the British population had been static, or rising only very slightly. Then in the space of a century it almost trebled—from 7.7 million in 1750 to 20.7 million in 1850. Why it happened is unknown. Over most of the period there were few significant advances in medicine or public health to account for it. Nor was there any marked rise in the average standard of living. If anything the rural labourers, who formed the majority of the population in 1750, lived in happier and healthier circumstances than the industrial workers crammed into the early 19th-century town slums. It must just be recorded that human reproduction and vitality follows unpredictable patterns. (Though it is easy to explain why, at a later date, because of administration and hygiene the population of most imperial possessions rose under British rule.) Britain was a dynamic country and one of the marks of its dynamism was the population explosion. Other countries at other times have had similar explosions of vitality; for example the racial vitality of Africans in the mid-20th century had been unforeseeable 50 years earlier. The British dynamism took a sometimes crude and roistering form but it was underpinned and set on orderly tracks by the Benthamite political reforms of the middle third of the 19th century.

Besides forming the biggest single source for the immigrants who were building up the U.S.A. into a world power, 19th-century Britain also populated two entirely new countries, Australia and New Zealand, and sent emigrants by the hundred thousand to Canada and by the thousand to southern Africa.

It was this pouring out of population to new territories which formed the basis of the characteristically British institution of self-governing colonies. Indeed the very word 'colony' in its original meaning had implied settlement by people from the colonising power rather than rule by officials over a subject people.

The biggest and the richest of the British-settled territories was Canada.

In area she was, in fact, the second biggest country in the world after the Soviet Union. Much of her three and a half million square miles of territory were, however, mountainous or frozen and unsuitable for mass human habitation. For all her size, her population in 1918 was only 8 million. But it was growing rapidly. In the four years ending March 31, 1920, she took in over 300,000 immigrants, about half of them from the U.S.A. and most of the remainder from Great Britain.

Practically the whole population was of European stock, the exceptions being about 100,000 American Indians and 3,000 Eskimos, plus a handful of Chinese immigrants. The Canadians had been more conciliatory towards the Red Indians than had the Americans to the south, there having been considerably less warfare. But three centuries of white immigration had entirely swamped the original population.

The first European settlement of Canada had been by France in the 17th century. A complete French community—New France—had been built up in Quebec. Then, in a war concerned principally with the politics of the European continent, Britain in the mid-18th century, using forces drawn largely from her American colonies further south, had conquered the French settlements. Although there was little subsequent immigration from France, the French-Canadians maintained their language, religion and culture. In 1918 they formed about a quarter of the total population.

Substantial English-speaking immigration came as a result of the American War of Independence 30 years later. Some 40,000 American 'loyalists' who had supported the British side in the war moved northwards so they could continue to live under the British flag. Although they were passionately pro-British they were also American in their outlook upon life and Canada acquired a quasi-American air which was to persist. An attempt by British administrators to set up a replica of British society in Canada—it was even proposed to start an hereditary House of Lords—ended in failure. Thus there existed three disparate strains in the Canadian population—British, French and American—and the people tended to feel the lack of a national identity. The over-emphasis with which successive generations of Canadian leaders tried to extol 'the Canadian way of life' is evidence of the search for a national identity.

During the early 19th century immigration continued slowly but steadily, much of it from the U.S.A. Had it not been for the distant but mighty force of Britain, Canada would almost inevitably have been incorporated into the United States. The construction of the Canadian Pacific Railway in 1872 opened up the empty lands of the vast Canadian west and the rate of immigration sharply increased, many of the newcomers being of Central European origin. But the British–French–American stock continued to predominate and in 1918 accounted for about 90 per cent of the population.

The way in which the government of Canada had developed over the previous century had been of crucial importance for the future of the British Empire. Canada had formed a laboratory of government in which new constitutional mechanisms had been devised. These mechanisms were eventually to be applied throughout the Empire and, indeed, were to be the legal framework of dissolution.

The basic conundrum which had existed had been how to combine a Governor appointed from London with a legislature elected by the local people. Britain, herself a parliamentary country, had been bound by her very nature to introduce legislatures wherever she ruled; even the most unsophisticated of African colonies contained legislatures of nominated people in which laws could be settled by debate and where there was European settlement the legislatures had, of course, to be elected. Yet, sooner or later, the natural course of politics would be certain to produce an issue on which elected legislatures disagreed with the Governor. What would happen if the elected legislature refused to enact what the Governor considered to be essential laws? What if it refused to vote taxes? Conflict on such lines had produced the War of Independence in which 13 British American colonies had broken away to form the United States of America.

Of course the conundrum was in the last resort insoluble. One side or the other had to give in. The Canadian mechanism, as it ultimately developed, was one in which the British surrendered in a fog of camouflage.

The root ideas had been drawn from the British constitution itself, in which a conflict, actual and potential, existed between hereditary King and elected parliament. It had been resolved in the 18th century—though few at the time had recognised it—by the device of executive administration by ministers who acted in the name of the King but in practice were a committee of parliament. Once the party system in the House of Commons had become established, such a committee could operate only if it came from the majority party. This meant that the real head of government was no longer the King but the leader of the majority party. The reality of the change was cloaked by the respect and deference with which ministers treated the monarch's views but, by the middle of the 19th century it had become clear that the monarch was bound to do what he was told to by the Cabinet.

This was the system applied in Canada.

Commonly it has been traced back to the Durham Report of 1839. The Earl of Durham—'Radical Jack'—was an aristocratic Whig sent out to look at Canada after rebellions had occurred among both British and French settlers. He recommended the union of Upper Canada (British) with Lower Canada (French) under an elected legislature. His aim was not to introduce government responsible to the legislature but to submerge raw right-wing French nationalism under British liberalism. But it turned out that a combination of British and French radicals secured control of the new legislature. The Governor, Sir Charles Bagot, took the decisive step of appointing their leaders to office. Bagot and not Durham was the true progenitor of the new system.

Tory opinion back in England was worried about Bagot's action. The old Duke of Wellington, clear-headed enough to see the implications, was reported to be 'thunderstruck.' But the Tory administration in London split and fell from power over the repeal of the Corn Laws and a new Governor-General, the Earl of Elgin, was sent out by the Whigs. He set responsible government on a permanent basis. He did so entirely upon the basis of custom, no change being made in the written constitution. Newfoundland and the maritime colonies on the east coast followed suit and by the middle of the century responsible government had become the norm in Canada.

The implications of it, though, were smaller than what later became known as 'dominion status.'

Elgin and the other Canadian governors were sent out by the British Colonial Office in London. If Elgin's instructions from London had run counter to the advice of his Canadian ministers, it would have been London he would have had to obey. He was specifically required to consult London before giving assent to certain classes of legislation. He himself set a theoretical limit beyond which he would not accept the advice of his Canadian ministers. 'No inducement on earth,' he said, 'would prevail with me to acquiesce in any measure which seemed to me repugnant to public morals or Imperial interests.' Foreign affairs, including relations with the neighbouring United States, remained an entirely British responsibility, as did the major aspects of defence. For sea defence Canada was dependent upon the Royal Navy and garrisons of British troops remained on her soil until 1871.

Nevertheless Canadian ministers and under them Canadian civil servants had acquired control over the machinery of government. Had there been any serious conflict with Britain, it would have required the most massive British expeditionary force to intervene effectively. Since, in such a conflict, the Canadians could have looked confidently to the United States for support, Britain would probably have lost. By the middle of the 19th century the association between Great Britain and Canada rested not upon power but upon mutual consent.

In 1867 the Canadian colonies, except for Newfoundland, united under a federal government. The necessary legislation, the British North America Act, was passed by the British parliament and specifically laid it down that the Canadian constitution should be 'similar in principle to that of the United Kingdom.' There was some idea of calling the new federation the 'Kingdom of Canada' but this was rejected in part because it would offend the United States and in part because it simply did not correspond with the legal position. The British Crown was regarded as an indivisible entity. Canada did not have a monarch of her own but was, according to the Act, subject to 'the Sovereign of Great Britain and Ireland.' Instead of 'kingdom' the vaguer word 'dominion' was employed to express Canada's status. As a result 'dominion' passed into constitutional jargon as a technical term. If a territory wanted 'dominion status' it meant it wanted to be ruled on the same principles as Canada. The British North America Act remained the constitution of Canada. Up to the time of writing, the only way the Canadian constitution can be revised is by an amending Act of the British parliament.

No substantial cause for conflict with Britain arising, Canada acquired over the next three generations from 1867 most of the practical attributes of national sovereignty. Political authority rested with her Prime Minister, who was consulted by the Colonial Office about who should be appointed Governor-General. In 1918 the Governor-General was the ninth Duke of Devonshire, a 50-year-old grandee who had held junior office in British governments before being sent out in 1916 on a salary of 50,000 dollars a year. He was just the type of person normally appointed. Some of his immediate suite, including the future British Prime Minister,

Harold Macmillan, were British but all real power belonged to the Canadian politicians. There was a developed two-party system, Conservatives and Liberals succeeding each other in office. The Prime Minister, Arthur Meighen, was a member of the British Privy Council and entitled to attend meetings of the Imperial War Cabinet when he visited London. Significant matters in Anglo–Canadian relations were settled not by Devonshire reporting to the Colonial Office but by Meighen communicating directly with the British Prime Minister, David Lloyd George.

Newfoundland, which had refused to enter the new Dominion of Canada, had developed on similar lines, although in miniature. Her population of some 260,000, mostly of British stock and dependent upon fishing, had acquired the apparatus of responsible government. Of course there was no question of so tiny a unit conducting foreign affairs or defence but, proudly claiming to be the oldest territory of the British Empire, she conducted her own internal affairs. Unlike Canada and the other big dominions she did not sign the Treaty of Versailles or join the League of Nations but her Prime Minister, R. A. Squires, a lawyer, attended the Imperial Conference of dominion Prime Ministers.

After Canada, the second biggest of the white dominions was the island-continent of Australia. If someone had dug deep enough under the Canadian House of Commons at Ottawa he would eventually have come out somewhere near the Australian capital, Melbourne. He would have found the weather topsy turvy but the public institutions instantly comprehensible and far more familiar to him than those he would have found by making the easy little journey to Washington. During the preceding century Australia, almost automatically, had followed British and Canadian precedents in shaping her government.

European explorers had vaguely known of the existence of Australia since the 17th century but it was not until the 18th century Captain Cook had begun to chart its coasts that it had become at all well known. Cook had hoisted the British flag on the south-east coast in 1770, calling it New South Wales, and this had become the site of the first British settlement. The only inhabitants of the continent were then a few hundred thousand aboriginals who to the early settlers appeared to be little higher than animals. The aboriginals could not read or write, knew nothing of the wheel and were prey to superstition. It was said that some tribes did not realise that babies resulted from sexual intercourse. The only

The public school spirit. Major Sir Ralph Furse, who from 1910 to 1948 was the leading influence in recruitment for the colonial administrative services

'Palestine is not Rhodesia'. Chaim Weizmann, leader of world Zionism, with his wife in 194

David Ben-Gurion, first Prime Minister of Israel

interesting thing about them, to the early settlers, was their weapon, the boomerang. They were classed with the kangaroo as a curiosity and, on occasion, actually hunted for sport.

In 1918 Australia had a population of about 6 million, nearly all of British origin. Although geographically she was remote from Europe she had adopted a strict 'white Australia' policy and would admit as immigrants only people of European ancestry. This applied even in Northern Australia where the climate was tropical and, by the old spine-pad doctrines, unsuited to permanent white settlement. The Australians set about to prove that people of European origin could live and carry on hard manual work in sugar plantations in hotter weather than had previously been thought possible. At the negotiations to write the covenant of the League of Nations the Australian Prime Minister, W. M. Hughes, fought fiercely against a Japanese proposal to include in the text a declaration on racial equality. He saw it as a threat to 'white Australia.' Eventually, with British support, he managed to defeat it.

The Governor-General of Australia, Lord Forster of Lepe, was an insubstantial figure and power rested with Hughes. Aged 54 in 1918, Hughes had risen to power through waterfront trade unionism in Sydney and the Labour Party. Australia in 1905 had been the first country in the world to elect a Labour Government. Like Lloyd George in Britain, Hughes had combined a radical approach in internal affairs with a belligerent external policy; he had been determined to fight and win the world war. He had ousted a less warlike leader in 1915 to become Prime Minister and then, when in 1916 his Labour Party had split over the issue of forcing men to fight by law, had formed his own National Party which, with Liberal support, had been able to carry the legislature. He was a thin, nervy man, prone to indigestion, ruthless in his political methods. For the moment, in 1918, he dominated Australia. In Britain he had become something of a national hero. He believed that nothing but benefit could accrue to the world from the maximum possible expansion of the British Empire. This, in his view, did not mean that Australian interests should be subordinated to those of Great Britain. If anything, it should be the other way round. Australia should be allowed the fullest voice and influence in the determination of imperial policy.

Australia had her own little chain of colonies set around the Coral Sea off her north-east coast. She and Britain had combined to take over Papua in 1907; since 1907 this territory had been

L

administered entirely by Australia. Early in the 1914–1918 war she had conquered the German islands in the Papua area and, also, German New Guinea. In fact one reason she had come so enthusiastically into the war in 1914 had been to get control of these German territories. At Versailles Hughes fought to get them under full Australian sovereignty but, eventually, he had to settle for mandatory status. Under the treaty Japan got the former German Pacific territories north of the equator, Australia got New Guinea and New Zealand got Western Samoa.

New Zealand, the other self-governing dominion in that part of the world, lay 1,000 miles from Australia across the stormy Tasman Sea. It was the most patriotically British of all the dominions and, indeed, economically was just an outlying British farm. Settlers, many of them from Scotland, had flowed in steadily but slowly during the 19th century and by 1918 the population stood at about 1,200,000. In 1905 New Zealand had become the first country in the world to enfranchise women. There was also an indigenous population of about 50,000 Maoris, an intelligent, attractive people who during the 19th century had on occasion come into violent conflict with the immigrants. Now they were hopelessly outnumbered but they had not dwindled into the insignificance of the American Red Indians or the Australian aboriginals; under the enlightened guidance of their leader, Sir James Carroll, a man of mixed European–Maori blood, they were beginning to integrate themselves into European society. Although there were to be many difficulties on the way, New Zealand was to prove to be the only place in the entire British Empire where differences between immigrant and indigenous races were to be solved by integration rather than by separation.

The cardinal point in New Zealand's policy was to maintain close links with Britain. Her leaders were painfully conscious that the country was militarily too weak to defend itself. In the 1914–1918 war nearly one fifth of the New Zealand male population had served overseas in the British cause—a higher proportion than from any other dominion—and, as a kind of reward, the titular head of the administration, the Earl of Liverpool, had in 1917 been upgraded in title from Governor to Governor-General. The effective ruler was William Ferguson Massey, Prime Minister since 1912. Massey, an Ulsterman who had gone out to New Zealand to farm, was the leader of the Reform Party, the organisation of the small farmers. Massey and other New Zealanders were suspicious of the growing trend for British dominions to be treated as independent countries; they wanted the British Empire to act as a single international unit, the dominions helping to formulate British policy rather than running their own. While this was obviously in New Zealand's interests—it was preferable to be an influential section of a major world power than just a weak little country in the Pacific—it drew little support either from the other dominions or, for practical purposes, from Britain herself. The dream of the British dominions forming a sort of federal unit was essentially a New Zealand dream.

New Zealand had its own colonies—the Cook Islands and, conquered by its own forces in 1914 and to be held under League of Nations mandate, the former German territory of Western Samoa.

The remaining white dominion was the newly-formed Union of South Africa. It was 'white' in the sense that political power rested with the one and a half million European population; the Africans, Indians and people of mixed races formed in fact four fifths of the inhabitants. In 1918 the non-white peoples of the Union were little regarded as a political factor; despite their overwhelming numbers and their economic value as cheap labour, they were dismissed as primitives who neither wanted nor were capable of early participation in public affairs. Talk of 'racial conflict' in South Africa in 1918 did not refer to whites versus blacks but to British versus Boers.

The Boer population, of Dutch origin and of ancient admixture with African blood, had lived in southern Africa for two centuries. The British had captured their main colony, Cape Colony, during the Napoleonic wars and held on to it on the traditional pretext of the route to India. The Boers had disliked British domination and moved inland to try to set up their own independent republics. In the South African War of 1899–1902 the British had conquered the Boer republics; then in 1909, in what had been represented as a triumph of liberal idealism, had united the British and Boer territories into the Union of South Africa with the rights of dominion self-government. It was evidence of the compromise on which the arrangement was based that the administrative capital of Pretoria lay in the Boer heartlands but parliament met in British-dominated Cape Town nearly 1,000 miles to the south. In the Boer provinces, Transvaal and the Orange Free State, only white people were allowed to vote. In the British-dominated provinces, the Cape and Natal, there existed a restricted franchise for Africans, coloureds and immigrant Indians; it was on a scale too insignificant to affect the basic policies of the Union. The qualification for actually becoming a member of the Union legislature was to be a 'British subject of European descent.' These franchise arrangements formed part of the constitution and could be altered only by a majority of two thirds of the members of both houses of parliament voting together. The Judicial Committee of the Privy Council in London was the ultimate arbiter in deciding the validity of South African legislation.

In 1918 South Africa was regarded as an experiment which, on the whole, was going well. The more intransigent of the Boers had risen in rebellion on the outbreak of war in 1914 but they had been suppressed, with 300 deaths, with no aid from Britain. (The British garrison had been reduced from 8,000 to 1,000 men at the start of the war.) The Prime Minister, Louis Botha, and his principal deputy, Jan Christian Smuts, were liberal-minded Boers who had once fought against the British but now regarded participation in the British Empire, on a self-governing basis, as the best hope for their people. Their aim was to build a united South African nation—a united white nation, that is. 'The different elements in our white populations ought really to be used to build up a stronger and more powerful nation than would have been possible if we had consisted purely of one particular strain. All great Imperial peoples really are a mixture of various stocks . . .' said Smuts.

A spry little man, sparkling with ideas, Smuts, who became Prime Minister in 1919, was the first statesman from Africa ever to emerge as a world personality. He was a professional lawyer who had also proved to be an able soldier; his education in Britain had contributed towards a wider outlook than was characteristic of his people. After putting down the 1914 rebellion—a task which had included the execution of an old friend—he had gone on to direct the conquest of the German colony of South-West Africa. Then he had commanded imperial troops in East Africa. In 1917 he had burst upon London, providing hope and encouragement for the British in the worst period of the war. This former enemy of the British, attending the Imperial War Cabinet and delivering stirring speeches about the unity of the many races in the Empire, became a popular hero. There had been some talk of sending him to command the offensive to capture Palestine but, instead, he had stayed on in London as a member of the British War Cabinet. It was a unique arrangement, never to be repeated, that a dominion statesman (he remained South African Minister of Defence) should be one of the seven men at the top of British affairs. After 1918 he became one of the leading advocates of the League of Nations; in particular he helped pioneer the system of mandating conquered German territories instead of them being handed over outright to the victorious powers. South-West Africa passed to his own South Africa under such a mandate.

In Canada had been devised the essential mechanisms of the dominion system. In South Africa had been demonstrated the possibility of using these mechanisms to turn former enemies into supporters of the British Empire. It was, however, in an unforeseen quarter that the mechanisms were turned to their ultimate destiny, that of cloaking the dissolution of the British Empire.

The place was Ireland which, in 1918, was still an integral part of the United Kingdom, sending M.P.s to Westminster in the same way as every other part. Ireland, in a sense, was the oldest British colony. Kings of England had claimed to be Kings of Ireland ever since Henry VIII in the 16th century. However, the arrangement had never worked properly. The reasons were part economic— much of the land of Ireland had been owned by absentee British proprietors who had shown little regard for the interests of their tenantry—and part religious, most of the Irish having continued, under persecution, to hold the Roman Catholic faith while the rest of the United Kingdom had become Protestant.

During the 19th century the Irish had sent to Westminster a formidable bloc of Nationalist M.P.s who had demanded 'home rule,' by which they had meant internal self-government under continued British sovereignty. These M.P.s had exerted a significant although negative influence upon the development of imperial institutions. They had operated outside the main party system and bartered their votes in return for concessions on Ireland. At times they had come near to paralysing the parliamentary system as when, from 1910 to 1915, they had held the actual balance of power in the House of Commons and could decide, by reference to purely Irish interests, whether Liberals or Conservatives should hold office. Such a nuisance had they been that the British, in considering how to unify the Empire, were rarely tempted to follow the French example of allowing colonies to elect members of the metropolitan parliament. The Irish had shown how inconvenient it could be to have M.P.s who did not fit into the orthodox pattern of domestic politics.

Exactly why the British had failed to grant home rule must be reckoned as much a question of psychology as of straightforward political calculation. The objections appear to have been predominantly ones of prestige; it was essential for British world power that the home base, the British Isles, should operate as a single unit. There was also the question of religion. In the early period of the Irish Nationalist movement, Protestants as well as Catholics had advocated home rule. Later, however, under partly artificial stimulation, the predominantly Protestant area in the north-east had objected to the point of armed rebellion to being placed under a Catholic-controlled administration in Dublin. In the years immediately before 1914 there had been a majority in the British House of Commons in favour of home rule but the change had been held up by the House of Lords, the Ulster Protestants agitating violently on the sideline.

In this absurd situation emotions became so aroused that the combatants on both sides lost contact with reason, and even with humanity. In 1916 a group of Irish extremists had seized public buildings in the capital, Dublin, and proclaimed an Irish Republic. The British had put them down with such severity, including summary executions, that the mass of Irish public opinion moved to the revolutionary side. After the 1918 general election most of the Irish M.P.s refused to attend Westminster; instead they set themselves up in Dublin as an independent Irish parliament, supported by the irregular Irish Republican Army. In a context of atrocity and counter-atrocity the British tried to rule by force but after two years of appalling fighting had to admit defeat. Meanwhile the six Protestant counties of Ulster—which included a substantial Catholic minority—were granted home rule on the 19th-century model; that is they elected their own parliament at Belfast for local affairs but continued as a section of the United Kingdom with M.P.s also at Westminster.

By 1921 the proposition that no imperial power, however powerful, can in the long run hold down an intelligent, organised population intent upon independence, had become obviously proved in Ireland. The British began to negotiate and the curious contrivance was devised of southern Ireland being treated as if it were an overseas dominion. Indeed it was specifically laid down in the treaty that Ireland should be administered on the same lines as Canada with a Governor-General acting on the advice of ministers responsible to the elected legislature. A mechanism invented to provide a degree of unity between distant but friendly peoples was employed to paper over a surrender to armed rebels. Essentially it was a perversion of the 'prestige' on which the

British Empire so largely depended; rather than admit that the Irish had won, the British had to disguise what had happened by pretending that, in some mysterious manner, they were still loyal to the Crown. It was not, as in South Africa, a calculated grant of self-government to former rebels with the idea of winning their loyalty but a face-saving manipulation. It set some of the pattern for the future, that of the national self-deception which by the middle of the century was to poison British life.

So little understood were the implications of dominion status that at first a minority of Irish, under the half-Spanish fanatic Eamonn de Valera, refused to accept it. They mistook the shadow for the substance and actually started a civil war against their former colleagues who had negotiated the treaty. It was evidence of the absurdity which Irish politics had reached that the moment the dream of generations had been realised, that of a freely-elected and independent Irish parliament, the most extreme Irish Nationalists rebelled against the decisions of that parliament. De Valera conducted a nasty little war against his fellow countrymen in which, among many others, Michael Collins, the best of the Irish leaders, was murdered. When he had been militarily defeated, de Valera returned to straightforward politics, took a formal oath of allegiance to the British Crown and, having been elected to power, proceeded to exploit dominion status to its logical conclusion, that of complete independence. With the Governor-General selected by Irish ministers and bound to follow the advice of Irish ministers, there was nothing that the British legally could do to interfere.

Thus it was not in the far-flung overseas territories that the ultimate formula for dissolution was devised but in what in 1918 was still regarded as a part of the imperial homeland. The fragile idea of self-government combined with the sovereignty of the British Crown could work only so far as genuine loyalty was felt towards the Crown; where no such loyalty existed, the formula was one not for imperial unity but for imperial disintegration. The Irish Free State pointed the way.

Moreover, the Irish disaster peripherally weakened British influence in other ways. The Irish had been among the most energetic of overseas settlers and had moved in large numbers to the United States. Even in 1918 there were more Irishmen in the U.S.A. than there were in Ireland. Irish emigrants and their descendants retained an attachment for their ancestral country and were bitter over British treatment of it; the existence of an anti-British vote among Irish Americans made it the more difficult for the British to attract United States support in maintaining the imperial dream. (Also over the matter of Palestine there was to develop an anti-British vote among American Jews; there could scarcely have been a more formidable force for the British to combat than the combination of the Irish with the Jews.) At the same time, though, the Irish example of successful guerilla warfare against a powerful British army was not to be followed by anybody else for a generation. Other subject territories were either too young in nationalist aspirations to follow it or, as in the case of India, the nationalist leadership attempted a high-principled formula of non-violent resistance. It was not until the 1950s, when the Empire was already in an advanced state of decay, that rebellions of the Irish intensity in Kenya and Cyprus heralded the final downfall. What the Irish did do was to implant, in a generalised way, in the minds of distant subject peoples the notion that the British might not, after all, be invincible.

In 1918, before the Irish had won their victory, the theory of dominion status, although it was so riddled with contradictions, did appear to be working well. By voluntary choice the dominions had provided huge contributions to the British war effort. A high degree of imperial unity still existed on the legal level; in the official list of British colonies Canada, for example, although a potential member of the League of Nations, was sandwiched in alphabetical order between British Honduras and Ceylon. South Africa was listed between Somaliland and the Straits Settlements. Elected dominion statesmen such as Hughes of Australia and Smuts of South Africa, freely conferring in London with British ministers and freely acknowledging British leadership, could be represented as the harbingers of a new and greater age in which political freedom could be combined with an ever mightier British Empire.

Kipling expressed the 1918 view of what the attitude of a dominion ought to be to the Mother Country:

'A Nation spoke to a Nation,
A Throne sent word to a Throne:
"Daughter am I in my mother's house,
But mistress in my own." '

PART II

*Twilight*

CHAPTER 7

# The Statute of Westminster

ADDRESSING an audience in Adelaide Town Hall, Australia, on a stiflingly hot January day in 1884, Lord Rosebery, later to become Liberal Prime Minister of Great Britain, said that Australia was becoming a nation in its own right.

'Does this fact of your being a nation,' he went on, 'imply separation from the Empire? God forbid! There is no need for any nation, however great, leaving the Empire, because the Empire is a commonwealth of nations.'

This is commonly held to have been the first use of the word 'commonwealth' to describe the British Empire. Strictly it is an almost meaningless word, capable of being applied to any kind of communal organisation. Literally it means 'common welfare,' the 'wealth' part of it referring not to financial riches but carrying its older connotation of 'welfare.' The English had used 'commonwealth' to describe their short-lived republic during the 17th century and it was applied, too, to the Australian federation of 1901, the Australian colonies joining together to form the 'Commonwealth of Australia.' The American states of Kentucky, Massachusetts and Pennsylvania include 'commonwealth' in their official designations. Rosebery appears to have alighted upon the word more or less by chance but, having once used it, he continued to do so and others rapidly took it up. As early as 1886, Cardinal Manning, Archbishop of Westminster, was referring to the Empire, in a letter, as 'our Commonwealth' without considering it necessary to explain the term. It became especially popular among the imperialist wing of the Liberal Party, of which Rosebery himself was a leading figure; 'Commonwealth' sounded more compatible with Liberal principles than did 'Empire.' It was, however, essentially a vague word, serviceable more for peroratorical passages in political speeches than for purposes of exact definition. Some applied it to the whole Empire and others only to the self-governing white dominions. Some considered the British Commonwealth to be a part of the British Empire; others thought the Empire was part of the Commonwealth; others, again, thought the terms were synonymous. 'Commonwealth' carried the implication of partnership with rather than subordination to Britain but was otherwise a word of ornament.*

The enhanced status won by the dominions as combatants in the 1914–1918 war brought 'Commonwealth' into official use. It was held to be more accurate to describe self-governing countries, furnishing their own armed forces to fight in a world war, as members of the 'British Commonwealth of Nations' than as subject territories of the 'British Empire.' There was no legal enactment of the change nor any precise definition. It was slow, too, to percolate among the British public; for decades after it had become customary for sophisticated politicians to use 'Commonwealth' in their speeches, the ordinary people continued to talk of 'the Empire.' King George V, at the point of death in 1936, was said to have murmured among his last words 'How is the Empire?' Up to 1947 the British minister in charge of relations with the self-governing dominions was termed 'Secretary of State for the Dominions;' then in that year his office became that of 'Secretary of State for Commonwealth Relations.'

So far as any change can be detected in official terminology it came in the communiqué of the 1917 Imperial War Conference; this referred to the dominions as 'autonomous nations of an Imperial Commonwealth.' But 'Imperial Commonwealth,' presumably an attempt to compromise between 'Empire' and 'Commonwealth' did not catch on. The more favoured term was 'British Commonwealth of Nations,' devised by a journalist, Lionel Curtis, and popularised by Jan Smuts of South Africa. 'British Commonwealth of Nations' achieved some technical recognition in 1922 when it appeared in the schedule of the Act of Parliament conferring dominion status upon the Irish Free State; this schedule referred in one clause to 'the Community of Nations known as the British Empire' and then, a few lines further down, to 'the British Commonwealth of Nations.' (It was following the wording of the Anglo–Irish Treaty of 1921 and so was not the work of the ordinary parliamentary draftsmen.) It was as members of the 'British Empire Delegation' that the dominions' representatives attended the Versailles Peace Conference of 1919 and it was the 'British Empire' which was allotted a permanent seat on the Council of the League of Nations; the individual dominions, except for Newfoundland, joined as ordinary members. Up to

* The word 'Empire' itself derived from the Latin 'imperium' meaning supreme command. The English had originally used it in such expressions as the 'Imperial Parliament' and 'Imperial State Crown' with reference not to overseas possessions but to their own independence of the Holy Roman Empire.

1947 the meetings in London of the dominion Prime Ministers were called the 'Imperial Conference;' then in that year the designation was changed to 'Commonwealth Prime Ministers' Conference.'

More than any other single individual it was Smuts of South Africa who put 'Commonwealth' into common parlance. He did so, in particular, in an able speech, afterwards much quoted, at a banquet in London on May 15, 1917. It is worth quoting now not just for purposes of definition but to summarise the ambitions of those who at this period really thought that the British Commonwealth of Nations would be a lasting force in the world.

'I think,' said Smuts, 'that we are inclined to make mistakes in thinking about this group of nations to which we belong, because too often we think of it as one State. We are not a State. The British Empire is much more than a State. I think the very expression "Empire" is misleading, because it makes people think we are one community, to which the word "Empire" can appropriately be applied. Germany is an Empire. Rome was an Empire. India is an Empire. But we are a system of nations. We are not a State, but a community of States and nations. We are far greater than any Empire which has ever existed, and by using this ancient expression we really disguise the main fact that our whole position is different, and that we are not one State or nation or empire, but a whole world by ourselves, and all sorts of communities under one flag.

'We are a system of States, and not a stationary system, but a dynamic and evolving system, always going forward to new destinies. Take the position of that system today. Here you have the United Kingdom with a number of Crown Colonies. Beside that you have a large Protectorate like Egypt, an Empire by itself. Then you have a great Dependency, like India, also an Empire by itself, where civilisation has existed from time immemorial, where we are trying to see how East and West can work together.

'These are enormous problems, but beyond them we come to the so-called Dominions, independent in their government, which have been evolved on the principles of the free constitutional system into almost independent States, which all belong to this community of nations, and which I prefer to call "The British Commonwealth of Nations." '

Then Smuts looked into the future and laid down the conditions in which, in his view, the British Commonwealth of Nations could survive as a concrete political force.

'The question arises: How are you going to keep this Commonwealth of Nations together? If there is to be this full development towards a more varied and richer life among our nations, how are you going to keep them together? It seems to me that there are two potent factors that you must rely upon for the future. The first is your hereditary kingship, the other is our conference system. I have seen some speculations recently in the newspapers about the position of the kingship in this country—speculations by people who, I am sure, have not thought about the wider issues that are at stake. You cannot make a republic of the British Commonwealth of Nations.

'In regard to the present system of Imperial Conferences, it will be necessary to devise better machinery for common consultation than we have at present. . . . What is necessary is that there shall be called together the most important rulers of the Empire, say, once a year, to discuss matters which concern all parts of the Empire in common, [It may be noted how easily Smuts slips back from 'Commonwealth' to 'Empire.'] in order that causes of friction or misunderstanding may be prevented or removed. We also need a meeting like that in order to lay a common policy in common matters concerning the Empire as a whole, and to determine the true orientation of our common Imperial policy. There is, for instance, foreign policy on which the fate of the Empire might from time to time depend.'

The very imprecision of 'British Commonwealth of Nations' pleased the British. It fitted the flexibility of their institutions. The vague idea of 'partnership' was even more flattering to British national pride than the concept of ruling 'natives' in remote parts of the world. But flexibility in words and institutions is tolerable so long as it does not entail, also, self-deception and the use of vague words to hide reality. The 'Commonwealth' doctrine of Smuts and his fellows helped the British to embark upon an era of self-deception and self-flattery on a scale which has rarely otherwise been seen in mass psychology. Many of the British entered a kind of mirror-world in which every weakening of imperial bonds could be represented as if it were a new cord of steel. The roistering self-confidence with which the British had conquered a quarter of the world turned into a complacent vanity. Through Smuts—although he himself did not intend it—the Boers had their revenge.

The 'Commonwealth' doctrine led not to a stronger and more durable form of Empire but to the dominions drifting further and further apart until the organism had dissolved as an effective unit.

Within 30 years two dominions were at war with each other. 'Commonwealth' doctrines turned out to be just the lubricant with which the Empire was dismantled rather more smoothly than might otherwise have been the case.

The crucial decisions which rendered the British Commonwealth meaningless as a political organism were taken in the 1920s. They had two aspects, negative and positive.

Negatively, the vital point was the failure to follow Smuts's proposals and set up machinery by which Britain and the dominions could conduct a common foreign policy. In the past such a mechanism had not been necessary; foreign policy had been the sphere solely of the British Foreign Office. Under the new system, with the dominions becoming recognised as international entities in their own right, London could clearly no longer be the only authority. Either new constitutional machinery must be set up or, sooner or later, the dominions would be bound to drift away from the London lead; this would be the more essential if it were ever to be possible for crown colonies, containing non-British populations, to become part of a united Commonwealth.

At the time of Smuts's 1917 speech some start had in fact been made. During 1917 and 1918 a so-called 'Imperial War Cabinet' with representatives of the dominions and of India met in London to co-ordinate the war effort and to prepare for the peace conference. (The word 'cabinet' applied to it was a misnomer; it was more in the nature of a conference, the members remaining responsible to their own governments.) At the Versailles Conference the British and dominions representative formed the British Empire Delegation, which presented generally a united front to the foreigners.

The difficulty was to convert such makeshift wartime arrangements into a permanent structure. It was, indeed, an insurmountable difficulty. Was Britain, a great world power, really able to think in terms of surrendering sovereignty to a super-cabinet in which she might be outvoted by such comparatively weak little countries as South Africa and New Zealand? In the 1920s less than five per cent of the population of the British Empire lived in the self-governing dominions. Then could a super-cabinet function effectively unless there were an Empire parliament to which it were responsible and which could enact binding legislation? How could such a parliament be elected? Elections on a population basis would enable Britain (even without India and the colonies) to outvote the combined dominions' representatives by two to one.

How could the dominions, in the first flush of nationhood, accept a new form of subordination? Amateur constitution-makers hovered for years on the fringes of such questions. Ingenious schemes were produced. But nobody took much notice; it could be sensed, if not reasoned, that the task was impossible. No mechanism could combine the irreconcileables of dominion sovereignty and a united British Commonwealth. Unity could last only as long as everyone wanted unity.

The wartime arrangements were allowed to lapse. The final flicker of them appeared in the 1921 Imperial Conference which resolved that 'the whole weight of the Empire should be concentrated behind a united understanding and common action in foreign policy.' But this was mere aspiration with no practical step being taken to implement it. Within a few months the Lloyd George administration in London went to the edge of war with Turkey without consulting the dominions at all; the first the dominions heard was a request for troops. At the next Imperial Conference, that of 1923, the notion of 'common action in foreign policy' was not pursued. In the same year Canada and Ireland appointed their own diplomatic representatives in Washington and Canada negotiated the Halibut Treaty with the United States entirely on the signatures of her own representatives. (The Americans, however, sought an assurance from the Foreign Office in London that the Canadians were entitled to sign treaties on behalf of the British Crown.)

The significance of what was happening was not at once clear. There existed, for example, a fog of confusion over British Empire membership of the League of Nations. The 'British Empire,' so described, was a member and held a permanent seat on the Council. Canada, South Africa, Australia, New Zealand and India were also members but the United Kingdom, as such, was not, she being merged in the 'British Empire' designation. The Irish Free State joined in 1923. The position was the more confusing in that one dominion, Newfoundland, was not a member of the League while India, whose foreign policy was under complete British control, had full membership. Many outside the Empire, especially Americans, thought that the multiple representation was a trick by Britain to get six votes instead of one; in fact this was a contributory factor towards the Americans refusing to join. Confusion became yet more confounded in 1927 when Canada was elected to a non-permanent seat on the Council, thus destroying the notion that the 'British Empire Delegation' from London was

Michael Mouskos, who aged 37 became Archbishop Makarios III of Cyprus. His aim was to drive out the British

'No power in the world can suppress our movement'. George Grivas, military leader of the Eoka guerilla rebellion in Cyprus

the permanent spokesman on the Council for the whole Empire and Commonwealth.

Another cause for obscurity was that the dominions at this stage were more eager to assert a theoretical right to an independent foreign policy than to carry it out in practice. New Zealand did not even claim the right, its government producing a legal opinion to the effect that international representatives of the dominions were sharing in the formulation of common imperial policy rather than representing their own countries. All the dominions continued to leave almost all the work of diplomatic representation to the British Foreign Office and to be content just to be informed about what Britain was up to.

So far from Smuts's ideal of annual meetings to determine common policy being realised, the intervals between Imperial Conferences steadily widened. Meetings of the Conference between the wars were held in 1921, 1923, 1926, 1930 and 1937. The long gap in the 1930s was allowed to occur while the expansionist ambitions of Germany, Italy and Japan were posing problems for the whole Empire.

The positive steps towards Commonwealth dissolution were the Statute of Westminster, which removed the ultimate supremacy of the British parliament, and a tacit agreement to split up the Crown itself.

They followed the failure to establish machinery for a common foreign policy. The initiative came from Ireland and South Africa, both of which contained powerful elements hostile to the concept of a British 'family.' The South African demands were particularly disappointing to the British. Smuts, the prophet of the 'Commonwealth of Nations,' ranked as a greater figure in the world at large than in his own country and in 1924 his electorate ejected him from office. The new Prime Minister, J. B. M. Hertzog, was leader of the Boer Nationalists and disliked the British connection. Hertzog's ultimate aim was to turn South Africa into a Boer-controlled republic; under his leadership the union jack ceased to fly in South Africa and 'God Save the King' ceased to be the national anthem. Hertzog arrived at the 1926 Imperial Conference determined to remove the vestiges of British control over South African affairs. The Irish, who were also more interested in affirming their own independence than in maintaining Commonwealth unity, shared Hertzog's approach. Once the demands had been put forward the Canadians and the Australians had, in self-respect, no option but to claim similar rights. Mackenzie King,

M

the little bachelor who served as Prime Minister of Canada for the record period of 22 years, was the more willing to press for independence because he had just emerged from a bitter dispute with his Governor-General, Lord Byng, appointed from London. King wanted future Governors-General to be of his own choosing.

The British brought in the subtle old Arthur Balfour. He had already set his mark upon the Empire with his ambiguous pledge to allow Jews to settle in Palestine. Now he turned his skill at the use of language into preparing what was supposed to be a definition of the status the dominions had acquired. They were, he wrote, 'autonomous communities within the British Empire, equal in status, in no way subordinate to one another in any aspect of their domestic or external affairs, though united by a common allegiance to the Crown and freely associated as members of the British Commonwealth of Nations.' It sounded a bit like the Niceaen creed and, on strict analysis, is incapable of a clear political meaning; at the time, though, it was a definition much admired and quoted. Its true virtue was that it comforted nationalist Boers and Irish by referring to their autonomy and independence while reassuring British loyalists with the phrases about Crown and British Commonwealth.

The Imperial Conference appointed a committee to work out the legal implications of dominion independence and from its work resulted the Statute of Westminster, passed by the British parliament in 1931. This was a tidying-up operation by which the British formally surrendered legislative powers they had in practice ceased to exercise. In future the British parliament was to legislate for a dominion only at its own request. (This had a bearing on the constitution of Canada which could be amended only by the British parliament.) Also the Statute gave the dominion parliaments the characteristically sovereign power of being able to pass legislation of extra-territorial effect and, by repealing the Colonial Laws Validity Act so far as it applied to them, gave them the right to legislate in contradiction to Westminster. Judicial unity was ended by permitting the dominions to limit or abolish appeals to the Empire's supreme court, the Judicial Committee of the Privy Council in London. All but New Zealand ultimately did so.

The Statute of Westminster aroused wide interest, it being hailed as the foundation stone of a permanent new Commonwealth arrangement. Of at least equal significance, however, was the more subtle process of splitting up the Imperial Crown and reducing its status in the dominions to that of a mere mascot. King

George V recognised clearly what was happening—and worried about it—but few others did. Instead of being the sovereign of a single Empire he became, in practice, the separate sovereign of each dominion. 'I cannot,' he minuted in November 1929, 'look into the future without feelings of no little anxiety about the continued unity of the Empire.'

The change was significant because of the actual manner in which monarchy worked in the British tradition.

According to established doctrine, as it had been refined in the 19th century, the monarch was bound to act on the 'advice' of such ministers as could command a majority in the elected house of parliament. Such 'advice,' when formally tendered, was binding and the monarch had no option but to accept it. (If he did refuse it, his ministers would resign and he would face the task, probably impossible, of finding successors who could also control parliament.) The monarch retained, however, the right and duty of advising his ministers what 'advice' to give him. He was entitled and expected to keep in close touch with public administration and cabinet business so that his advice to the ministers would be worth considering. It was held that the virtue of such constitutional monarchy was that it placed at the head of affairs a functionary free of the ordinary corruptions of ambition and so able to offer disinterested guidance on the national interest. Moreover, a King during his reign acquired a longer experience of government business than any minister; it was a salutary check upon a minister to require him to discuss business with an experienced person whom he had to address as 'Sir.' It was the nature of this system that such virtues as it had could only emerge if there were close and continuous relations between monarch and ministers.

In the dominions the Governors-Generals were supposed to follow the same procedures as the King in London. They were bound to accept formal 'advice' from their ministers and they were entitled to suggest what the 'advice' might be. On the rare occasions—notably the episode concerning Lord Byng in Canada in 1926—when they tried to defy their ministers and find new ones, they generally came to grief. Neither their prestige nor their experience could match that of the Crown. They were just officials appointed for a five-year term; the politicians who had appointed them might play-act at treating them with deference but they were difficult to take seriously. Up to 1926, however, their position was buttressed by two factors. Firstly, they were nominated by the British Colonial Office, the local dominion government being allowed no more than the right of being consulted. The binding 'advice' to the King on appointing a Governor-General came from a British minister. They were all British and they arrived in their territories as distinguished strangers, the possessors of great names in the powerful mother-country. There was a mystery about them which attracted awe. Secondly, their prestige was aided by the fact that they were officially the link between the British government which had appointed them and the local dominion governments. This function had been somewhat eroded by the custom of dominion Prime Ministers communicating direct with London but they were still performing some of the functions of British ambassador in addition to those of ceremonial figurehead. In case of disagreement between Britain and a dominion the Governor-General might find himself in the influential position of middleman.

The 1926 Imperial Conference abolished the buttresses of the prestige of Governors-General. It determined that in future they should no longer represent the British government but only the King personally. Separate high commissioners should represent the British government. A Governor-General's responsibility should be solely to his own dominion and to the King; he should have nothing to do with the British Colonial Secretary. (In 1925 the British had split the dominions off from the Colonial Office and put them under a separate Dominions Office; but until 1930 the positions of Dominions Secretary and Colonial Secretary continued to be held by the same person.)

There remained the problem of who was to have the decisive word in the selection of Governors-General. Was the London government still to be the channel through which binding advice reached the King? Or were the dominion governments to have a right of direct access? King George V saw dangers in the latter course and tried to insist that formal approaches to him should continue to come through his British ministers. He felt it would make nonsense of the constitution for him to be bound by formal 'advice' from more than one source and that, in any event, he did not have the continuous contact with dominion ministers which would enable him properly to influence them. Formal 'advice' from, say, Australia would be liable to have the character of peremptory instructions.

The question first arose with the selection of a new Governor-General of South Africa in 1929. Hertzog followed tradition to the extent of choosing a British aristocrat, the Earl of Clarendon. But he tried to insist that the formal 'advice' to the King should come from him and not from the British Secretary of State. The King resisted and the compromise was reached by which Hertzog made what was termed a 'submission' to Buckingham Palace and the British Prime Minister, Ramsay MacDonald, formally 'advised' the King to accept the 'submission.'

A few months later the question arose in a more acute form over Australia. The Labour Prime Minister, Arthur Scullin, chose Chief Justice Sir Isaac Isaacs, an Australian, as the next Governor-General. This was the first time the appointment of a non-British Governor-General of a dominion had ever been mooted. The King at first flatly refused to agree. He said a Governor-General should not be a citizen of his own dominion. Also Isaacs was unsuitable as the King's confidential representative because the King had never met him; in any case Isaacs was too old. The King told Lord Passfield, the British Dominions Secretary, that the appointment could not be sanctioned. The British Cabinet, uncertain of its duties in the matter, consulted the British Law Officers who produced a doctrine which was indeed extraordinary. They said British ministers no longer had the right to 'advise' the King on Australian matters and that Australian ministers had no right to 'advise' him directly on anything; therefore the King should act entirely on his own responsibility. This was not welcome to the King either; the idea of his exercising naked discretion without ministerial 'advice' was foreign to the principles on which British monarchy had developed. It could bring the Crown into political controversy.

Passfield found a way out of the dilemma by getting the King and Scullin to agree to the matter being referred to the Imperial Conference which was meeting later in the year. The Conference took the crucial decision that the King 'should act on the advice of His Majesty's Ministers in the Dominion concerned.' As a sop to the King it added that formal 'advice' should not be tendered until there had been 'informal consultation with His Majesty.' The King then had an angry audience with Scullin in which he appealed to him to drop Isaacs. Scullin refused and, eventually, the King gave way. 'It seems to me,' wrote Lord Stamfordham, the King's Private Secretary, 'that this morning's incident was one of the most important political and constitutional issues upon which Your Majesty has had to decide during Your twenty years reign.'

So the King was now bound to follow the 'advice' of seven different governments, 'advice' mostly coming from a distance from politicians he hardly knew. In the natural course of events various items of 'advice' from different quarters would be bound sooner of later to conflict. Within a decade King George VI had German bombs raining upon Buckingham Palace while the Irish Minister in Berlin conducted normal diplomatic relations on credentials signed by him. Within 17 years the King was even to be at war with himself when the Dominion of India fought the Dominion of Pakistan. What it really meant was that the dominions for all practical purposes became republics. The Governors-General became figureheads holding their posts at the will of the local Prime Ministers.

The reality of the change was cloaked by the sentimental popularity of the Crown among dominion inhabitants of British descent. It was a link with history. They regarded it with enthusiasm even while their leaders were overthrowing its real influence. King George V, with his worries about the continuance of imperial unity, did his best to foster such sentiments. At the beginning of his reign he had gone so far as to propose to visit each dominion and be crowned there, as he actually was in India. This came to nothing but he did send his heir, the Prince of Wales, on a series of Empire tours. Superficially they were a gigantic success. The Prince, sailing across the world in a battlecruiser, received a tumultuous welcome in every dominion he visited. Crowds thronged around him wherever he went, cheering madly and trying to touch him. Such extravagant popularity for a young member of the Royal Family was novel and, perhaps, less than salutory. The Prince was greeted not with the dignity traditionally hedging monarchy but with an hysteria more suited for his contemporary, the film actor Rudolph Valentino; he became an object of curiosity rather than of awe. The King kept writing to his son to tell him to beware of his dignity but the Prince could only reply that the mobs were uncontrollable.

It was that Prince who, as King Edward VIII, provided clear proof of how the imperial Crown had been split up. After 11 months on the throne he chose, in 1936, to renounce the throne so he could marry an American divorced woman. Under the Statute of Westminster it was not sufficient for just the British Parliament to pass the Abdication Act to make the renunciation effective; since British Acts no longer applied to the dominions, each dominion had to pass its own legislation. In Britain the Abdication Act was passed on December 11 and Edward's brother, George VI, started his reign on that day. Canada, Australia and New

Zealand timed their legislation to synchronise with the British date. In South Africa, however, a retrospective Act was passed to date the new King's reign from December 10. The Irish, for their part, legislated to start the new reign from December 12. So for three days there were different Kings reigning in different parts of the British Commonwealth. The situation was further underlined in the new wording of the coronation oath sworn by George VI. In it he pledged himself to uphold the laws not just of the Empire, but of each separate dominion, the names of which he recited in turn.

Two episodes of the 1930s illustrated contrasting trends in the meaning of dominion status.

The first was the case of Newfoundland, the smallest of the dominions (and the oldest British overseas territory). The 300,000 fishermen and foresters of Newfoundland were too weak to aspire to international status as a sovereign country and had not joined the League of Nations. Thirty years later it was to be acceptable for countries even smaller and poorer than Newfoundland to claim the rights of sovereignty but in the 1930s such a conception hardly existed. At the same time Newfoundland had full status as a dominion. Her Prime Minister attended the Imperial Conference and she was covered by the Statute of Westminster.

A combination of the world economic depression with a degree of mismanagement by the Newfoundland administration bank-rupted the country in the early 1930s. Thereupon, Britain, with the consent of the Newfoundlanders, in 1934 abrogated dominion status and set up a government by a mixed British–Newfoundland commission. This reversion of a nominally sovereign country to virtual colonial status was regarded as entirely a domestic matter for the British Empire and attracted little international attention. It was just a rearrangement of the affairs of a country already under the British Crown. The episode showed how close-knit the British Empire could be considered still to be; 30 years later, the bankruptcy of a Commonwealth territory would have been regarded as an international rather than a British problem.

The other episode showed the exactly opposite tendency, how dominion status could be used to establish complete national sovereignty. It happened in Ireland where, in 1932, the republican purist, Eamonn de Valera, won office as Prime Minister. A decade earlier this narrow, fanatical man had actually risen in arms against his fellow countrymen rather than accept dominion status and a divided Ireland. Now he proceeded to show how the status of the Irish Free State could be manipulated to destroy the British connection. A series of laws—to which the Crown had no option but to assent—abolished practically all the remaining links. The oath of allegiance was removed, the Governor-General was reduced to a nonentity and, finally, in 1937 the monarchy itself was abrogated. The Irish Free State adopted a republican-style constitution with an elected president as head of state; the King was to act formally for the new state in foreign affairs. The new republic claimed as its rightful territory the whole of Ireland, including the six Protestant counties in the north-east. In practice any hope of getting the embattled Unionists to link up with the rest of Ireland was further weakened by de Valera's radical policies. Control of both parts of Ireland rested with fanatics.

Besides constitutional changes, de Valera also quarrelled with the British over money. Under the treaty establishing the Free State, the Irish had agreed to pay annuities to Britain, representing the cost to Britain of compensating landlords whose property had been distributed among the Irish small farmers. Many of the landlords had been absentee Englishmen and their mode of conducting their estates had been a potent encouragement to the growth of Irish nationalism in the 19th century. De Valera claimed that the land had been stolen by the landlords in the first place and stopped payment of the annuities. Although both British and Irish administrations at that time were working under the same Crown, the British found that there was no juridicial framework in which the dispute could be arbitrated. The Judicial Committee of the Privy Council specifically confirmed that under the Statute of Westminster, the Free State parliament could legislate as it liked. De Valera offered to refer the dispute to an international tribunal. The British insisted that the tribunal should consist only of Commonwealth citizens and this de Valera rejected. There followed a trade war, with the two sides taxing each other's exports, just as if Britain and the Free State were entirely independent of each other. Then the British, making about their first really conciliatory decision on an Irish matter, in 1938 dropped their claim in return for a nominal outright payment. For good measure they also abandoned the three naval bases which, under the treaty, they were entitled to maintain on Irish soil. The bases would have been of value in protecting British shipping during the 1939–45 war but the calculation was that they would be useless without the support of the local population. De Valera, declaring that he would never fight for Britain so long as his country was partitioned, in fact declared neutrality at the outbreak of war, a neutrality that would have been unrealistic had the British kept the bases. With the bases operating, Ireland would have been a legitimate target for German attack.

Such use by de Valera of dominion status counted for more than the opposite example of Newfoundland. Within a decade nationalist leaders in the colonies—notably Kwame Nkrumah in the Gold Coast—were claiming dominion status, reckoning it would give them all they wanted while reducing the resistance of the British. De Valera had shown that to be a dominion could be a transitional rather than a permanent condition.

An underlying factor in the slow weakening of the bonds between Britain and the British-settled dominions must have been the sharp decline, between the wars, in emigration from the mother country. For two decades the British appeared to lose much of their former pioneering spirit. Up until the 1914–1918 war, emigration had been proceeding at the astonishing rate of about 300,000 people a year. Britain had thus annually sent overseas the equivalent to the population of a large city. The outflow stopped with the outbreak of war and, after the peace, it was not renewed on the old scale. During the 1920s the numbers leaving Britain were balanced, approximately, by the numbers coming into Britain from the dominions. In the 1930s the pattern shifted even further, with actually more immigrating into Britain from the dominions than going out to them. Thus dominion attachment to the British way of life ceased to be refreshed by the constant influence of new arrivals; it became more normal to be a Canadian, or an Australian, by birth than by immigration and the concept of Britain as 'home' tended to become more and more artificial. For many ordinary people the main Commonwealth link became games of cricket, test matches between England and Australia arousing high excitement in both countries.

Superficially, the reason for the decline in emigration from Britain was the world depression, which interrupted the growth of the dominion economies. There may, however, have been some deeper and more mysterious cause. Despite being drenched in torrents of imperialist propaganda, despite unprecedented government encouragement of emigration, despite an unemployment rate at home rising to ten per cent and more, the British voted with their feet by declining to settle in the Empire. The dream-Empire was more satisfying than the real thing.

It was a favourite theme of British politicians, especially those of the Conservative Party, to point to the glories of the Empire and of British destiny. Their problem, though, was to find ways of advancing from rhetoric towards constructive courses of action. Solutions on the political level were obviously out of the question; despite the old ideas of an imperial federation, the Statute of Westminster had shown that imperial unity and development would come, if at all, in some manner other than through formal political institutions. Some attached faith to the power of propaganda, believing it was sufficient only to proclaim loudly enough that the Empire had a destiny for such a destiny to appear. There was the great Empire Exhibition at Wembley, London, in 1924, at which the King-Emperor so far compromised his dignity as to be filmed while riding in a miniature train with his knees up. Empire Day—Queen Victoria's birthday—was celebrated with much pomp, schoolchildren all over the Empire being assembled under the union jack to hear imperialist harangues and to pipe up 'Land of Hope and Glory.' Such propaganda did, however, tend to backfire. Rather than stir the British up, it tended to create complacency; if the Empire were so great and glorious, what further strengthening could it need?

If neither politics nor propaganda were of use, how about economics? At the beginning of the century Joseph Chamberlain, the man who had virtually invented the conception of the British Empire, had proposed to turn it into a single economic unit by a system of tariff preferences and this, by the 1920s, had become orthodox Conservative policy. Then Lord Beaverbrook, the brilliant millionaire Canadian who had entered zestfully into British politics and newspaper publishing, took Chamberlain's scheme a stage further. Beaverbrook devised 'Empire Free Trade' which would have surrounded the whole Commonwealth and Empire with massive tariff walls against 'foreign' imports but would have allowed complete free trade within the Empire itself. Through his newspapers and with platform campaigns, Beaverbrook whipped up 'Empire Free Trade' until it became, briefly, the best-known political cause in Great Britain. For a moment he came near to capturing the Conservative Party for it and there was talk of his replacing Stanley Baldwin as leader. Beaverbrook's scheme would undoubtedly have strengthened the Empire but it bristled with difficulties. It was doubtful, for example, whether the dominions would allow their infant manufacturing industries to be exposed to unrestricted British competition. The British, in their turn, would have been unlikely to agree to foreign food being taxed. Then the Empire was by no means a natural economic unit; British trade with China was greater than with India, with South America greater than with Canada. Beaverbrook ignored the attitude of the Indian and colonial peoples who, as they gained in political understanding, would surely resent their economies being shaped by the requirements of Britain and the dominions. Already, indeed, local pressure had caused the British administration of India to tax the import of cotton textiles so that, to the distress of Lancashire, the Indians could establish their own cotton weaving industry. By the late 1940s, 'Empire Free Trade' could have been an embittering rather than a unifying force.

The Conservatives in office did, at the Ottawa Conference of 1932, establish a system of 'imperial preference' with Britain and the dominions agreeing to let in each other's goods at reduced rates of tax. This was, however, only a modest measure and it is difficult to trace what fundamental results, if any, sprang from it. (Save, possibly, that the existence of protected markets in the dominions tended to weaken the competitiveness of British industry.) Beaverbrook's fuller scheme was never more than a chimera. It postulated the British Empire as a lasting world force while, in truth, it was really only a haphazard collection of territories drawn transiently together during a particular phase of world history.

CHAPTER 8

# The half-naked fakir

GANDHI called off his first 'passive resistance' campaign against
the British in India because, in 1922, a group of villagers at
Chauri Chaura fell so far away from the ideal of non-violence as to
burn to death 21 policemen. His decision shocked and irritated
most of his followers who felt that the eccentricity of one village
should not be enough to divert the main course of Congress policy.
But Gandhi insisted that the Chauri Chaura incident proved that
the Indian masses were not yet sufficiently permeated with 'soul-
force' to operate a proper non-violent campaign. There was, too,
tactical sense in the move. The campaign had impressed upon the
British and upon world opinion generally that the National
Congress was the most powerful political force in India but, at the
same time, the fabric of British administration had shown no sign
of early collapse. It was better for him to call off the campaign of
his own accord than to appear to have been forced by the British
into surrender. Abandonment of the campaign would give
Congress the opportunity to consolidate its forces and for the
lesson of what had happened to strike home to the British. Then
there could be another offensive. Sharp blows repeated at intervals would be more effective than continuous pressure.

On their side the British began to realise that the Indian
Empire was in danger of becoming unmanageable. Apart from a
few left-wing members of the Labour Party nobody in Britain yet
thought that power should be handed to Gandhi and the Nehrus,
who were 'agitators,' but the recognition did grow in London that
Indians of some kind would have to be allowed power. Slowly the
strategy developed of trying to create a self-governing Dominion of
India which would be a loyal member of the close-knit British
Commonwealth of the day. The hope was that the Indians would
come to prefer such a solution to total independence under the
Congress 'extremists.' Exactly how Gandhi and the Nehrus were
to be ousted from their position of national leaders the British did
not work out. They devised no settled tactics for implementing
their policy and knew for certain only that it would take a long
time—50 or 75 years—before it could possibly come to fruition.

Really it was based on British vanity. They could not conceive how, in the long run, intelligent and educated Indians could decide other than that British ways were best.

What actually happened was that the Congress steadily strengthened its hold on the Indian people. Gandhi was released early from prison on the ground that he was ill and no British propaganda—not even the incessant dinning into schoolchildren that India had been in chaos before the sahibs arrived—could compete with Gandhi walking around with his staff and his hypnotic eyes. Villagers would tramp 20 miles just to catch a glimpse of a train in which he was travelling. Jawaharlal Nehru, the Congress secretary, flashed from meeting to meeting to preach the need for 'freedom.' The vigorous vernacular newspapers fulminated daily against the British. Even the central and provincial legislatures, elected on a narrow franchise and weighted with official and nominated members, proved unmanageable. The Congress moderates, led by old Motilal Nehru, dominated them. Year after year the central legislature threw out the budget and essential legislation had to be promulgated through the Viceroy's emergency powers. The Congress extremists refused to have anything at all to do with the legislatures. A handful of terrorists systematically disobeyed Gandhi's teaching of non-violence and embarked on outright murder and sabotage, raising funds to buy bombs by robbing post offices. The numbers involved were extraordinarily small but they kept British nerves on edge; every British official now stood in constant danger of assassination. When the white Viceregal train puffed across the sub-continent there were guards posted at 20-yard intervals along the whole length of the track, each man at night carrying a flaming torch.

Moreover, the great British bureaucracy itself was beginning to crumble. Partly because of the shortage of British candidates and partly through a deliberate policy of trying to get educated Indians to associate themselves with the British Raj, more and more Indians were admitted to the privileged ranks of the Indian Civil Service. Between the wars the number of British Civilians fell from about a thousand to about five hundred, the empty places being filled by Indians. Even the key office of District Collector came often to be held by an Indian. The new Indian officials maintained the day-to-day framework intact but they felt no lasting allegiance to Britain. The more rapidly the British quit, the better would be their own chances of promotion. Prudence and patriotism alike inclined their private thoughts towards

Indian nationalism. The result of 'Indianisation' was not, as had been hoped, to attach the cream of Indian ability to British rule but merely to provide an efficient administration ready for the Congress to take over.

As late as 1925 Lord Birkenhead, the Conservative Secretary of State for India, was declaring in a letter to the Viceroy, Lord Reading: 'To me it is frankly inconceivable that India will ever be fit for Dominion self-government.' (He was, in a sense, to be proved right. India, as he knew it, did not achieve independence; partition had to come first.) But Birkenhead realised that in face of the nationalist ferment some sort of change or advance would have to be made in the Indian constitution. According to the Montagu–Chelmsford constitution of 1919 there was supposed to be a review after ten years. Birkenhead decided to expedite this review, partly because of the nationalist pressure and partly because he feared Labour was about to win office at home and he wanted the review to take place under Conservative auspices. In 1927 he appointed an all-party committee from the British parliament to proceed to India and to conduct an inquiry. It was known as the Simon Commission after its chairman, Sir John Simon, a cold, brilliant lawyer who led the right wing of the British Liberal Party. Among the ordinary members was the Labour M.P. for Limehouse, Clement Attlee; just 20 years later Attlee as Prime Minister was to surrender British India.

The Simon Commission showed the British administration at its most inept. All Indians, moderate and extremist alike, were infuriated because it had no Indian member. They thought it the ultimate insult that the future of their country should be decided entirely by foreigners. Even the Indian Liberal Party, usually regarded as friends of the British, decided to join in boycotting it. The British at first stuck to the commission and so aroused maximum hostility. Then, after two years, they suddenly caved in, virtually ignored the commission's report and began to negotiate with the Indian leaders direct. It was a fall between two stools. One factor in the change of policy was that Labour did in 1929 replace the Conservatives in office at Westminster after an election fought entirely on British domestic issues. The Simon Commission muddle was a most graphic illustration of the difficulties that can arise when a power with democracy at home attempts to run the affairs of distant countries.

The Viceroy of India was now Lord Irwin, heir to Viscount Halifax. He was a tall, intelligent aristocrat who loved fox-hunting and believed implicitly in the privileges of his own order. He had been born without a left hand. Many chose to regard him as typical of the British aristocracy but although he looked the part he was, in fact, an individualist. He was cleverer than the ordinary aristocrat. He also had a strong religious streak in him, not the 'muscular Christianity' of the public school but a mystical faith in Anglo-Catholicism. Historically his family had been Whigs but he had made his career in the Conservative Party. At the time of his appointment—which was suggested to the Cabinet by George V—he sat in the British Cabinet as Minister of Education. He was aged 44.

Irwin left for India early in 1926, being seen off at Victoria Station, London, by the Prime Minister, the Archbishop of Canterbury and a representative of the King. He arrived at Bombay at Easter and the story was spread that he ignored the official reception and went straight off to church. In fact this was not so—he and his wife sat on two thrones under a ceremonial arch at the dockside and heard ceremonial addresses of welcome—but the church legend formed part of the role attached to him that he was as much a 'holy man' as Gandhi. He worked hard at his job, travelling India attended by an entourage of private secretaries, aides de camp and 80 domestic servants. Around him snapped the dogs to which he and his wife were devoted. He fought unsuccessfully with Birkenhead to get Indian members appointed to the Simon Commission. Because of his physical height and commanding, feudal manner he looked the perfect Viceroy. He wore his ceremonial costumes as to the manner born. 'When I go home,' one of his friends remarked, 'I shall suggest that Edward Wood [his family name] be impeached for exceeding the King in grandeur.' The only time he looked funny was when he rode a horse, which he did nearly every day for sport; Indian horses were mostly too small to accommodate his dangling legs. He was the most considerable figure ever to have been Viceroy of India and momentarily, indeed, he bridged what had otherwise become an unfathomable gap between the British and the Indian Congress.

By nature Irwin was a conciliatory man. Also he was capable of learning from experience. After two years in India he realised that only two true alternatives existed for British policy. Either dominion status should be promised or the British should prepare and carry out a programme of repression of unprecedented severity, holding India by naked force. He regarded the latter idea as both impracticable and undesirable and so he came down on dominion status. He thought that once dominion status had been definitely promised it might be possible to get the Indians to agree to it being introduced only gradually. The third possibility, that of holding India indefinitely within British authority and giving self-rule only in social and welfare matters, he realised no longer existed. Almost the whole of British officialdom in India disagreed with him; so did his own Conservative Party at home, and so did the King-Emperor himself. They all thought the old ways could continue indefinitely. The Simon Commission, too, touring India to the accompaniment of boycott and black flags, decided that only the most modest extension of the Montagu–Chelmsford constitution was required; it recommended responsible government in the provinces, subject to governors' reserve powers, but the executive at the centre to remain responsible solely to the Viceroy. Irwin, however, believed that the Congress, Gandhi and the Nehrus were real and not illusory forces with whom it was essential to come to terms; he saw that they had captured the Hindu majority of India.

At this stage Irwin did not actually meet the Congress leaders very much. He had a couple of formal encounters with Gandhi— the first confrontations ever between a Viceroy and the principal Indian politician. He had remote dealings with old Motilal Nehru who was leading the opposition in the central legislature but he did not see Jawaharlal Nehru at all. Irwin's principal dealings were with the supposedly 'moderate' Vithalbhai Patel who was president of the legislature. Egged on by Congress, Patel constantly embarrassed the administration by giving rulings in favour of the opposition. He delved deep into British parliamentary history in search of precedents for wide use of a Speaker's power and once, coolly, ruled out of order a complete government Bill. Patel was the most painful of the Viceroy's minor problems. The Viceroy tried charm on him and, even, gave him medicine to cure his constipation but the effect was always undone when Patel next met Motilal Nehru.

While the Viceroy's thinking moved towards giving a pledge of ultimate dominion status, the Congress jumped far ahead. During 1928 Motilal Nehru drew up a design for a Commonwealth of India modelled specifically on the constitutions of the existing British dominions. Under it the Indian Empire and the title King-Emperor would have been abolished. The British monarch would have become just 'King of India' ruling through ministers responsible to an Indian parliament elected on adult suffrage. Congress meeting at Lahore gave the British an ultimatum to grant such dominion status within a year. The left-wing of Congress, including Jawaharlal Nehru, regarded it as a most moderate demand—they themselves really wanted complete independence, not just dominion status.

The following year, 1929, the Labour Party came into office in London, forming a weak administration dependent on Liberal votes in the House of Commons. The new Prime Minister, Ramsay MacDonald, had already spoken in general terms about dominion status for India and so Irwin's ideas fell on fertile ground. Irwin got on well, too, with the Labour Secretary for India, William Wedgwood Benn. 'I think,' he wrote to his father, 'Wedgwood Benn ought to be rather good at the India Office. He is a nice fellow, keen, with lots of ideas, and a gentleman, which is worth a great deal.' Irwin came home on leave, consulted the new ministers and then back in India issued a public statement in which he pledged dominion status 'as the natural issue of India's constitutional progress' and went on to promise a 'round table' conference in London at which everybody could have their say. The agenda of the conference would not be fettered to the Simon report.

Just as he was issuing this statement Irwin was moving house into the magnificent viceregal palace at New Delhi which had been completed during his absence in London. It was the centre-piece of the new capital, the fitting home for the King-Emperor's representative. It had 300 rooms, a Durbah hall with crimson hangings and a dining room to seat 120. Portraits of former Viceroys hung on the walls and the garden was planted with a profuse mixture of Indian and British flowers. It was an unlooked-for irony that the first major act of the first Viceroy in occupation should be to announce the prospective abdication of the British. Oddly enough, too, 1929 was the year in which a regular air service was established between Britain and India, cutting down the journey time to 54 hours, compared with four weeks by sea. While Britain and India were thus brought physically closer together than ever before they drifted politically farther apart.

Irwin's sweeping away of the Simon Commission even before it had reported aroused fury in London. Winston Churchill, calculating that the loss of India was imminent, turned his power of invective on Irwin. The previous Viceroy, Reading, denounced dominion status in the House of Lords. So did Birkenhead,

N

Irwin's former chief at the India Office. The Conservative shadow cabinet sent him a telegram of protest. So angry a reaction gravely weakened the effect of Irwin's pledge; Indians assessed it as a concession by a weak and temporary Labour government rather than as a considered change of heart by Britain. They were thus the less disposed to abandon their own schemes in order to work with the Viceroy. 'It really makes my blood boil that people with mentality like that, not knowing the problem as you and I have to deal with it, should have such capacities for making mischief,' Irwin wrote to Benn of the telegram from his former cabinet colleagues.

The Congress policy remained unaltered—dominion status by the end of 1929 or total independence. Irwin's pledge of dominion status at some point in the indefinite future was not an acceptable substitute, particularly as British opinion appeared to be so doubtful about it. On December 31, 1929, the Congress voted for 'complete independence of India,' declined to take part in any 'round table' negotiation, instructed its members of legislatures to resign their seats and authorised the All-India Congress Committee to launch a programme of civil disobedience.

The previous civil disobedience campaign which had ended in 1922 had been mainly a passive affair—refusal of taxes and of co-operation with civil authorities. The new one, which Gandhi launched immediately, included a positive programme of committing petty, non-violent crimes so as to embarrass the administration by overfilling the prisons. Gandhi started it with a brilliant stroke of propaganda. One of the staples of the Indian revenue was the government salt monopoly. It was an offence for anyone to possess salt which he had not bought from the monopoly. In substance there was nothing particularly oppressive about the system; it was just a way of collecting taxation. However, it was the form of taxation which everyone in India, millionaire or outcast, had to pay and Gandhi decided to challenge it.

He led a procession of his followers 240 miles to the coast. The journey took 20 days, Gandhi skipping ahead at a pace which even the youngest found it hard to keep up with, and drawing crowds at every village he passed. Then on the seashore at Dandi in southern India he solemnly broke the law by picking up a piece of salt left behind by the sea. The demonstration aroused all India—the salt monopoly was something everyone could understand and it *did* seem harsh that it should be a crime to pick up salt on the seashore. Moreover, it attracted worldwide and sympathetic news coverage, the little saint in his loincloth appearing on the beach to advantage before the newsreel cameras.

From salt the movement extended to other peaceful breaches of the law. Crowds thronged the prisons demanding to be locked up. Women, including Jawaharlal Nehru's delicate wife, Kamala, joined in for the first time. Lawyers and even government officials courted arrest. Most ominous of all, two companies of a crack Indian army regiment refused orders to assist the civil power; Irwin sent a special note to the King-Emperor about that. On the fringes of the campaign hovered non-Gandhian terrorists committing murder and arson. Even before the official campaign began there had been an attempt to blow up the viceregal train with the Viceroy in it. The police lost their tempers under the strain and became unnecessarily harsh on the Congress crowds, lashing out with their batons; this aroused more unfavourable publicity for the British. 'In 18 years of reporting in 22 countries I have never witnessed such harrowing scenes,' wrote the American United Press correspondent Webb Miller. 'From where I stood I heard the sickening whack of the clubs on the unprotected skulls.' But there were no serious atrocities, nothing to match Amritsar. By the end of the year the government had Gandhi, the Nehrus and some 36,000 other congressmen in gaol and Congress itself had been banned. The government was holding the situation, but only just. British rule was being stretched to its capacity.

In this context the first 'round table' conference in London, held according to Irwin's announcement, proved to be a farce. It could have no meaning without Congress participation. More embarrassment came with the illness of Motilal Nehru locked up in Naindi prison. The distinguished old man plainly was dying of cancer. The government built him a special veranda in prison, allowed him a free choice of diet and let him take a daily newspaper but his condition worsened and Irwin ordered him to be let out. Then he let Jawaharlal out too so he could be with his father in his last days. Motilal died on February 22, 1931, and great crowds assembled for his cremation by the Ganges; he had been a Roman figure, the prop and patriarch of Congress. In his opposition to British rule he had advanced regularly, testing each step before he took it. While the son served his early prison sentences Motilal had taken to sleeping on his bedroom floor to see what prison was like. By the last summer of his life his anxiety had been lest the government should spare him from prison and so prevent his sharing the fate of his followers. Irwin sent a message of condolence to his widow.

The only way to break the deadlock, Irwin decided, was by a new and unprecedented initiative. He released Gandhi unconditionally from prison and then invited him to negotiate, his aim being to persuade Gandhi to call off the passive resistance campaign and to join a new 'round table' conference. Gandhi, writing that he wanted to meet 'not the Viceroy but the man inside the Viceroy,' agreed to come.

Thus on February 17, 1931, Gandhi, in his scanty dress and clasping his bamboo staff, appeared at the new Viceregal Palace, a plenipotentiary come to talk on equal terms with the British Raj. Hundreds of the Viceroy's domestic servants crowded the entrance to watch him. The veil of the temple was rending; a rebel straight from prison was being recognised as a national leader. In London Churchill declared that he was revolted by 'the nauseating and humiliating spectacle of this one-time Inner Temple lawyer, now seditious fakir, striding half-naked up the steps of the Viceroy's palace there to negotiate and parley on equal terms with the representative of the King-Emperor.' Churchill's denunciation had reason in it. So far as the fall of the British Empire can be epitomised in a single event it was when Gandhi entered Irwin's palace. He was the first and the greatest of a succession of nationalist leaders who in the years ahead were to pass straight from prison into the conference chamber.

Irwin and Gandhi negotiated for four weeks, Gandhi squatting cross-legged on the floor. The actual agreement they reached was so favourable to Irwin's point of view as to infuriate the other Congress leaders. Gandhi called off passive resistance and agreed to attend the conference in London. Irwin, in return, agreed to release from prison all the passive resisters save those who had committed violent crimes. Gandhi's true victory lay in the meetings themselves and in the wording of the agreement; with its reiterated phrase 'it is agreed that . . .' at the head of each clause, it read like a treaty between equal, sovereign powers rather than an arrangement between Viceroy and private citizen. The 'prestige' to which the British had always attached such importance could never be the same again. They had accepted the Congress as the principal voice of India.

There could be no going back. In London the new National Government, predominantly Conservative, accepted the changed situation, leaving only Churchill and a splinter group to continue to protest. Irwin finished his term of office. His successor, Lord Willingdon, was an old India hand who cracked down sharply on disorder but he, too, was tied by Irwin's actions. The actual 'round table' conference in London proved useless, Gandhi at his most awkward angering the Moslem and 'untouchable' representatives by insisting that he alone spoke for all India. It broke down and the British, more or less on their own, devised a system for self-government in the provinces, with ministers responsible to the legislatures. The Governors were to retain, of course, their emergency powers. The central government was to continue to be responsible to the Viceroy alone. The Congress launched another wave of resistance but its followers appeared to be exhausted and under Willingdon's firm hand the police were able to cope. Jawaharlal Nehru went back to prison again but was released when his wife fell mortally ill. He took her to Switzerland where she died; their only child, their daughter Indira, was now an undergraduate at Oxford.

The new constitution, based in many of its details on the Simon Report, was administratively a sharp break with the past. Hitherto there had not been much need for formal differentiation between the powers of the Viceroy in the centre and the governors of the various presidencies and provinces; they had all been the representatives of the same King-Emperor. Now India was given a sophisticated federal constitution, the relationships between the provinces and the centre spelled out in detail. The Government of India Act of 1934, which brought it into operation, was the longest that the British Parliament had ever passed and it proved to be a durable one, many of its provisions passing unchanged into the constitution of the Republic of India 15 years later. The British aim, though, was not to prepare the way for a republic but to get the hundreds of princely states into the same federal system. It was a complicated undertaking which went ahead very slowly. In reality the princes were puppets of the British and they were to collapse completely the moment British power was removed. Gandhi called their jewels and elaborate ceremonial clothes 'the badges of their slavery.' At the same time, though, the British were bound by treaties, a separate treaty for each prince, to maintain them in power. Unless the British were to break their plighted word, they could only persuade and not order them to come into the federation.

While the princes were posing constitutional problems for the British, Gandhi and Nehru were facing even worse constitutional problems of their own. They had brought India to the verge of self-government, but it was not a united India. Gandhi's troubles in London with the Moslem leaders had exemplified the jagged and widening gap between the Moslem Indians and the Hindu majority. As the defeat of the British was to rank as their greatest success, so was their inability to conciliate the Moslems to rank as their historic failure. It was not entirely through want of trying. From the beginning the Congress had been designed as a secular body representating the members of all the religious communities of India. Gandhi himself was by no means a strict Hindu; he preferred to seek 'truth' in all religions; Nehru was an outright agnostic. There always had been Moslem members of the Congress and there were to continue to be such even after the creation of Pakistan. During the 1920s Gandhi and the Congress leadership had gone out of their way to conciliate the Moslem community; there had been five Moslem presidents of the Congress in ten years. 'Hindu–Moslem unity is not less important than the spinning wheel; it is our breath of life,' said Gandhi. Nevertheless by sheer weight of numbers the Hindus dominated the Congress and it was easy for Moslem communalist leaders to represent it as a Hindu organisation.

Racially the Moslems and the Hindus were practically the same and there was no definite linguistic division between them. Nor was there any clear geographical boundary between them, both groups being represented in all parts of India. The Moslems did form majorities in eastern Bengal, western Punjab, Kashmir, the north-west frontier province and Sind but many Hindus also lived in those areas and many Moslems lived outside them. It was essentially a patchwork pattern, hardly more definite than, say, that of Protestants and Catholics in the U.S.A. Historically the Moslems had been the ruling community which had made converts from the Hindus. More recently, in the British period, the Hindus had become the better educated and economically more enterprising group. The purist Hindus, who had their own organisation, the Hindu Mahasabha, repudiated the idea of building a secular India and wanted a definitely Hindu regime to replace the British.

The disputes between the two communities were not just doctrinal, like those between the Catholics and Protestants in Ireland. They extended also into social life over such matters as the sacredness of the cow. Orthodox Hindus regarded Moslems as outcastes in whose company it was not possible to eat a meal.

Moslems regarded Hindus as superstitious pagans. The rank and file on both sides were volatile in defending their faiths and it was part of the common pattern of India for riots and even murder to flare out of trivial disputes between the two faiths.

From the beginning of representative government the British had recognised the Moslems as a separate community and allowed them to elect their own representatives to the legislatures. This certainly did not diminish the division between the communities and the Congress leaders condemned the British for running a 'divide and rule' policy. But during the 1914 war the Moslems had been agitated by the British fighting the leader of their religion, the Sultan of Turkey, and their organisation, the Moslem League, had formed an alliance with the Congress. The Moslems were, however, much less active than the Hindus in pursuing civil disobedience, Gandhi's doctrines being remote from their way of thought. During the 1920s the Congress and the Moslem League followed independent policies and were generally hostile to each other.

The leading Moslem was a very tall, very thin, very rich Bombay lawyer called Mahommed Ali Jinnah. Born in 1876, he had qualified as a barrister at Lincoln's Inn, London, and built up a flourishing legal practice. During the early years of the 20th century he played a prominent role in the Congress. In 1910, when the Moslem League had adopted a programme of seeking self-government for India, he had joined it while maintaining his membership of the Congress. He broke with Gandhi over non-co-operation in 1920 and entered the new central legislature as the leading Moslem spokesman; his group for some years held the balance of power in the legislature. Sometimes he would support the government and sometimes oppose it. He was a brilliant but enigmatic figure. Unlike Gandhi and the Congressmen he wore European clothes and maintained close social links with Englishmen. He owned an opulent house in Hampstead, London; many regarded him as being too fastidious and too aloof to be an effective nationalist leader but he stood higher in prestige among the Moslems than anyone else. So far as can be ascertained, he was willing in principle to work with the Congress so long as the Congress allowed the Moslem community separate electorates and more seats in the legislatures than its strict numbers would justify. Only so could the rights of the Moslem minority adequately be protected. The Congress leaders took the disastrously simple view that the Moslem fuss was really the fault of British 'divide and rule.' They refused to take it seriously. The new India, they argued, should be a secular state with all religions treated equally. The Congress, as the representative of the Indian people as a whole, was the only legitimate inheritor of the British Raj; special rights for any religious minority could only entrench superstition, reaction and national division. The Moslems reacted violently at what they regarded as cavalier overriding of their rights and on the younger and more forceful of them dawned the revolutionary dream of building their own Moslem state in India.

The actual genesis of the new state happened not in India but at Cambridge University, England. In 1932 a group of Moslem Indian students there, led by C. Rahmat Ali, devised the name 'Pakistan'—P for Punjab, A for Afgans on the frontier, K for Kashmir, and S for Sind, the whole meaning in Urdu 'Land of the Pure.' At this time Jinnah had retired altogether from Indian politics and was living at his London home. In 1934, however, he returned to India and became Qaid-i-Azam ('Great Leader') of the Moslem League. Up to then the League had been a largely middle class body but Jinnah set about with energy to build it up as a mass movement, the Moslem equivalent of the Congress. He toured India with fiery oratory calling upon the Moslems to rally to defend their rights. At this stage 'Pakistan' was still just the dream of a few extremists; Jinnah's aim was not to set up a separate state but to provide a vigorous Moslem party to contest against the Congress the elections in 1935 for the legislatures under the new constitution. But he had rallied the Moslem masses to his side as effectively as Gandhi and Nehru had rallied the Hindus.

Thus the 1935 elections took place in the entirely new context of there being two Indian nationalist parties, the Congress and the Moslem League, instead of, as in the past, just one, the Congress. In the election the Congress won control of six of the 11 provinces. The League won two provinces and the other three had no clear majority. Jinnah at this stage was still willing to co-operate; he had won his seats and now he claimed a share in the government of the Congress-controlled provinces. Nehru and the Congress, however, made the fatal error of continuing to regard the Moslem League as a temporary aberration caused by British influence. They refused to share power and set up purely Congress administrations. Jinnah, furiously resentful, built up the Moslem League even further and became steadily more extreme. If the Moslems were not to be allowed to share power with Congress they must aim at establishing their own state. In 1940 the Moslem League finally adopted 'Pakistan' as its objective.

The British had intended the 1935 constitution to be only a transitional step. At least a further generation should pass before self-government at the centre could be allowed and actual dominion status would be a step beyond that.

The British had not expected the Congress to do so well in the elections, the chimera persisting that from somewhere 'moderates' would appear to lead the Indians into sensible co-operation with the Raj. Nevertheless they allowed the Congress to form ministries in the six provinces. Neither Gandhi nor Nehru took office. Gandhi was in one of his phases of withdrawal from politics, concentrating on religious work and on the uplift of the outcastes. Nehru devoted himself to co-ordinating the work of the Congress ministries forming, indeed, what amounted to a shadow central government. He virtually appointed and dismissed ministers in the Congress-controlled provinces, drew up economic plans and directed the methods of administration. In theory the new ministers were supposed to be dependent on their British advisers but, in practice, it was Nehru's word from Allahabad that counted. Simla, with its bureaucratic and social rituals, retained military power but for day-to-day purposes Nehru was already Prime Minister of most of India. The British had supposed dominion status still to be two generations away at least but by the late 1930s it was becoming clearer and clearer that the next step could only be independence. There could be no further intermediate stages. The only questions were what particular crisis would finally smash the remaining fabric of British rule and what would happen to the Moslem minority.

The crisis that came was the Second World War.

# CHAPTER 9

# New opponents

THE major enterprise between the wars in protecting the British Empire was the Singapore naval base. It cost about £60 million and was laid out in a former swamp, a whole river being diverted to make way for it. Much of the money for building it came from the neighbouring colonies it was intended to protect—Straits Settlements, the Malay states and Hong Kong. In theory it also formed a keystone of British Commonwealth defence for the whole of India, the Far East and Australasia and its creation had been approved by the 1921 Imperial Conference. But the only self-governing dominion actually to contribute towards the cost was New Zealand.

The need for the base sprang largely from the growth of Japan as a first-class power. Up to the start of the century it had been possible for European countries to dominate the Far East without elaborate forces. Gunboats, such as those which sailed hundreds of miles inland up the rivers of China, plus a few cruisers, were sufficient to protect British trade and possessions. Serious military challenge could come only from another European power. In the early 1920s Japan had recently been an ally. Nevertheless she possessed a fleet of battleships and, as the decade proceeded, it became increasingly clear that she aimed to be the dominating power in the Far East. The China seas and the Pacific were no longer the political vacuum they had been on the arrival of the British a century earlier. Moreover, there were signs of stirring in the chaotic mass of China itself; the young Chiang Kai-Shek and his Nationalists were emerging under their prophet, Sun Yat-Sen, with the ambition of uniting their country as a modern industrial state. Such changes could threaten not only the colonies in China and Malaya themselves (including Malayan rubber) but also the balance of security of the imperial territories of India and Australasia. A whole new flank was at risk and it was necessary to construct a new Gibraltar in the Far East. Until Singapore was finished, the nearest dockyard to India at which a battleship could be serviced was Malta.

That, at least, was the strategic conception. But there were many tactical difficulties in implementing it. Having spent £10,000 million on the 1914–1918 war, the British at home considered themselves impoverished. Against a background of depression in the older exporting industries, successive governments set about a series of 'economy' campaigns. Winston Churchill as Chancellor of the Exchequer laid down the doctrine that defence preparations should be based on the assumption that war was unlikely during the following ten years. The 1924 Labour Government managed for a moment to halt the Singapore programme altogether.

There followed the doubt about whether there were enough warships to make the base worthwhile. Up to 1914 Great Britain had pursued the 'two power' standard of maintaining the Royal Navy at twice the strength of the next largest navy in the world. This principle had lain at the very heart of imperial thinking; without the capability of commanding the world's sea routes, the scattered British Empire could not possibly be secure. Yet, during the war, the United States of America had, for the first time, constructed a substantial navy. Should Britain now attempt to maintain the 'two power' standard against Americans who at that time, patently, had no ambitions towards world-wide power? The question had only to be asked to be answered. It would be a futile waste. Policy should be aimed at the reduction of armaments, not competition in producing them. Accordingly, in the 1922 Washington Naval Treaty, the British formally abandoned the 'two power' standard and accepted a proportion of '5-5-3' with the Americans and the Japanese—for every five British battleships, the Americans should have five and the Japanese three.

This summary abandonment of maritime supremacy seemed so much an obvious thing to do at a moment when the British were more than ordinarily sickened of war that the only people who worried about it were a handful of grumbling admirals. Thus two powers which had hardly existed upon the world scene when the British Empire had been created were now between them stronger than the British at sea. Moreover, allowing for the fact that the British fleet was spread all over the world, the Japanese were likely to be stronger than the British in Far Eastern waters. The only way Britain could form a Pacific Fleet strong enough to tackle the Japanese would be by denuding herself in home waters and the Mediterranean. She was no longer in a position to defend the whole Empire at once. In terms of military calculation the only hope would be an alliance with the United States; but neither then nor later were the Americans, who cherished the traditions of their own 18th-century revolt against colonial status, prepared to conduct their policy in terms of protecting the British Empire. This not unreasonable attitude by the Americans was to be one of the decisive factors in ultimate imperial dissolution.

The battleship was assumed to be the queen of the seas and, indeed, the most effective of any weapon of war—land, sea or air. With her thick armour, gigantic guns and her 30-knot speed she formed the mightiest fighting unit man had ever devised. Movements of the battleships of any fleet sent tremors across the world—naval intelligence staffs customarily maintained maps upon which they pinned the position of every battleship of every country. Orthodox naval doctrine was that the only enemy a battleship need fear was another battleship. Nothing else had guns big enough to sink her. Actually, the capabilities of battleships were largely paper capabilities drawn up by naval theoreticians. Modern battleships had engaged in only one fleet action, Jutland, and that had been too confused a scuffle to prove anything beyond the importance of armour. The battleship had hardly been tested at all in action against bombs or torpedoes dropped from aircraft; whether her armour and guns were sufficient protection against aerial attack was between the wars a matter for active controversy. Most experts thought a battleship could defeat an aircraft but, in the event, they were to be proved wrong. The battleship, in truth, was as untested in actual war conditions as were nuclear weapons a generation later.

The 21 square miles of Singapore dockyard were designed for the specific purpose of servicing battleships. There was an air base, too, and a permanent garrison of 7,000 soldiers but it was the battleships that really mattered. By the time of the official opening of the base in 1938 it had two huge dry docks, each capable of taking the biggest battleships. One of them, a floating dock, had been towed, in an epic of navigation, all the way from the Tyne in England. Despite these facilities there were, however, rarely any battleships actually stationed at Singapore; they would be sent out from the Home Fleet or the Mediterranean if they were needed. The danger existed, therefore, of the Japanese battle fleet reaching and destroying Singapore before the British battleships arrived. So the base was fitted with the most elaborate fortifications that existed outside the French Maginot Line. Guns of 18-inch calibre, said to be the biggest in the world, pointed out to sea from shell-proof concrete emplacements. Singapore was proudly proclaimed to be impregnable. The planners, however, took no account of the possibility of attack from the landward side, through Malaya; their thoughts and the guns were directed at the sea.

The Singapore base was in cost the largest single constructional work carried out in the British Empire between the wars. It was proof of an intention to maintain the world-wide Empire. Besides being a European power, an American power, an African power, a Middle Eastern power and the ruler of India, Britain wanted to continue to be a power in eastern Asia and the Pacific. Singapore in its symbolic aspect became a part of that fragile 'prestige' upon which so much of the imperial structure depended. There was, however, practically no attempt to analyse the fundamentals of the situation. The British, undefeated in a major war since the 18th century, seemed to take it for granted that they were bound to win any conflict that arose. Yet in Japan the British were facing for the first time a real danger on the outer fringe of Empire; instead of the archaic opponents they had been accustomed to encounter in such quarters, Japan was a coolly efficient modern power. To defeat Japan on its own would be a task requiring the whole resources of Great Britain. If there was war in Europe as well as in the Far East, British resources would be stretched beyond a safe limit. If the Middle East were added, too, the Empire would stand on the brink of disaster. To be sure of survival, the Empire could not contemplate war in more than one place at once. Actually, of course, despite the rhetoric of the imperialist politicians, the preservation of the Empire was far from being the sole, or even the principal, consideration in British foreign policy.

Over most of the colonial empire, internal opposition to British rule was, between the wars, an inconsiderable factor. India, obviously, had reached the brink of revolt but in the colonies there appeared to be no nationalist forces which could effectively challenge British rule. Indeed, so far as the matter was considered at all, the British reckoned that the longer their rule continued, the more attached would the colonial peoples become to the Empire spirit. Africa, despite the resistance of the Emperor Haile Selassie to Italian colonisation, could be counted as politically a stagnant continent. Haile Selassie's success in attracting a degree of international sympathy, including British sympathy, for his cause showed that colonialism, as it had been taken for granted in the 19th century, was becoming obsolete; few, however, saw this as a reason to doubt the value of the colonial system as it already existed. The expansion of colonies was no longer respectable but the maintenance of them was quite all right.

Spasmodic troubles arose in the Caribbean colonies, most of which had been British possessions for three centuries. With their main crop, sugar, in constant depression, the populations were undernourished and prone to epidemics. There was, however, a steady progress towards universal literacy and, as a consequence, increasing unrest. Under such leaders as Alexander Bustamente of Jamaica and Uriah Butler of Trinidad it expressed itself in the form of vigorous trade unionism, strikes leading to riots and killings. The background to this unrest was far from creditable to British colonialism. So far were the British from attempting any vigorous programme of development or aid that in 1931 they ludicrously accepted from the Trinidad legislature (not a popularly elected body) a grant of £5,000 a year for five years to help the United Kingdom in its budgetary difficulties.

Between 1934 and 1938, in particular, the islands seethed with unrest. The British, characteristically, attempted first to deal with it by police actions and the dispatch of troops. This failing, they equally characteristically sent out a commission of inquiry with a brief thoroughly to examine the situation. The resulting report, the Moyne Report (named after the chairman, Lord Moyne) was ready in 1940 but it was so devastating an indictment of British administration that publication of the bulk of it was withheld until 1945 lest German propagandists made use of it. The report recommended the rapid extension of self-government and the provision of economic aid, thus setting what was to be the characteristic post-war pattern for the colonial Empire.

In the Middle East, what most engaged British attention was, as always, the problems of Egypt, the country which because of the Suez Canal commanded 'the windpipe of the Empire.' Since 1922 Egypt had nominally been independent but it proved impossible to get a decent working arrangement with her. The British garrison remained in Egypt both to guard the Canal and to provide a general reserve for the whole of the Middle East and Africa. The development of oilfields in Iraq, Persia and, later, Kuwait, formed an additional justification for the British staying; it was taken for granted the oil would not be safe unless there were a British military presence. (Before the 1939–1945 war, however, oil was only a secondary consideration.) The Egyptians resented the British occupation of their country; the easiest way for an Egyptian politician to whip up popular support was to blame the British for anything that happened to be going wrong in the country at any particular moment. There was a standing quarrel, too, about

Sudan. Nominally Sudan was a 'condominion' of Great Britain and Egypt but in practice it was run by the British alone. The Egyptians regarded Sudan as their natural hinterland and their King proclaimed himself 'King of the Sudan.' Support for the Egyptian claim came from many of the Sudanese Arab intellectuals and there were periodic riots in the capital, Khartoum; many of the less sophisticated of the Sudanese people, especially the Africans in the south, did, however, prefer the British to the Egyptians.

Political activity in Cairo revolved around three fixed points — the British High Commissioner, the King and the nationalist politicians, some of them corrupt, of the Wafd Party. It was an impossible situation and one which by its nature could not last; Egypt might have been manageable as a British colony, just manageable, but the apparatus of independent government could not be reconciled with the presence of an unwanted British garrison. The British, on their side, pointed to the contribution they made to the Egyptian economy and to the services of British officials in modernising the administration; they became tense with anger at Egyptian 'ingratitude.'

It took 14 years after nominal independence in 1922 for the British and Egyptians to negotiate a treaty to regularise their relations. Every step was punctuated by violence. In 1924 Sir Lee Stack, Governor-General of Sudan and Commander-in-Chief of the Egyptian army was shot down in the street in Cairo. The British exacted a £500,000 collective fine, secured the trial and execution of seven men involved in the conspiracy and expelled Egyptian army units from Sudan. They occupied the customs posts at Alexandria until their orders had been carried out. This tough attitude, confirmed by the arrival of a new High Commissioner, the Conservative politician Lord Lloyd, failed to produce results in the form of a treaty the Egyptians would sign. The Labour Government of 1929 dismissed Lloyd—to his fury— and tried a softer approach, offering to withdraw the garrison to the canal zone and to allow Egypt to conduct normal international relations. Still the Egyptian nationalists, under Nahas Pasha, refused to sign; they were hoping to get the British out altogether.

Finally, in 1936, both sides conceded enough to make a treaty possible. Under it Egypt was allowed full international status but the British garrison, to be removed gradually to the canal zone, was to be allowed to stay for at least another 20 years. Egypt joined the League of Nations and began exchanging ambassadors with other countries; the office of British High Commissioner was replaced by that of British Ambassador. There remained, however, ambiguity in Egypt's status. When Britain declared war in 1939 Egypt was bound by the treaty to break off relations with Britain's enemy, Germany; she did so but went on to proclaim herself 'non-belligerent' and the strange situation arose of her territory becoming the scene of fierce warfare without her being a combatant. This, naturally, further exacerbated Anglo–Egyptian relations. Under wartime pressures the British were not too choosy about their methods and intervened as strongly as ever in Egyptian affairs; at one point they surrounded the royal palace with troops to make the King dismiss his ministers. Ordinary British soldiers thought of themselves as fighting to defend Egypt against Nazi aggression and could not comprehend the ingratitude with which the Egyptians appeared to regard them. It was a poisonous situation, one in which hatreds were nourished on both sides.

The British had two reserve bases in the Middle East. Both, in their own way, were as troublesome as Egypt.

British rule in Cyprus had begun in the 19th century with a fund of goodwill. The Greek-Cypriots, who formed 80 per cent of the population, preferred the British to their former Turkish masters; also they hoped that British rule was only a stage towards 'Enosis'—union with Greece. The British had established honest, efficient administration, set up a legislature with elected members and allowed such freedom of speech that the people enjoyed a cultural and intellectual renaissance. Up to 1914 the island remained technically a part of the Turkish Empire and although the British then formally annexed it they gave it no definite status. Instead of being a colony or a protectorate they called it, vaguely, a 'British possession.' It had a high commissioner, not a Governor. In 1915 the island was offered to Greece as an inducement to her to declare war upon Germany.

By the 1920s, however, the old goodwill was running out. The memory of Turkish oppression was becoming too faded to offset dissatisfaction with alien British rule. The legislative council no longer appeared as an epitome of liberalism. It had nine elected Greek members, three elected representatives of the Turkish minority and six British officials. In practice the British and Turks usually voted together and so, with the Governor's casting vote, could pass what laws they wanted without Greek consent. The dangerous situation grew of the Greek representatives forming a permanent opposition and of using the council as a political platform rather than as an opportunity of sharing in the government. British officials, despite their honesty, became less popular. Many of them, arriving from less sophisticated territories, treated the Cypriots as a subject race instead of as fellow-Europeans. One arrival from East Africa was supposed to have proclaimed within Cypriot hearing: 'I can understand a white gentleman, and a black gentleman, although I don't let him touch me; but these betwixts and betweens I don't want to understand.' Such extreme lack of tact was uncharacteristic but it did epitomise the mood of some British officials. It was rare for the British to mix socially with the Cypriots—they preferred to talk shop among themselves. In 1925 Cyprus was proclaimed a proper crown colony and a Governor, Sir Ronald Storrs from Palestine, was appointed. Storrs's declared aim was to make the island a permanent part of the British Empire, of educating the children to think of themselves as British rather than as Greek or Turkish.

Why the British should have been so eager to consolidate Cyprus in the Empire is far from clear. The island had originally been acquired with a view to possible use as a base, a purpose for which it was not particularly suitable as it lacked a deep water harbour. Shortly after acquiring Cyprus the British had occupied Egypt and this was so much the better strategic centre that the notion of stationing a garrison in Cyprus was abandoned. By the 1920s British forces on the island amounted to a single company of infantry. Nor was there much thought of using Cyprus as an alternative if Egypt became too hot to hold; the alternative to Egypt commonly discussed was not Cyprus but Palestine. Cyprus was only the third string. In terms of strict British and imperial interests there could have been no practical objection to allowing the population self-determination. (Turkish objections were not, in the 1920s when Britain had just dismembered the Turkish Empire, a serious obstacle.)

The main reason why self-determination was not allowed was a combination of inertia with ignorance. Cyprus was one of the smallest of Britain's 50 or so colonial possessions and none but a few experts were acquainted with its conditions. The campaign for 'Enosis' was regarded as just a curiosity. How could anyone seriously prefer rule by Greeks to rule by British? At the Storrs level (he was an unusually vigorous and enterprising Governor) it was an axiom of sound administration to make the British Empire

o

as British as possible. At the high policy-making level in London— so far as such a level existed at all—politicians and officials were too occupied with other matters to consider the exceptional case of the only territory in the Empire which wanted to join up with a foreign country.

The establishment of colonial rule under Storrs on a firm basis jolted the Cypriot nationalists into realising that, the way things were going, they might never get 'Enosis.' Allied to this political concern were economic problems—poor harvests and a complicated controversy over the 'tribute' which had formerly been exacted from the island for the benefit of Turkey. The policy of trying to make Cyprus more British broke down in rioting in 1931, Storrs' own residence being burned down. The disturbances were ill-organised and the arrival of two cruisers and troops from Egypt rapidly suppressed them. The legislative council was suspended and the Governor, ruling as an autocrat, appeared to keep the island well in hand. Cyprus faded from the headlines again and most British people forgot she even existed. But, under the surface, the desire for union with Greece waxed stronger and stronger. The people blamed everything that went wrong on the island on the British and 'Enosis' was held out as the cure for all ills. There began to accumulate a store of bitterness which within 20 years was to spill out in the most successful rebellion conducted against British rule since that of the American colonies. The situation exemplified one of the inherent weaknesses of an imperial system such as that of the British; the territories within it were so numerous and so varied that so tiny a one as Cyprus rarely attracted the attention of statesmen.

The problem of Cyprus was aggravated by too much obscurity. Exactly the opposite weakness—too much publicity—confounded the problem of Palestine 200 miles across the water. Everything that happened in Palestine was a subject of world-wide interest. For Arabs, Christians and Jews it was a Holy Land. Jewish settlers had relations and friends across most of Europe, together with influential supporters in the United States. The Arab population could call upon the sympathy of the Arab world from Morocco to Muscat. The British purpose of maintaining Palestine as basically an Arab country, while allowing limited Jewish immigration, made enemies on both sides. The fault lay not so much in the British administration itself but in the original inconsistencies in the Balfour Declaration and the mandate themselves and in political events in Europe outside British control.

The first British High Commissioner, the Jewish Herbert Samuel, tried to hold a balance between the Arab and Jewish communities but succeeded only in antagonising both. His successor, Field Marshal Lord Plumer, was a tactful soldier who sought, with some success, to lower the temperature. He stood carefully to attention during the playing of the Zionist anthem 'Hatikvah;' when an Arab delegation complained, Plumer said there should be an Arab anthem too and offered to help them get one. He loved to wander through the tunnel-like streets of Old Jerusalem, observing the people and wearing what he called 'plain clothes;' actually with his bowler hat, stiff white collar and furled umbrella he stuck out among the multitudes like a bishop in a lingerie shop and everyone knew who he was. It was the golden era of the British mandate and conditions in Palestine contrasted favourably with those next door in Syria, where the French were at war with nationalist rebels. Under Plumer the British security forces were actually reduced. The main proportion of the British police in Palestine came from the Royal Irish Constabulary which had been disbanded in the Free State.

Under the surface of Plumer's calm administration, which lasted from 1925 to 1928, rough forces were at work. Anti-Jewish measures in Poland stimulated emigration to Palestine—most Jewish arrivals in Palestine at this time were from Poland. Moreover, Weizmann, with skill, was consolidating the Zionist movement to associate it more closely with the main body of Judaism. From being a sect among Jews, the Zionists became an accepted part of the whole international Jewish community; Jews who did not themselves wish to go to Palestine nevertheless supported those who did. Money was raised to buy more and more land from Arab absentee landlords. Weizmann raised capital from world Jewry to develop the agricultural settlements which, by a combination of science, money and dedicated labour, were proving that land hitherto considered marginal or barren was capable of producing plentiful crops. The work of such settlements, many of them run on idealistic principles of common ownership, was of crucial significance not just for Palestine but for the whole underdeveloped world; it showed what could be achieved. The Arabs, too, were organising themselves under Haj Amin El Husseini, Mufti of Jerusalem. In theory the Mufti was just a religious leader but Haj Amin was a subtle, ambitious man who also exerted political power. Under a suave, apparently civilised manner, he concealed an unbalanced hatred of everything Jewish.

He was not only an opponent of Jewish immigration but also a genuine anti-Semite. Superficially he could appear so reasonable and charming that it took the British years to realise how absurd and dangerous were his inner principles.

Plumer's successor was Sir John Chancellor, who had previously been Governor of Mauritius and of Trinidad. Leopold Amery, the Colonial Secretary in London, was one of the more fervent believers in the British imperial mission. He was also a pro-Zionist, believing that such a policy would not only secure British authority in the Middle East but also attract the friendship of world-wide Judaism. He selected Chancellor as the most experienced man available for Palestine. Unfortunately, though, Chancellor turned out to be ill-equipped to deal with communal tensions; he knew little of either Arabs or Jews or of the motives which impelled them.

Trouble began with squabbles at the Western Wall (nicknamed the Wailing Wall), Jerusalem. This is the only remaining part of Herod's temple and for two millenia had been a sacred object of Jewish pilgrimage. It was, indeed, the main physical symbol of the Jewish faith, their Mecca and Holy Sepulchre rolled into one. Every devout Jew wanted to pray there. Unfortunately the wall was overlooked by the Mosque of Omar, an especially holy place for Moslems, and by the house of the Mufti of Jerusalem himself. The aggressors at the Wall appear to have been the Moslems, egged on by the Mufti. Noisy Moslem services were arranged to coincide with Jewish days of penance, a muezzin was installed to call the faithful to prayer over the heads of the Jewish pilgrims and road works were started to turn the pavement before the wall from a blind alley into a thoroughfare. The Mufti's aides spread inflammatory rumours that the Jews were planning to take over the Mosque of Omar.

During 1928 and 1929 there were a series of worsening scuffles and minor riots at the Wall. Ill-feeling between the two communities increased. Then, in August 1929, after what should have been an innocent incident, the disagreements turned to outright violence. A Jewish boy kicked his football into an Arab's garden. The owner of the garden protested and a brawl took place between a handful of Arabs and Jews in which one Jew was murdered with a knife. The Jews, outraged, gave the victim a public funeral at which were uttered threats of vengeance. Arab mobs in Jerusalem and other parts of Palestine reacted with mass attacks on Jews, killing 133 and wounding 339. For three days the country lay in anarchy, Arab police refusing to stop Arab attacks and the British refusing to use Jewish police; not until troops had been brought up from Egypt were the murders checked. To what extent this Arab offensive was organised is difficult to establish. The Mufti himself was careful to avoid open incitement but the apparent efficiency and synchronisation with which the Arabs armed themselves and chose their objectives suggested a degree of planning somewhere in the background. The Jews themselves were convinced that the outbreaks were planned and that the British were grossly negligent in checking them; some extremist Jews even alleged that the British had connived at the massacre.

Until this breakdown in order the Jews, on the whole, had trusted the British and made comparatively little preparation for their own self-defence; during the disturbances 116 Arabs had been killed by the British forces and only six by the Jews. Now, however, the Jews decided they must have their own security organisation; they began to create a semi-secret army, the Haganah. Vladimir Jabotinsky, a fanatical terrorist from Poland, gained some influence for his doctrine that it was only by crude force that the Jews could survive in Palestine.

Meanwhile there was a change of government in London, the pro-Zionist Amery giving way to the Socialist Sidney Webb, Lord Passfield, who tended to sympathise with the Arabs. For reasons connected with British domestic politics and which had nothing to do with the actual situation in Palestine, the trend of policy changed overnight. Passfield sent a commission to inquire into the disturbances and on receiving its report decided that excessive Jewish immigration was the root of the trouble. He proposed to limit future immigration to a final total of 50,000, reckoning that this would fulfil the pledge to allow a Jewish 'national home' while maintaining the existing Arab predominance in Palestine. Whatever the merits or otherwise of this proposal, it fell oddly as the outcome of a situation in which the Jews had been the victims of mass murder. It looked as if the Jews were being punished for having been attacked while the Arabs were being rewarded for having attacked them. World Jewish opinion turned solidly against Great Britain.

Then again British domestic politics came into play. The administration to which Passfield belonged was in the unusually weak position of depending upon Liberal votes for a majority in the House of Commons. The Liberal leader, Lloyd George, had presided over the cabinet which had issued the original Balfour

Declaration. Weizmann came to London and whipped up a great anti-Passfield agitation, drawn from the Conservative and Liberal parties, the British Jewish organisations and many members of the Labour Party itself. The Labour Government caved in under the pressure, dropped the 50,000 limit and affirmed its sympathy with Jewish settlement. The Palestinian Arabs, who had no Weizmann to tread expertly in British politics, felt betrayed. All they now knew for certain was that murder was capable of making an impression.

Thus the combination of inept administration on the spot with vacillation from London caused the British to lose the confidence of both sides in Palestine. No episode could show more graphically the inherent unsuitability of an open political system like that of Great Britain for the administration of tumultuous colonial peoples.

Nor was there any possibility of a quiet breathing space in which Palestine might simmer down. In 1933 Adolf Hitler came to power in Germany on an insanely cruel programme of anti-Semitism. Jews had long been accustomed to persecution in Russia and Poland but they had regarded Germany as a safe place. The German Jews were among the most assimilated in the world, German in their culture and political loyalties, Jewish only in religious profession. They had shown relatively little interest in Zionism. Yet with Hitler in office, not even Germany was now a secure home. Where else could Jews turn to as the ultimate stronghold but their 'national home' in the promised land of Palestine? Their only hope of winning proper human rights was to construct their own nation-state in the land to which they were attached by age-old tradition. Under Hitler's impact, Zionism took on a new urgency and a new violence. When the British tried to restrict immigration, the Jews conducted elaborate conspiracies to circumvent the regulations, justifying them in propaganda campaigns explicable only in terms of the dreadful emergency they faced. (Jewish nationalism had a stronger rational basis than most nationalisms.) The British were presented to the liberal part of the world as inhuman rulers, denying the rights of the Jewish people to their home. At the same time the Germans and Italians were active with propaganda among the Arabs, attacking the British as thieves who sought to give Arab lands to interlopers from Europe. The Mufti of Jerusalem allied himself with the Nazis and ended his career by assisting with Hitler's 'final solution' of genocide.

The British, themselves divided into pro-Arab and pro-Zionist factions, could not win. A colonial problem turned into an international problem. They fumbled with ideas of partition but really no peaceful solution existed. The longer the Palestine mandate lasted, the more enemies the British Empire made.

# CHAPTER 10

# Liberty and justice

WHEN on September 3, 1939, Great Britain declared war upon Nazi Germany, the Empire was still intact. A quarter of the world still lay under the sovereignty of the King in London. Since the high water mark of 1918, the Empire had shed only three territories, Egypt, Iraq and Weihaiwei. Of these, Egypt and Iraq still contained British garrisons and could be counted as Empire satellites. Only Weihaiwei, ceded to China in 1930, now lay definitely outside the British sphere, it having been occupied by Japan in the course of her invasion of China. With authority reaching to every continent, the British Empire was literally a world power; indeed in terms of the extent of its influence it was the *only* world power. The United States limited its authority to its own continent and to the Pacific; the Soviet Union was a smaller unit than the former Russian Empire. Both the U.S. and the U.S.S.R. were pursuing introspective policies, confining their main attention to their own internal affairs. Of the European powers, Germany had no overseas colonies at all, Spain was in chaos, Italy's empire was confined to northern Africa. The only country with a world influence comparable with that of Great Britain was France, which had substantial territories in Africa and in south-east Asia; but the population of the French territories was less than half that of the British Empire.

Nevertheless the British Empire was much more fragile than it might appear at first sight. It contained the gravest political and military weaknesses. India, the biggest component, was in imminent danger of becoming uncontrollable; her next step could be only towards self-government and so to independence as a world power in her own right. The white dominions had acquired full equality of status with the United Kingdom and could quit the imperial framework at any moment they chose; in the cases of South Africa and Ireland, which contained powerful elements hostile to the British connection, such severance was liable to happen at any moment. In the Middle East the British position in Egypt had become precarious and the garrison was due to be evacuated altogether in 1956. Palestine was a liability. Cyprus seethed with hostility to British rule. There were formidable military threats from Italy in the Middle East and Japan in the Far East.

In the colonies of Africa and the West Indies, British rule was not in such immediate danger. The steady upbuilding and professionalisation of the administrative services suggested, indeed, that in the future British control was likely to become firmer rather than weaker; this, certainly, was at least the short-term intention of the Colonial Office. Nobody thought of such territories achieving sovereign status; the most they could achieve, long years ahead, would be self-government within the Empire framework. Yet even in these territories there were a few who were watching India and reading the history of Ireland. The methods of the Nehrus were being studied with rapt attention. What finer career could an ambitious young man have than to be a liberator of his country? It was noted how the Indian leaders had been able to paralyse British administration. It was seen how they could outflank the local British rulers by appealing direct to sympathisers in the British House of Commons.

Militarily the British Empire was undermanned and underequipped, its armed forces being in no way proportionate to its size. Even the self-governing dominions, for all their assertions of independence, were too weak to defend themselves unaided againsd a strong, modern enemy; their administrations still tended to think in terms of just a 'contribution' towards imperial defence, leaving the main burden to London. In the London-governeti territories the only notable force was the great Indian army of 260,000 men. In previous generations the Indian army had been an essential adjunct of imperial expansion, it having been well able to defeat unsophisticated, ill-equipped enemies. But the Indian army of 1939 was not prepared for modern war. It had practically no artillery or tanks. Nor was the Indian navy or air force equipped for anything more than police actions. Allowing for the fact that India, bubbling with subversion, required a garrison of 50,000 men from Great Britain, the Indian Empire could no longer be counted as a net military asset. In Africa and the West Indies there were a few battalions of locally-recruited troops but they were not equipped to tackle a modern enemy. The main burden of defending the imperial complex of 500 million people rested on the 45 million inhabitants of the British Isles.

The mother country maintained forces inadequate for this duty. The army of 154,000 men (in 1938) was smaller than those of her potential opponents in Europe alone. The Royal Navy was still powerful but no longer the unchallengeable mistress of the seas. If the Royal Navy were sent to the Far East in sufficient quantity to match Japan, the sea routes of the remainder of the Empire, including the British home waters, would be left dangerously vulnerable. In the air Britain was acquiring excellent bomber and fighter forces but in numerical strength she was still below her potential enemies.

Traditionally, of course, there had been little need to protect the overseas Empire from attack by modern powers. The decisive fighting in the 1914–1918 war had taken place on the mainland of Europe and the Empire, with its contingents of extra manpower for the trenches in France, had been a reserve of strength. Such fighting as had taken place outside Europe had been mostly of an unsophisticated character.

In 1939, however, the British Empire was confronted by three hostile powers in three different areas; by Germany in Europe, by Italy in the Middle East and by Japan in the Far East. To take on just one of these enemies would be a formidable task. To take on two at once would place the Empire in extreme danger. To take on all three would be to invite disaster. The only mitigation would be the support of the other great imperialist country, France.

The fact that the power calculation was rarely made in such terms illustrates a further weakness in the imperial structure, a fatal weakness. The failure to make it sprang in part from a vague idea that the British 'always won.' Apart from the struggle with Irish nationalism, the British Empire had been undefeated in major war since the 18th century. But it was not just that undoubtable psychological fact. The fatal weakness was that the preservation of the Empire was simply not the prime aim of British policy. In the final analysis, British interests depended not on the world-wide Empire but upon the continent of Europe. The actual declaration of war came not because of any threat to the Empire but because Germany had chosen to attack the Central European country of Poland. There appears to have been absolutely no consultation between Britain and the dominions before the British pledged themselves to support Poland's integrity. In terms of strict imperial advantage, it was nothing but lunacy for a hard-pressed Empire to meddle in Central European frontier problems which did not affect it. But, of course, the British were not thinking in terms of imperial advantage. To some extent they were swayed by the consideration of preventing Germany from becoming too powerful lest, at some stage in the future, she might become a threat to British interests but that in 1939 was only a speculative consideration. The German leader, Adolf Hitler, had written and spoken most generously about his ambitions; never, though, except in the marginal case of the expropriated German colonies had he posed any threat to Britain or the Empire. The emotional steam behind the war was less the interests of the British Empire than a British dislike of the nature of Hitler's regime and sympathy for the victims of his aggression. Liberalism was more important to the British than imperialism. Ironically the actual declaration of war which precipitated the fall of the imperial structure came under a Prime Minister, Neville Chamberlain, who was a son of the great Joseph Chamberlain, the virtual inventor 50 years earlier of the concept of the British Empire as a political entity. 'It is an evil thing we are fighting,' said Neville Chamberlain in his first wartime broadcast. The King-Emperor wrote in his diary: '. . . the country is calm, firm & united behind its leaders, resolved to fight until Liberty & Justice are once again safe in the World.'

Apart from half-hearted approaches to Italy, there had been little attempt to detach from each other the three potential enemies of Britain and the Empire. Nor had there been much attempt to construct reliable alliances. Britain did, in fact, declare war in alliance with France, whose interests were basically similar to her own, but the French were lukewarm about the enterprise and militarily as ill-prepared as the British. It was generally assumed that if there were a war in the Far East with Japan, the United States would also be engaged but no Anglo–American treaty existed. Some attempt was made to secure an alliance with the Soviet Union but the approaches were so weak that the Soviet leader, Joseph Stalin, decided his security would be better served by joining up with Hitler; Stalin took a colder view than the British of the way to maintain his power.

So for non-imperial reasons, the British entered a war in which they had nothing to gain and an Empire to lose. Among leading politicians, only David Lloyd George, who had seen more closely than anyone else how close the British Empire had come to defeat in 1917, cast doubt upon the enterprise.

The declaration of war by Britain in 1939 was sufficient to involve all the colonies. There was no consultation with the colonial peoples and, indeed, no machinery existed through which they could have been consulted. As in 1914, the proclamation in London was sufficient to involve the remotest tribesman who had never heard of Warsaw. Such, however, was British prestige that in most of the colonies the process was taken for granted. So far as the articulate minorities among the colonial peoples considered the merits of the war, they favoured it. The German regime, with its emphasis upon the 'Nordic' race, was unattractive to them and they were happy to fight against it. The main exception was the Arabs who, over the matter of Jewish settlement in Palestine, sometimes found the anti-Jewish character of German and Italian propaganda not unattractive. The exiled Mufti of Jerusalem worked actively with the Nazis.

The constitutional position of the dominions was less definite.

Both Australia and New Zealand went to war at the same moment as Great Britain, regarding themselves bound by the British declaration. Robert Menzies, the Australian Prime Minister, said in a broadcast to his people: 'It is my melancholy duty to inform you officially that, in consequence of a persistence by Germany in her invasion of Poland, Great Britain has declared war upon her and that, *as a result*, [author's italics] Australia is also at war'. Such prompt association with Britain sprang partly from motives of loyalty to the mother country but also from the knowledge that both Australia and New Zealand depended upon British support against the expansionist aims of Japan.

Canada struck a different note. Her Prime Minister, Mackenzie King, had long insisted that Canada would go to war only with the specific approval of her own parliament. Accordingly Canada remained at peace for a week after the British declaration until parliament could be assembled and there was some speculation about the possibility of her taking a non-belligerent position. But when her House of Commons met it decided unanimously in favour of war. The actual declaration came in a proclamation by George VI, acting as King of Canada upon the advice of his Canadian ministers.

In South Africa the Prime Minister, Hertzog, actually decided in favour of neutrality. On September 4, the day after the British declaration, he introduced a resolution into the Union parliament that 'the existing relations between the Union of South Africa and the various belligerent powers will, in so far as the Union is concerned, persist unchanged and continue as if no war is being waged.' But the Hertzog administration contained a pro-Commonwealth element led by Jan Smuts, Minister of Justice. A year earlier, when war had threatened between Britain and Germany over Czechoslovakia, the whole South African cabinet, including Smuts, had favoured neutrality. Now, however, Smuts introduced an amendment to Hertzog's resolution to the effect that 'relations with the German Reich should be severed' and that South Africa should 'continue its co-operation with its friends and associates in the British Commonwealth of Nations.' To the surprise of almost everyone, including Hertzog and Smuts themselves, the amendment was passed by 80 votes to 67. Hertzog then wanted to appeal to the electorate and asked the Governor-General, Sir Patrick Duncan, to dissolve parliament. Duncan (the first South African to hold his office) refused and Hertzog accordingly resigned. Smuts became Prime Minister and upon his advice South Africa declared war. As in 1914–1918 Smuts, one of the few South Africans interested in world affairs, went on to play a significant role in directing the Commonwealth war effort and ended up by helping to draft the United Nations charter. Within South Africa, however, opposition to the war persisted and moderate Boer nationalists of the Hertzog type combined with fanatical extremists in a new, definitely anti-Commonwealth Nationalist Party which was to win the first post-war election. Smuts's apparent victory of September 4, 1939, contained the seeds of disaster for his policies because it enabled the Boer extremists to gain control of the opposition.

The remaining dominion, Ireland, with her republican-style constitution, was still formally linked with the Commonwealth for purposes of external relations. But her Prime Minister, Eamonn De Valera, immediately proclaimed neutrality and both British and Germans recognised her status, even though bases in southern Ireland would have been of utility in the battle against German submarines. The six Protestant counties in the north were, of course, bound by the British declaration and entered the war with enthusiasm; but because of the strong Catholic minority in the counties, the British did not attempt to apply conscription in Northern Ireland as they did in the rest of the United Kingdom.

Thus the self-governing dominions proved two things by their actions in September 1939. Australia, Canada, New Zealand and the Smuts faction in South Africa proved that considerable reserves of loyalty to the British connection still existed. The dominions, generally, were content to associate themselves with the British cause. At the same time, however, the procedures in Canada, South Africa and Ireland showed how in the supreme issue of war and peace the British Commonwealth was no longer automatically united.

In India the position in some respects was even more strange. Since 1919 the Indian Empire had existed as a distinct international entity. She had signed the Versailles Treaty and joined the League of Nations. Whether or not she should be bound automatically by a British declaration was doubtful both legally and morally. There was at least a case for arguing that she should, if only as a formality, make her own separate declaration of war. Also she had a vigorous political life, with recognised national leaders, and an elected central legislature; there was a moral case for consulting public opinion before making a declaration. Constitutionally, however, the control of foreign affairs lay with the Viceroy, Lord Linlithgow, and his council. Linlithgow did not declare war on behalf of India; he just announced that 'war has broken out between His Majesty and Germany.' The process was therefore as automatic as it had been in 1914. Nor was it just a token declaration; units of the Indian army had already been sent to the Middle East and to Singapore to fight for the British Empire. The leading Indian nationalist, Jawaharlal Nehru, was bitterly resentful, as were all his Congress associates. 'The idea of a great country like India being treated as a chattel and her people utterly and contemptuously ignored was bitterly resented,' he wrote five years later. 'Was all the struggle and suffering of the past twenty years to count for nothing? Were the Indian people to shame the land from which they sprang by quietly submitting to this disgrace and humiliation? . . . One man, and he a foreigner and a representative of a hated system, could plunge four hundred millions of human beings into war without the slightest reference to them.'

On the actual merits of the war, the Indian Congress Party was inclined to agree with Britain. That is except for the pacifist Gandhi who thought force should not be met by force; he wrote a letter to Hitler asking him to call off the invasion of Poland. The prevailing Congress view, though, was that German Nazism was even worse than British imperialism and should be resisted by force. Nehru, in particular, took a close interest in world politics and was as opposed to Hitler as any European left-wing intellectual. What Congress found difficulty in stomaching was a war fought, according to British propaganda, for 'democracy' being conducted in India upon autocratic lines. If power were handed immediately to the Indian politicians, they would co-operate with the British as independent allies. The British, to try to keep the situation under control, were rapidly driven into the position of promising self-government immediately after the war if only the Indians would for the moment keep quiet. As practically every outside observer during the late 1930s had commented, the British Raj could not survive a war. Linlithgow's declaration on September 3, 1939, was the last exercise on a major matter of that British sovereignty which had bound India since the decay of the Moghuls 150 years earlier. It is odd that this virtual suicide should have resulted from a dispute about the frontiers of Poland.

Because of the British attitude, the Congress ministries in the provinces all resigned office and the administration went back to the Indian Civil Service. During the first six months of hostilities, the 'phoney war' period, India seemed momentarily to have slipped back to an Edwardian calm. There was some expansion of the army and a development of war industries but the war seemed remote. The machinery of government, the pomp of New Delhi and Simla proceeded as automatically as dinner being served on an ocean liner up to the moment of hitting an iceberg.

So far as it is possible to ascertain the immediate British war strategy, it was to hold Germany on the French border, avoid excessive bloodshed and hope for a European settlement when everyone had become tired of fighting. So long as Germany was being held in France, there could be some hope of Italy and Japan keeping out of the conflict.

As it happened, though, the Germans in a series of brilliant offensives managed to eliminate France from the war and secure control of the whole Western European mainland from Norway to Spain and to threaten the British homeland itself with invasion. Italy immediately declared war and attacked in the Middle East, seizing British Somaliland and posing threats to Egypt, Sudan and Kenya.

According to available evidence, it would have been possible in this crisis for the British to have come to terms with Hitler. They would have abdicated their concern with the European mainland and acquiesced in Hitler's primary purpose of expanding eastwards. Hitler, on his side, would have underwritten the worldwide British Empire. In such partnership Great Britain and Germany could have dominated the world. Despite the imminent danger to the homeland, the British hardly considered such a course of action. Any minister who had proposed it would, in the mood of the summer of 1940, have been instantly ejected from office. Instead under a new and belligerent Prime Minister, Winston Churchill, the British resolved to continue the war on their own. There was no serious hope, without allies, of defeating Germany and Italy; the decision to go on was an ethical one and demonstrated how the British political system was unsuited, save in temporary and accidental circumstances, for the maintenance of an Empire.

Churchill had been among the most active opponents of Indian self-government but, as early as August, 1940, so urgent was the need to win Indian support, his government promised that the post-war constitution of India should be determined by an elected constituent assembly. Almost unnoticed in the press of events, the British thus abdicated their claim to legislate for India and it was Churchill, of all people, who was in charge. At almost the same moment, the British parliament passed, too, the first Colonial Development and Welfare Act which converted £10 million of old loans to the colonies into gifts and authorised the further expenditure of £5 million a year of United Kingdom taxpayers' money on development schemes. For the rest of the war, colonial self-government advanced at a faster rate than ever before. The combination of war propaganda about 'democracy' with the acceleration of economic development and the recruiting of troops led nevitably to a broadening of government. Examples were Jamaica which acquired full adult suffrage and the Gold Coast which was allowed its first African representation in the legislature. No actual transfer of power took place but the pace was towards local control.

Although preservation of the Empire had not taken absolute priority in the policy of the Government, Churchill said he had no intention of giving it up and directed much of his war strategy on trying to hold it. 'I have not become the First Minister of the Crown in order to preside over the liquidation of the British Empire,' he declared. Had the Germans successfully invaded the United Kingdom, Churchill intended that the war should continue to be prosecuted from the remainder of the Empire, with Canada as the seat of leadership. (The King, though, despite his position of sovereign of a world-wide Empire, intended to remain in Britain even if there were a German occupation. A man of duty, King George VI felt that in the last resort the British were his people more than any others of his subjects and that his place was with them.)

After the autumn of 1940, and the beating back of German air

'Seek ye first the political kingdom'. Kwame Nkrumah of the Gold Coast (Ghana) on his release from prison, 1950. He was immediately appointed head of the government

Home after 34 years. Hastings Banda of Nyasaland (Malawi)

attacks, an invasion of Britain ceased to be such an immediate threat. Hitler appeared to fear getting bogged down in fighting the British while his real ambitions were to the east. Under Churchill's vigorous leadership, the British built up their war industries and armed forces but the prospect of re-entering Western Europe was a remote one; the main British attack upon Germany before 1944 was from the air. Land fighting from 1940 to 1944 was based mainly upon imperial considerations, especially upon the Middle East. The most famous British formation of the war, the 8th Army, won its reputation in battles swaying backwards and forwards over the desert between Egypt and the Italian colony of Libya. So much significance did the Churchill administration attach to Egypt and the Suez Canal that late in 1940, when invasion of the homeland was still an immediate peril, the United Kingdom defences were denuded of tanks for the benefit of the desert army. The Mediterranean being closed for the safe passage of British shipping, troops and equipment had to go all the way around southern Africa to reach the war zone. Even after the British had acquired powerful allies in the United States and the Soviet Union, the Middle East continued as a major theatre of war.

The big success in the Middle East was the defeat of Italy. During 1941 a British offensive recaptured British Somaliland and went on to conquer Italian Somaliland and Mussolini's prize of Ethiopia, which he had seized from its local African dynasty five years earlier. There was some talk among British officials on the spot of turning Ethiopia into a permanent British protectorate rather than returning her to independence under the Emperor Haile Selassie (who had spent his exile in Britain). Had this been the First World War instead of the Second, Haile Selassie might well have never seen his throne again but now the climate of both British and international opinion was against imperial expansion. Haile Selassie did at first find British interference in his administration irksome but the idea of adding Ethiopia to the British Empire was never more than a passing shadow of an ambition. The Italian colony, Libya, did fall for a time under British control but this was always recognised as temporary and in 1951 it was set up as an independent kingdom.

Momentarily, in 1941, the British had managed to place the whole Horn of Africa and its hinterland under a single political authority. Unfortunately, the opportunity was not taken to rationalise the frontiers, which related more to old carve-ups

P

between European interlopers than to the natural divisions of the local people. In particular it would have prevented future trouble if the Somali section of Kenya, which ethnically and geographically has nothing to do with the rest of the country, had been added to former Italian Somaliland.

The campaigns in the Middle East and Africa, including the brilliant conquest of Ethiopia, would have been difficult or impossible to run without Empire and Commonwealth support. South Africa was an essential staging post for supplies. The South African whites, too, despite their political divisions, managed to supply troops on a generous scale; their Prime Minister, Smuts, had such seniority and experience that Churchill would listen to him as he listened to few others. In 1941 Smuts was given the rank of Field Marshal; whether this was supposed to be in the British army or the South African army or both was not clear. The King conferred the rank on the advice of the London government but Smuts wore the uniform of it while acting as South African Commander-in-Chief. The Indian Army, too, was prominent in the Middle East, its battalions being closely brigaded with British troops and its officers still predominantly British. The Australians and New Zealanders also fought in the Middle East but they were mostly withdrawn after war began with Japan; from 1942 to 1944 the British Minister of State in the Middle East was the Australian, Richard Casey, whose career illustrated how flexible the dominion system could be. He was variously a member of the Australian Cabinet, a British minister and Governor of Bengal. In the African colonies there was for the first time a substantial enlistment of African troops; the enlarged knowledge of the world such troops obtained and the propaganda that they were fighting for 'democracy' was to prove to be a powerful ingredient in the African nationalism which arose immediately after the war.

The strategic scene changed abruptly when, in June 1941, Hitler embarked upon his grand enterprise of invading the Soviet Union. Churchill, despite his long record of anti-Communism, instantly declared for the Soviet side. From the point of view of preserving the Empire, the Soviet Union was far from an ideal ally. Her administration was dedicated to the ultimate aim of upsetting established government throughout the world and replacing it on principles laid down by Marx, Lenin and Stalin. She had habitually criticised British imperialism and had welcomed any form of opposition to it. Nazi Germany would have been much the better ally had preserving the Empire been the primary British objective. At the same time, though, the Russian autocrat, Stalin, was a realist whose purpose was to defend and consolidate his regime. For a while he had been an ally of the Germans but now they had turned upon him he was happy to work with the British. He did not meddle in the Empire—it was to be a decade and more before Marxism was to appear as a discernible force in the colonies.

Actually the first result of Anglo–Russian co-operation was a neo-imperialist venture to occupy Iran (Persia) with the aim of eliminating German influence. Russian troops occupied the north of the country and British the south. The Shah was exiled to Mauritius where he continued to be treated with royal honours. The Governor, Sir Bede Clifford, made an enormous silk flag to fly over his residence. The local military band did not know the Persian national anthem so Sir Bede, thinking of the supposed Persian attachment to opium, ordered it to play 'When the poppies bloom again.' The Shah's occupied capital, Teheran, was to be the scene of the first meeting between Churchill, Stalin and the United States President, F. D. Roosevelt.

A somewhat similar episode took place in Iraq, though involving Britain alone. Under the treaty of 1930, which had ended the British mandate, Iraq was bound to accept a British garrison and to assist Britain in war. In 1939 Iraq had accordingly broken off relations with Germany. Nevertheless Iraqi nationalist sentiments, combined with resentment over Zionist immigration into neighbouring Palestine, had awakened a strong pro-German feeling. An army revolt in 1941 set up an anti-British government which set siege to the Royal Air Force. The British, narrowly anticipating the arrival of German forces, sent a small military expedition which, without undue difficulty, quelled the revolt and set up a more acceptable government. In 1943 Iraq formally entered the war on the British side. Iraq territory formed an essential supply route for the supply of British and, later, American materials to the Soviet Union.

Zionism in Palestine had further exacerbated relations between Britain and Egypt. Despite the presence of enormous British forces she remained a constant political embarrassment. On the British declaration of war in 1939 she had obeyed the treaty and broken off relations with Germany but she had proved awkward over Italy. For weeks after the Italians had declared war, Italian diplomats had remained freely in Cairo and it had taken the most vigorous British pressure to get them out.

The Zionists themselves, of course, hated Hitler who had persecuted their people so cruelly and was moving towards the mass murder of the 'final solution.' But this was not entirely to the British advantage for the German persecutions had sharpened yet further the Zionist determination to establish a proper Jewish state in Palestine. The British were still thinking in terms of holding a balance between Jewish immigration and the local Arab population; their attitude was in part an instinctive 'divide and rule' (although a correct calculation in terms of cold power might have been to plump either for one side or the other rather than antagonise both) and in part a genuine bewilderment over how rightly to interpret the inconsistencies of the Balfour Declaration. Even the formation of a Jewish army to fight the Germans and Italians caused years of bickering, the Zionists wanting it to have autonomous status and the British wanting to integrate it with their own forces. Fanatical Jews—unrepresentative of mainstream Zionism—indulged in a terrorism which culminated in the assassination of the British Minister of State in the Middle East, Lord Moyne, a formal Colonial Secretary. This event caused great horror among the British for assassination had never been a normal tactic of opponents of their rule. It stimulated a slight but unpleasant tendency towards anti-Semitism* among the rank and file of British forces in Palestine.

By the autumn of 1941 the British Empire stood in mortal peril. It was far from certain that the Soviet Union could indefinitely withstand the German onslaught. Even with the bulk of the German army engaged in Russia, the British had experienced the utmost difficulty in maintaining their power in the Middle East. If the Soviet Union were beaten, Hitler could mop up the Middle East at his leisure.

If the war were to spread to Japan and the Far East, the British Empire, already fully extended, might well start to lose territory.

---

* The author here and elsewhere in this book has endeavoured to maintain a distinction between anti-Zionism and anti-Semitism.

# CHAPTER 11

# The greatest disaster

By 1941 it had long been the settled policy of Japan to try to extend her political influence over all eastern Asia. She had little in the way of an idealistic concept of 'liberating' territories from European control but rather the intention of constructing for herself an Empire on similar lines to those of the European powers, especially her neighbour, Russia. Her main struggle had been with the decaying giant of China over which, so far as can be ascertained, she wished to assert much the same kind of suzerainty as the British were about to relinquish over India. It was necessary for the paramountcy of Japan to drive European colonisers out of the region and to replace them with Japanese colonisers; also the British possessions in Malaya and Burma, the Dutch East Indies, French Indo-China and the American colony of the Philippines (scheduled for independence in 1946) were obvious prey in their own right. More remotely, Japan looked too towards bringing India and Australasia within her sphere. She had modern, experienced forces, expertly led and backed by a civil administration which directed the life of the country according to military requirements.

Although the Japanese imperial forces had enjoyed 40 years of success in every campaign they had undertaken, including one against a European power, Russia, there remained among the British a disinclination to believe that any Asiatic troops could be a match for the white man. Indeed the existence of the British Empire was inexplicable save on such an assumption. While the possibility of a Japanese attack when Britain was already engaged in Europe and the Middle East did cause concern, the full consequences were unforeseen.

From their own point of view the Japanese might have been well advised to confine their onslaught to the British Empire and not involve the United States. Although there had been some tentative contacts, including visits of American warships to Singapore, there existed no certainty at all that the Americans would declare war in support of the British Empire in the Far

East. In the summer of 1940 the British had been so concerned at the possibility of facing a Japanese attack on their own that they had attempted appeasement by closing the road from Burma along which supplies flowed to Nationalist China. The closure of the road angered the Americans, who were anxious to help the Chinese in every way except actually fighting for them, but the Churchill administration had calculated that at that moment appeasement of Japan would pay better than a gesture to the United States. Then in 1941 Churchill sought to involve the Americans by making a unilateral declaration that Britain would treat a Japanese attack on American territory as if it were an attack on her own. No reciprocal American declaration was forthcoming. There were just desultory staff talks between British, Americans and Dutch with no definite commitments.

As it turned out, though, the over-confidence of the Axis powers caused the war to start on the best possible basis for Britain. Japan, on December 7, 1941, launched brilliantly planned attacks on the British Empire and the United States simultaneously, destroying the American fleet at Pearl Harbour and making landings in Malaya. Moreover, Germany at once declared war upon the United States, a gratuitous action on Hitler's part since he was not bound to do so by treaty. His calculation must have been that the United States could do him no more harm in Europe than she was already doing by supplying Britain with war materials. Fully occupied in the Far East, the Americans would not also fight in Europe.

Thus the result of German and Japanese actions was to draw together the United States, the Soviet Union and the British Empire into an alliance of such potential strength as to be sure of victory, provided it avoided a knock-out in the early stages. To Britain the value of the alliance was only military; for the political purpose of preserving the British Empire it was unsuitable. The British entered into intimate relations with partners who were profoundly antipathetic to the imperial spirit, or at least to the classical form of the imperial spirit. It was quite different from the former Anglo–French alliance in which both parties, when it came to the point, had recognised automatically the right of each other to possess an empire. Moreover, in military power and resources the other two members of the alliance were superior, or about to become superior, to the British Empire. That this should so plainly have been so when, in fact, the British Empire and Commonwealth contained population and territory greater than those of the other two put together, is a further indication of the flaws which existed in British imperial power.

The early Japanese onslaught was worse than the British had dreamed possible. Up to the very last moment there persisted a staggering complacency among most of the organs of defence and administration. Implicit faith was attached to the fortress of Singapore which for 20 years had been constructed to meet the contingency of a Japanese attack. The round of bureaucracy and social life continued in its accustomed rhythm; the Japanese were able to drop bombs on a Singapore still brightly illuminated at night. Because after the fall of France in 1940 they had been able to seize French Indo-China, the Japanese had a base from which it was easy to invade Malaya. While their troops, carefully trained for such work, were hacking their way through the Malayan jungles, there were still daily tea dances at the Raffles Hotel, Singapore. It was as if the British were afraid to wake up from their imperial dream.

When Japanese attack had become imminent, Churchill had weakened British defences in the west by sending out to the Far East the latest British battleship, *Prince of Wales*, which had just been brought into service. With her went the battle cruiser *Repulse*. These two vessels were among the most powerful in the world and symbolised the sure shield traditionally provided by the Royal Navy for British dominions and colonies. A brief attack by Japanese aircraft sank them both in the Straits of Malacca. The blow to prestige was devastating. It had come because the British command had neglected what should have been the obvious precaution of providing the great ships with air cover. It appeared that Japan had vanquished the Royal Navy. On Australia and New Zealand, in particular, the disaster had a traumatic effect. Hitherto they had always sheltered complacently behind the Royal Navy, confident that the distant homeland of Britain was a sufficient support for their defence. In a moment this complacency was shattered and with it the old military unity of the Commonwealth; to both dominions, the United States became at least as valuable an ally as the British.

With the American fleet also crippled by the Pearl Harbour attack, the Japanese forces ranged freely and rapidly across British, American and Dutch possessions. Hong Kong fell on Christmas Day, 1941, and Manila, capital of the Philippines, eight days later. In London, though, it was still assumed that Singapore was a secure bastion and 30,000 more British and Empire troops poured in to reinforce the garrison. Churchill ordered that if Singapore were attacked, it should be held to the last man; the calculation was that Singapore was capable of withstanding a prolonged siege and of providing the foothold for an ultimate Anglo–American counter-offensive. But the fortifications of Singapore were directed towards the sea, an attack from the land side being regarded as unlikely or impossible because of the difficulty in getting through the Malayan jungles. Most of the big guns were fixed in concrete so they could not be turned towards the land. The specially-trained Japanese troops made their way through the Malayan peninsula, the British troops, unprepared for jungle fighting, simply falling back before them towards Singapore itself.

On February 15, 1942, Singapore capitulated with a British garrison of 100,000 men, most of whom had not fired a shot. Instead of being another Malta, Singapore had proved to be a trap. In the actual circumstances of the moment there was no sane alternative to surrender. Continued resistance would merely have enabled the Japanese to shell and bomb the place to pieces; moreover, water was on the point of exhaustion.

This was the worst single military defeat the British Empire ever suffered. The effects reverberated through India and the colonies. Hitherto the British had been regarded as invincible on their own ground—the fortitude with which they had defended the United Kingdom in 1940 had aroused the admiration of even the most nationalist of the Indian and colonial politicians. Now they had been driven to abject surrender by an Asiatic army in what they had claimed to be a supreme stronghold. British authority had rested more upon prestige than upon any other single factor. Now the Japanese had ripped away the invisible cloak. Churchill described the fall of Singapore as 'the greatest disaster to British arms which our history records.'

The Japanese went on to occupy Burma and to pose threats to India, Australia and New Zealand. They mopped up the Philippines and the Dutch East Indies. Burma proved to be conclusively lost to the British Empire; the British officials escaped to Simla and went through the pantomime of conducting a government in exile but they were never to get back their authority.

Only to a most limited extent were the Japanese welcomed as liberators and they themselves by their actions did little to encourage popular support for their occupation. Despite vague talk of a 'South-East Asia Co-Prosperity Sphere,' the main effect of

Japanese conquest was to substitute one imperial power for another. In India, especially, the dominant Congress Party politicians had long supported the Chinese against the Japanese and had no test for the semi-Fascist nature of the Japanese state. A Japanese-sponsored 'Indian National Army,' formed in Burma, attracted only the most limited response. In Burma itself the nationalists at first accepted office as a Japanese puppet government but soon turned against the invader. There was little disposition for Asia to arise on Japan's behalf or to fight for her against counter-attack from the United States and the west. Nevertheless the Japanese blows permanently crippled the British capacity and will to govern. Captured British civilians and soldiers, subject to harsh and humiliating treatment, had difficulty in recovering their former pose as lords of creation. The humbler virtues of liberalism and humanitarianism acquired popularity as the proper contrast to Japanese rigour.

The association between the British Empire and the United States immediately became an exceptionally close one. The leaders of the two countries associated on intimate terms and arrangements were made for joint Anglo–American command of fighting troops. It was at this stage a partnership of equals, the greater potential resources of the Americans being matched by the greater immediate fighting capacity of the British. Very early the Americans took the crucial decision, which suited the British, to concentrate first upon Europe and North Africa and to leave the main counter-attack against Japan until Germany had been defeated. In return the Americans were in a position to influence British policy. Exactly what were the war aims of the United States from 1941 to 1945, beyond a desire to crush the regimes which had challenged it, is hard to discern. Certainly, though, American aims did not include the restoration of British imperial power. American philosophy was based upon Abraham Lincoln's phrase of 'government of the people, by the people, and for the people' and the weight of American influence was in favour of that method of administration being extended in the British Empire, especially in India. 'Quit fighting a war to hold the empire together,' demanded *Life* magazine in 1942. Moreover, the Americans were opposed to the tariff arrangements which hindered trade between the Empire and the rest of the world.

The principal and immediate American influence was exerted upon British policy in India. As early as March, 1942, Churchill reported to the King-Emperor that Roosevelt, the American

President, was pressing for an immediate pledge of dominion status to India. The Americans were embarrassed to find themselves in alliance with the largest subject territory in the world; over the preceding years Nehru, Gandhi and the Congress had become well known to the American public and were regarded as the Indian national leaders. The very word 'Congress' was potent in American ears; much less was known about the Congress Party's rival, Jinnah's Moslem League. The British, reliant upon virtually free gifts of American supplies under the 'lend-lease' system and eager to secure the fullest American participation in the European and Mediterranean war theatres, were obviously in a weak position to withstand Roosevelt's views, even if other circumstances had not been pushing them in the same direction.

At a more local level, the arrival of thousands of American servicemen in India was an upsetting influence upon the Raj. Their informal manners, their disregard for the hierarchical nature of British–Indian society presented the white man in India in a new and less awesome light. By going about without sun helmets and not suffering sunstroke they made even the headgear of the British look silly. Indian intellectuals and civil servants mixing with them acquired a broader outlook upon the world. Hitherto the British, either as friends or opponents, had tended to bound the entire Indian horizon. Now they became, instead, just one white country among several—and one which had lost Singapore, Burma and Malaya to an Asiatic enemy.

The pledge, given in the near-panic conditions of August 1940, to allow the Indians to elect their own constituent assembly can be seen in retrospect to have marked the watershed in British policy. For the first time the British had explicitly renounced their claim to determine the future of India. Both the Congress and the Moslem League had, however, rejected the offer. The Congress had hoped that by holding out it might acquire immediate self-government. The Moslem League (committed since March 1940 to the aim of a separate Moslem state, Pakistan) had made the unacceptable stipulation of equal Hindu and Moslem representation in any central government. On the breakdown of negotiations Gandhi had launched a new civil disobedience campaign. It had been largely his own private affair and based upon purely pacifist opposition to the war. Most other Congress leaders had refused to co-operate—it had been an indication of the complexity of the British–Indian relationship that the Congress, as a whole, had not wished to take advantage of the imminent threat of German invasion of the United Kingdom—and the campaign had been the weakest Gandhi had ever run. Nevertheless both Gandhi and the other Congress leaders had been interned.

By 1942 India was faced with invasion herself, from victorious Japan. The imperative need to attract full Indian participation in the war, coupled with American pressure, caused the British Cabinet to make a new offer. This time Churchill openly and definitively broke with his opinions of the past to accept a detailed scheme for Indian independence. He regretted what he was doing but regarded it as desirable for his overriding aim of winning the war. Under the scheme the Indian nationalist leaders were immediately to join the Viceroy's council. After the war the provincial legislatures would elect a constituent assembly which would negotiate a treaty with Great Britain to settle the future form of Indian government. The Moslem provinces were to be allowed the right to contract out. The right to secede from the British Commonwealth and Empire was explicitly stated.

To present the scheme to the Indian leaders, who had been let out of prison just before the Japanese war, Churchill selected a minister who above all others would be likely to attract their confidence. He was Stafford Cripps, a successful lawyer and a left-wing Christian Socialist. Just before the war he had actually been expelled from the British Labour Party for being too far on the left. Cripps represented revolt against established society within Britain. He was, too, a vegetarian. He and the Indian leaders could talk to each other in the same language. (That such a man should have been serving as Churchill's ministerial colleague was evidence of how far the war had disrupted the ordinary pattern of British administration.)

Cripps arrived in India and communicated the proposals to the Indian leaders before giving them in detail to the Viceroy. He also sought advice from the United States representative in Delhi, Louis Johnson. Such ignoring of the customary channels antagonised the British officials on the spot and alarmed the King-Emperor in London but it very nearly brought results. Nehru was strongly tempted to accept the offer but was overborn by Gandhi. On April 10 the National Congress formally rejected it, the ground being that the proposed Viceroy's council would not immediately have the full powers of a dominion cabinet.

The Congress Party, on Gandhi's proposition, went on to pass the 'Quit India' resolution calling upon the British to surrender all control immediately. This, with the Japanese poised to invade, was not one of Congress's more acceptable actions and, with American acquiescence, the British locked the Congress leaders up again. The Congress calculation, so far as the decision had been made upon a reasoned basis at all, was that if the British forthwith quit India the Japanese would be less eager to invade. It was not a calculation which appealed to London or Washington. There followed what amounted to an armed revolt, with riots and outbreaks of sabotage right across India, but it lacked effective leadership or proper weapons. At a cost of 900 lives it was suppressed but it served as a warning of what greater disorder might arise in the future.

Churchill thought of sending his own successor-designate, Anthony Eden, out to India as the new Viceroy to replace Linlithgow, who had been administratively efficient but politically passive. Eden was Foreign Secretary and, as such, at the heart of British politics; he would have been the most senior politician ever seconded to rule India. He himself was willing to take the post but the King opposed his going on the ground that he could not be spared from London and would be wasted in Delhi. Churchill tried to get around this difficulty by suggesting that Eden, using the resources of air travel, should combine the Viceroyalty of India with membership of the London cabinet. This interesting constitutional notion was also opposed by the King and Churchill gave in. He chose instead, as the penultimate Viceroy, Field Marshal Sir Archibald Wavell, who had been Commander-in-Chief of India. It was the first time a Commander-in-Chief had stepped up to Viceroy and, indeed, the first time a professional soldier of high rank had ever been given the office at all. Wavell was a soldier of unusual sensibility, by no means inept at political matters, but inevitably his appointment suggested that the British were putting India on ice until the end of the war. A soldier had been made caretaker until the Japanese had been defeated and then the imperial structure would be dismantled. There could be no going back from the salient principles of the Cripps offer.

Further, what had become potentially available for India could not in logic be withheld from India's neighbours—Ceylon, Burma and Malaya, the more especially as the two latter were occupied by the Japanese.

The changed spirit brought by the Japanese war also affected Australia and New Zealand which, hitherto, had been emotionally the closest to Britain of all the self-governing dominions. With the

Americans now their ally, their horizons widened. Australia, in particular, now acquired for the first time a foreign policy of her own and by the closing years of the war she was regarding herself less as a satellite of Great Britain than as a leader of and spokesmen for the smaller countries which had gathered around the grand alliance of Britain, the United States and the Soviet Union. Australia provided the first chairman of the United Nations general assembly and her representatives resisted the authority claimed by the great powers, including Britain, in the security council.

Within Britain herself, too, the grand alliance had its influence. From 1941 to 1945 the alliance with the Soviet Union acquired a remarkable public popularity. As the stories spread of the gargantuan scale of the fighting in Russia, the British acquired a feeling of guilt about their own relatively passive posture. Since very little was known about the Russians it was easy to idolise them. King George VI presented a sword of honour to what was then called Stalingrad; the biggest crowds of wartime London gathered to look at it in Westminster Abbey. Few saw incongruity in such a gift from such a donor, displayed at the shrine of St. Edward the Confessor, being sent to an atheistical regime which repudiated the leading principles upon which the British Empire was based. While anti-imperialism at this period was by no means the most prominent of the Soviet principles it was difficult for anyone to see virtue in those principles without losing faith in the traditional conception of the British Empire. The process was almost exactly opposite to what had happened in the 1914–1918 war; then the stress of martial emotion had strengthened imperial patriotism. This time, however, the posters in the war factories exhorted workers to higher production not for the sake of King and Empire but on behalf of unpronounceable strongholds somewhere east of the Carpathians.

The alliance with the Americans was closer and therefore more realistic. The American social system, language and methods of public administration were so similar to those of metropolitan Britain that many British people tended to regard the United States as a bit of the Empire which had, unaccountably, got broken off. In the months before the invasion of France, American troops by the hundred thousand poured into Britain and Northern Ireland. There were some instances of friction, the British regarding the Americans as people who had shirked their responsibilities in the fight against Nazism, the Americans regarding themselves as saviours. The American disregard for British middle class notions about leadership and the 'civilising mission' must have exerted at least a negative effect.

Moreover, at the high political level the Americans tended during the war to trust the Russians nearly as much as they trusted the British. Roosevelt and Stalin could share in common a suspicion about the imperialist designs of the perfidious British; indeed there is reason to suppose that it was suspicion of the British which led Roosevelt so readily to accept Russian hegemony over eastern Europe.

Apart from the alliance there were other wartime influences at work upon the British people. It was a total war requiring involvement by the whole community. The propagandists did not regard it as sufficient to say all this effort was required just to defeat the German Reich. The notion was also propagated that in fighting Germany the people were, in some unexplained way, fighting for the enhancement of their own living standards. Fostered especially by left-wing and Socialist advocates, it took a grip on the minds of people. Soldiers in hutments, housewives rising at dawn to attend the factory, airmen blasting German cities were persuaded that their efforts would bring about not just victory but also a new world. The feeling was the more powerful because the promises of 'a land fit for heroes' made at the end of the previous war had been far from fulfilled. Depression in the older, basic industries between the wars had brought about a continual high level of unemployment, ranging between one and three millions. The reaction to the failure of the 1918 pledges was not to distrust such undertakings but to be determined that this time they should be properly carried out. The reward for the wartime ordeal should be a society ordered on principles more efficient and more just than in the past. The British, ordinarily a conservative people, swung into a mood favouring radical change. The Labour Party leaders who were to benefit from this mood were not, on the whole, men who had paid much attention to the Empire in the development of their policies; of the Labour Party politicians who had seriously considered the Empire, many were actively anti-imperialist. To most voters the Empire was either an irrelevance or a place where hardship had been suffered during war service. It appeared obvious that the Empire had not prevented the dole queues.

At the same time, though, there was little disposition to regard the Empire as a lost cause. The leading Labour Party spokesman on colonial affairs, Creech Jones, who later became Colonial

Secretary, was talking in terms of developing the colonies economically for the benefit of their inhabitants rather than of working for early independence. He thought—and this was a common view at the time—that South Africa would become the leading influence on the African continent. Harold Macmillan, who only 15 years later was to be Prime Minister presiding over the final dissolution of the Empire, served for a time during the war as Colonial Under-Secretary. While in this post he made, in June 1942, a long speech in the Commons in which he specifically repudiated the likelihood or the desirability of the colonies becoming independent. (He was talking specifically of the colonies, not India.) 'The war has shown us,' he said, 'certain inescapable facts of which we will learn the lesson. Self-government without security means nothing. Independence without defence is vain. The future of the world is in larger organisations and not in breaking it up into a number of small countries. It is in the light of these events that we should think of our future relationship with the colonies as a permanent and not a transitory thing.'

Most of the troops which defeated Germany in Europe were Russian and American. The British had managed, as they had not in 1914–1918, to conserve their manpower but, by 1945, the balance of power was such that they could no longer command the world. What Washington wanted and what Moscow wanted were the decisive influences. In the Far East the British re-entered the territories which Japan had conquered but, save possibly in Burma, this could not really be counted a British victory. Even apart from new nuclear devices, the Japanese faced certain defeat from the overwhelming American and Russian forces now free to concentrate on her.

The ending of the Second World War brought the British little feeling of triumph or elation. They were proud to have fought in it for longer than anyone else and reckoned that their cause had been good. But they had no sense of being conquerors. The prevailing public sentiment was relief that the ordeal was over, the predominant public wish was to reform internal United Kingdom institutions and the Labour Party was returned to power with an overwhelming majority. Churchill, the man who had determined not to preside over the dissolution of the British Empire, was swept from office in the moment of victory.

By 1945 the mainsprings of the British Empire were broken.

# CHAPTER 12

# The Labour Empire

ALTHOUGH nominally a victor, Great Britain found herself at the conclusion of the war of 1945 in a weaker position than in 1939. The trading mechanisms by which she had earned her livelihood had been shattered. She had sold overseas investments, run up debts and become dependent on United States assistance for the maintenance of an appropriate standard of living for her people at home. Many of her capital assets—from housing to industrial machinery—were worn out. Even the electricity supply was not working properly. The overriding determination of the public, which had for the first time returned a Labour Government to power, was to repair the damage and, further, to construct a society at home from which the worst hardships of the past would have been eliminated. The world-wide Commonwealth and Empire, so far as it attracted attention at all, was widely regarded as an irrelevance to the central problems. When it obtruded itself, it was regarded as a burden to be endured rather than as a glory to be enjoyed. Such countries as Palestine became objects of actual dislike.

The immediate obtrusion was the sub-continent of India. From having been the glory of the imperial crown it had turned into a chaotic entanglement from which everyone, or nearly everyone, wished to escape. In 1945 the wheels of the British Raj still creaked around. There was talk even of recruiting by competitive examination in Great Britain a further generation of the Indian Civil Service. As late as October, 1945, an Indian Army commission of inquiry, consisting of three British officers and one Indian, produced a report on post-war military organisation; it envisaged half the Indian army officers continuing to be British and one division of the Indian army being available for imperial service overseas. But few outside the administrative framework now shared such dreams. Despite the subsisting British bureaucracy, India lay in the real control of her own politicians—Gandhi, Nehru and Jinnah. Such was the rivalry between the majority National Congress and the minority Moslem League that the practical issue was how Britain could get out without

'Fifty per cent Jewish, fifty per cent Polish but one hundred per cent British'.
Roy Welensky of Central Africa

Harold Macmillan, the first British Prime Minister in office to visit black Africa, in a surf boat at Accra, Ghana

THE WIND OF CHANGE

Colonial Secretary Iain Macleod with the Tanganyika nationalist leader, Julius Nyerere

leaving anarchy behind. There was a limit to the period for which the crumbling administrative framework could be expected to endure. Many of the senior British officials were serving beyond the customary retiring age and were worn out by the combined effects of war and of nationalist agitation. During the six war years they had been allowed little or no home leave. The middle and lower ranks of the administration were almost entirely Indian and of the old élite body, the Indian Civil Service, half was now Indian. In the past Indian bureaucrats had been loyal to the British but now partly from conviction and partly with a view to their future careers they were coming to terms with the nationalist politicians. The army remained loyal for immediate purposes but the Royal Indian Navy, which had been established during the war, mutinied in February, 1946.

The only method of restoring British control would have been to land an army of many hundreds of thousands of men and to have purged the administration of anti-British elements, replacing them with clerks from Britain. Even without the pressure of American and world opinion, without the new United Nations, without the consideration that she had just fought a war in the name of self-determination, the British had neither the resources nor the will-power for such an operation. Had they attempted it, they might well have failed. After all, the tiny country of Ireland, next door to Britain, had successfully defied the British after the previous war. Nor was there any benefit, save imperial glory, that the British could have hoped to gain.

Even Winston Churchill, who during the 1930s had been the leading advocate of strong British rule over India, had changed his mind. As early as 1942 the King had recorded in his diary a conversation with him. 'He [Churchill] amazed me by saying that his colleagues & both, or all 3, parties in Parliament were quite prepared to give up India to the Indians after the war. He felt they had already been talked into giving up India. Cripps, the Press & U.S. public opinion have all contributed to make their minds up that our rule in India is wrong and always has been wrong for India. I disagree and have always said India has got to be governed, & this will have to be our policy.' By 1945 the King, too, was accepting that his dream of following his father's example and being crowned on Indian soil as Emperor of India would never be realised and that India would have to go her own way.

Any remaining hesitation the British might have had was eliminated by the election of the Labour Government. The new

Q

Prime Minister, Clement Attlee, could appear at first sight to be an insignificant man but he possessed to an unusual degree the capacity to make decisions and to stick to them. For reasons both of principle and of policy, Attlee determined that the British must quit India and quit as soon as possible.

The simple course would have been to have followed the lines of the wartime Cripps offer and to allow the Indians to elect a constituent assembly, to which power could have been handed over. Technical points about timing and procedure would have been the only ones requiring discussion. Such a straightforward line was, however, excluded by the bitterness of the conflicts between the Indian politicians. The Hindu-dominated National Congress wanted to take over the whole of British India. It had many Moslem members in its ranks and refused to agree that religious differences should any more be a consideration under Congress rule than they had been under the British. At the same time, though, the Moslem League, with its demand for a separate Moslem state 'Pakistan,' had consolidated its hold over most of the Moslem minority of the population. Almost until the last moment, Nehru and the Congress refused to admit the validity of the Moslem League's popularity—they insisted on regarding it as a temporary effervescence encouraged by the British for reasons of 'divide and rule.'

Immediately after the war the Viceroy, Wavell, held general elections for the central and provincial legislatures. Although these were conducted on the old, restricted franchise, the results showed beyond doubt that the Congress and the Moslem League between them controlled Indian public opinion. Wavell's next step, taken either in consultation with or on instructions from the Labour Cabinet in London, was to try to get Nehru and the Moslem leader, Jinnah, to serve together in a caretaker administration which would prepare a federal constitution to give Hindus and Moslems self-rule in their own provinces while defence and foreign policy were reserved to an all-India government. Despite intensive negotiation, including a visit by Nehru and Jinnah to London, where they met the King-Emperor, this scheme got nowhere. Jinnah was now coolly confident that if he held out long enough he would get an entirely sovereign Pakistan. Nehru was content to blame the difficulties on the past and present actions of the British.

During the summer of 1946 the enmity between the Hindus and the Moslems exploded into vicious riots, which by chain reaction spread right across the sub-continent. Hundreds or possibly thousands were murdered. India, clearly, had reached a condition of suppressed civil war and it was doubtful whether the British administration was capable of suppressing it for much longer.

Wavell's reaction to the failed negotiations and to the threat of anarchy was a military one. He thought in terms of ordered retreat. The British should steadily and inexorably withdraw their forces from India and leave it to the Indians themselves to fill the vacuum with what form of administration they could. The south of India should be the first to be evacuated and the north should be held temporarily as a stronghold for members of the British community. He drew up a detailed plan and presented it to London as the only workable policy remaining.

How much chaos Wavell's plan would have caused and whether it would have been greater or less than the chaos that actually did ensue a year later must be a matter for conjecture. He was certainly a humane man, an expert on India and working with the best intentions. Nevertheless the Cabinet in London refused to accept the plan, save as a possible emergency measure, and decided to recall him.

To be the new and last Viceroy, Attlee made a bold choice. He picked the 45-year-old Viscount Mountbatten of Burma. A cousin of the King and the husband of a millionairess, Mountbatten already had a remarkable record behind him. As a young man he had managed to combine the life of a socialite playboy with a devotion to the profession of naval officer. Early in the war he had been a successful destroyer captain and a film about his exploits had commanded wide public attention. Churchill had placed him in charge of Combined Operations—the commandos—in 1941 and two years later had exalted him to the high level of Supreme Allied Commander in South-East Asia. His substantive rank had then been only that of a naval captain but from his headquarters in Ceylon he had supervised the campaign in Burma and commanded British, American, Indian, Australian and New Zealand naval, land and air forces. He had drive, he could be ruthless and he was not unsympathetic to the general policies of the Attlee Government. Another of his leading characteristics was charm and a gift for persuasion; from a few people these qualities rebounded and he had enemies as well as many fervent admirers.

At the end of the war Mountbatten's purpose had been to revert to his regular rank and resume his ordinary naval career. In 1946 he had been selected to command a cruiser squadron. But it took little persuasion to get him to accept India. He was the first member of the Royal Family ever to become Viceroy—one of the curiosities of the British Empire, as compared with most empires in world history, was the limited extent to which the Royal Family had been concerned with acquiring or administering it. Queen Victoria had possessed few of the Roman or military qualifications which might have been held to be implicit in the title she assumed of Empress (imperatrix) of India. Mountbatten, however, was that statistical rarity, a royal person possessed of unusual talents. His royal birth was reckoned less a qualification for his office than an adventitious aid in his dealings with Indian princes.

His method in India had the ruthlessness commonly associated with him. Immediately on his appointment and before leaving England he decided that there must be a time limit, after which the British would leave. The time limit must be publicly announced. Only by presenting the Congress and Moslem League with an ultimatum would there be any hope of their coming to agreement. Mountbatten decided that the right time limit was 17 months ahead, June 1948. The Attlee Cabinet accepted his suggestions and sent him out to India with them as his mandate. It was not entirely dissimilar from Wavell's plan but it was conceived in political rather than military terms.

Mountbatten arrived in India in March, 1947, and came rapidly to the conclusion that swift partition was the only answer. Nehru at last agreed and, on the Viceroy's prompting, joined the Moslem League leaders in a temporary central government to prepare the split. Mountbatten's were rush tactics. In June, after three months in India, he announced, with the agreement of the Attlee Cabinet, that to wait until June, 1948, was too long. The date of withdrawal would be advanced to August 15, 1947. This left only three months for the creation of two new administrations, for dividing the armed forces and for defining the frontiers of the two new states. A British barrister, Sir Cyril Radcliffe, headed a commission which raced around to fix the exact boundaries; the Hindu and Moslem members of the commission often failed to agree and in the more difficult cases the awards were made by Radcliffe's casting vote. The treaties between the King-Emperor and the hundreds of princely states were unilaterally abrogated. Nominally the princes attained independent status but it was recognised by everybody that without British support they would fall inevitably either to Pakistan or to India. At Westminster, Attlee introduced on July 3 the India Independence Bill which, without opposition, was rushed through all its stages in one week. The Bill set up India and Pakistan as self-governing dominions, on the same lines as Canada and Australia, and deprived the King of his title as Emperor. It was recognised that dominion status could be only a temporary condition; once they had control of their own affairs, the two new countries would decide for themselves their form of government.

The new country of Pakistan, organised in such a hasty manner, consisted basically of the western Punjab and eastern Bengal, together with Baluchistan and Sind adjoining the Punjab. It was to contain about 80 million of the 400 million of the sub-continent's population. Between the Punjab section and the Bengal section lay a thousand miles of Indian territory. Even such elaborate frontiers were incapable of matching the Hindu–Moslem patchwork of population and, in the weeks before and after August 15, millions of people fled from their homes to seek refuge in territory that was to be of their own religion. The sub-continent boiled with resentment and, with no authority capable of checking it, the resentment led to massacre. Stories of atrocities spread from province to province, multiplying in horror as they were retold, and whole communities of Hindus and Moslems sought bloody revenge. Complete trainloads of refugees crossing the Punjab were murdered, men, women and children. Exactly how many died has never been properly computed—it certainly ran into hundreds of thousands and may well have been over a million. India suffered destruction on a scale similar to that which Europe had recently been undergoing through aerial bombardment, but the bitterness lasted for longer in India than it did in Europe.

The only hope of checking the tumult was to get properly constituted Indian and Pakistani administrations into power as soon as possible. Mountbatten pressed forward with his date of August 15 and the senior British civil servants, who felt as if the world were collapsing around them, worked night and day to preserve at least a skeleton bureaucracy for the new masters. It was not thus that they had imagined their careers ending when they sailed out as young men to take their places in the serenity of the British Raj. The dream of the men of Simla had turned to nightmare.

Nehru agreed that for a transitional period Mountbatten, on ceasing to be Viceroy, should serve as Governor-General of the new Dominion of India, a constitutional Governor-General, acting on the advice of ministers. The British suggested that Moun batten should serve also as the first Governor-General of Pakistan, thus making himself a link and a mediator between the two new countries. But Jinnah insisted on taking the Pakistan governor-generalship himself, it being the post most suitable for the founder of the nation. He thus became the first person of non-British descent to serve as a dominion Governor-General; he behaved as an independent head of state rather than as the personal representative of the King. Nehru, who was leader rather than founder of India, was content to be Prime Minister.

In brief, dispirited ceremonies at New Delhi and Pakistan's capital, the port of Karachi, the British Raj came to an end at midnight on August 14–15. The union jacks fluttered down from a thousand public buildings never to be raised again. The flag from Lucknow, the latest of the succession that had flown day and night over the residency since the Indian Mutiny, was sent to the King for him to keep at Windsor Castle. Regiment after regiment of British soldiers rattled by train down to Bombay where they embarked for the last time in the homebound troopships, bands playing 'Auld Lang Syne' and 'Will Ye No Come Back Again?' British imperial India, which within the lifetime of those troops had stood as an unquestioned reality, had become so dead that future generations would have the utmost difficulty in envisaging how it could ever have existed.

With the loss of India, the British Empire, as governed from London, lost four fifths of its population.

Bereft of British support, most of the princely states melted like ice. Despite their nominally sovereign status, the princes could not resist being sucked into either India or Pakistan. They were allowed to keep some of their palaces and private fortunes and were granted pensions; but they became ghostly figures—the aristocracy of the new India was not them but the families which had served the Congress. In theory each prince, as his final act of sovereignty, decided which to accede to, India or Pakistan, but in most cases considerations of religion and frontiers made the choice an inevitable one.

In only two cases out of hundreds did the choice involve serious trouble. In the great state of Hyderabad, of a size and population equal to those of several European countries, the ruler, the Nizam and his administrators were Moslem but the majority of the people were Hindu. The Nizam at first attempted to maintain his independence but when his subjects revolted the Indian army marched in and took control. The state was completely surrounded by

Indian territory and the Nizam, unable to obtain effective aid from Pakistan, capitulated.

In the other problem state, Kashmir, a similar problem existed but the other way round—the ruler was Hindu while the majority of the people were Moslems. The scandalous Maharajah—he of the blackmail case in London 20 years earlier—had an apparently free choice. His beautiful territory among the Himalayan foothills shared common frontiers with both India and Pakistan. The resulting conflict was to bring a long-lasting tragedy.

Both India and Pakistan coveted Kashmir, which is about twice the size of Ireland and a favourite place for vacations for people from all over the sub-continent. Cool lakes and clear streams cascading down the hillsides make it a lovable contrast to the baking plains below. Nehru himself was particularly attached to Kashmir; his family had originated there and he delighted in returning for a rest in what he regarded as his ancestral surroundings. The Maharajah, after considering for a moment the possibility of retaining independence, decided to ignore the fact that most of his people were Moslems and acceded to India. Nehru accepted the accession without considering it necessary to consult the wishes of the inhabitants.

Almost immediately, irregular bands of Pakistanis entered Kashmir to raise armed revolt against the Maharajah and the Indians. To what extent this essentially spontaneous movement was aided by the Pakistan Government is difficult to ascertain but certainly official Pakistan was sympathetic. Nehru, on his side, believed that his new India was a national, not a religious state, that people of any religious persuasion should be capable of living within it. If he relinquished Kashmir he would be recognising that India was not a natural home for Moslems. He moved in his army to resist the irregular incursions and Pakistan, on a semi-official basis, began to assist the attackers. The pathetic possibility developed of these two chaotic, raw countries engaging in full-scale war against each other. They were like two, gigantic crippled children, hitting each other with their crutches. The armies, recently split from the old army of British India, were organised on similar lines, wore similar uniforms and conducted their administration in the same English language. The remaining British officers found themselves faced with the serious possibility of having to fight against each other; their disinclination to do such a thing accelerated their withdrawal, thus making the military arrangements more chaotic than ever.

Had such a dispute occurred between two members of the older British Commonwealth it would have been inconceivable to fight over it. At the judicial level the Privy Council would have heard both sides and made a judgement, as it had done when Canada and Newfoundland had quarrelled over Labrador 20 years earlier. Alternatively, the influence of the Crown, of Great Britain and of the Imperial Conference would have been sufficient to force a political agreement. So much, however, were India and Pakistan dominions of a novel kind that Commonwealth mediation was out of the question. Instead what were nominally two sets of subjects of the same King took their differences to the United Nations. This, alone, was enough to show that after only a quarter of a century the high phrases of Balfour's definition of imperial unity had ceased to be meaningful.

Nobody was more distressed at the bloody culmination of his exli's dreams than the aged M. K. Gandhi. He had given his life to fepounding the virtues of peace and non-violence but now found his country achieving independence in a carnage worse than it had known for at least a century. He took no official ministerial post but devoted himself instead to preaching, fasting and praying for peace; it was largely through his influence, exerted from Calcutta, that the massacres involved in the partition of Bengal were lesser than those which happened in the Punjab. He preached against all religious intolerance and against the Hindu caste system. More than any other individual, this idealistic little lawyer had been responsible for the overturn of the British Raj. He towered on the world scene as a political leader and moral teacher. But he could not tame the passions of his own countrymen. On January 30, 1948, five months after independence, he was shot dead at his prayer meeting. His assassin was a Brahmin from Poona, a member of an extremist Hindu group which objected to his teachings on tolerance. So Gandhi who for 30 years had fought against the British died in the end at the age of 78 at the hands of an Indian. His death was not entirely in vain. It shocked millions so badly that it caused them to realise the horrors towards which communal hate was taking them. The beginnings appeared of a newer, more peaceful spirit. How far British sentiment had changed from regarding him as a 'half-naked fakir' was shown in the message from King George VI to Mountbatten: 'Will you please convey to the people of India our sincere sympathy in the irreparable loss which they, and, indeed, mankind, have suffered.'

Nine months later, Gandhi's former colleague, Mohammed Ali

Jinnah, founder of Pakistan, died from heart failure at the age of 69. His methods had been different from Gandhi's. He had never explicitly renounced his westernised characteristics and remained a barrister fit to appear in the London High Court. Nevertheless he had succeeded in so whipping up the Indian Moslems that within a decade he had converted the conception of Pakistan from fantasy into reality. His successor as the principal Pakistani personality was another lawyer, Liaquat Ali Khan, who had been Jinnah's second-in-command since 1936 and had served as Prime Minister since Pakistan's inception. Ali Khan was yet another lawyer: the four most prominent figures in the creation of India and Pakistan—Gandhi, Nehru, Jinnah and Ali Khan—had all dined as barristers in the London inns of court.

As a logical consequence of Indian independence the territories around also had to get their freedom. There could be no purpose in withholding it.

Burma, which had been conquered by the Japanese, slipped out of the British Commonwealth almost by stealth. Few cared to notice her departure. During the war the occupying Japanese had established a nominally independent State of Burma under the leadership of Aung San, a lawyer who had collaborated with the Japanese army in the early stages of the war. Aung San was not, however, just a puppet and he rapidly acquired the characteristics of a genuine nationalist leader. He quarrelled with the Japanese and in 1944 changed sides back to the British, forming as the main organ of Burmese politics the Anti-Fascist People's Freedom League. The Burmese nationalists helped the British to eject the Japanese from their territory but they had no intention of allowing the British to return to pre-war methods. The British made some show of trying to restore the old constitution and sent out a Governor who appointed Aung San and other nationalists to his council. But the old administrative framework, with a hierarchy of officials similar to that in India, was never restored. Aung San won an overwhelming majority in a general election on the issue of immediate independence and to this the British agreed. In July 1947 there was an awkward interruption in the process when Aung San and most of his colleagues were assassinated in a bomb explosion but, after a short pause for breath, his successor Thakin Nu, a former schoolteacher who had been Foreign Minister in the Japanese-sponsored administration, continued the negotiations. He signed a treaty with the British in October, 1947, and on January 4, 1948 at 4.20 a.m., a date and an hour chosen by astrologers, Burma became an independent republic outside the British Commonwealth. Despite the care of the astrologers, the new state was to lead a troubled existence, military, Marxist and tribal insurrections being punctuated by assassinations.

There could have been no place for the Burmese republic in the British Commonwealth as it had traditionally been organised, a partnership of like-minded governments acknowledging the sovereignty of a single monarch. 'We want no unwilling partners in the British Commonwealth,' Clement Attlee told the House of Commons in London while expounding the Burma Independence Bill. He might have added, sotto voce, that the British, who had been hanging Japanese generals, were embarrassed at handing power to Burmese who had collaborated with those generals. Burma was better forgotten. But under the newer conception of the Commonwealth, which was shortly to develop, Burma would have proved a perfectly adequate member had she wished to join.

Just south of India lay the island colony of Ceylon where progress towards independence was much happier. Indeed Ceylon stands as a model of what the British liked to consider as their settled method of steadily training a country for self-government. Since 1931 Ceylon had enjoyed an unusual constitution, based on that of a British municipality, the government being in large measure under the control of committees of the elected legislature. It was the only British colony in which every adult was allowed the vote. The leading personality was a hefty tea planter, D. S. Senanayake, who had found it possible to combine a belief in nationalism with collaboration with the British. Ceylon was admitted to full dominion status on February 4, 1948, Senanayake —who really was a considerable man—declaring: 'We glory in the fact that this transformation has been effected without shedding one drop of blood.' It was a fact worth glorying in because the racial and religious differences among the people were not inconsiderable and, under less enlightened leadership, might have led to a repetition of the disturbances over the water. The lion flag, emblem of the former Singhalese Kings, was hoisted at the ancient capital of Kandy but Ceylon was content to retain dominion status under the sovereignty of the King in London. Her first two Governors-General were Englishmen.

Had every colonial territory reached independence in the manner of Ceylon there would have been point in the utterances of many London politicians about the partnership of the multi-racial British Commonwealth. What, however, was a much more urgent matter than Ceylon was the determination of India, immediately after independence, to convert herself into a sovereign republic. This at once posed the question of whether it would be preferable to continue the Commonwealth as a close association of like-minded governments under the King's sovereignty, and shed territories which would not co-operate, or to change it into a much vaguer association which could accommodate anybody. The choice, made after very little consideration, was for the latter.

According to every British imperial tradition, the essential tie which kept the dominions together was the sovereignty of the King. Whatever local governments happened to exist, whatever autonomy they happened to enjoy, the peoples of the Common-wealth shared the common status of being the King's subjects. As recently as 1926 the Balfour definition had laid it down pre-cisely that imperial unity existed in 'common allegiance to the Crown.' An Australian or a Canadian military officer held the King's commission just as did a British one. Appointments to public office and assent to legislation were everywhere given in the King's name. Until 1948 it appears to have occurred to nobody, politician or lawyer, that the British Commonwealth could continue to exist without the Crown.

Jawaharlal Nehru was insistent about India becoming a republic but, provided that was permitted, he had no objection to remaining within the Commonwealth. Despite his long fight against the British and his repeated imprisonments, he retained something of a British cast of mind and a taste for some British culture. He spoke most effectively in English and, probably, even thought in English. Moreover, his aim in external affairs was to make India a mediating force in the world, a gigantic democracy dedicated to peace. Continued intimate contacts with Great Britain and the Commonwealth would be of assistance in this work. Within the Commonwealth, too, India would be able to exert extra pressure towards destroying the remainder of the British imperial system. There might, too, be extra economic aid available. All such considerations were, however, secondary in Nehru's mind and the minds of his colleagues compared with the essential matter of making India a republic. It was an indignity not to be endured that a great nation should be ruled in the name of an alien monarch who dwelt 4,000 miles away and who sym-bolised the imperialism of the past. If becoming a republic entailed quitting the Commonwealth, then India would quit.

The Attlee Cabinet decided in March, 1949, to scrap the Balfour

definition and seek a new formula which would enable republican India to stay in the Commonwealth. Correspondence between
the King and Attlee shows that one motive impelling the Cabinet
was the belief that if India left the Commonwealth it would assist
the spread of Communism in Asia. A broader consideration, which
is difficult to pin down but which certainly existed, was that the
British could not bear to admit that their world influence was
shrinking. They wanted to keep some of the forms of the former
Empire alive even after the reality had died. It was palatable for
the British to regard India as not just another sovereign nation but
as a people which had freely associated itself with the imperial
land which had inspired so many of its political institutions. The
British were willing to go to extreme lengths to maintain this
fiction, even to that of changing the titles of their monarch.

The actual formula was worked out at a conference of Commonwealth Prime Ministers in April, 1949. The new dominions as well
as the old attended this conference and much satisfaction was
derived from the attendance of 'coloured' Prime Ministers from
India, Pakistan and Ceylon. When photographs were taken of
them with the King in Buckingham Palace, the British rejoiced in
the notion that these new visitors were the recipients of the
democracy that had been 'granted' to them by the British.

The reality was different. What went on in that Commonwealth
Conference and who proposed what is not clear but the result was
the dissolution of the British Commonwealth as it had hitherto
existed. The Balfour definition might have had its metaphysical
aspects but at least, after careful study, it could be taken to mean
something. The 1949 declaration was incapable of precise inter-
pretation. Even nomenclature was obscure. In the first paragraph
the declaration refers to 'the British Commonwealth of Nations.'
The final paragraph uses the indefinite term 'the Commonwealth
of Nations.' Whether the latter was meant as an abbreviation of or
as a substitute for the former is not stated; certainly there is no
explicit announcement of a change in name. But in practice the
term 'British Commonwealth' passed out of most official terminology and was replaced by just 'The Commonwealth.' The British
monarch was declared to be 'Head of the Commonwealth' but was
assigned neither duties nor rights in this capacity. It might be
remarked, following Hobbes, that the Head of the Commonwealth
was not other than the ghost of the deceased British Empire,
sitting crowned upon the grave thereof. The purpose of 'The
Commonwealth' was defined in one vague sentence: 'The United

Kingdom, Canada, Australia, New Zealand, South Africa, India, Pakistan and Ceylon hereby declare that they remain united as free and equal members of the Commonwealth of Nations, freely co-operating in the pursuit of peace, liberty and progress.' The co-operation was to prove, in fact, to be strictly limited and the Asiatic territories, in particular, pursued independent defence and foreign policies. In 1950 Australia and New Zealand signed with the U.S.A. a defence treaty to which Great Britain was not a party.

In 1947, on India and Pakistan becoming independent, the British had abolished the Dominions and India offices in Whitehall and replaced them with a single new department, that of the Secretary of State for Commonwealth Relations. It was staffed in London by members of the home Civil Service and in the high commissions overseas by staff recruited from a variety of sources. Rapidly, however, it acquired the characteristics of a subsidiary Foreign Office. The most obvious difference between foreign and Commonwealth diplomacy became one of language—English was used instead of the customary French of the diplomats. The Commonwealth Office retained, too, residual functions in arranging the organisational details of Commonwealth conferences—a wartime proposal by Australia that the Commonwealth should have a secretariat responsible equally to all the members had foundered—and as a channel of communication between such Commonwealth countries as did not maintain high commissioners on each other's territory. As late as 1943 Australia and New Zealand had not exchanged high commissioners; right into the 1960s Britain continued to be the only Commonwealth member with a complete set of representatives in Commonwealth capitals. By the early 1950s the high commissioners had become so similar to the ambassadors from foreign countries as to be virtually indistinguishable; for ceremonial purposes they became ranked with the ordinary diplomatic corps and were allowed diplomatic immunities and privileges. The British Foreign Office continued to act on behalf of Commonwealth countries in capitals where they did not maintain ambassadors of their own but this implied no control over the foreign policies of those countries.

Then in 1948 came the decisive change in British domestic law. The British Nationality Act of that year, passed in anticipation of India becoming a republic, dissolved the common citizenship which had lain at the roots of the old Commonwealth and Empire. Up to 1948 every citizen of the Empire (save for certain 'protected persons') had possessed the same status of 'British subject'—that is a subject of the British King. Most of the dominions had had, in addition, their own local citizenship arrangements, relating mainly to taxation and the right to vote, work and acquire property, but in the United Kingdom there had been no local citizenship at all. A British subject born in Calcutta was entitled to the same rights in Great Britain as a Cockney born within the sound of Bow Bells; both were 'British subjects.' The new Act established a local, British citizenship for the people of Britain and the Whitehall-governed colonies. It also devised the term 'Commonwealth citizen' as an optional alternative for the historic term 'British subject;' in practice the newer term came almost totally to replace the latter. Apart from certain advantages, varying from time to time and from place to place, to be a 'Commonwealth citizen' did not count for much. What did matter for international purposes was whether one was a 'citizen of the United Kingdom and Colonies,' a 'citizen of Canada,' a 'citizen of the Republic of India' and so on; that was what decided the form of one's passport. Britain did not at first restrict the entry of Commonwealth citizens into the United Kingdom but, with the forms of separate United Kingdom citizenship established, was free to do so and in the end actually did so.

At the same time the term 'dominion,' which had been coined less than half a century earlier to describe the self-governing Empire countries, was becoming unpopular and passing into disuse. In its place the words 'member of the Commonwealth' were the only really acceptable ones.

All these changes—to jump forward a little—caused complications with the title of the British monarch. Hitherto the King had borne the same title everywhere, it having been understood since the Statute of Westminster that any change would be made by unanimous agreement among the imperial countries. The form which (except for Ireland) dated from the accession of Edward VII had been: 'George VI, by the Grace of God of the United Kingdom of Great Britain and Northern Ireland and of the British Dominions beyond the Seas King, Defender of the Faith, Emperor of India.' Plainly he had ceased to be Emperor of India—the final use of the signature George R. I. (Rex Imperator) had been for the last Indian Honours List published in January 1948. Equally plainly, 'British Dominions beyond the Seas' was becoming inadequate for such countries as Australia and entirely out of place for such countries as Ceylon. The title 'Defender of the Faith' was unsuitable for non-Christian countries. Also the new conception of headship of the Commonwealth had somehow to be introduced to suit republican members.

The search for a new formula taxed the ingenuity of lawyers, courtiers and politicians and was not completed by the time of the King's sudden death in 1951. His successor, Queen Elizabeth II, was proclaimed in London, on no very clear authority, with the vaguest of formulae: 'Elizabeth II, by the Grace of God Queen of this Realm and of all Her other Realms and Territories, Head of the Commonwealth, Defender of the Faith.' It can rarely have happened before that a monarch had been given a 27-word title which mentioned the name of not a single territory over which she was supposed to reign.

The following year a conference of Commonwealth Prime Ministers formally abandoned the principle that the sovereign's title should be the same everywhere; instead each country was to call her by a different title. Thus perished the conception of common monarchy. In Great Britain, under the Royal Titles Act of 1953, the sovereign became: 'Elizabeth II, by the Grace of God of the United Kingdom of Great Britain and Northern Ireland and of Her other Realms and Territories, Queen, Head of the Commonwealth, Defender of the Faith.' It was a clumsy title but not quite so vague as the original by which she had ascended the throne. 'Other Realms and Territories' was weak compared with the simplicity of 'British Dominions beyond the Seas;' it was as tautological as saying that a King is King of his Kingdom. In the monarchical Commonwealth countries the name of the country concerned—Canada, Ceylon and so on—replaced 'United Kingdom of Great Britain and Northern Ireland.' Some of them also dropped 'Defender of the Faith.' In the republican countries the Queen's only title was 'Head of the Commonwealth' but she was more normally referred to as just the British Queen.

Together with the Statute of Westminster of 1931, the British Nationality Act of 1948 and the Royal Titles Act of 1953 dissolved the constitutional bonds between the self-governing members of the Commonwealth and put nothing legally meaningful in their place. Each of the Acts was a recognition of a system which had already come to exist in practice—they were declaratory rather than innovating Acts.

The new formula was devised just too late to keep Ireland within the Commonwealth. Since 1937 the Irish had reconciled republican-style institutions with Commonwealth membership by a measure known as the External Relations Act by which the

King had formally accredited their diplomatic representatives. She had taken no part in Commonwealth conferences since the start of the war. Finally, in 1948, she broke the last tie by repealing the External Relations Act and starting to conduct her foreign affairs in her own name. Had the newer conception of republics within the Commonwealth enjoying the full rights of independence been established and had the bitterness arising from past history been allowed more time to settle down, she might have settled for the same status as India. In fact she turned out to be in some respects better off outside than inside the Commonwealth. The British continued, as always, to treat her for nationality purposes as if she were a part of the United Kingdom. Irish citizens were allowed to travel freely to Britain and to acquire at once the rights of British citizenship. Thus the Irish were treated more favourably than Commonwealth citizens whose entry into Britain was later to be strictly controlled. The point was that geographically, economically and demographically Ireland formed part of the British Isles and it would have been inconvenient to allow political factors to interfere with free movement of people. The Attlee Government did, however, treat the repeal of the External Relations Act as an occasion for affirming continued British support for the Protestant administration which held the six counties in Northern Ireland as part of the United Kingdom.

As in Ireland so also in South Africa there continued to exist powerful elements which were hostile to any connection with Britain. In 1939 the immediate result of the vote in the South African legislature on the declaration of war had been in favour of fighting with Britain. In the longer term, however, the changes in the party structure resulting from that vote were to produce quite a different result. The pre-war Nationalist Party, under Hertzog, had been none too friendly towards the Commonwealth connection but it had been prepared for most practical purposes to work with the British. The war issue split the old Nationalists, some of them joining up with Smuts and the British politicians in the pro-war United Party and others going off to extreme Boer quarters. The process had been accelerated by the death of Hertzog in 1942. The extreme Boer politicians were a group which up to 1939 had been only a splinter—the 'Purified Nationalists' under Dr. D. F. Malan, a former minister of the Dutch Reformed Church. The 'Purified Nationalists' took a mystical view of Boer destinies, believing that the Afrikaaner had a divine right to control South Africa. They believed in racialist principles and sympathised with the German Nazis, their papers running anti-Semitic campaigns of a kind that must have been pleasing to Adolf Hitler. The Malan Nationalists established themselves as the focal point of opposition to the war and by 1945 had grown into the principal opposition party and the alternative government.

In the eyes of most people in Great Britain the figure of Smuts so dominated the South African scene that it was difficult to think of Dr. Malan, in his tidy black suit, as being anything more than an eccentric. How could a pro-Nazi possibly get control of a country which had just fought so loyally in the war? Smuts himself did not discourage this complacency; he behaved as if his leadership of South Africa were part of the immutable order of nature. Nevertheless it was clear that some gesture ought to be made to bring home to the South Africans the reality of the Commonwealth and in 1947 George VI, with his Queen and two daughters, paid the country a State Visit. In part it was regarded as a routine affair. The King intended to visit all the dominions in time. He had made a successful trip to Canada in 1939 and only the war had prevented him from continuing the programme. But the actual selection of South Africa in 1947 sprang partly from political calculation by the King, the British Cabinet and Smuts that it would do South Africa good to see her sovereign.

To outward appearances, the visit went well. The King and his family sailed out in H.M.S. *Vanguard*, the biggest and the last battleship the Royal Navy ever built, and were welcomed by enthusiastic crowds headed by a gratified Smuts. Dressed in a white uniform of admiral of the fleet, the King toured the Union by special train and went, too, to Southern and Northern Rhodesia. It was the first time a British reigning monarch had travelled on the African continent, one half of which was ruled in his name. The King's only contact with the black African majority of the population were meetings with selected tribal chiefs and displays of tribal dancing—everybody appeared to take it for granted that contacts of such a kind were sufficient. Despite the friendliness of the crowds there were, however, some unpleasant portents. The Malan Nationalists, intelligently, eschewed any outright criticism of the King but their newspapers either avoided mentioning him altogether or gave him only the briefest mentions. The warmth of the welcome in the streets came from the British rather than the Boer segment of the white population.

During the tour, the heir presumptive to the throne, Princess Elizabeth, celebrated her 21st birthday. Many took it as evidence

R

of the vitality of the Commonwealth that such a significant event in her life should occur while she was in South Africa. She marked the occasion by broadcasting to the Commonwealth and Empire from Government House, Cape Town. 'I declare before you all,' she said, 'that my whole life, whether it be long or short, shall be devoted to your service and the service of our great Imperial Commonwealth to which we all belong.' The term 'Imperial Commonwealth,' which she used, presumably after taking advice, was one which in informal parlance had been popular during the war and dated back at least to 1917. It is difficult to trace any usage of it in official pronouncements subsequent to the broadcast.

The circumstances of her 21st birthday must have impressed upon Princess Elizabeth the world-wide nature of her inheritance and for many years afterwards she adopted a distinctively Commonwealth approach to her work. She actually acceded to the throne, four years later, while on African soil, her father having died suddenly while she was in Kenya. But within four months of her 21st birthday India was independent and the Imperial Commonwealth, as she had known it, had lost its main prop.

Racial disagreements in South Africa, apart from the latent antagonism between Boers and British, did not arise during the South African tour. The Labour Cabinet in London had fully endorsed its taking place and had vetoed a suggestion from the King that he might cut it short because of a fuel shortage that was crippling Britain during an exceptionally cold winter. Yet within less than a decade the situation was to change so much that it was to become inconceivable that any British administration, let alone a Labour one, should be eager to set a seal of approval upon South Africa. But in 1950 it was the Labour Government which deposed Seretse Khama, Chief of the Banzamwato tribe, Bechuanaland, because he had offended racialist opinion by marrying a white girl.

The explosive growth of racial conflict sprang from two sources —from the South African whites themselves and from the growing self-consciousness of the black Africans who formed four fifths of the population.

Smuts had been widely regarded as a Liberal, and, indeed, after the war had been elected to honorary office in the international organisation of Liberal parties. He believed in representative government and the rule of law. Such principles he had applied consciously and carefully to the affairs of white men but he had never worked out how, if at all, they should be applied to

Africans. 'I feel inclined to shift the intolerable burden of solving that sphinx problem to the ampler brains and stronger shoulders of the future,' he declared. Smuts believed that Africans were proper human beings—he had to state this because some of his compatriots took a contrary view—but he considered they were so hopelessly unsophisticated as to require the paternal care of white men. He commonly used what was already becoming an old-fashioned term, 'the native problem.' In his long life Smuts had few dealings with Africans save as servants. He disliked the more educated Africans who wanted to integrate themselves with white society—'The proper place for the educated minority of natives is with the rest of their people, of whom they are the natural leaders, and from whom they should not in any way be disassociated,' he said. He disliked, too, the Indian community which had settled in the eastern part of South Africa. That community, fired by the political progress in India, started after the war a vigorous campaign for proper civil rights, including the right to vote. Smuts was adamant in resisting it and, as a result, the new Indian Government broke off diplomatic relations with South Africa—the first occasion on which two Commonwealth countries did this.

In the 1948 South African election, the year after the King's visit, the Malan Nationalists propounded a doctrine which was clearer and more comprehensive than anything Smuts had put forward. The racial 'problems' of South Africa should no longer be left to the wisdom of the future but should be settled in the present generation by apartheid—complete separation of the races. Malan warned that, unless the apartheid principle were adopted, white civilisation would be submerged in what he called 'the black sea' of Africanism. The only remedy was to cut off the non-white South Africans from any share, or the hope of any share, in public administration and to segregate them residentially from the whites. So far as possible, Africans should live in their traditional rural tribes and the process by which they had been migrating into the towns should be halted. The Nationalists made this doctrine into their principal campaign issue, soft-pedalling their older republicanism and anti-Semitism. They did not expect actually to defeat Smuts but they thought they could build up strength to become serious contenders in the next election, due in 1953.

Smuts's United Party had no clear answer to the Nationalist campaign and, indeed, there could be no logical alternative to the apartheid policy other than a programme for the integration of Africans and Europeans into one society. Smuts's deputy, Jan

Hofmeyr, did make one or two cautious gestures in an inte-
grationist direction—and earned much opprobium for doing so—
but the mass of the United Party was content with white dominance
as it already existed. The Nationalists found that apartheid was
even more popular among the white electorate than they had
hoped and this, added to passing economic difficulties for which
the Smuts administration got the blame, was enough to give the
Nationalists and their allies an unexpected victory, with a majority
of five seats in the legislature. Malan, who became Prime Minister,
called it 'a miracle.' He had not actually won a majority of the
white vote but the arrangement of constituencies, with extra
weight allowed to rural Boer farmers, had exaggerated his parliamentary strength.

Thus just a year after King George had opened in state the
parliament of South Africa that parliament passed under republican control. 'Oom Paul' Kruger, whose statue glowers over
Pretoria, had won at last. Hofmeyr died a few months after the
election and Smuts died two years after. Thereafter the Nationalists faced no serious challenge, the United Party, although still
numerous, becoming a nostalgic, conservative, pro-British group
looking back to the past. The innovators were the Nationalists
who, in office, held faithfully to their principles and passed law
after law to put them into effect. They had to change the constitution itself to get coloured voters removed from the rolls in Cape
Province. The whole South African population was classified into
different racial groups—white, Indian, coloured and African—and
organised accordingly, political power remaining with the whites.
South Africa developed into a unique society, a collective dictator-
ship. The parliamentary system continued actively in operation,
the law courts continued to be fair and the newspapers claimed and
practised vigorous freedom in reporting and comment. This was
possible because all but a tiny minority of whites, who ran those
institutions, were complacent about what the government was
doing. From the angle of the non-whites, however, the system was
unjust and oppressive. So eager were the Nationalists to consolidate
white opinion on their side—British as well as Boer—that they
held up for a decade the formal abolition of the monarchy. They
did, however, oblige the King to appoint Governors-General of
their own political persuasion; thus the monarch's personal
representatives were men who did not believe in the monarchy.

The vigorous initiatives of the South African Nationalists did
much to stimulate racial tension but its creation was by no means

entirely their doing. It would have appeared under whatever politicians had been in power in South Africa. By the late 1940s urbanised Africans in most parts of the continent were becoming resentful of European political control. They disliked in their daily lives the operation of the colour bar and they began to consider that only government by Africans could produce sound administration for their countries. The tragedy for the continent was that the African population which, educationally, was the most advanced—the South African—was also politically the most repressed. The Africans in less advanced territories were left to make the running. The example of India inspired African politicians with the belief, the reasonable belief, that if they kept at it, they could swing public opinion against the colonial administrators and get the British and other colonial powers to quit. The British, on their side, had lost with India much of their former prestige and self-confidence.

Up to 1945 African nationalism had been largely an American and West Indian phenomenon; the sporadic tribal risings which had taken place on the African continent itself had been unrelated to any broad political concept. Under the leadership of William du Bois, Marcus Garvey and George Padmore on the other side of the Atlantic, descendants of African slaves had formed their own associations with a view to elevating the condition of their people. Although their membership was primarily American, they had never failed to think of Africa, which they regarded as their ancestral home. As early as 1900 there had been a Pan-African Congress in London. Few of the delegates at it had ever actually been to Africa but they sent a petition to Queen Victoria asking for better treatment of Africans in South Africa and Rhodesia. A second Pan-African Congress was held in Paris in 1919 with a view to influencing the Versailles peace conference. Again the Americans and the West Indians played a leading part and, too, delegates from the French African colonies were prominent. It did not appear to occur to this congress that the Africans should claim political independence. The most extreme demand was that 'the natives of Africa must have the right to participate in the Government as fast as their development permits.'

Further congresses were held between the wars in London, Brussels, Lisbon and New York, providing a medium through which students from Africa came into contact with the older generation of American and West Indian leaders. They attracted little public attention. The British Colonial Office appeared to ignore them and the mass of the African people knew nothing about them whatsoever. Then in 1945 the movement reached its climax and its conclusion in an obscure meeting in Chorlton town hall, Manchester, in October, 1945. This was the fifth, or according to some computations the sixth, Pan-African Congress. It was at this Congress that, for the first time, Africans from Africa were in control and, also, at this Congress that the immediate objective was established of campaigning for political independence. The delegates, who included Kwame Nkrumah from the Gold Coast, Jomo Kenyatta from Kenya, Wallace Johnson from Sierra Leone and Peter Abrahams from South Africa, passed the historic resolution: 'We demand for Black Africa autonomy and independence, so far and no further than it is possible in this One World for groups and peoples to rule themselves subject to inevitable world unity and federation.' The congress agreed that so far as possible the campaign for political independence should be based on non-violence and the teachings of M. K. Gandhi—but that violence was to be accepted as a last resort.

The Manchester congress was to be the last for 13 years. When next the leaders of Black Africa met together they did so in Accra, capital of independent Ghana, and included representatives of eight sovereign states. The obscure men of Manchester had returned home, stirred up the people, changed the face of a continent and destroyed the bulk of the remaining British Empire.

The Labour administration which took office in 1945 had not the least conception that within 20 years the African colonies would be independent states. As the Labour Deputy Leader, Herbert Morrison, put it during the war, independence for such colonies would be 'like giving a child of ten a latch-key, a bank account and a shot-gun.' According to Socialist principle it was held that colonial peoples should be helped along a gradual road towards self-government but it was supposed that Africans were so unsophisticated that the process would take generations. Also, by the ideas of the time, it was difficult to conceive of African colonies, each with a few million people, being either big enough or rich enough to maintain the apparatus of political sovereignty. Through mixed motives of imperial self-interest and Socialist idealism the new administration decided that the best course for the present was a degree of economic and educational development. This was not just a Labour Party notion—colonial administration had in any event acquired a momentum of its own and, as is the nature of bureaucracies, had elaborated its routines and activities. For example the Brooke family could not be allowed back to reign in Sarawak after the temporary Japanese occupation. Tidiness demanded that it became an ordinary colony.

In the years after 1945 the Colonial Office became almost unrecognisably different from the lethargic institution of 20 years earlier. The 'dinosaurs' had departed and their places were filled many times over by eager experts in various fields of colonial administration. Where, for example, forestry had once been covered part-time by one general administrator it was now a complete department, staffed by officials and specialists. In 1939 the London staff of the Colonial Office had totalled 465. By 1950 it reached 1,289. Moreover, the new officials, unlike their predecessors, actually went out to look at the colonies. Travelling expenses for Colonial Office London-based staff in 1939 had totalled only £3,100. By 1950 the same item rose to £51,875. The swollen staffs could no longer be accommodated in the old Downing Street building. That was handed over to the Dominions Office and the colonial administrators rented what they regarded as temporary premises from the Church of England in Great Smith Street, Westminster. As a result of wartime bombing there existed a magnificent empty site bounded by Whitehall, the Houses of Parliament and Westminster Abbey. This site was earmarked for a new Colonial Office which in architectural pretension was to match the splendour of an organisation which controlled 50 colonies. It was to be the physical symbol of the world-wide British Empire. Actually it was never built.

Similar expansion took place in the local administrations of the colonies themselves. Between the wars the numbers of recruits sent out from Britain into the Colonial Service had varied between 551 in the busiest year, 1919, and 70 in the slackest year, 1932. In the five years after 1945 the numbers sent out were 1,715, 806, 957, 1,341 and 1,510. The appointment of more and more technical specialists accounted for part of the increase but the major factor was a trebling in general administrators. Areas once controlled by a single district commissioner were now split up into fractions, each under its own commissioner. In the colonial capitals the old 'secretariats' were split up into separate government departments on the pattern of a European state. Practically all the senior administrative posts still went to British expatriates with locally-recruited staff allowed only clerkships and specialist posts; since 1942, though, there had been no formal colour bar.

Recruited according to plans devised by Ralph Furse during the war, the new administrators were mostly public school men who had served as officers in the wartime forces. They were selected on record and interview—with no competitive examination as for the old Indian Civil Service—and then given a course at Oxford, Cambridge or London universities before being sent out for a career which they expected to last for the whole of their working lives. Although he was now running a proper personnel department, Furse still conducted many of the interviews with candidates himself and his was the main influence in setting standards. He regarded the introduction of London University as a training centre, in addition to Oxford and Cambridge, as something which needed to be explained. 'I added London,' he wrote in his autobiography, 'partly because they were, without any help from us, showing signs of an enthusiastic desire to promote colonial studies, partly because I suspected that my rather ambitious proposals would have no chance in the political atmosphere to be expected after the war, unless a "modern" university were added to the team.'

Furse retired in 1948 but carried on for two years more as an adviser. He had been possibly the most influential British civil servant of his generation. By the time of his departure it could be reckoned that almost every senior administrator in almost every British colony had originally been recruited by him. His standards had been those of the British public school. What neither he nor anyone else had foreseen was that his post-war generation would find their most crucial function not in routine administration but in handing over power to new masters.

Another feature of the post-war years was a rise in the numbers of emigrants from Great Britain to the dominions and the colonies. Some were war veterans anxious to escape from a country which they felt had not given its people a fair chance in the inter-wars depression—many such people went to Australia. Others among the emigrants were rich or enterprising people who disliked the restrictions and austerity of Britain under Socialist administration. Others, again, had just the wanderlust and pioneering spirit which had been traditional among the British for a century past.

The main beneficiaries of the outflow were the dominions but there was also, for the first time, a substantial settlement in some African colonies. The white population of Southern Rhodesia went up from 80,000 in 1945 to over 200,000 a decade later; the Southern Rhodesian administration, controlled by local whites, almost bankrupted itself in its eagerness to bring in immigrants. In Northern Rhodesia the development of the copper mines increased the white population from 5,000 in 1945 to over 60,000 a decade later. In the case of Kenya, the British Government assisted ex-officers to acquire farms in the White Highlands, and the white population of the colony rose from 12,000 in 1945 to over 50,000 a decade later. It was assumed by the Labour Colonial Office that white settlement in Africa would bring economic benefits to all concerned. Political problems arising from such settlement were still considered in terms of striking a balance between the powers of the Governor and of a white legislature elected locally. Southern Rhodesia was a special case—a colony with a local Prime Minister and cabinet responsible to the local white legislature, the Prime Minister for many purposes being regarded as if he were running a dominion. Capital poured into the white settled areas from both Britain and the United States, Salisbury in Rhodesia and Nairobi in Kenya acquiring the air of modern European cities.

Although imperial matters had never been a primary concern with the Labour Party as they had been with the Conservatives for half a century, there existed within the Labour ranks a number of specialists who had long studied colonial affairs. The primary organ of study had been the Fabian Colonial Bureau of which a former trade union official, Arthur Creech Jones, had served as secretary. In 1946 Creech Jones entered the Cabinet as Secretary of State for the Colonies—the Colonial Office was the only department in which he ever held ministerial office. He was a short, intelligent man who knew a lot about his subject. Many of his officials and colonial Governors were uneasy at working with a Fabian Socialist but they respected his actual knowledge. Had the issue of independence, arising during the 1950s, not short-circuited all his plans, Creech Jones might well have ranked as the greatest man who ever held his office. He was certainly one of the few colonial secretaries to care deeply about his job instead of regarding it as just a step on the political ladder.

Creech Jones directed and guided the expansion of the colonial administrations according to a conscious policy of trusteeship. There had always been some strain of idealism in British colonialism but Creech Jones brought it out more clearly than ever before. In 1939 the total cost to the British taxpayer of administering the colonies had been £5.5 million. By 1950 the same figure was £41.5 million, the greater part of the increase accounted for by economic development. (These figures refer to *public* income and expenditure; they take no account of the benefits derived by private British interests from the colonies.) In absolute terms £41.5 million was not a large sum—within 15 years Britain would be handing out over £200 million a year in aid to the former colonial territories—but the fact that it was provided at all was proof of a changed attitude. The principal organ for economic development was the Colonial Development Corporation set up in 1948 as a semi-autonomous body resembling a British national-ised industry. Financed partly by the Government and partly by loans raised on the Government's guarantee, the C.D.C. concen-trated mainly on supplying the colonies with public utilities—roads, electricity, water, irrigation, forestry. It generally left manufacturing industry to private enterprise.

Some of the British money was wasted. The biggest scheme of all under the Labour Government was one for growing groundnuts in Tanganyika, the theory being that it would at once develop the Tanganyikan economy and provide margarine for the straitened British people. Bulldozers cleared the bush, a whole new town was built, experts poured in by the hundred. Africans who had never seen a motor car found themselves surrounded by the latest in European technology. The scheme had, however, been disas-trously ill-prepared. Insufficient account had been taken of the nature of the soil and of the tropical pests that would be en-countered. The Government had repeated on a gigantic scale the errors of many private farmers who had been too optimistic about what could easily be grown in the tropics. Even Lord Delamere in Kenya had lost two fortunes before he finally began making money out of his farms. The groundnuts scheme foundered, having cost £36 million and produced not one commercial nut. A similar failure at the same time was an extraordinary attempt to turn the little West African colony of Gambia into an egg-producing country. Gambia was a good place for groundnuts, having produced them profitably for years, but it was hopeless for eggs. The scheme foundered to a loss of £5 million without a single egg having been exported. These two tragic and expensive failures were a dead loss to Great Britain and the residual benefits they left for the colonies concerned were not worth the money—the total of £41 million could have been much better spent.

Although they were impoverished and in much need of development, the colonies as a whole were at this time of crucial importance in maintaining the pound sterling as an international currency. At the outbreak of the war in 1939, Britain and the self-governing dominions, except for Canada, had agreed to co-operate in managing their currency reserves. Thus was formed what became known as the 'Sterling Area.' It included the whole British Commonwealth and Empire, except Canada, with the addition of other countries which were closely associated with Britain—Egypt, Iraq, Transjordan and, for a while, Iceland and the Belgian Congo. The theory was that strict controls were required over the exchange of sterling for 'hard' currencies, notably the American dollar, but that free convertibility, or almost free convertibility, could continue among the sterling countries themselves. The system had the minimum of formal arrangement; the finance ministries and central banks of the participating countries, with Britain first among equals, simply collaborated on a friendly basis. That such a sophisticated monetary mechanism could operate in so club-like an atmosphere was a proof of the deep ties of kinship which at that period still existed within the British Commonwealth. Overseas countries and colonies which earned dollars or other foreign currencies put them into a pool in London at the disposal of the whole Sterling Area. The countries did not actually have their dollars confiscated; they were given the equivalent in sterling, at the fixed rate of exchange. During the war the whole currency exchange resources of the Commonwealth and Empire were at the disposal of the war effort which, in effect, meant mostly at the disposal of Great Britain, and most Commonwealth countries and colonies built up substantial sterling balances in London. After the war the theory was that each territory could take out of the dollar pool roughly the same amount as it contributed to it.

Some colonies had a reasonable complaint in that their currency transactions were controlled not by themselves but by Great Britain. This was felt with special force in the Gold Coast, Nigeria and Malaya which, between them, contributed from their exports of raw materials enough dollars to make the difference between solvency and bankruptcy for the Sterling Area as a whole. Instead of these colonies getting the dollars they earned they were given, instead, sterling balances in London. To make things worse, they were not even allowed free access to those balances—the British released them in dribs and drabs. In 1949, when sterling was devalued, the balances lost about a third of their value. It was easy for nationalist politicians to accuse the British of theft, of purchasing American films and American tobacco at the expense of the colonies, but in fact the situation was less simple than that. The

British themselves, taking one year with another, drew no more out of the dollar pool than they had contributed to it by their own exports. The true beneficiaries were, to some extent, those colonies which had no dollar earnings and, to a much greater extent, the self-governing dominions. Simply because they were self-governing and could, if they wished, withdraw from the Sterling Area altogether, the independent Commonwealth countries could always put pressure on London for more dollars. Australia benefited a little but the two countries which went really out of balance were India and Pakistan. The dollars from the cocoa of the Gold Coast peasant were expended on capital equipment from America for the industry of India.

Looked at narrowly, the gains and losses to Britain herself of running the Sterling Area and of maintaining the pound sterling as an international currency roughly cancelled each other out. As time went on it was to become a liability rather than an asset. The outstanding advantage in the eyes of many British politicians and bankers was emotional rather than economic, the delight to be derived from possessing a currency in which was conducted about one third of the world's trade. The pound sterling was treated as if it were a symbol of virility rather than just money. On a broader basis, it could be reckoned to be in the interests of mankind generally that, in an era of currency restrictions and exchange difficulties, there should be the great Sterling Area in which trade flowed freely. Without the Sterling Area, the transition from war to peace economies after 1945, which was difficult enough as it was, would have been even more painful. But the colonies were not consulted about whether or not they wanted to co-operate—there was no means of consulting them. By decisions taken at remote desks in London they were required willy nilly to contribute their dollar resources for the common good. It was notable, though, that after they had secured their independence the majority of them chose freely to remain within the Sterling Area; the demand of the new politicians on winning power was not for control of their own foreign exchange but for the spending of the sterling balances in London.

It was in the African colony most affected by the Sterling Area system, the Gold Coast, that political trouble broke out—although very much more was involved than the problem of currency. The Sterling Area was one of several sticks for Gold Coast politicians to use in beating the British, not the cause of their antagonism.

The Gold Coast was a small and relatively prosperous colony which produced most of the world's cocoa. Most of the six million inhabitants still lived in their tribes but there were, as well, significant groups of urban Africans and African farmers producing crops for cash. The Gold Coast also contained the most numerous middle class of any British African colony; there were African doctors and lawyers and even African judges. The British took pride in the progress that had been made there and regarded it as a model colony. The Gold Coast people should be grateful for the benefits they had received from enlightened British administration. In 1946 the Gold Coast and its large neighbour Nigeria were given constitutions which, by African standards, were very advanced. Each of the two colonies acquired a central legislature with a majority of unofficial members. The franchise qualifications were narrow, the powers of the assemblies were circumscribed and all executive authority remained with the British administrations but it could be claimed that at least a beginning had been made with parliamentary methods. The Labour Colonial Office in London saw the constitutions as the first step in a long process of 'training' Africans for self-government—a process that would take many years even in West Africa, let alone in less advanced territories elsewhere on the continent. In 1946 no British minister or civil servant dreamed it possible that the Gold Coast could become independent within only a decade.

To operate the new constitution the Gold Coast intellectuals formed a political party called the United Gold Coast Convention. It was a middle-class body dominated by lawyers and was something like what the Indian National Congress had been before the arrival of Gandhi. The leader was Dr. Joseph Danquah, a 52-year-old barrister of royal birth who wanted to replace the name 'Gold Coast' with 'Ghana' after a West African empire which had existed in pre-European times. Although they demanded greater self-government for their country, Danquah and his associates were sympathetic to British culture and British political principles. They had little contact with the African masses.

In 1947 Danquah invited Kwame Nkrumah to return home from London to become organising secretary of the United Gold Coast Convention. Nkrumah, then aged 37, had been editing in London a paper called *The New African*, modelled on the British *New Statesman*, and dedicated to carrying out the principles of the 1945 Pan-African Congress in which he had played a leading part. He had been away from home for 12 years and had taken degrees in Great Britain and the United States. He arrived back in the Gold Coast determined to carry into practice the political theories he had formed during his years in exile. His fundamental idea was that progress for Africans could come only under African rule and that therefore the first priority must be to defeat colonialism. 'Seek ye first the political kingdom' was his slogan. Although his ethical principles were different to those of Gandhi, his primary political weapon was the same—to convert nationalism from an intellectual, middle class notion into a creed which would appeal to the illiterate masses.

About 30,000 men of the Gold Coast had served in the army during the war, most of them outside their own country. They had acquired a sophistication and a knowledge of the world which was novel in ordinary Africans. They had been assured that they werę fighting for democracy. These men, disciplined and dissatisfied, formed superb material for Nkrumah's movement. He recruited them into his party and led them in a series of protests and demonstrations against the colonial administration and against the prices of goods in the shops. Within a year he had the colony in turmoil, although few British administrators at this stage took him seriously.

The situation exploded in February, 1948. A procession of ex-servicemen marched towards the Governor's castle in Accra with a petition about prices, a more or less disorderly crowd surrounding them. There was some error or misunderstanding about the route they had agreed with the police that they should take. A junior police officer tried to bar their way with a tiny cordon outnumbered hundreds to one. The demonstrators began to push through the cordon and the police opened fire. Just as at Amritsar two decades earlier, those shots spelled the beginning of the end of British rule. What had been a peaceful demonstration turned into a furious mob and for three days rioting spread through Accra and through the other centres of population in the Gold Coast; 29 people were killed.

The Gold Coast riots had an influence throughout the Commonwealth and Empire. They could be likened to the fall of the Bastille in 1789. In South Africa they coincided with the general election campaign and so helped Malan into power. In London and the colonies they were a matter for amazement—everybody had considered the Gold Coast as one of the most stable territories. Creech Jones appointed a commission under a British barrister, A. A. Watson, Recorder of Bury St. Edmunds, to find out what had gone wrong. Watson, aided by a British trade union official and an Oxford don, reported that the Gold Coast administration had failed to take account of the political frustration felt by educated Africans, that 'the most serious problem of the Administration in the Gold Coast is the suspicion which surrounds Government activity of any sort.' He went on to recommend an immediate extension of self-government.

Creech Jones accepted the Watson Report and appointed the Coussey Commission, an all-African body under a local judge, to draft a new constitution. This was a new departure in colonial administration and one that has not subsequently been repeated; the customary method of drafting colonial constitutions has been to bring at least some outsiders into the drafting body or to have a conference presided over by a British minister. Creech Jones considered, presumably, that only an all-African commission could overcome the deep-rooted hostility to colonial rule which had been revealed in the Watson Report.

The Coussey Commission, not surprisingly, recommended a rapid and drastic advance in self-government. It said the Gold Coast should have a proper national assembly, elected on universal franchise exercised through electoral colleges. Eight of the Governor's executive council of 11 members should be Africans responsible to the assembly, the colonial regime retaining control only of finance, law and order and the Civil Service. To many members of the British colonial service this report caused consternation. Universal franchise in a territory where only ten per cent of the population was literate was regarded as unworkable. The idea of placing Africans in charge of public departments—putting them above white bureaucrats—appeared to be a reversal of the normal order of nature. At the same time, though, once the Watson and Coussey commissions had reported it was impossible for the Colonial Office to retrace its steps other than by resorting to harsh and dictatorial methods. The Governor of the Gold Coast, Sir Charles Arden-Clarke, had earlier repudiated the need for commissions of inquiry but now he agreed that the proposed new system should at least be given a trial and he dedicated the remainder of his service to trying to give the new African ministers a good start.

Meanwhile the United Gold Coast Convention had itself fallen into dissention. The reaction of the older leaders, including Joseph Danquah, to the 1948 riots had been one of distress and they had attempted to curb Nkrumah's activities. They demoted him from secretary to treasurer of the party. Nkrumah thereupon broke away altogether. He founded his own newspaper, the *Accra Evening News*, as his personal mouthpiece and started a mass youth movement which owed allegiance to him personally. Finally, in 1949, he founded a new political party, the Convention People's Party, which campaigned forthright for dominion status. Support for the Gold Coast Convention rapidly melted away, Nkrumah proving himself capable of winning the support both of the young intellectuals and of the masses of uneducated Africans. Within three years of his return home he was the national leader of the Gold Coast.

The British by now recognised that Nkrumah was an influential figure but there appears to have been some residual hope in the colonial administration that he was the product only of some passing hysteria and that he might yet be cut down to size. Nkrumah rejected the Coussey proposals, declaring that they did not go far enough, and in 1950 launched a campaign of 'positive action' based roughly on the methods which had been used by the National Congress in India. The Governor declared a state of emergency and locked him up.

In England Creech Jones lost his parliamentary seat in the 1950 general election and so had to give up his post as Colonial Secretary. His successor was James Griffiths, a former miner much trusted in the British Labour Party. He had the habit of emphasising his sincerity by beating his chest while talking. Griffiths, unlike Creech Jones, possessed no expert knowledge of the colonies but he was determined, on grounds of general principle, to encourage democracy in the colonies. In consultation with Arden-Clarke he agreed to allow a general election in the Gold Coast on the Coussey constitution. Exactly what the British expected the result of the election to be is hard to discern. They appear to have had at least the hope that with Nkrumah away in prison the Convention People's Party had lost its mainspring and that the older, more conservative politicians would have a chance of winning. Whatever their hopes, the British organised the election with exemplary fairness, the district commissioners dutifully undertaking the novel task of registering voters and explaining to them how the system worked. Because so many of the voters were illiterate the system, later to become familiar in Africa, was adopted of giving each candidate an animal symbol—a fish, an elephant, a lion—under which he campaigned and against which the elector put his mark on the ballot paper. The peaceful and competent manner in which the election was conducted gave hope to many that European-style government might, after all, be possible in Africa.

The actual results, from the British point of view, were far less satisfactory. Out of 84 seats in the new assembly Nkrumah and his supporters won 48, including all the urban seats. Nkrumah himself, although in prison, beat his Gold Coast Convention opponent in Accra Central by 22,780 votes to 342. For a moment the British hesitated about what to do. Might they not after all scrap their liberal policy and revert to direct colonial rule? This possibility had only to be examined to be rejected. The Gold Coast people had expressed their wishes in an unmistakable manner and it would cause a world-wide uproar to flout them. The Communist countries would acquire a propaganda weapon. Such Commonwealth countries as India would intervene. The matter might even reach the United Nations. The British themselves, after the loss of India, no longer bore in the depths of their souls the will to rule. Above all Griffiths himself, and his Labour colleagues, believed profoundly in democracy—they had devoted their political careers to the proposition that the mass of the people should control their own affairs.

Nkrumah was let out of prison and, under the title 'Leader of Government Business,' joined the Governor's executive council. A year later his title was changed to that of Prime Minister. He himself had previously repudiated the Coussey constitution but at least two motives appear to have impelled him to work under it. Firstly, he genuinely realised that he and his colleagues needed administrative experience. Once they had that experience they could mount a stronger case than ever for dominion status. (Nkrumah customarily spoke in friendly terms of the Commonwealth and claimed what he called dominion status rather than independence.) Secondly he was not a man of the self-sacrificing type of Gandhi or Nehru; the prospect of office and its perquisites was more attractive to him than martyrdom. Against a background of overwhelming public rejoicing he agreed to work in partnership with the Governor to administer his country. The people, wild with joy, held a celebration demonstration in the open air at which they sacrificed a sheep and closed the proceedings with Cardinal Newman's hymn 'Lead, kindly light, amid the encircling gloom.'

The advent to office for the first time of African ministers in a British African colony was an event of critical importance. One

S

riot in one comparatively small territory had been sufficient to start a revolution. It was the beginning of a chain of events which in a decade had virtually abolished the British African Empire. At the time, however, it did not give rise to excessive public attention in Great Britain. People in Africa were much interested but outside the continent the event was regarded as hardly more than a curiosity. It was possible, for example, for John W. Wheeler-Bennett to write the official biography of King George VI in nearly 900 pages, devoting much space to the Empire and Commonwealth, without even mentioning the Gold Coast or the name of Nkrumah. The expense of the groundnuts failure took up at least tenfold as much time in the British House of Commons as did the revolutionary decision to grant to black Africans powers for which for half a century or more they had been regarded as unsuitable. If, as the British were fond of asserting, they had acquired their Empire in a fit of absence of mind, it could be held that they also lost much of it while in a similar condition.

The colonial territory which did attract public attention during the period of the 1945 Labour Government was Palestine. Because of the international repercussions of Zionism the attention was world-wide; in particular, many Americans came to judge the British Empire by the conduct of Palestine. The Labour Foreign Secretary, Ernest Bevin, was unwise enough in so many words to stake his public reputation on his ability to provide a solution.

When the British had taken over Palestine in 1917 the population had consisted of about 600,000 Arabs and 56,000 Jews. By 1945 the Arabs had increased in numbers to over 1 million; this was partly a natural increase and partly one caused by immigration, Jewish-developed Palestine having been attractive to Arabs from other areas. The Jews, principally through immigration, had increased to over 600,000. Thus while the Palestinian Jews were now a substantial community they were still considerably outnumbered by the Arabs; as in Rhodesia and Kenya, the newcomers found that the native population, far from fading into insignificance, was growing in strength. At the same time the Jews who had settled in Palestine and the Jews who wished to go there had a far deeper enthusiasm than ordinary colonial settlers. They were not just seeking a new way of life but attempting to preserve their very existence as a cultural and religious community. Before and during the war they had suffered extreme persecution at the hands of the German Government, about six million of them having actually been murdered. Only by forming their own nation-state in Palestine, the land of their scriptures, could the Jewish people ever hope to survive.

The immediate issue which faced the British at the end of the war was that of immigration. Several hundred thousand Jews from Europe, survivors of Nazi persecution, were anxious to settle in Palestine. At the same time the Palestinian Arabs were objecting to any more Jews coming in at all; they could maintain that it was for Europeans to solve a problem that had been created in Europe. The British had considerable sympathy with the Arabs for reasons both of principle and of policy. On principle it was obvious that the Arabs had a case and in the conditions of the moment nobody other than the British was likely to assist them. Politically, Britain wished to win the sympathy of the Arab countries so as to safeguard Middle East oil and communications. Moreover, it was considered, probably falsely, that the Arabs were easier than the Jews to administer on a colonial basis; the simple Arab peasant would show more deference to a British district commissioner than would a Jewish chemist from Frankfurt. It could be claimed that the admission of half a million Jews in less than 30 years had already amply fulfilled the pledge of the Balfour Declaration to create a 'Jewish National Home.'

The Jews, on their side, under the leadership of the Polish-born David Ben-Gurion had already established on sophisticated lines what amounted to a shadow government with its own army, the Haganah. During the war there had been continual clashes with the British administration over the smuggling of firearms for the Haganah, smuggling in which Ben Gurion had been implicated. The Jews maintained that the weapons were required to defend Jewish agricultural settlements from attack by Arab marauders; the British maintained that no administration could tolerate the existence of a private army. Ben Gurion's organisation was also active in the bringing of illegal immigrants to Palestine, sad ship-loads of men, women and children who kissed the soil of the Promised Land at the moment of their arrival. The British seized such ships and placed the passengers in transit camps in Cyprus. Conditions in the camps were none too pleasant and the dwellers in them were full of bitter resentment because they were not in Palestine. Ben Gurion's organisation in its propaganda tried to depict the Cyprus camps as being the same as the German concentration camps and that further aggravated ill-will between the Jews and the British. Indeed the Zionists made a sustained attempt to equate opposition to Zionism with anti-Semitism and, even, to claim that the British were as bad as the Nazis. The only justification for such unscrupulous propaganda, which went well in the United States, was the dreadful experiences the Jews had so recently undergone in Germany.

Even that extenuation could not justify the activities of the extremist Jewish groups, the Stern Gang and the Irgun Tsva'i Leumi, which indulged in murder and terrorism and showed, simply, that Jews at their worst could be as bad as other peoples at their worst. In 1946 the Irgun blew up a wing of the King David Hotel, Jerusalem, one floor of which contained the British army headquarters. No regard was paid to the fact that the attack would harm civilians more than it would the military. In fact 91 people were killed, British, Jewish and Arab, and the effect was to fill the British police and security forces with anger against the Jews. Of course, mainstream Zionism opposed such actions. 'I warn you,' cried the veteran leader Chaim Weizmann, now going blind, 'against bogus palliatives, against short cuts, against false prophets, against facile generalisations, against distortion of historic facts. If you think of bringing the redemption by un-Jewish methods, if you lose faith in hard work and better days, then you commit idolatry and endanger what we have built. Would that I had a tongue of flame, the strength of prophets, to warn you against the paths of Babylon and Egypt. "Zion shall be redeemed in Judgement"—and not by any other means.' But the Irgun pressed ahead and the Arabs, too, began to organise terrorist gangs. In the summer of 1947 the Irgun hanged two British sergeants from a tree near Tel Aviv, adding an extra horror by fitting one of the bodies with an explosive booby trap. The British police momentarily ran amuck and murdered several innocent Jews. Politically, the Irgun—which was always a small minority among the Jews— was claiming the whole land of Palestine as a Jewish state to be placed under Jewish government.

The American administration, which in that period knew and cared little about Arabs, took the Jewish side and exerted continuous pressure upon the British to admit more immigrants. If the situation had arisen only a couple of years later when, under the 'Truman doctrine' the United States had begun to resist Communist advance in the Balkans and the Middle East, the American attitude might have been different. As it was, though, a vital influence in Washington's attitude was the domestic Jewish vote. One of the odder features of Zionism and one which could only be accounted for by the dreadful impact of Hitler was the eagerness with which capitalist American Jews subscribed hundreds of millions of dollars to create socialistic settlements in Palestine. In 1946 a joint Anglo–American plan proposed to let in 100,000 immigrants; this infuriated the Arabs and would still not have given the Jews a majority in population. Then Ernest Bevin, the British Foreign Secretary, pressed ahead with a design to partition Palestine into Jewish and Arab provinces, with Jerusalem remaining under direct British administration. When this plan proved unacceptable and because of the mounting disorder impossible to enforce, Bevin became bitter and voiced what sounded very like anti-Semitic views. In fact before he had to deal with the Palestine issue Bevin had not been at all anti-Semitic, indeed rather the reverse. But he was a tough trade union leader who liked getting his own way. He thought he was doing his best for the Jews and became exasperated when they criticised him and murdered British soldiers; by 1948 his opposition to Zionism was shading into anti-Semitism, a process not discouraged by Ben-Gurion's Jewish Agency which liked so much to confuse the two things. Creech Jones at the Colonial Office was, however, a convinced pro-Zionist and considered it entirely admirable that Jews from the United States and Europe should settle in the Middle East.

When the British found that their plans for Palestine were unworkable and that the situation was making them enemies on all sides they chose simply to abdicate. This was in 1947, the year when they had done the same in India. The reasoning appears to have been similar to that over India—to force two rival communities to come to terms by leaving them on their own. Palestine was, however, quite different from India. There had been no proposal by the Indian Moslems, as there was by the Palestinian Jews, to import vast numbers of immigrants to swamp the existing majority population. Moreover, because of the terrorist campaigns relations between the British and the Jews were so bad that there could be no question of the British helping to establish the administrative framework of successor states. The British merely notified the United Nations that they intended to quit in June 1948 and then set about winding up their administration.

The United Nations produced a plan for partitioning Palestine between Jews and Arabs with Jerusalem, the Holy City of three religions, as an international zone. Neither Jews nor Arabs accepted it and both sides prepared for war. On the eve of the British withdrawal, the Jews declared the State of Israel with Weizmann as President and Ben-Gurion as Prime Minister. The surrounding Arab countries immediately invaded with the intention of destroying the new state and of driving the Jews into the sea. The Jews considered themselves threatened with final extinction; pogroms in Eastern Europe and Germany had inflicted the most grievous damage upon them and now their national home on what to them was sacred soil lay in mortal danger. Although outnumbered and outgunned, the Jews, in an epic of heroism, turned back the Arab armies and held the modern quarter of Jerusalem, largely Jewish-inhabited. For the first time since the Hasmoneam the Jews proved themselves capable of military achievement and so established a glowing self-confidence in themselves. There were atrocities on both sides during the fighting and four fifths of the Arab inhabitants of Jewish territory fled away to safety; they assumed that the conquering Arab armies would speedily restore them to their homes. How far this mass movement of population was a Jewish responsibility is difficult to establish. Certainly extremist Jews of the Irgun type did their best to terrorise the Arabs and frighten them away. At the same time, though, many Jewish and Arab neighbours, especially in Haifa, bade each other a cordial farewell and expected to see each other again as soon as the politicians had stopped the fighting. The invading Arabs contributed to the exodus by exaggerated propaganda broadcasts about Jewish atrocities.

By the end of the first phase in the fighting the Jews had established control of the areas where their settlements were the most numerous—the eastern coastal strip, the Galilee region and the new city of Jerusalem. The remainder of Palestine went to the new Kingdom of Jordan which, in 1946, had been set up, in close alliance with the British, to replace the former Emirate of Transjordan. The State of Israel had also acquired international recognition, the United States and the Soviet Union having been among the first to establish diplomatic relations. There followed a period during which the United Nations attempted to achieve a settlement. It was to be based mainly on the areas already held by the two sides except that Jerusalem was to be an international zone. Any hope of it being accepted was destroyed by the assassination by Jewish extremists of the United Nations mediator, the Swedish Count Bernadotte. Another war broke out in which the Jews gained more ground, notably the huge, empty area of the Negev desert. Finally in the summer of 1949 Israel signed a series of truce agreements with the Arab states which left frontiers as they had been established by the fighting. These were essentially military truces not political settlements and sporadic fighting continued to break out for many years afterwards. The Arabs retained as their ultimate objective the destruction of Israel, but in fact it was the Israelis who succeeded in increasing their territory. The Israelis moved their capital to the portion of Jerusalem they had occupied but most countries refused to recognise the legitimacy of their being there and ambassadors continued to reside at the main centre of Jewish population, Tel Aviv.

That the new Israel should have been established in hostility to the British was a missed opportunity. Balfour's dream of an alliance between the British Empire and world Jewry faded for ever. Yet if it had not been for the pressure for extra Jewish immigration resulting from the actions of the German Nazis, the Jews might well have been pleased to achieve independence as a British dominion. Their state, based anyway in large measure on British laws, British administrative methods and even British-style letter boxes and police uniforms, might have had a more secure existence within the Commonwealth than it actually suffered as a besieged Jewish enclave. During the trial of Adolf Eichmann, the Nazi war criminal captured by Israeli agents in South America, the lawyers on both sides quoted British precedents and decisions of the Judicial Committee of the Privy Council. The English language became, after Hebrew, the principal language of the new state. But as things were in 1947 and 1948 there was no prospect of the Israelis wishing to join the Commonwealth, still less of the British wanting to accept them.

With vigour and enterprise the Jews set about building their new country, making it a model for the Middle East. They even began to make the Negev Desert produce crops. Politically they ran a liberal democracy which, apart from certain restrictions on the remaining Arab inhabitants, appeared as a miracle of stability and tolerance in Middle Eastern conditions. Their constitution, like that of Great Britain, was uncodified. The leaders, especially in the early days, went around with open-necked shirts to symbolise the informal but businesslike character of the new state—parliamentary deputies dressed in the debating chamber as if for the seaside. The open-necked shirt, together with the beards and frock-coated ghetto dress of the orthodox minority, became as typical of Israel as the sun helmet had been of the old British Empire. But the character of Israel turned out to be not entirely what had been expected.

To build up population and to fill the places left by the refugee Arabs, the new administration, sustained by overseas funds, conducted a massive immigration programme which by 1960 had trebled the Jewish population. Under the 'Law of the Return' any Jew was entitled to come in. Once, however, the backlog of refugees from Nazi persecution had been cleared up, comparatively few Jews from Europe wanted to come. Those in Eastern Europe were, in any event, actively hindered by Communist governments from moving. From the United States came plenty of money but very few immigrants. By the 1950s the bulk of the new immigrants were 'oriental' Jews—Jews who for many centuries had lived contentedly in Arab countries and were distinguishable from other Arabs only by their religion. They knew nothing of the essentially European cause of Zionism. As a backwash of the Arab–Israeli war they were forced out of their traditional homes and obliged to settle in Israel where culturally and educationally they tended to form a separate class from the European Jews who dominated the state.

Thus one outcome of Zionism, an idea born in Central Europe, was to shuffle around about two million inhabitants of the Middle East—Moslem Arabs ejected from Palestine and Jewish Arabs brought in. With intense energy and idealism, however, Ben-Gurion and his associates worked towards the goal of creating a united nation.

The failure to harness the energy of the Jews either to the British Empire or to the economic development of the Middle East was one of the major tragedies of the post-war years. But it did not just rest there. The establishment of Israel sparked off a chain of further events which positively weakened the British Empire.

The Arab countries, in particular Egypt and Syria, felt humiliated at their defeat by 600,000 Jews. The younger army officers thought they had been let down by their political leaders and that a political and social revolution was required if the Arab peoples were to win their rightful place in the world. Arab army officers were untypical of most military men in that their political views tended towards the left and towards social change. As a direct result of the Arab–Israeli war there developed a newer and sharper Arab nationalism coupled with a dislike of traditional Arab leadership by kings and sheikhs. Israel itself was regarded as an outpost of imperialism, as evidence of Western aggression against the Arabs.

'I particularly remember,' wrote one Egyptian officer of the

Palestine war, 'a young girl of the same age as my own daughter. I saw her rushing out, amidst danger and stray bullets and, bitten by the pangs of hunger and cold, looking for a crust of bread or a rag of cloth. I always said to myself, "This may happen to my daughter." I believe that what was happening in Palestine could happen, and may still happen today, in any part of this region, as long as it resigns itself to the factors and the forces that dominate it now.'

The writer was Gamal Abdel Nasser.

# CHAPTER 13

# The last initiative

THE Conservative Party, which in 1951 returned to power under Winston Churchill, proclaimed itself the party of the Empire. Benjamin Disraeli had acquired the Suez Canal and made Queen Victoria into Empress of India. Joseph Chamberlain had pressed British expansion in Africa and advocated the economic union of the Empire. A. J. Balfour had brought the Jewish Zionists into the Empire and devised the 1926 formula by which the British Commonwealth was supposed to combine quasi-independence for the white dominions with continued imperial unity. Lord Beaverbrook, whose 'Empire Free Trade' campaign had formed the most vivid imperial propaganda between the wars, had worked mainly through the Conservative Party. Also Churchill between the wars had opposed self-government for India. For four generations practically every statement of Conservative policy had pointed to the value of maintaining and strengthening the Commonwealth and imperial system. 'Land of Hope and Glory' had been commonly sung at Conservative rallies. (The Labour Party, characteristically, had preferred Blake's 'Jerusalem' with its emphasis upon *England*'s green and pleasant land.)

It might have been supposed that the accession of such a party to power would reverse the trend of the Socialist period, in which India had become independent and a start had been made upon self-government in Africa. In fact, though, Conservative thinking upon Empire was based upon sentiment rather than upon clearly considered policies. It consisted of a bundle of muddled and even contrary attitudes which few Conservatives bothered to try to analyse. The Empire was easier to deal with as a muzzy, sentimental symbol of British glory than as an actual political problem. In 1939 a Conservative Government had declared war upon Germany in a dispute which had had nothing to do with the Empire; compared with the frontier disputes of Central Europe and distaste for the Hitler system, the interests of the Empire had been secondary. Similarly after the war, in opposition, the Conservatives had attached high priority to the unification of the non-Communist section of Europe and, with Churchill playing a leading role, had devoted much of their creative energy to this end. To be 'European' had become the fashion among younger Conservatives; the Empire had become something just for formal obeisance.

Then the Conservatives, or practically all of them, were liberal in their ideology; they considered it self-evident that free elections, free speech and impartial law courts were essential features of sound administration. The impact of Fascism and Communism had made them yet more outspoken about such principles. But the colonial Empire, which Conservatives also notionally believed in, was based upon autocratic rule by alien officials. The two things— liberalism and colonialism—were in the last resort inconsistent. In a muddled way the Conservatives and others talked of a doctrine of 'trusteeship' by which the colonial officials were to guide the subject peoples towards ultimate self-government. But this begged as many questions as it answered. Suppose a subject people did not want to be guided? Suppose such a subject people as the Cypriots were already equipped with the attributes of European civilisation? Suppose a subject people disliked the Westminster pattern of government? Suppose there were disagreement about the rate of progress? The moment a colonial people ceased to accept British administration the only way to continue was by force. Yet to use force was alien to liberal principles and, moreover, practically difficult. There was also the quasi-mathematical law that the more self-government was allowed, the more the appetite for it grew. Once the process had started it was bound to accelerate in pace. No territory wanted to be behind another; the granting of a little power to a local politician put him in a stronger position for claiming more power. In this formula (which appears both practically and theoretically correct) the doctrine of 'trusteeship' is not a meaningful factor.

The Conservatives won power on a policy statement of 32 pages entitled 'Britain Strong and Free.' In the middle of this statement were two pages devoted to the Commonwealth and Empire. 'To retain and develop the great and unique brotherhood of the British Empire and Commonwealth is a first task of British statesmanship,' it said. (The indefinite article in 'a first task of British statesmanship' is a good illustration of the muzziness of approach; a thing is either first or it is not.) The statement went on to proclaim: 'The Conservative Party, by long tradition and settled belief, is the Party of the Empire. We are proud of its past. We see it as the surest hope in our own day. We proclaim our abiding faith in its destiny. We shall strive to promote its unity, its strength and its progress.' Considering that the two major world powers, the United States and the Soviet Union, were opposed to any such enterprise and that important currents of opinion within the dependent territories themselves were also unsympathetic, this was indeed an ambitious proposal. Yet the statement proposed no new measures for giving the Empire a destiny beyond an advocacy of meetings of Commonwealth Prime Ministers being held more frequently so as to integrate the Asian ones with the older white dominions. Of the central dilemma, that of a government run at home on liberal principles attempting to run autocratically an overseas empire, the statement had nothing to say. It extolled, in connection with the colonies, the conceptions of 'individual freedom, democracy and the rule of law' and warned of the dangers of Communist subversion. The aim should be to guide the colonies along 'the road to self-government within the framework of the British Empire.' These words bear a distinct meaning—self-government implying less than sovereign independence and the avoiding of any pledge about Commonwealth membership implying something less than equality with the dominions. Somehow the colonial peoples, notably in Africa, were to be coaxed to vote freely in favour of a subordinate status within the imperial system, controlling their own internal affairs but subject to the overriding control of London. How this remarkable objective was to be achieved, the statement did not set out.

The development of jet airliners in the 1950s, bringing Africa within a night's journey of London, was, in a sense, to bind the Empire more closely together than ever before. It was to become routine during this decade for British ministers to zoom out to the colonies to handle local problems directly instead of delegating them to local governors. Yet within 13 years of this supposedly imperialist party taking office, the British Empire had practically ceased to exist. The 'surest hope' had turned out to be a delusion.

From the start, imperial affairs were allowed only a low priority in the government's thinking. Churchill himself, his mind filled with foreboding that the Korean war might develop into a third world war, devoted most of his constructive energy to foreign affairs. His last public service should be to secure a realistic settlement between the United States and the Soviet Union. His mind constantly dwelled upon such matters. Subsidiary to them was the task of hardening Western European defences against a presumed danger of invasion by the Soviet Union. Whether or not West

Germany should be rearmed, whether or not there should be a 'European Army,' were questions as much at the forefront of government and public thinking as had been the frontier problems of Czechoslovakia and Poland 15 years earlier. United States influence had much to do with it, the Americans wanting to lighten their European responsibilities. Once again, as if by instinct, the British put Europe first; in 1954 the process culminated in the British taking on the unprecedented commitment of maintaining an army of 60,000 men in Germany.

Such essentially non-Commonwealth matters were the administration's first priority. The second priority was the domestic affairs of Britain herself and to these the energies of the most effective of the younger ministers, R. A. Butler and Harold Macmillan, were devoted. The way for the Conservatives to consolidate themselves in office was to stabilise the social reforms the Labour Party had introduced and to combine them with a rising standard of living for the mass of the population. Such concentration upon consumer interests was to produce such a degree of success as to enable Macmillan ultimately to announce: 'You've never had it so good.' This was a reversal of traditional Conservative practice, which had been to provide circuses rather than bread. Now no imperial circus was required to bolster Conservative propaganda.

The Commonwealth and Empire thus took, at betst, only third place in this proiessedly imperialist administration's f hinking. This was probably fortunate. Had the whole resources oi Great Britain been mobilised in the early 1950s to the consol dation of the Empire, the ultimate result might well have been no different and the means of reaching it more painful. The British watched with attention the misfortunes of the French, who tried to maintain their overseas Empire by unsuccessful wars.

Between 1951 and 1965 Conservative imperial policy ran through three phases. (To some extent overlapping but in outline clear.) The first, and shortest, was a positive attempt to strengthen and underpin the imperial concept on a basis called 'partnership.' This lasted until about 1954. Next came a defensive period in which the British tried to stand pat against movements of revolt; the Suez war of 1956 was one aspect of this period. Thirdly came the outright decision to abandon the Empire; this was crystalised in Harold Macmillan's 'wind of change' speech in 1960 and coincided with the first British attempt to join the European Economic Community.

The story started with the Empire still intact in Africa, the

West Indies, the Mediterranean and South-East Asia. Also Britain was still the leading power in the Middle East, with many of the local Arab governments subsisting as British satellites. When the Persians had nationalised the British oil refinery at Abadan there had been talk of using actual armed force to get it back. At the same time the Empire had also, plainly, suffered serious wounds. In losing India it had lost its centre of gravity. With India gone, it was as much by habit as by strict political necessity that the British continued to dominate the communications routes. The disinclination to use force against Persia over Abadan had shown vividly that the buccaneering methods of the 19th century were ceasing to be relevant. Outright revolt was going on in Malaya, the West Indies were discontented and on the African continent was appearing a modern kind of nationalism which had not been seen before. Already an African administration was in office in the Gold Coast.

The Colonial Secretary, Oliver Lyttleton, was a business executive of aristocratic background who had entered politics in middle life at Churchill's behest. He was an efficient administrator but his purely political instincts were defective; he was not that rare kind of politician who can sense what the future will be. He thought it businesslike to amalgamate small colonies to make big ones and, with the full backing of his party, he set stolidly about this task. The Commonwealth Office at first had no continuing guidance at all—there were four Commonwealth Secretaries in the Government's first three and a half years—and there was little apparent attempt to mould the new Commonwealth, with its Asian members, into a unified force.

Lyttleton was impressed by three major schemes for joining together groups of colonies to form powerful new imperial units. Two of them were in Africa: the proposed Central African and East African federations both of which were expected to operate largely under the leadership of white settlers until such time as the local African population had become sufficiently imbued with British ways to be enabled to share in the control. The third scheme was to unite the British islands of the Caribbean into a West Indies Federation, converting them from isolated minnows into a considerable country off the American eastern seaboard.

Of these schemes the most immediately practicable was that for Central Africa and, indeed, the preliminary moves towards a federation there had already been undertaken by the Labour Government. It was to consist of Southern Rhodesia, Northern

Rhodesia and Nyasaland. The two Rhodesias having been reinforced by recent and massive white immigration, mainly from South Africa and Britain, it was reckoned that the conditions for success already existed. Southern Rhodesia, in particular, had for nearly 30 years been a self-governing colony with all effective power in the hands of its white settlers; it had constructed a sophisticated and localised system of government which had almost nothing to do with the rest of the British colonial apparatus. From Southern Rhodesia could come the bulk of the experienced manpower to run a federal administration. In racial matters at this time Southern Rhodesia could hardly be distinguished from South Africa; no black Southern Rhodesian had ever sat in the local legislature, nor was any to do so during the whole federal period. Nevertheless the Southern Rhodesians lacked the systematic doctrine of 'apartheid' which was being applied in South Africa and Cecil Rhodes's *bon mot* of 'equal rights for all civilised men' (although not fully characteristic of Rhodes's philosophy) commanded some theoretical acceptance. The control by Southern Rhodesian whites (who in 1951 numbered 180,000 as compared with over two million Africans) of their country's affairs was at variance with normal Colonial Office doctrine. By this doctrine the government of a colony should be a neutral arbiter between the races rather than representative of one of them and it was on such lines that Northern Rhodesia and Nyasaland were run; in these two northern territories executive power belonged to officials appointed from London, not to white settlers.

The problem, therefore, was to construct a federation which could reconcile the doctrine of settler control with that of maintaining a balance between the races. The solution, propounded by Godfrey Huggins, leader of the white Southern Rhodesians, and Roy Welensky, leader of the white Northern Rhodesians, was that of 'partnership.' The whites were to be the senior partners and the blacks the junior ones but as, over the generations, the blacks acquired education and a taste for European-style manners and institutions, they could be admitted to equal rights. For the moment, as Huggins put it, the partnership would be like that between a rider and his horse.

The actual population figures were: Southern Rhodesia 2,400,000 (178,000 European), Northern Rhodesia 2,183,000 (66,000 European) and Nyasaland 2,596,000 (6,800 European).

To implement 'partnership' required a constitution which was possibly the most complicated in the whole world. At the centre was to be a federal government controlling defence, most finance, trade, transport and external affairs. This federal government was to be responsible to a largely white-elected legislature, over half the members coming from Southern Rhodesia; within its sphere it was to have neo-dominion status with a Governor-General as ceremonial figurehead. The three territorial governments were to control such matters as education, welfare and police; of them one, Southern Rhodesia, was to continue to be run by a government responsible to a white-elected legislature with no effective control from London and the other two were to be run by executive Governors appointed by and responsible to London. So in many major matters the federal government was to enjoy substantial independence but in many minor ones the local administrations in the north remained subject to the Colonial Office. Then there was to be an African Affairs Board to be a check on discriminatory legislation against Africans (it was to prove to be a useless body) and a series of franchise arrangements of considerable complexity. The population of the federation was only about the same as that of Belgium and the majority of the inhabitants were poor and unsophisticated. To saddle them with four different administrations, each complete with legislature, bureaucracy and judiciary, was a venture indeed. That it worked at all was evidence of the zeal of the white minority who were its mainspring. But by the very nature of its construction, with so many competing authorities, it was liable to shake itself to pieces in any serious political storm.

The justification was that in the course of time the complexities and anomalies could be ironed out and that, meanwhile, the federation would form a natural economic unit to the benefit of all the inhabitants. Northern Rhodesia's copperbelt would provide wealth, Southern Rhodesia would provide skilled white manpower and Nyasaland, short of resources of her own, could form a reservoir of African labour for the whole. Politically the federation would form a counterbalance to Boer nationalism in South Africa and the black African nationalism typified by the Nkrumah administration in the Gold Coast. It would form in the heart of Africa a bastion of the true ideals of the British Commonwealth.

This sophisticated fabric, and the imperial dream it embodied, suffered from the start from a mortal defect. It was that most of the population disliked it.

Of this majority disapproval there could be no doubt from the beginning. Almost every articulate expression of African opinion in the two northern territories—chiefs, nationalist agitators, trade unionists, ministers of religion, the handful of African business and professional men—protested against it on the ground that it extended the power of the Southern Rhodesian white settlers. The Africans of the northern territories had been taught to believe that British colonialism would lead towards their developing institutions of their own; they felt a sense of betrayal. They were allowed no formal voice in the matter, no opportunity of accepting or rejecting their scheme. Despite every protest they could make, including petitions to the Queen recalling the treaties that had been made in the name of her great-great-grandmother, federation was imposed by a party vote in the British parliament, the Labour and Liberal parties opposing the necessary legislation. The final vote in the London House of Commons was 304 for the federation and 260 against. The only voting in the territories themselves was a referendum of the Southern Rhodesian voters, of whom all but 380 were white. In this referendum the idea of federation won comfortably, although there was a sizeable opposition. The voting was 25,570 to 14,729. The minority were mainly white supremacists of the Southern Rhodesian Dominion Party which wanted Southern Rhodesia to be independent on her own, with no truck with the 'black north.'

Among both the ministers in London and among the white settlers themselves there was a serious miscalculation about the effectiveness of black African opposition. Huggins and Welensky held that most Africans, being rural and illiterate, had no knowledge of the issues involved. So long as they were not misled by 'agitators' they would come in time to recognise the advantages of federation. The British Government, although it had its own sources of information through colonial administrators in the field, chose to accept the Huggins–Welensky argument. It had no reason to do so except its own will; no conceivable pressure by pro-federation settlers could have forced London to act unless London had wanted to. Business pressures may have had something to do with it but the overriding consideration appears simply to have been to strengthen the Empire by creating a new white-controlled dominion in the heart of Africa.

It happened that the inauguration of the federation came in the same year as the coronation of Queen Elizabeth II. This was an event which aroused the deepest interest among the British organs of opinion; the crowning and annointing of a female monarch who had acceded to the throne at an unexpectedly early age was represented as evidence of British greatness. During and after the

T

war the British had been living in conditions of economic strin-
gency and the coronation provided a refreshing glamour. It was
widely held that the ceremony inaugurated a 'New Elizabethan
Age' and it was explained that the British had always been among
their most glorious under a Queen Regnant. The reasoning,
obviously, was faulty; Queen Anne and Queen Victoria had
contributed nothing to the international triumphs of their days and
the new Queen was acceding in conditions in which the scope for
royal initiative had never been smaller. Her resemblance to
Elizabeth I of England was only her name. Although she
attempted to attach meaning to her title as Head of the Commonwealth and took an obvious interest in Commonwealth matters,
Elizabeth II, like her predecessors, remained an essentially British
monarch. She lived in Britain, spent most of her time on British
matters and had far closer relations with British ministers than
with any ministers in the Commonwealth. When she went to a
Commonwealth country it was definitely on a 'visit' and if it
happened to be a republican Commonwealth country the formali-
ties of her reception were practically the same as if she were making
a state visit to a foreign country. Nevertheless the coronation fever
of 1953, with leaders of the world-wide Commonwealth in the
great procession in the rain between Westminster Abbey and
Buckingham Palace, gave the British a momentary renewal of
self-confidence in their imperial mission. For a moment the loss of
India could be disregarded. With the young Elizabeth on the
throne and the ancient Churchill at Downing Street, it seemed
possible to dream again of a land of hope and glory. The dis-
content of a few ill-clad, uneducated Africans, living in huts and
locations in Central Africa, was a small thing against the evident
majesty of the British Commonwealth and Empire. The arti-
ficiality and irrationality of the coronation fever was part of the
mood in which the British placed Northern Rhodesia and
Nyasaland under white settler government.

The effect within Central Africa was to accelerate the growth of
political consciousness among Africans. So far from coming
gradually to accept the principles of 'partnership,' with themselves for the time being as junior partners, their hostility grew
from generalised distrust into organised movements of opposition.
Within less than a decade the largely rural and unsophisticated
Africans of the federation had reached the degree of political
consciousness of those of the Gold Coast. Even in Southern
Rhodesia, where the 'natives' had been quiescent since the 1890s,

the nationalist infection began to spread, it being hurried on by infection from the two northern territories.

To a limited extent this growth of African opposition was the fault of the federal government itself, which showed a remarkable disregard for African susceptibilities. For most of the federal period the colour bar was maintained in full vigour; Huggins treated a debate on it in the federal legislature as an occasion for humour. Not until 1959 did an African achieve government office and that was only as a junior minister. Salisbury, capital of Southern Rhodesia and fortress of white supremacy, was chosen as the federal capital; it was a place where African members of the legislature were not allowed to stay at hotels or eat in restaurants. Possibly Huggins and certainly Welensky were held back from more liberal attitudes by the practical requirement that to remain in office they had to satisfy a white electorate of less than super-human generosity. The white artisans of Salisbury, Bulawayo and the copperbelt accurately foresaw that African advancement could only weaken their own privileged position. Rather than teach Africans to drive trains, the federal authorities imported Greeks to fill railway vacancies. Throughout the history of the federation, the authorities appeared to regard it as more important to direct propaganda at the outside world, to attract capital and white immigrants, than to attempt to sell the concept to their own Africans. The extravagant damming of the Zambezi at Kariba to provide more electricity than the federation needed in the fore-seeable future was essentially a public relations exercise. The £78 million worth of concrete together with the largest man-made lake in the world provided a dramatic illustration of federal enterprise. Africans, however, found it less impressive; some of them resisted to the point of death the flooding of ancestral lands and it was believed that Kariba, which lay just inside Southern Rhodesia, had been chosen for political reasons in place of a smaller and more economic scheme which had been advanced for a dam at Kafue in Northern Rhodesia.

Even, though, if it is granted that the federal administration was inept, the true flaw of the federation lay in its basic concept and in the nature of the Africans themselves. One of the salient facts of the latter 20th century was to be the tumultuous vitality of Africans. Far from dwindling like Red Indians they showed a vigour comparable with that of 19th-century Europeans. Their birth-rate bounded upwards. Where the vigour ultimately will lead, what constructive achievements it will produce, remain unforeseeable at the time of writing; but beyond doubt the awakening of Africans brought a new factor into world affairs.

While the Central African Federation was being established by the firm, even ruthless, exercise of imperial authority, an entirely different line of development was continuing in West Africa. The actual elevation of Kwame Nkrumah to authority in the Gold Coast had taken place under Labour administration but the Conservatives confirmed and encouraged it. Lyttleton agreed to Nkrumah dropping the title of 'Leader of Government Business' and becoming 'Prime Minister' instead. At this time Nkrumah and the African-elected legislature still lacked the full attributes of internal self-government, control of finance, justice and the Civil Service still resting with the Governor, but Nkrumah, showing moderation and skill, did not kick unduly against the restrictions. He still claimed what he called dominion status but for the moment was content to serve an apprenticeship. Between him and the Governor, Sir Charles Arden-Clarke, there flourished a sound partnership and it was commonly remarked that the Gold Coast had never been more efficiently administered. White settlers in Central Africa and elsewhere grumbled about Nkrumah, rightly seeing him as the portent of the end of white supremacy, but the British at home mostly took pride in the Gold Coast and Members of Parliament, in their perorations, took to holding it out as an example of the enlightment of British colonialism.

Nkrumah's moderation had brought momentarily to reality the British dream of training colonial peoples in British methods and British manners so that they would associate freely in a united Commonwealth. The success of the Gold Coast experiment had an immediate effect in the great colony of Nigeria, almost next door. With Ceylon now a dominion, Nigeria was easily the biggest colony of the British Empire. It was not a natural unit, the urban peoples of the coast being entirely different from the Moslem traditionalists in the north, and the problem was how to underpin bureaucratic unity established by Lugard with a federal system based upon popular election. In the mid-1950s it was still common-ly assumed by the British that to establish such a federation would take a full generation but the Nigerian politicians peacefully but insistently pressed for independence by 1960. The Nigerians got their way—Nkrumah had achieved for them as well as for the Gold Coast the essential break-through.

How to reconcile settler imperialism in Central Africa with African nationalism in West Africa was a difficult, if not impossible, task. It was held that West Africans were more sophisticated than those in the Rhodesias; while West Africans could be safely allowed control over their own affairs, the Central Africans required the 'partnership' of a resident white population. But this was a thin theory and one which, by its nature, was unlikely to satisfy Central Africans. By tolerating and assisting black nationalism in West Africa, the London government was further undermining the chances of the Central African Federation.

The third great region of British Africa—the East African territories of Kenya, Uganda, Tanganyika and Zanzibar—stood politically midway between the settler-controlled territories in the south and the emerging black nationalism of the west. The hope of turning Kenya into another Southern Rhodesia still flourished among many white settlers there. More remotely, also, some of the settlers dreamed also of an East African Federation, running under predominantly white control on the Central African model. Kenya settlers would provide leadership, Uganda would provide natural wealth and Tanganyika would provide manpower. The establishment of such a federation had been a talking point for a quarter of a century and the Labour Government in 1947 had set up the East African High Commission to run common services for the territories. In the early 1950s, when there still appeared to be room to manoeuvre in colonial policy, it was undoubtedly the long-term hope of the British Government to create an East African dominion which, like that of Central Africa, would be a permanent part of a functioning British Commonwealth. Lyttleton kept dropping hints in his speeches about such a federation but, as it turned out, the ball never got rolling. New-style nationalism apart, the traditional authorities in Uganda were strong enough to put up effective resistance to any idea of domination from Nairobi. The Kenya whites themselves were divided over the project, the more cautious wanting to concentrate on their own 'white man's country' rather than dilute their resources over the black multitudes of Uganda and Tanganyika. Despite renewed immigration since the war, there were still hardly enough whites in Kenya to populate a proper town—in 1953 the white population was only 30,000. Moreover, the white Kenyans, although influential in the legislature, had no real political power; unlike the Southern Rhodesians they did not control their own police and armed forces. White leadership, too, was aspiring rather than effective; the rakish Delamere tradition persisted and Kenya European leaders were at their best amateurish and at their worst just silly. There was no Welensky in Kenya—had there been he would not have been let into the clubs—nor even a Huggins. Another, although potential, obstacle to East African Federation was the status of Tanganyika as a United Nations Trust Territory (a continuation of its former status as League of Nations mandate). The Tanganyikans would have had the opportunity to present opposition in New York, a right not open to the Africans of Northern Rhodesia and Nyasaland.

Before all such varied obstacles to an East African Federation could be overcome, the key territory, Kenya, had been swamped under the most violent wave of African nationalism of any British territory.

The idea of federalising the West Indies was different in kind from the African schemes. It had no element of ambition among recent immigrants. The scheme was directed towards administrative tidiness, towards turning small units into a single big one. Talk about it had continued under both Labour and Conservative administrations, the chief impetus coming from London rather than from the colonies themselves. In 1953 a conference in London drew up a plan for uniting the West Indies on the model of Australia but such were the jealousies and doubts among the territories that it was another five years before it began to come into force.

In fact the main impact of the West Indies upon Great Britain was not the tangled problem of getting the colonies to agree to federation (all, now, had elected legislatures) but the movement of West Indians into the metropolitan country. The process had started during the war and, with full employment in Britain, it accelerated during the 1950s until by 1967 there were an estimated 300,000 West Indian immigrants living in Britain. There were some strains; West Indians—keen cricketers—had been educated to regard themselves as British and were surprised to be treated as strangers when they arrived in the 'mother country.'

How determined the Churchill government was to maintain the imperial fabric in the early 1950s could be seen not only in Central Africa but, also, in the special cases of British Guiana and Malaya. In British Guiana the (East) Indian majority of the population returned to power a Communist-influenced administration under the dentist Cheddi Jagan; the Admiralty dispatched a cruiser, Jagan was dismissed and the Governor resumed full power. This was not, however, the straightforward suppression of a national leader. The Negroes, who formed nearly half the population, were distrustful of the Indian Jagan and the Negro leader, Forbes Burnham, switched from being Jagan's ally to Jagan's opponent. In Malaya the war continued against the Chinese Communist insurgents and a brilliant soldier, General Sir Gerald Templer, was dispatched in 1952 both to govern the territory and to direct military operations.

The apparent success of British power in both British Guiana and Malaya was to some extent misleading. Special factors existed. In both territories the opponents could be labelled as 'Communists' (although it was Jagan's American wife, Janet, rather than Jagan himself to whom Marxist affiliations could be imputed) and, therefore, sympathy could be secured from the United States. In particular the Americans disliked the apparition of Jagan on the actual mainland of the South American continent. Elsewhere in the colonial empire, Communism simply did not exist as a discernible force; it was to be a decade and more before it became even the slightest factor in Africa. It was the French who in both Indo-China and Africa encountered Marxist opposition; indeed it could be counted that the outstanding success of British colonialism was that opponents of the British were, on the whole, content to demand British-style institutions. Also the Malayan civil war, although murderous and difficult, was being run with the consent and approbation of most of the Malay people; it was a rising by Chinese immigrants, not by Malayans. Thus the essential condition for success for a guerilla rising, that of the sympathy of the non-combatant population, did not exist.

Speaking in the House of Commons in London to a motion on the Central African Federation on March 24, 1953, Lyttleton declared: 'This is a turning point in the history of Africa. If we follow this scheme, I believe that it will solve the question of partnership between the races. To defer or reject it now is to resign our responsibilities as a colonial power; it is to sink into inglorious inaction and to hope that, contrary to every lesson of history in these matters, inaction will lead to peace. It will not; it will lead to discord.'

For almost the last time, the British Parliament was hearing the voice of Empire.

PART III

*Sundown*

CHAPTER 14

# *Revolt*

REBELLION against and armed opposition to British rule had been a characteristic of the British Empire, in one part of it or another, throughout most of its history. Even in the high days of Victorian expansion when getting new colonies had hardly been more troublesome for the home government than picking apples, a year rarely passed without some kind of battle on some distant frontier. Even the triumphant Cecil Rhodes, seizing 440,000 square miles of Africa and naming them after himself, had to fight armed African tribesmen within two years of the arrival of his pioneer column. The 'Mad Mullah' in Somaliland was a plague for 20 years. While at any given moment there had been at least passive consent to British rule over most of the Empire, there had always been at least one particular trouble spot. During the formative period of the Empire such conflicts had caused the British relatively little concern. As the Victorian Prime Minister, Lord Salisbury, put it, they were 'but the surf that marks the edge and the wave of advancing civilisation.' Despite the occasional setback, such as the fall of Khartoum and the death of General Gordon, the British had found by experience that in the long run they could always defeat a non-European enemy. Rebels against the Empire had had little or no access to outside assistance and they had been defective in coherent political principle. An uncooperative chief resisting the district commissioner in Africa had little in common with, for example, the King of Burma who was fighting the Government of India; indeed the chief had never heard of Burma and knew the British only as enterprising strangers who happened to have entered the only bit of the world he knew at all. There had been little infection from one territory to another.

By the 1950s, however, these conditions had changed and the British Empire faced a series of decisive trials by force. They came from peoples who in the past had been incapable of posing a serious military problem. The developed nature of world communications meant that they took place in conditions of publicity. Although the issues in many of them were more subtle than plain rebellion against alien oppression, the British could hardly help appearing in an unfavourable light before world public opinion. Moreover, as a professed supporter of the United Nations, the British Government no longer possessed untrammelled powers of decision.

The first and instinctive reaction of the London Government was to resist. The initial phase of the Conservatives advancing in new imperial enterprises (as exemplified by the Central African Federation) gave way to a dourly defensive phase. Because of past experience the British at first assumed that colonial rebellions could be overcome without undue difficulty but this turned out to be incorrect. The military problems of the Empire grew into matters of the first magnitude and caused the utmost embarrassment.

The crucial battles were fought in Kenya, in Cyprus and, most decisively of all, in the old imperial hoodoo, Egypt.

The Kenya struggle was the most surprising and remains the most difficult to understand. The basis was the Kikuyu tribe, a vigorous group living in the part of Kenya most appropriated by white settlers. Partly from their nature and partly from their especially close contact with Europe, the Kikuyu were among the most restless Africans on the continent. From the Kikuyu had arisen a leader of ability and personality, Jomo Kenyatta, who in 1946 returned home after 15 years' absence in Europe. With Kwame Nkrumah of the Gold Coast, who had returned home at about the same time, Kenyatta had helped to draft the principles of African nationalism. Now he sought to put the principles into practice. He founded in 1947 the Kenya African Union, a body led mainly by Kikuyu but which had gone out of its way to enlist support from other Kenya tribes. Kenyatta and his movement made rapid progress, using Kikuyu grievances about land which had been 'stolen' for European settlement to combine into one force the tribal traditionalists and the younger, educated Africans. By the late 1940s Kenyatta was addressing rallies of 30,000 and more and the settlers had taken to demanding his deportation. Actually his objectives at this stage were more moderate than those of Nkrumah in the Gold Coast. When in 1951 the Labour Colonial Secretary, James Griffiths, visited Kenya, no demand was made for an African administration on the Gold Coast model. All Kenyatta asked for was an increase from four to twelve in the number of African members on the legislative council, popular election to replace nomination by the Governor. (At that time there were 27 elected and official Europeans in the legislature; a typical Kenya election of the period consisted of a couple of white farmers competing for the votes of a few hundred of their neighbours.) The settlers threatened to 'take matters into their own hands' if the Colonial Office gave way to Kenyatta's demands and, in fact, all Griffiths agreed to was one extra, nominated African in the legislature.

Thus it appeared obvious to African nationalists that the existence of a white, immigrant community in Kenya was an obstacle to their political advance. This, added to the land grievances, was the background to armed revolt, the Mau Mau.

The aims and organisation of Mau Mau and, even, the meaning of the name are still less than clear. It sprang from Kikuyu secret societies, bound together by oath, and was stiffened by ex-servicemen who had belonged to the British forces in the war. At its most developed stage it had a shadow government and parliament but the direction was less than intelligent; had the organisation acted decisively while it still had the advantage of surprise, it might have come near to overwhelming the colony. It was a partly political, partly superstitious and partly criminal body; in the ultimate analysis it must be counted as a form of violent resistance to British colonialism and settlement.

The early disturbances, in 1950 and 1951, were sporadic and appeared more as a nuisance than a danger. Despite agitation from the settlers, the administration took them less than seriously. Then, as they worsened, a new Governor, Sir Evelyn Baring, changed the policy. He declared a state of emergency, banned African political parties, suspended most civil liberties and arrested 200 African leaders, including Kenyatta. The following year Kenyatta was tried for and convicted of managing Mau Mau and sentenced to seven years' imprisonment; the trial, which attracted wide international attention, had unsatisfactory features and the nature of Kenyatta's involvement with Mau Mau remains uncertain. What was certain was that among Africans, especially the Kikuyu, Kenyatta acquired the status of a martyr and so, in the long run, his influence increased. Moreover, the identification of Kenyatta with Mau Mau increased the popularity of the latter and it was able to count upon much passive support among the mass of the African population, not least in the capital, Nairobi. In 1953 and 1954 the British found themselves in battles in up to battalion strength against strong guerilla groups.

It was a muddled, sordid and cruel war. Some African leaders held aloof from it altogether and others actually supported the British. Mau Mau itself concentrated much attention on recruiting fellow-Africans into the organisation. Those who agreed to join swore oaths to the accompaniment of elaborate, often obscene, rituals. Those who held back from such things were killed, sometimes with torture. Mau Mau killed about ten times as many Africans as it did Europeans. The largest number of deaths was of Mau Mau members themselves; many were killed in battle and others were summarily tried and executed. The hangings totalled over a thousand, the gallows in Nairobi crashing away at a rate which had never been seen before on British soil. At the peak, 80,000 Kikuyu were held in concentration camps.

The Europeans, leading a form of siege life and constantly armed, declared their determination to eliminate the movement altogether but, at the same time, even the most self-confident of them acquired a new outlook upon Africans. The common form of address for any African of any age had been 'boy' and the settlers had customarily treated them as children; useful children, tricky children but definite inferiors. Mau Mau was not just hated and despised by the Kenya Europeans; they were also alarmed by it. It appeared that African opposition could actually hurt. Many Europeans could scarcely have been more surprised had their farm animals staged an Orwellian revolt. Politically the British began to retreat. The aim was to defeat Mau Mau by force and, at the same time, to conciliate moderate African opinion in the hope that a new leader would arise to replace Kenyatta.

In the light of Mau Mau and against the background of historic Colonial Office principles, the British began to develop a new doctrine, that of 'multi-racialism.' It was the colonial version of the 'partnership' preached by Sir Roy Welensky in the Central African Federation. From about 1954 to 1959 it was the leading theme of British colonial policy in eastern and central Africa. The leading exponent was Alan Lennox-Boyd, who in 1954 succeeded Lyttleton as Colonial Secretary. A brusque giant of a man, six feet six inches tall, Lennox-Boyd had married an heiress of the Guinness brewing family and had devoted most of his life to politics. Aged 50 at the time of his appointment, he had long been interested in colonial affairs and was determined to make his mark. Such was his energy that while he was in office it was customary to refer to him as one of the greatest Colonial Secretaries—and so he would have been had his plans worked out.

'Multi-racialism' implied the admission of educated Africans to a share in government but it differed from the 'one man one vote' of the Gold Coast in that it did not envisage Africans within the foreseeable future getting control of their countries. Not only was the franchise to be limited to the minority of educated Africans but, also, the Africans as a whole were to achieve no more than 'equality' with the minority immigrant races. Executive government was to be gradually transferred to ministers responsible to the legislature, among them representatives of all races. The British-appointed Governor would tend slowly to sink into the background but he would retain emergency powers in case the elaborate design broke down. Lennox-Boyd believed in this policy and used a mixture of persuasion and authority to implement it. Certainly in giving a limited recognition to African aspirations it marked a sharp break with Conservative policy of the past; that Lennox-Boyd welcomed African leaders to his private home in London and treated them as normal guests was regarded, at the time, as something worth remarking upon.

In Kenya, Lennox-Boyd set about revisions of the constitution which by 1957 had brought 'multi-racialism' towards full flower. The new arrangement was riddled with checks and balances. There was a legislature of 14 elected Europeans, 14 elected Africans, six elected Asians, two elected Arabs, 12 'specially elected members' (four each European, African and Asian) and 44 official and nominated members. There was provision for two Africans to sit among the 12 members of the Governor's executive council, which acquired some of the characteristics of a ministry responsible to the legislature. The understanding was that this constitution would last for at least ten years so that the 'multi-racial' spirit should have a chance to grow. Most European settlers were doubtful about it but their main leader, Michael Blundell, an intellectual farmer who in his youth had trained as a Lieder singer, accepted the new spirit and tried to work it. While Blundell lacked the stature of Welensky in Central Africa and, anyway, at this period was by no means excessively liberal, he became, briefly, the favourite son of the Colonial Office. He failed, though, because at first many, and later most, Europeans distrusted his policies and he got practically no support at all from Africans. The leading Africans formed a solidly nationalist phalanx, refusing to enter the executive council and pining for the imprisoned Kenyatta.

In the neighbouring colony of Uganda there arose a different kind of conflict. Uganda had no white settlers to speak of and historic British policy had been to develop it as an entirely African state. The arrival of a progressive, reform-minded Governor Sir Andrew Cohen (one of the few Jewish members of the Colonial Service) had the odd effect of uniting traditionalist Africans and modern nationalists into joint opposition to the British. This arose through the leading African personality, the young Kabaka (King) of Buganda; the Buganda royal dynasty was an old one which had provided settled government long before the arrival of the British. Buganda, which formed a quarter of the whole colony of Uganda, had its own administration and its own parliament, the lukiko. The Kabaka's ministers, who literally crawled in the royal presence, were proud of their traditions and with their direct link with Great Britain, which had been by treaty with Queen Victoria. Their country had originally been a protectorate under the Foreign Office and they had resented their transfer to the Colonial Office and their subordination to the Governor of Uganda. It was a quaint arrangement, the continued vitality of Buganda proving an irritation alike to reforming Governors, such as Cohen, and to African nationalists who wanted 'one man one vote' rather than tribal dynasties. Royal Buganda was an obstacle towards converting Uganda into a proper nation-state.

The Kabaka was Edward Frederick Mutesa II, commonly called 'King Freddie' in newspaper headlines. Part playboy and part serious politician, he had acceded to the throne in 1939 when he was aged 15, the Archbishop of Canterbury ruling that he was the only son of his father to have been born in proper Christian wedlock. He went to Cambridge University in England and, to his pride, was made an honorary captain in the Grenadier Guards. In the early 1950s, during intervals from holidays in Europe, he pressed for the separation of Buganda from Uganda and for its ultimate independence under his own sovereignty. Matters came to a head in 1953 when the Colonial Secretary, Oliver Lyttleton, implied in a speech in London that the aim of British policy was to set up an East African Federation including Uganda, complete with Buganda. The Kabaka, supported by his ministers and people, started what amounted to a non-co-operation policy, which infuriated Cohen. Backed by London, Cohen arrested him, placed him on an aircraft and exiled him to England, where he was given an allowance of £8,000 a year tax free. His sister, Princess Nalinya, dropped dead from shock when she heard the news.

Cohen bade Buganda to choose a new Kabaka but the entire

kingdom refused to co-operate. Moreover, nationalist Africans in the rest of Uganda, who normally disliked Buganda traditions and Buganda separatism, had no option but to rally to the Kabaka's support. For two years the colony was in an uproar, 'King Freddie' with his Guards tie becoming the popular hero. What with Mau Mau going on in neighbouring Kenya, the British had hardly any option but to climb down and after two years the Kabaka was allowed back, his standing strengthened. As it turned out, Buganda separatism was eventually to be defeated (and 'King Freddie' exiled again by an African national government) but what mattered at the moment of the Kabaka's return was that it had been demonstrated conclusively that there existed such a thing as African public opinion and that the British could be made to bend before it. Moreover, the episode showed how unwilling Africans were to accept the guidance of a Governor who was genuinely devoted to their advancement; nationalists preferred leaders of their own, even so unexpected a leader as the Kabaka. To what extent the fear of another Mau Mau was an active influence upon the British is difficult to assess; but Mau Mau was an obvious part of the context.

To the south, in the sprawling trust territory of Tanganyika, conquered from the Germans in the First World War, 'multi-racialism' reached momentarily a point of perfect balance in the constitution of 1955, the first in which the Africans had been allowed any substantial say at all. The territory contained 8 million Africans, 140,000 Asians and 20,000 Europeans; a symmetrical legislature was created in which the three races were allotted seven seats each. Even this advance had owed as much to the United Nations Trusteeship Committee and to the initiative of the British themselves as to any internal agitation. Tanganyika, a poor country administered in classical Colonial Service style, had long been a political vacuum. 'There is no insistent clamour for reform. The pace of political and constitutional developments must be matched with the capacity of the bulk of the population to absorb change,' said an official report in 1951. In 1954, answering proposals for phased self-government produced by a United Nations visiting commission, the Tanganyika administration declared: 'The suggestion that Tanganyika could achieve self-government in less than twenty years is based on erroneous assumptions.'

As it turned out the blankness of Tanganyikan political life proved to be all the better opportunity for an intelligent, ambitious

v

leader; he had a clean sheet on which to start. Such a leader arose
in the Roman Catholic schoolmaster Julius Nyerere, born in 1921.
A tense, clever man with a small head, Nyerere in 1949 had been
the first Tanganyikan to study at a British University (Edinburgh).
He returned home with his mind full of political ideas and in 1954
started the Tanganyika African Union as the first effective
political party the territory had known. As Nkrumah had done in
the Gold Coast, and Kenyatta in Kenya, Nyerere caught the ears
of the people, both the traditionalists and the younger literates,
and converted their notion of politics from a local, tribal one into a
dream of sovereign independence. This at first amazed the British
but there were no serious disorders. As Nkrumah had done in the
Gold Coast and Kenyatta wanted to do in Kenya, Nyerere combined vigour in whipping up the African masses with a moderate,
statesmanlike approach to the British. He went out of his way to
keep declaring that the immigrant races were as much Tanganyikan as any native African. The Tanganyika Europeans actually
grew proud of Nyerere and took to boasting how much better he
was than nationalist leaders in other colonies. Although self-
government and then independence were to come to Tanganyika
at a pace far faster than the British had planned, the process was
largely peaceful. But, again, Mau Mau in Kenya was a part of the
total context.

One factor in Nyerere's success was the territory's status under
the United Nations. Unlike the old, European-controlled League
of Nations, the United Nations from the beginning took its trusteeship responsibilities seriously. (Some of the actual members of the
League of Nations commissions had been quite diligent; but the
mandated territories had rarely attracted political interest in the
League.) The majority of United Nations members, including the
two most powerful, the United States and the Soviet Union, were
unsympathetic to the imperialist concept and the more new
members joined, the stronger the anti-imperial bias became. The
General Assembly Trusteeship Committee, with representatives of
former colonies among its members, was an effective, informed
body of which the British administration had to take account.
While the committee had no power to interfere in the administration of Tanganyika, the British had to answer its questions, report
to it annually and listen to its recommendations. The Foreign
Office in London, engulfed in a cold war with the Soviet Union
and eager to expound in the world forum the virtues of liberal
democracy, could not allow a remote place like Tanganyika

to become a diplomatic embarrassment. Nyerere had a world audience at his disposal.

Mau Mau was only the taster for the more fundamental military challenges of the mid-1950s. The scene was the Middle East, the traditional pivot of the Empire. Lately it had also become the principal source of British oil and at this time it was taken for granted that a degree of imperial suzerainty, backed by military strength, was necessary to keep the oil flowing.

Despite the Palestine disaster, the British at the beginning of the 1950s were still the dominant force in the Middle East. The Mediterranean Fleet, although diminished, still steamed along the sea routes with bases at Gibraltar, Malta and Aden to support it. In Egypt the British maintained a garrison of 60,000 soldiers; the Suez base was the biggest base maintained by any country outside its own borders. Iraq still lay under British influence. The army of Jordan (the Arab Legion) was commanded by a British officer, Sir John Glubb. The British could recall with satisfaction how in two world wars they had maintained their Middle East position; there had been no destruction of prestige to compare with what had happened with the Japanese in the Far East.

It was possible to doubt the continued utility to Great Britain of so elaborate an apparatus. The assumption that the route to India and Australia and the oil depended upon a gigantic military occupation of the Middle East had not been properly assessed. Any tendency to look at it in a new light was weakened by the cold war with the Soviet Union, then at its worst; as in the days of Disraeli the spectre kept arising of a Russian conquest of the Middle East. More important, there existed a subtle but real consideration of prestige, the British control of the Middle East symbolising the continued reality of Empire and Commonwealth both to the British themselves and to the world at large. No Australian or Indian could sail through the Middle East, with its union jacks, without recognising that the senior member of the Commonwealth was a great power.

For a quarter of a century the maintenance of the British garrison in Egypt had been a subject for bitter dissension between British and Egyptians. An Egyptian army revolt in 1952 ended the monarchy and brought to power a raw, radical nationalism which further exacerbated the situation, even though the British themselves had not lifted a finger to save the king. The inspirer of the revolt was Gamal Abdul Nasser, a 34-year-old man in a hurry to establish himself and the 'Arab nation' in a position of dignity and power and to inaugurate social reform. At first he did not claim full authority and for two years allowed the older General Neguib to occupy nominally the senior position. Under the Anglo–Egyptian Treaty of 1936 the British garrison had the right to remain until 1956, when the arrangement would be renegotiated. This treaty had been renounced by the monarchist government in 1951 and three years of negotiation followed with successive Egyptian administrations, the country being in an apparently chaotic condition. Indeed the fact that Egyptian administrations were rising and falling so frequently in those years led the British to take the ultimate victor less than seriously as an Egyptian representative. It was supposed at first that he was just another hotheaded young revolutionary whom another turn of the wheel would soon cast down. Such refusal to accept Nasser as a national leader explains much in British policy that otherwise must baffle the observer. At the time of the Suez War of 1956, Nasser had been formally in office as President of Egypt for only four months.

Riot and sabotage against the British garrison made its position increasingly difficult in the early 1950s. The Egyptian Government even cut off its water supply. A mob in Cairo destroyed £4 million worth of British property and buildings; the rioters actually broke into the Turf Club where they murdered the Canadian Trade Commissioner and nine British subjects. At an unofficial, local level, there were British retaliations, including the burning down of a complete Egyptian village. Shut in their encampments, surrounded by barbed wire, the British soldiers led lives of misery and it was doubtful whether in such conditions the garrison had any military utility at all. The old consolations for Egyptian service of night clubs and approachable sisters of street touts were no longer available. The Turf Club itself was not safe. Instead of being an outcrop of British strength, the Egyptian garrison became a liability, its resources turned to its own self-defence.

To such unpleasant circumstances were added the sheer cost of the base, its vulnerability to nuclear attack and the doubtful utility of keeping so substantial a section of the British army behind barbed wire in Egypt when soldiers were needed for Europe, Korea, Malaya, and, latterly, Kenya. In any event, the legal right to stay would expire in 1956.

Against this background, the Churchill government, for all its imperialist posture, decided to make concessions. A new treaty in 1954 provided for the total withdrawal of the garrison; but the British were to leave behind their installations, in the charge of technicians, and to have the right to return in the event of a serious threat to the Suez Canal from an outside power. It was an arrangement which gave the British most of what they really required and, indeed, more than they might have expected. At the same time, though, it was the greatest British retreat since the abdication in India. Once again the legions were sailing back home. The Prime Minister, Churchill, made no effort to conceal his belief that the process was profoundly distasteful to him; he had, after all, directed much of the British effort in the Second World War, to the defence of this area. Anthony Eden, the Foreign Secretary who negotiated the agreement, was subject to serious criticism from the right wing of the Conservative Party, a 'Suez Group,' being formed within the party actively to organise opposition in the House of Commons. Egypt became a subject which put on edge the nerves of both Eden and his party.

To set against the setback in Egypt there came a minor British triumph in Sudan, nominally an Anglo–Egyptian condominion but in practice run by the British. The persistent aim of the Egyptians had been to get sole control of Sudan as an integral part of Egyptian territory and during the early 1950s they acquired American support for this end. The British, proud of the club-like and dedicated little administrative service which ran the country, were loathe to hand it over to the less efficient methods of Egypt; also, for general political reasons, they did not want to add to Egyptian strength. As a counterpoise to Egyptian aspirations they developed self-government within Sudan at an unusually fast rate, rejecting meanwhile Egyptian demands for a plebiscite. In 1955 the Sudanese parliament voted for an independent republic and this was formally set up on January 1, 1956, outside the Commonwealth. While Sudan was far from being in the forefront of African nationalism, its very existence as an independent country was an example, to add to that of the Gold Coast, to whet political appetites in other African countries.

In evacuating Egypt there was no intention of relinquishing power in the Middle East. What was required was a new site for a military base and it was ready to hand in the island of Cyprus which, in fact, had been acquired by Disraeli from Turkey 75 years earlier with just such a use in mind. Cyprus was a fully-fledged crown colony; it appeared that no complications could arise with her as had arisen in trying to maintain a British garrison in such an independently sovereign country as Egypt. Without considering it necessary to consult the local population, the

British Government blandly announced that Cyprus was to be the site of a new and permanent British base. From this it followed that the island must expect to remain permanently within the British Empire.

Speaking about Cyprus in the House of Commons on July 28, 1954, Henry Hopkinson, Minister of State at the Colonial Office, declared: 'It has always been understood and agreed that there are certain territories in the Commonwealth which, owing to their particular circumstances, can never expect to be fully independent. . . . Nothing less than continued sovereignty over this island can enable Britain to carry out her strategic obligations to Europe, the Mediterranean and the Middle East.'

Thus from a relatively obscure minister, who shortly afterwards was retired to the House of Lords, came the last full-blooded statement of imperial claim by an official British spokesman. Because Cyprus was essential for imperial defence, she could 'never' expect to be independent. It was a straightforward assertion of power and the power was assumed to be real; Cyprus was a poor island with only a 600,000 population and so could offer no serious challenge to London.

In fact it would have been difficult to have obtained any constitutional expression of Cypriot opinion. There was no local, elected legislature. The leaders of the Greek 80 per cent of the population were as determined upon Enosis—union with Greece—as they had been during the riots of 1931. They had swung to Britain's support during the war, when Britain had been fighting in support of Greece, but they had hoped that victory against Germany and Italy would produce such a liberal atmosphere that their wishes would readily be granted. In 1948 they had rejected an offer from the Labour government of a constitution which would have given them limited self-government and had continued to press for Enosis.

The conversion of Cyprus into a permanent and major British base, together with Hopkinson's use of the word 'never' about their aspirations, removed any reasonable hope that continued peaceful agitation could fulfill their aspirations. Either they must challenge the British Empire outright, and by force, or else they must put away their dreams. The Colonial Office found difficulty, as was common during this period, in accepting that nationalist leaders in the colony represented the true will of the people. Certainly in Cyprus it was only with the utmost reluctance that the local administration was to yield to the notion that British rule really was unwanted; Cyprus was so much a special case—a colony with a European population devoted to a non-British culture—that officials arriving from previous service in, perhaps, equatorial Africa or the West Indies, often failed to get to grips with it. So did some who ought to have been there long enough to know better. Nevertheless the bare fact that the permanent withholding of self-determination would be likely to cause some kind of trouble must have been appreciated. The British calculation must have been that it would form no more than another bit of surf breaking on the frontier of Empire and that it could be the more easily handled because the island was acquiring a powerful garrison.

The emergence of two Cypriot leaders of exceptional ability, one a priest and the other a soldier, turned the trouble into much more than just surf.

The priest was Michael Mouskos, a sharp-witted farmer's son from western Cyprus. He had a vocation to the church and, after study at a local monastery and in Athens, he got a scholarship from the World Council of Churches to visit the United States. Such was his reputation among his own countrymen that, while still midway through a theological course at Boston University, he was called back to Cyprus to become Bishop of Kitium. Two years later, in 1950, he was elected Archbishop of Cyprus and took the title of Makarios III. He was then aged only 37 but the beard and black robes of his office gave him a patriarchal aspect and people tended to treat him as if he were much older. The office of Archbishop carried with it the additional title of Ethnarch, or national leader, and for centuries of both Turkish and British rule the head of the church had been regarded by Greek-Cypriots as their political as well as religious spokesman. To symbolise the splendour of his dual office, the Archbishop always signed his name in red ink and, on high festivals, wore robes of imperial purple.

While the young Makarios punctiliously performed his religious duties, his main skill and ambition lay in political matters and he was determined that he should be the man to fulfil the ancient ambition of joining Cyprus to Greece. His office as prince-bishop had medieval overtones but his actual political approach was in harmony with the methods of the 20th century. One of his early acts was to organise a Greek-Cypriot plebiscite in which 97 per cent of his people voted for union with Greece; then in 1954 he got the Greek Government to place the matter before the United Nations.

The soldier was Lieutenant-Colonel George Grivas, a retired officer of the Greek army. Five years older than Makarios, Grivas was Cyprus-born and had adopted a military career against the wishes of his parents. He had played his part in the stiff resistance put up by Greece to Italian and German invasion but had won no outstanding reputation. He had left the army at the end of the war and had devoted himself to his vast postage stamp collection and to dabbling in Greek right-wing politics; he had twice stood unsuccessfully for parliament as an ultra royalist. He could be ill-tempered and vain but his deep Greek patriotism could attract the devotion of younger men.

In the early 1950s Makarios and Grivas worked together in a Cyprus liberation movement, Makarios heading the political side and Grivas the military side. The two men had little in common: Makarios, the elegant, fork-tongued politician, had a flexibility alien to the rough Grivas who tended to see opposition as something that should just be shot down. The bishop had a better knowledge than the soldier of how the world worked. Their partnership was one of convenience only and was disrupted by periodical disputes. Nevertheless each depended on the other. Grivas provided brilliant leadership for a guerilla war against the British. Makarios as the national leader, his portrait prominent in every Greek-Cypriot home, provided that context of a sympathetic local population which is essential for the success of guerilla operations conducted against a superior enemy. The result was an almost miraculously successful campaign.

Grivas enlisted about a thousand young Cypriot men into his guerilla army, Eoka, trained them and then late in 1954 commenced operations with an attempt to assassinate the Governor, Sir Robert Armitage, with a time bomb. Further explosions and attacks followed but the British at first took them less than seriously. Soldiers, relaxing gratefully after the unpleasantness of Egypt, were irritated rather than annoyed. 'We thought we were among friends. What a pity,' said an official army spokesman. The attitude changed as it became clear that the administration was faced with an unusually intelligent and well-organised enemy. Even the Cypriot Communists found they had been manoeuvred into the position of supporting the bishop and his royalist ally. 'NO POWER IN THE WORLD CAN SUPPRESS OUR MOVEMENT. We are all determined to die for our cause. We shall push the British imperialists into the sea,' proclaimed Eoka pamphlets.

One reaction came from the Turkish-Cypriots who formed about one fifth of the total population. Remnants of the centuries of Turkish rule, the Turkish-Cypriots had as their ultimate ideal the reunion of the island with Turkey. Meanwhile they supported the British as a lesser evil than the Greeks. As the Eoka campaign developed, the British became more and more dependent upon the Turks for administering the island, especially in the police, and gave them some favour and encouragement. No obstacle was raised to the registration of a 'Cyprus is Turkish' political party. It was something like the early period of Moslem agitation in India; while the British angrily denied they were working to a 'divide and rule' policy, they did in practice find it not unwelcome that a section of the population opposed the main nationalist movement.

Turks and Greeks alike enlisted the support of their mainland governments, thus turning Cyprus into an international issue. It was the more awkward because Greece and Turkey were allies in the North Atlantic Treaty Organisation and were supposed to form a joint bulwark against southwards expansion by the Soviet Union. This factor brought in the United States, which was helping to finance the defence arrangements of both, and the Americans regarded unity against Communism as being more important than any local, colonial difficulty or, for that matter, than the maintenance of the British Empire. What with the United Nations also being brought in, what in the old days would have been a domestic matter for the Empire turned into an international issue. No longer could the British run the Empire without outside interference.

For a moment the British hesitated. Alan Lennox-Boyd flew out to Cyprus, the first Colonial Secretary ever to go there, and in public statements hinted that 'never' should not be taken too literally. Eoka celebrated his arrival with the biggest set of bomb explosions yet. Then the British called a conference in London of themselves, Turkey and Greece but this had no result beyond illustrating how Cyprus had become an international as well as an imperial problem.

Next the Cabinet in London decided upon a warlike line. The Governor, Armitage, was replaced by Field Marshal Sir John Harding, who had just retired as Chief of the Imperial General Staff. Harding's brief was to destroy Eoka. It was reckoned that he would be able to do what Templer had done to the rebels in Malaya; it was assumed (by wishful thinking rather than upon any definite evidence) that Eoka was unrepresentative of the general Cypriot population and that, in any event, no organisation of ill-equipped and ill-shaven Greek guerillas could withstand the might of the British Empire. The British by 1955 had lost much of their old self-confidence but enough of it remained to make them assume that the Cyprus rebellion could be no more than a passing difficulty. Politically, the hope was that once Eoka had been suppressed, the main body of Cypriots would accept internal self-government and voluntarily play their role within the Empire.

In the first stages of Harding's administration, the two policies—military repression and political conciliation—were conducted simultaneously. Emergency regulations set up detention camps in which Eoka suspects could be held without trial, made the carrying of arms a capital offence and forbade public meetings. Juvenile offenders, who loved conducting anti-British riots in their schools, were made liable to flogging. In the Troodos mountains where Grivas (whose identity was still unknown) had his secret headquarters, the first pitched battles took place between British units and Eoka bands. At the same time Harding and Makarios negotiated on internal self-government. Makarios's tactic was to say he would accept it, provided it was regarded as only a temporary phase and did not rule out ultimate self-determination. He also insisted that internal self-government must include control of the police and that there should be an amnesty for Eoka members. To the British his attitude appeared temporising and insincere.

Eastern prelates, with their beards, brimless top hats and broken English, had hitherto tended to be regarded by the British as vaguely humorous figures, capable of lightening works of fiction. 'I have been telling how I was expulsed from Sofia. The Bulgar peoples say it was for fornications, but it was for politics. They are not expulsing from Sofia for fornications unless there is politics too.' Thus spoke the Archimandrite Antonios in Evelyn Waugh's novel *Put Out More Flags* (1942). Makarios failed to fit this kind of characterisation and so he was cast by the British, instead, as a sinister man of infinite guile. In his black robes, fingering his crucifix while dealing with Eoka gunmen, the young archbishop looked like an incarnation of evil. Certainly at this stage Makarios was indeed less than frank; unlike Grivas he was not convinced of the efficacy of straight military force and believed he should use the arts of negotiation to get the best possible terms for his people. The British, not only the general public but also the officials in Cyprus, found him so easy to dislike that they lost any sense of cool judgement over him. On March 9, 1956, they abruptly lost patience with him and, as he was setting off on a visit to Greece, church bells pealing, arrested him and flew him off to exile in the Seychelles. Within 48 hours Eoka had managed to get a time-bomb into Harding's bed. Makarios himself, when he had got over the shock, was amused—the Seychelles were a comfortable prison and he was sure of his own indispensibility. On the island, though, the civil war became crueller than ever, terrorism answered by executions, arbitrary imprisonment and collective fines.

In 1955, Winston Churchill, full of years and honour but well past the peak of his capacity, had retired as Prime Minister and been replaced by Anthony Eden. Had Eden never become Prime Minister his political career would have been reckoned on all sides to have been both successful and honourable. People trusted him and because of this he had been a distinguished international negotiator. His tragedy was that he came to the highest office at a moment when older conceptions of the Empire and Commonwealth were in decay and he lacked the genius which could have given him a vision of the future. That the decay should be a painful process was inevitable; the British misfortune was that Eden, always a tense man and now also a sick one, tended to think in slogans and to fail, pathetically, to use guile as a substitute for strength.

Eden's purpose was to prevent the withdrawal from Egypt marking the start of a general British retreat in the Middle East. No further ground should be yielded to the militant Arab nationalism typified by Nasser and Cyprus must be held firmly within the Empire. It was an indication of Eden's lack of balance that he went so far as to equate the anti-British propaganda of Radio Cairo with the aggressive designs of the pre-war European dictators Hitler and Mussolini; drawing such a parallel might have been justified as just a piece of counter-abuse but Eden appeared really to believe in it. To give in to Nasser, he thought, would be like the unsuccessful old policy of 'appeasement' in Europe. In 1955 was signed the Bagdad Pact, a military alliance of Britain, Iraq, Turkey and Pakistan designed to seal off Soviet expansion from the north and to form an obstacle to the cruder new nationalisms. Turkey and Pakistan joined for their own purposes but Iraq, the former British mandatory, was still at this time regarded as something of a British client-state. The young King, Feisal II, had received a British education and his Prime Minister, the deaf old Nuri es-Said had for 30 years championed the British connection. The Bagdad Pact formed the political basis and the Cyprus garrison the military basis for Eden's policy. The British Empire was set upon a collision course with the newer Middle East nationalisms.

One irritation for the British was the delinquency of the Kingdom of Jordan in which they reckoned they had a proprietary interest. In Eden's view: 'Jordan was a country for which we had special responsibility; we had brought it into being.' It consisted of the former Emirate of Transjordan, a relatively backward area, plus that part of Palestine which had not fallen to Israel. The young King Hussein—he had succeeded aged 18 in 1953 after his father had fallen ill with schizophrenia—was temperamentally as pro-British as his cousin Feisal in Iraq but he was well aware of the difficulties of his position. The sophisticated Palestinian Arabs had little loyalty to his dynasty or to the British connection. Hussein's hope of survival was to act as a modern nationalist leader rather than as a feudal survival. He refused to join the Bagdad Pact and then, in March 1956, went on to demonstrate his independence in a yet more striking manner. The leading personality in Jordan, after Hussein, was Lieutenant-General John Glubb (Glubb Pasha) who had commanded the Jordanian army, the Arab Legion, for 18 years. He was practically old enough to be Hussein's grandfather. He had spent most of his adult life in Arab countries and, in a paternalist way, was devoted to Arab interests as he saw them. He was the last and one of the greatest of the line of British Arabphiles who had donned Bedouin headdress and sought to establish brotherhood with the men of the desert.

Hussein sent for old Glubb and dismissed him at a moment's notice.

This was a horrible injury to British pride and yet nothing could be done about it. Too much hostility towards Hussein might drive him into outright alliance with Nasser. Eden found himself in the uncomfortable posture of trying on the one hand to maintain the British connection without Glubb and on the other of withstanding right-wing British public opinion, furious at the humiliation. Such embarrassment must have made Eden the more determined to make a stand as soon as the right issue arrived.

That issue arose only four months later when Nasser nationalised the Suez Canal.

It happened at a particularly awkward moment for Eden. The King of Iraq and Nuri es-Said were paying a ceremonial visit to London. As usual on such occasions, the British were putting on a show of pomp to demonstrate how mighty they were. Escorted by the Household Cavalry, the Iraqi visitors jingled down the processional route, the Mall, to Buckingham Palace where they dined off gold plate. The next evening, July 26, 1956, they attended a more businesslike dinner at Eden's official residence, 10 Downing Street; the British Prime Minister, one of the world's most famous and experienced statesmen, received them at the door. Perhaps the cares of office appeared to weigh a little heavily on Eden's shoulders, but he could still exert charm. No man ever looked more like a British Prime Minister than Eden did. At the beginning of that dinner it could be reckoned that Eden, by virtue of his office, was the most powerful man in the affairs of the Middle East. The young King and the old Nuri could be grateful he was their ally.

Halfway through the dinner, a private secretary stepped into the room to tell Eden that the Suez Canal, the traditional windpipe of the British Empire, had been expropriated. The diners managed to finish off the meal but otherwise all was confusion. The Iraqis saw clearly, as Eden put it, that 'here was an event which changed all perspectives.' The King caused a flutter of alarm by pointing towards Eden's press secretary, who was lurking in the background in shirt sleeves, and hissing what sounded like 'Israeli!' Such was the agitation of the moment that it seemed as if the King feared assassination. In fact he was pointing past the secretary to a bust of Disraeli, the man who had bought control of the canal for the British Empire.

Nasser's action was not conceived primarily as an anti-British move. It had sprung from his desire to construct a dam, three miles wide, across the River Nile at Aswan to provide irrigation and electricity. In essence it was the most hopeful scheme for economic development ever undertaken by an Egyptian administration. The total cost was estimated at some £500 million which Nasser certainly could not raise on his own and in 1955 he had begun negotiations with the aim of borrowing the money from the United States, Great Britain and the World Bank, the American contribution being the key one on which the others depended. At the same time, in accordance with the still novel doctrine of 'neutralism' between Communist and non-Communist blocs, he had entered into active relations with Communist countries, acquiring arms from them and, even, trying to use them as a bargaining counter with the Americans. John Foster Dulles, the American Secretary of State, thought neutralism was nearly as undesirable as Communism itself and, on July 19, 1956, without consulting the British, abruptly broke off negotiations on the dam. Nasser, furiously angry, decided to pay for the dam by expropriating the canal. (He proposed to pay compensation to the dispossessed shareholders but calculated that there would be revenue left over to finance Aswan.)

The canal was the property of the Suez Canal Company, an Egyptian company in which the majority shareholder was the British government. The next biggest shareholder was France; the canal had originally been built under French direction and the company's headquarters were in Paris. The company's ownership of the canal was due to continue until 1968 when it would revert to Egypt.

Nasser was acting legally in taking it over. The abruptness of his action was unrepresentative of the more liberal traditions of public administration and his speeches abusing 'imperialism' made it sure that the transaction would take place in an atmosphere of ill-will. In the last analysis, though, he was as much entitled to nationalise the canal as the British Labour Government had been entitled to nationalise the British coal mines. The international aspects of the situation had nothing to do with actual ownership; they rested upon the Suez Canal Convention of 1888 by which Egypt and 23 other countries had undertaken to keep the canal open for shipping 'at all times and for all powers.' This convention had already been broken on occasion under the old ownership and, on the whole, it might have been assumed that it was Egypt's interest to attract as many customers as possible; the canal, like the oil of the Middle East, was an asset only so long as Europe would pay for it. British ships formed two thirds of the canal's customers.

To the British the canal was more than just a waterway. It was a symbol of imperial authority and one which in the recent past had figured in glorious military successes. Part of the proclaimed purpose of combatting Eoka in Cyprus was to retain a base from which to defend the canal. Its arbitrary expropriation by a man regarded as an unpleasant Egyptian upstart evoked the deepest emotions. Among Eden and his ministers clarity of thought gave way to atavistic impulse. Eden applied to the nationalisation the emotive word 'theft' (he was still employing it in his memoirs three years later) and immediately ordered plans to be prepared for the military invasion of Egypt.

The ally ready at hand was the other part-proprietor of the

canal company, France. In their handling of colonial problems
the French had been less skilful than the British. Their attempt to
hold on to Indo-China had proved a disastrous failure and one
which left a mess behind which was to trouble the world for years
to come. The British, at least, had managed to evacuate such
territories as India and Burma—and, even, Egypt—with a
measure of dignity for themselves and some framework of ordered
government left behind. The collisions between the British and
insurgent nationalisms in Kenya and Cyprus were trivial in comparison with the French colonial wars. Now the French were
engaged upon a struggle with Arab rebels in Algeria, a place they
regarded not as a colony but as a part of metropolitan France.
Their defeats in the Far East had made them the more determined
to win in Algeria. The rebels were receiving moral support and
some material aid from Nasser and the French were determined to
hit back at him; so far as they were concerned, Algeria was rather
more important than the canal.

Despite the similarity of their situations—imperial powers under
attack—France and Britain had hitherto in this period collaborated very little outside Europe. In the Middle East, indeed, they
had often been rivals. France's principal ally was Israel, with
which Britain's relations had been cool as a result of the incidents
of the Palestine mandate. While France had found common
interest with Israel in resisting Arab aspirations, the British had
preferred to rely upon allies among the Arabs themselves in such
places as Iraq, Jordan and the Persian Gulf. Moreover, the British
had little in common with the colonial policies of the dying Fourth
French Republic. Under the impact of the Suez nationalisation,
however, Eden decided to make common cause with the French
and the proposed invasion of Egypt was planned as a joint enterprise.

Eden attempted also to enlist United States support and did, in
fact, secure some measure of sympathy. Under Dulles, American
policy was dedicated to what was called the 'containment' of
Communism. Since Nasser had links with Communist countries
and had shown himself unworthy of American aid for Aswan,
there was a sound case from the American point of view of ensuring
that his ownership of the canal did not advance the power of the
Soviet Union. However, Dulles did not equate the containment of
Communism with the maintenance of British authority in the
Middle East; the two things were not necessarily the same at all.
He took a leading part in negotiations designed to get Nasser

voluntarily to accept a measure of international control over the canal and himself produced a scheme for a 'Suez Canal Users' Association' which would have helped to run the canal. What Dulles and his President, Eisenhower, would not do was to sanction an invasion of Egypt, still less co-operate with one.

For three months the negotiations dragged on while Nasser in Cairo exulted in having not just tweaked the lion's tail but having bitten off a piece of it. Eden became obsessed with the situation, appearing to regard the Suez Canal as the most important thing in the world. His wife said she felt as if the canal were running through their drawing room. But the actual invasion of Egypt turned out to be a more formidable operation than the armchair strategists had realised. Eden could not, like Gladstone, just telegraph the Mediterranean Fleet to bombard Alexandria. While far from being a first-class power, Egypt did possess an army equipped with tanks and an air force including jet bombers and fighters. She would have to be taken seriously and, indeed, attacked with an overwhelming superiority of force. When Gordon had fallen at Khartoum, the event had been so distant and British prestige so high that it caused hardly a ripple in world opinion. For Eden's Suez operation, however, the possibility of defeat at Egyptian hands simply could not be contemplated. The whole world, Communist, anti-Communist and neutralist would explode with laughter if the 'wogs' won. As it turned out, the martial qualities of Egypt were less than strong; she was diverted by fighting Israel and Nasser had made no serious preparations for meeting an Anglo–French invasion. Despite his fulminations against imperialism, it scarcely entered Nasser's head that the British would fall so far from respectability as actually to invade his country. He was as surprised as an atheist who finds the vicar picking his pocket. In their tunnels under Whitehall, however, the British military planners had to assume that Egypt could offer serious resistance. To seize the canal would entail the biggest combined operation since the landings in France in 1944—and there were no forces immediately available to do it. Planning and preparation took two months—some of the reservists, specially called up, got so bored with waiting that they actually mutinied. Moreover, the Cyprus base, which was supposed to be the springboard for military control of the canal, turned out to be useless save for air operations. This was because Cyprus possessed no deep water port, a fact which up to 1956 seems to have been disregarded in British strategic planning. Troops and heavy equipment would have to embark at Malta, six days' sailing distance from Egypt.

The preliminary preparations were largely secret, few outside the British and French administrations realising their massive scale. Almost to the last moment the possibility appears to have existed in Eden's mind that he might cancel the enterprise; aggression against Egypt did, after all, accord ill with the concept of international relations with which he had been commonly associated. The French, though, were determined to attack and, if possible, to overthrow Nasser. Their ally, Israel, provided the pretext and the method for Eden going ahead.

Israel had long been suffering from incursions by groups of Arab guerillas who, in defiance of the armistice agreements, penetrated her territory and attacked farms and villages. David Ben-Gurion, the Israeli Prime Minister, decided that the way to stop the raids was to mount a big counter-attack, using his army in strength. This, strictly, would count as aggression but Ben Gurion calculated that he could win a quick victory and then withdraw before anybody could interfere. If, after the event, he were arraigned before the United Nations, he would plead provocation. In the early autumn of 1956 the choice of which Arab country to attack had narrowed down to Egypt or Jordan. The British, brought into Franco–Israeli discussions, urged that there should be no attack upon Jordan since, apart from anything else, Britain had a treaty commitment to defend her. There followed the secret 'Treaty of Sèvres' by which the British, French and Israelis agreed upon an attack on Egypt.

The arrangement was decked with the clumsiest window-dressing. To please Eden, who hated the thought of appearing as an aggressor, it was agreed that the attack should not be mounted as a single operation. Instead the Israelis should attack first and then the British and French would step in to act as 'policemen' to protect the Suez Canal from damage in the fighting. The 'police' role would be directed entirely against the Egyptians, the Israelis having no intention of going anywhere near the canal. Although the existence of an actual agreement with the Israelis was concealed, the camouflage deceived practically nobody. In the British House of Commons accusations of collusion—including one from the Conservative benches—were made at once.

Israel attacked on October 29, striking deep into the 24,000 square miles of the barren Sinai Desert. Although the Egyptians had known in advance that an attack was likely and, moreover,

w

had garrisoned the desert with an ultimate view to using it as a springboard from which to attack Israel, they were completely routed. The Israeli army, consisting mostly of part-time reservists, eliminated all opposition.

Eden expressed shock at the Israeli action and told the House of Commons that the British Ambassador in Israel had been instructed five days earlier 'to urge restraint.' He went on to issue an ultimatum calling upon both sides to stop fighting and the Egyptians to accept an Anglo–French occupation of the canal zone. The Egyptians, naturally, refused and the British and French, without bothering to declare war, commenced military operations. There had been no consultation with the Commonwealth.

It is still difficult to write calmly about this episode, which so darkened the final phase of the British Empire. There had always been two strains, contrary strains, in British imperialism—the rough, aggressive strain and the other, more liberal one, which sought genuinely to provide sound administration for underdeveloped peoples. The British Empire is difficult to understand just because it was based upon two such contradictory principles. It was a shame that in 1956 the Eden administration decided to act as it did. Moreover the actual method of attack was clumsy. For the first six days, while the invasion armada sailed from Malta, the offensive was confined to air raids. While the bombs fell upon Egypt, Nasser had time to choke the canal with blockships and world opinion had time to coalesce against the British and French. When, eventually, the troops did arrive they landed successfully at Port Said and experienced little difficulty in fighting their way down the canal; they were stopped before they got to the southern end for political, not military, reasons. The decisive factor in the cease-fire appears to have been a sudden realisation by Eden's Chancellor of the Exchequer, Harold Macmillan, that the pound sterling was in danger of collapse and that there would be no American assistance so long as the aggression continued. Macmillan had earlier supported the operation; his change of attitude reflected a realism which in the following years was to end with the final dismantling of the imperial apparatus.

Exactly what Eden was aiming at is far from clear. According to his statements of the time, the occupation of the canal was to be only 'temporary.' If this were really so, it is difficult to see what purpose it could serve. Once the British and French had departed, the Egyptians could be as stiff as they liked. If, on the other hand,

Eden were thinking of a prolonged occupation until the Egyptians saw things the British way, he was reverting to a policy which had already failed. The British had agreed two years earlier to quit Egypt precisely because the local inhabitants had made life so difficult for the garrison. This time Nasser had taken the pre-caution of making a mass distribution of rifles to civilians in preparation for possible guerilla action. Any attempt permanently to hold down Egypt could well have resulted in the British and French bleeding to death in an Algeria-type situation, a situation the more uncomfortable because Egypt was a sovereign state and a member of the United Nations. Some hope appears to have existed among the British—it was reflected in propaganda broadcasts and in leaflets dropped upon Cairo—that the operation would cause the Egyptians to become disgusted with Nasser, who in 1956 was still comparatively new and untried, and overthrow him in favour of some leader more amenable to the British. In fact, of course, the operation was just the recipe for confirming Nasser in power. Had he been beaten by Israel alone he would certainly have looked silly but the Anglo–French intervention gave him an alibi.

In a muddled way, Eden attempted to argue that the onslaught was meant to pave the way for a United Nations force to protect the canal and to keep Egypt and Israel apart; this curious line of reasoning was hardly supported by the fact that Britain and France were saved only by their vetoes from defeat in the Security Council and were outvoted by 64 to 5 in the General Assembly. The truth was that the enterprise from beginning to end was an ill-conceived and harmful one, carried on by a Prime Minister who was physically unfit for his work. Swaying before the furious onslaught from the opposition in the House of Commons, Eden appeared to be far more agitated over Nasser than ever Churchill or Neville Chamberlain had been over Hitler. As Aneurin Bevan remarked in the House of Commons: 'There is something the matter with him.' It reflected, perhaps, a weakness in the British constitutional system that, so far as can be ascertained, neither his Cabinet colleagues, nor the Queen, insisted at once that he should hand the command of affairs to a fitter man.

As the Suez Canal had once reflected the power of the British Empire so the 1956 Suez War reflected its downfall.

It proved, first of all, that world politics were now so closely enmeshed in a single whole that it was no longer practicable for such countries as Britain and France to act independently. An attack upon Egypt was a matter for world concern and one which united almost everyone against them. It was unlike the Russian suppression of Hungary which happened at the same time (in part under the smoke screen of Suez); the Russians only had one power bloc opposing them, not both. Secondly it showed that the British Commonwealth of Nations had ceased to exist as a unified force in world affairs. Eden did not consult the Commonwealth about his plans and most of the members of the Commonwealth voted against him in the United Nations. Even little New Zealand, the most loyal to Britain of the old dominions, withdrew her cruiser, H.M.N.Z.S. *Royalist*, from the Mediterranean Fleet rather than let her take part in the assault upon Egypt.

The consequences were equally significant. Although the British had not been militarily defeated (Russian threats of nuclear rockets upon London had hardly been a serious factor), the fact that for political reasons their armed forces were unable to achieve their objectives was noted by every opponent of British imperialism. The triumphant Nasser established himself more strongly than ever as exemplar of the idea that it paid to defy the British. The delicate balance in the Middle East of the British operating partly through friends and partly through military power was destroyed. In less than two years Iraq had fallen to a new nationalist revolution and the King and Nuri had been murdered. Hussein of Jordan retained his throne only by the most careful balancing of Western against Arab nationalist interests and new American advisers replaced Glubb Pasha. Also the British themselves realised that old imperialist concepts were now a cause for embarrassment rather than for rejoicing; some popular self-delusion remained but the actual political decisions of the future were to be formed in a different context than had still been regarded as relevant in the days of Churchill and Eden.

On the whole, the British bowed out of Empire gracefully. Suez was the particular occasion on which they did so ungracefully. The Egyptians won at last.

# CHAPTER 15

# The wind of change

WHEN, just after the Suez War, Harold Macmillan succeeded Anthony Eden as Prime Minister of Great Britain, there were still about 45 separate governments controlled by the Colonial Office in London. (An exact count is difficult, it depending, for example, on how the central African and Pacific territories are computed.) The Colonial Service, in full vigour after its post-war modernisation, was still recruiting young men from the universities in the expectation they would have a life career in running and developing subject territories. The union jack still flew in every continent, portraits of the Queen hung in government buildings, the bands played, the governors wore white plumes in their hats, ceremonial and social life proceeded almost as if Kipling were still living. In particular, British colonialism was still the strongest single force in the continent of Africa.

The Commonwealth—at least as late as 1956 the leader of the Labour Party was describing it in a speech as the *British* Commonwealth—was still an intimate association, the leaders well known to each other and able to gather around a family-sized table. There were five 'white' members—Britain, Canada, Australia, New Zealand and South Africa—and three Asian members— India, Pakistan and Ceylon. The policies of the Asians and then Suez had destroyed the idea of common defence and foreign policy arrangements but the association still had a family air; the leaders gathered informally in the cabinet room at 10 Downing Street without the paraphernalia and etiquette of ordinary international conferences. It was exceptional for anyone less than a Prime Minister to represent his country. All the members, save India and Pakistan, maintained an allegiance to the Queen and conducted their affairs in her name.

The initial changes during the Macmillan period were the fruit of past developments and had little to do with the more recent crises in Egypt, Kenya and Cyprus. The battles over them belonged to the past and the transfer of power could be represented as part of a steady and long-term policy.

The first territory in this category was the Gold Coast, which had enjoyed substantial powers of self-government under Kwame Nkrumah for six years. This was to prove to be the longest apprenticeship for independence in any African colony. Nkrumah, while always pressing for dominion status, had worked cordially and efficiently with the Governor, Sir Charles Arden-Clarke; by the time Macmillan came to power, the British had largely overlooked the fact that they had originally locked up Nkrumah as an undesirable agitator and were now hailing the Gold Coast as a triumph of liberal principle. In March 1957 the British parliament passed an act conferring dominion status and changing the name of the country to Ghana, after a medieval West African empire, at Nkrumah's behest. British Togoland, which had been captured from Germany in the First World War and administered under mandate, was incorporated in the new dominion.

Nkrumah was happy to join the Commonwealth and, indeed, for the first three years was content to remain under the sovereignty of the Queen. He selected as Governor-General the Earl of Listowel, who had served as a minister in the British Labour Government. It was a measure of how little, even in Britain, the working of the Commonwealth was understood that *The Times*, London, went out of its way to congratulate the *British* government on the suitability of Listowel's appointment. In 1959 Nkrumah became the first person outside the royal circle to know that the Queen was expecting a baby, he being told even before Macmillan. This was because the Queen had been due to visit her new dominion but had to put the occasion off on account of her condition. Nkrumah instead visited the Queen's Scottish retreat, Balmoral, and was made a member of the Privy Council.

Despite such intimacy with the royal family and the cordiality of his relationship with the Commonwealth, Nkrumah's primary interests lay elsewhere. He did not want to be just an equal among Commonwealth Prime Ministers gathered in London; rather, in accordance with ambitions which stretched back to the Pan-African Congress of 1946, he saw himself as the potential leader of all black Africa. He assumed the title Osagyefo—'Redeemer'—and worked actively to promote the unity of African nationalist movements and opposition to colonial regimes. His capital, Accra, became (with Cairo) a centre for politicians exiled from other African countries. In 1958 he announced, more or less on the spur of the moment, a 'union' between Ghana and the formerly French territory of Guinea; in practice it amounted to very little but it did pose curious constitutional questions from the viewpoint of the

Commonwealth, Ghana then still legally forming a part of the Queen's dominions.

Had Nkrumah set about his pan-Africanism more calmly and been less obsessed with his personal position as a pioneer, he might well have established a lasting leadership. In his early days in power, everything was on his side. But although he had been an inspiring propagandist and, also, a philosopher capable of expressing African ideals in reasoned terms, his actual administration of the country was notable more for enterprise than for achievement. Internal opposition, some of it violent and unconstitutional, drove him into a condition approaching megalomania. When, after nine years, he was deposed in a military revolution, he had few friends left. Ghana, although the best 'prepared' of all the African countries for independence, was less than an unqualified success.

In 1957, however, it acted as an accelerator for African nationalism throughout the continent.

Ghana was the ninth member of the Commonwealth. Five months after she joined, a tenth, Malaya, was admitted, thus bringing 'non-white' members up to half the total. Never again was the Commonwealth to be predominantly a British family affair, with most of the members thinking in British or 'Western' terms.

Independence for Malaya came calmly. It was the logical consequence of independence for India and Pakistan and of the Japanese war. Only Communist insurrection and, to some extent, disputes between the various Malay princely states had delayed it. The success of Field Marshal Templer in putting down the insurrection had contributed towards the Cyprus disaster. It was not appreciated that Harding, appointed to Cyprus with a similar brief to that of Templer to restore order, was in fact confronted by different circumstances. The Communist rebels in Malaya had been mostly Chinese, operating without the support of the Malay people. Cyprus presented the different problem of a guerilla army operating *with* mass popular support. The leading Malayan personality, Tunku Abdul Rahman, was an aristocratic conservative of scholarly characteristics; he had insisted firmly upon independence but, having got it, was happy to work in close association with Britain. This was fortunate for upon Malayan rubber depended much of the strength of the Sterling Area; but the Tunku (this word is a title, not a name) for all his friendliness towards Britain was a radical on matters of race and soon he was

taking a leading part in ejecting South Africa from the Commonwealth.

Independent Malaya was a constitutional oddity, a monarchy
within the Commonwealth; the head of state, elected by the rulers
of the princely states, was allowed the prerogatives and rank of a
King, including the title of 'His Majesty.' This happened with no
fuss and little attention from lawyers; it can be taken as an illustration of how flexible the Commonwealth was becoming. Malaya
was the first Commonwealth country to cut free from the British
monarchy at the moment of independence, instead of going
through a preliminary phase as a dominion.

Another enterprise going ahead was that of federating the West
Indies, with a view to forming another independent dominion.
The legislation passed the British parliament in 1957 and the
federation came into being, on a basis of internal self-government
and not independence, at the beginning of 1958. The initiative for
it came largely from Britain and the smaller islands; in the big
islands of Jamaica and Trinidad, the most influential leaders
preferred to remain in local politics instead of seeking power in the
federal machinery.

A more lasting effect of the West Indies upon the Commonwealth was not the federation (which collapsed in 1962) but the
continuing emigration of West Indians to Britain, where well-paid
jobs were plentifully available. They could enter without formality,
it still being reckoned that Commonwealth citizenship implied
unfettered admittance to the mother country. Within a decade the
West Indian population of Britain had reached an estimated
300,000, forming the largest minority group. Also during this
period substantial numbers of Indians and Pakistanis came to
Britain to work and, also, growing numbers of students from every
part of the Commonwealth. At the moment of the fall of the
Empire, Britain looked more like the heart of a multi-racial
institution than she ever had done before. The children, instead of
being out of sight up in the nursery, were now claiming their seats
at dinner. They were not entirely welcome; in 1961 the British
broke with historic principle by subjecting Commonwealth
citizens to immigration control.

The Macmillan administration was an unusually young one;
of the 18 members of the cabinet, only five had served in the original Churchill cabinet of six years previously. Most of the ministers
belonged to a new generation which had not been active in public
life in the pre-war imperial heyday. The Prime Minister himself

concealed behind an old-fashioned manner a zest for novelty—part of his political success lay in his ability to cloak radical action behind conservative talk. He was an efficient administrator, maintaining an astute balance between prime ministerial initiative and a proper use of his colleagues' talents. After the ageing Churchill and the flagging Eden, Macmillan gave his young ministers a coherent sense of direction.

In imperial matters, the choice open to this clear-headed administration was whether to continue the policy of the mid-1950s, that of using force to retain the remains of the Empire, or whether to retreat. The Suez disaster, together with the prolonged war against Eoka in Cyprus, had demonstrated that force was both expensive and unlikely to work. The Mau Mau uprising and the success of Nkrumah had shown that even in Africa, the old assumptions of easy power were no longer valid. This latter point, curiously, was often grasped more readily in London than by the administrators on the spot. The 1955 Bandung Conference of 29 African and Asian countries, some of them still colonies, had shown that the leaders of the underdeveloped peoples were claiming a voice in world arrangements. Both the United States and the Soviet Union, hoping to enlist the new countries in the 'cold war,' encouraged such nationalist aspirations; in particular the United States wanted to avoid its anti-Communist policy being associated with the older style of 'imperialism.' Then there was the example of France, whose colonial wars contributed to the downfall of the Fourth Republic. The clear-cut actions of Charles de Gaulle, who on coming to power in 1958 gave up the attempt to hold Algeria by force and offered independence to the 'black' French colonies, commanded interest and respect. Another factor, indirect but increasingly influential, was the 1957 Treaty of Rome which bound together six west European countries in a customs union, the European Economic Community. The new grouping, from which the British at first held aloof, grew rapidly in strength and so caused the British to consider economic policy ever more in a European rather than a Commonwealth context. Thus a variety of disparate factors were working together against the continuance of the British Empire.

It is improbable that any outright decision was taken at the outset of the Macmillan administration to abandon the Empire. The available evidence suggests, indeed, that so far as there was a long-term imperial policy at all, it was to try to adapt the Empire to changed conditions rather than to abolish it. But at the same time that administration did from the outset recognise that to try to check violent nationalism by force would not work and, moreover, would attract international calumny.

The new attitude was exemplified by a rigorous reorganisation of the armed services which began under Duncan Sandys, Defence Minister, in the spring of 1957. Conscription, which had been the basis of the British army since 1939, was abandoned in favour of a smaller, mainly professional force designed mainly for the defence of Europe. Overseas commitments remained, of course, especially in the Middle and Far East but the wholesale disbanding of army units meant that manpower would soon no longer be available for major or prolonged colonial campaigns. (The Cyprus war was fought mainly by conscripts.) The nub of British defence policy was specifically stated to be the nuclear 'deterrent,' which was obviously useless for imperial purposes. Also there was a further reduction of ships in the Royal Navy, the historic Mediterranean Fleet being run down to almost nothing.

The first retreat was in Cyprus. Eoka had proved to be impossible to subdue by straightforward military methods and limits existed to the extent to which a country of the nature of Britain could go in counter-terrorism. The emergency regulations in Cyprus were stringent; concentration camps contained about a tenth of the adult male Greek population, torture was used to extort information, the gallows in Nicosia was busy; nevertheless a basic framework of law remained, the courts on occasion acquitting prisoners arraigned by the administration, and the House of Commons in London provided a forum in which Cypriot grievances could be ventilated. Grivas, despite the efforts of 30,000 soldiers to track him down, remained at large on the island and his guerilla army, constantly refreshed by new young recruits, became more rather than less effective. Every hanging of a captured guerilla made the Greek-Cypriot population rally more firmly against the British. From the moment of arrival at Nicosia airport, festooned with barbed wire and guarded by sentries, the visitor in those days was conscious of the atmosphere of terror; every bend in every road presented the possibility of ambush for a British vehicle.

The scheme of removing Archbishop Makarios to the Seychelles, where he was cut off from contact with his people, had miscarried. His absence had made him more rather than less influential. His photograph hung in the place of honour in every

Greek-Cypriot home, gazing sardonically down on British soldiers ripping up floorboards in search of illegal arms. The notion— generously expressed by the colonial administration on the spot— that Makarios was unrepresentative of his people and that Eoka's power stemmed just from terrorising the people at large, had never been a realistic one and by 1957 it could no longer be sustained at all. There would have to be negotiations and the only person to negotiate with was the Archbishop himself. Accordingly in March, 1957, three months after taking office, the Macmillan administration released Makarios. At first he was not allowed to return home and he established himself at Athens.

This was a crucial decision. Less than four years after declaring 'never' for self-determination in Cyprus, the British had begun to surrender.

It caused a Cabinet crisis in London. The Marquess of Salisbury, Lord President of the Council, was popularly reckoned to be the second most powerful member of the Government. His remote ancestors, the Cecils, had held high authority under Elizabeth I and James I; his grandfather had been Prime Minister to Queen Victoria and had presided over the heyday of British imperial expansion. The capital of the Central African Federation, Salisbury, had been called not after the English city of the same name but after the Marquess of Salisbury. As head of the House of Cecil, Salisbury was the outstanding example in current politics of the hereditary grandee; indeed he himself believed in and advocated a continuance of an hereditary element in the British constitution. His political career had been distinguished by his own personal achievement as well as by his family connection. Before the war he had resigned office rather than accept the 'appeasement' policy of Neville Chamberlain. Had he been a commoner and not a peer he would have been a strong contender against Macmillan for the office of Prime Minister itself. As it was he had taken a leading part in the sounding of Conservative opinion which had led the Queen to send for Macmillan to head the Government. Newspapers delighted in presenting him as the hidden eminence within the Government, the guardian of the doctrine, the maker of Prime Ministers. Besides all this, Salisbury was the leader of the imperialist wing of the Conservative Party; he had played a leading part in the setting up of the Central African Federation.

Salisbury opposed the release of Makarios. When Macmillan insisted upon going ahead with it, Salisbury resigned. For a moment it looked as if the heavens might fall in. In fact, though, there was no reverberation at all; nobody resigned with him and Salisbury, out of office, became just another grumbling peer. He learned that a kingmaker is not necessarily so powerful as a king and his followers on imperial matters were shown to be only an inconsiderable minority of the Conservative Party. By facing and beating Salisbury, Macmillan showed that the old faith in the imperial mission was no longer a force in British domestic politics. It had become hardly more important an issue than Sunday observance.

In Cyprus the fighting was beginning to change character and to assume something of the nature of a civil war between Greek-Cypriots and Turkish-Cypriots. The Turkish 20 per cent of the population had originally been convenient to the British as a counterpoise to Greek aspirations but now they were getting out of control. They began, even, to demand a partition of the island into Greek and Turkish areas and to conduct riots in support of this aim. Macmillan himself flew to Greece and to Turkey to try to get these two foreign countries to bring their nationals in Cyprus to agreement; the spectacle of a British Prime Minister craving the assistance of such comparatively minor powers in quelling disorder in a British colony was in itself evidence of how far the old spirit had declined. Eventually, after two more years, it was agreed at Geneva that Cyprus should become an independent republic, with safeguards for the Turks written into its constitution. To enforce the constitution there was to be a special law court, the first president of which was a German. The British were to remain theoretically 'sovereign' over the areas of their military bases.

Makarios was elected President of Cyprus and applied, successfully, for membership of the Commonwealth. The prelate, who had so recently been regarded as such an arch-criminal that a leading Cabinet minister had resigned rather than assent to his release, appeared benignly at Buckingham Palace to shake hands with the Queen. The Turks continued to be riotous and the Greeks ambitious to obtain unfettered control. As in Ireland, India and Palestine, disorder continued and within a couple of years United Nations forces were necessary to keep the peace.

Cyprus showed how weak the British colonial system had become. Suez, at least, had been a major military enterprise against a sovereign power equipped with modern weapons and associated with powerful friends. Cyprus was a tiny colony which in the early 1950s had appeared to be incapable of interrupting the majestic flow of British policy. The combination of guerilla rebellion with international action, within and without the United Nations, had been sufficient to force a British surrender. Moreover, it had demonstrated how defective were the strategic assumptions upon which Britain had been operating. The reason for the fuss over Cyprus had been its alleged value as a base. Yet the main Suez operation had had to be mounted from Malta. The idea of Cyprus playing a key role in British and imperial defence arrangements was proved to be a myth. The British insistence on retaining sovereignty over the base areas was a point of pride rather than of necessity. Demarcation of the areas took months of tortuous negotiation but hardly had the final agreements been signed than the British began to withdraw their forces. The principal Middle East base, which had originally been in Egypt, moved from Cyprus first to Kenya and then to the black rocks of the former punishment station, Aden. By 1967, a decade after the bloodiest Eoka fighting, a total British withdrawal from Cyprus was being canvassed—to the grief of the many Cypriots who had based their livelihoods on the presence of British forces.

Another significant point about Cyprus was its size. In past times it would have been regarded as ludicrous to allow the attributes of sovereign independence to a shrimp of an island with only 600,000 population. Such a country would plainly be incapable of providing for its self-defence and diplomatic representation. In the mid-1950s such lands as Switzerland (5 million) and Finland (4 million) were still regarded as 'small.' A Colonial Office study in the mid-1950s placed Sierra Leone (2.5 million) as the smallest colony which could ever be fit for sovereignty on its own. Cyprus helped to pioneer the changed system by which any organisation, no matter how tiny, could be recognised as an international entity. By 1965 Britain was surrendering independence even to the Maldive Islands with a population of only 97,000. In this revolution, the United Nations was an essential factor. Independence had meaning in so far as it carried with it the rights and duties of United Nations membership. Cyprus, or the Maldives, acquired exactly the same voting rights in the General Assembly as the United States of America. A mission to the United Nations was the only piece of diplomatic machinery it was necessary for them to maintain. Unlike the old days, when such powers as Britain and France had snapped up small, underdeveloped countries, the new world system provided a place (for what it was worth) for even the tiniest national community.

In Africa, now the principal section of the British Empire, the Macmillan administration at first lacked a clear-cut policy. It was obvious that, following Ghana, such other West African territories as Nigeria and Sierra Leone and even, possibly, tiny Gambia must move towards dominion status and that questions of timing and constitutional arrangement were all that needed to be settled. Also the positive, expansionist spirit of the early 1950s, exemplified by the creation of the Central African Federation, was now dead. The combination of Mau Mau, Mutesa and Macmillan made obsolete the conception of an East African Federation under the union jack. Yet the ideal subsisted, so long as Lennox-Boyd remained at the Colonial Office, of somehow creating 'multi-racial' societies in which, over a long period, British officials and settlers would lead Africans towards the splendours of Westminster-style government, in a modified form. The aim, so far as it was coherent, was to build a Commonwealth comprising every kind of African territory from white-controlled South Africa to black Ghana, with such 'multi-racial' lands as Central Africa and Kenya forming a bridge between the two extremes and, indeed, a model for them. As late as 1961, Macmillan was hoping to save the Central African Federation and he unfolded to a new British High Commissioner there, Cuthbert Alport, the possibility of the job being a great proconsulship in the tradition of Milner of South Africa and Cromer of Egypt. The crudities of African nationalism in the early Macmillan period were more evident than its strength. Retreat before pressure was a general posture, not an event regarded as imminent in Africa.

The process was exemplified at the scene of Mau Mau in East Africa. Right until the end of the 1950s white settlement was still being encouraged in Kenya. The city of Nairobi was growing into one of the showplaces of the African continent, clean new office blocks supplemented by tropical flowers planted by what was possibly the most able civic parks department in the world. White control still appeared to be absolute. The Civil Service was British in its senior grades and British or Asian in its middle grades; few Africans were above the rank of messenger. The African leader, Jomo Kenyatta, was held in detention in a remote, arid part of the country; his gaolers, it was said, plied him with cases of brandy in the hope he would drink himself to death. A few remnants of Mau Mau still subsisted in the forests but most of the members were in detention camps where attempts, sometimes brutal, were being made to 'rehabilitate' them. The administration hoped that

Kenyatta and Mau Mau belonged to the past and that a new generation of African leaders would arise to fulfil the 'multi-racial' ideal. Actually it was impossible for any African leader to prosper unless he identified himself with Kenyatta.

Yet the old magic of 'prestige' had faded. Practically no literate African was willing to settle for British-defined 'multi-racialism;' he would settle for nothing less than African control. In Tanganyika, which up to the mid-1950s had possessed no politics worth mentioning, Julius Nyerere built up his African National Union into the dominating popular force; whenever Nyerere pushed, the British gave way, and almost overnight the possibility arose of Tanganyika becoming a sovereign country. Because of his ability and apparent moderation, Nyerere was regarded as a model of what an African leader should be. He also held the reserve card of Tanganyika's status as a trust territory; if he quarrelled with the British he could always appeal to the Trusteeship Committee of the United Nations. In Uganda, too, the episode of the Kabaka, in which the British had retreated before popular agitation, provided fertile soil for nationalism.

The crucial challenge lay in Central Africa. The project for the Federation of Rhodesia and Nyasaland had marked the highest tide of British African aspiration. Rooted in the old faith in the 'civilising mission,' the aim had been to create a stable, prosperous dominion under the British Crown; in the first decades it would be under white administration but eventually it would flower forth into a model for the world of multi-racial partnership. From the start it had encountered trenchant African opposition in the two northern components but the British in the mid-1950s still believed that a combination of firm government with educational progress would persuade the Africans to accept 'partnership.'

As it turned out, advancing African education strengthened African nationalism instead of weakening it.

In some measure this was due to the attitude of the white settlers, who controlled the federal government and that of Southern Rhodesia. (The local administrations of Northern Rhodesia and Nyasaland were under Colonial Office control.) Few of the settlers were of the hardy, pioneering type; they were recent immigrants who had come out to Central Africa with no ideal beyond that of seeking a higher standard of living and a more equable climate than they had known at home. During the 1950s the white suburbs of Salisbury acquired the highest number of private swimming pools per head of population in the world, except for Beverley Hills, California. The aim of the settlers was to live according to the current Euro–American ideas of affluence. They had no desire to mix with Africans socially or, indeed, to deal with them in any way save as domestic servants. If they had had their way, the Africans would have been no more significant than the American Indians—Sir Roy Welensky, the federal Prime Minister, actually employed this comparison. The settlers were neither particularly liberal nor illiberal; they were just a cross-section of non-political British people who had been led to believe by everybody they trusted that it was their right to control the Rhodesias. In supporting Welensky with his 'partnership' doctrine they thought they were being radical compared with the apartheid of the South African Nationalists and their own right-wing opposition party.

Such a community, by its nature, was unlikely to produce an imaginative political spirit. Moreover, it was really too small—under 300,000 Europeans in the whole federation—to run a proper apparatus of government. At home they would have sustained, possibly, just a single city council and three or four M.P.s for Westminster. In Central Africa they had to provide politicians and civil servants for the federation and for three territorial administrations, each complete with legislatures, plus all municipal, commercial and industrial leadership. Thus holders of many important offices in the federation were of a personal quality lower than would have been considered suitable elsewhere. Their pattern of politics was to produce a single leader in whom they placed a higher degree of personal trust than was normal within a British political pattern. They would adulate that leader unless and until it dawned upon them that he was ceasing to advance their interests; then they would turn upon him and replace him with another, equally adulated.

The system evolved only one considerable leader, the Polish–Jewish railwayman and boxing champion, Welensky. Although his political origins had lain in the roughest white supremacist politics and his formal education had been slighter than that of most African nationalist leaders, Welensky had a good intellect and a sense of historical perspective. (Oddly, his educational attainments would not have been sufficient to entitle him to vote had he been an African.) Welensky saw with clarity that both from the viewpoint of world opinion and the actual future internal condition of the federation, 'partnership' could hope to succeed only if it meant something. His difficulty was that he had to try to lean two ways at once. To Africans and to the outside world he had to stress what plentiful opportunities existed for the educated African in a multi-racial society, opportunities wider than could exist in a purely black African community. But his electorate was overwhelmingly white and to retain its allegiance he had to convince it that African advance would not upset the serenity of the white suburbs. The example of Garfield Todd was sufficient to show what could happen if this serenity were upset. Todd, son of a missionary family, was the Prime Minister of Southern Rhodesia which then had an entirely white legislature. In 1957 he proposed some relatively liberal reforms to allow Africans a modest say in the government. Overnight his followers repudiated him and he was dismissed from power. Welensky, therefore, had to keep reassuring his electorate that he would permit no African advance which would weaken what he called 'our standards' (by which he meant white standards).

Naturally every speech Welensky made about 'standards' further antagonised African nationalist opinion and, also, made liberal opinion within Great Britain more suspicious of him. The Labour Party moved from a condition of irresolution about the Central African Federation into a policy of definite opposition to it. By the time of the 1959 general election in Great Britain, the absurd position had developed that whether or not the federation could continue appeared to depend on whether the British electorate returned Conservatives or Labour to power. The fate of Central Africa appeared to depend on an election fought on British domestic matters and in which Central Africa was not an issue; so far as Central Africa was concerned, it was as much a gamble as was spinning a coin. This was the ultimate contradiction of a country democratic at home trying to run an overseas empire.

Any residual hope of getting advanced Africans to accept 'partnership' was wrecked by the social colour bar which, because of white opinion, Welensky failed to modify until the last days of the federation. It was a bitter experience for a prospering African to find himself barred from hotels, restaurants and residential areas in his own country. There were even separate entrances for whites and Africans in the Southern Rhodesian post offices. Every potential African 'partner' was subject in his daily life in the capital of the federation to intolerable humiliations. Welensky called such disabilities 'pin-pricks' but to the victims they were much more than that.

x

In the long run, however, it is unlikely that even the most generous of approaches to Africans would have enabled the federation to survive. The essential factor which had not been considered in its creation was the rise of African nationalism.

At first the main trouble was in Northern Rhodesia which, with its copper revenues, was the richest section of the federation. The pioneering African leader was Harry Nkumbula, a warm-hearted, boisterous man who had organised the original resistance to federation. Although regarded by whites as an 'agitator' he was, in fact, relatively moderate and by the late 1950s had been superseded by a more radical leader, the young Kenneth Kaunda. Born in 1924, Kaunda was a practising Christian; he was more ascetic than Nkumbula, who enjoyed the good things of life. Although frail and frequently ill, Kaunda organised his mode of living so that prison could never be a hardship to him. Extreme in his views in the sense that he demanded universal adult suffrage, he believed deeply in non-violence and did much to influence the Northern Rhodesian nationalist movement in that direction (although with less than complete success). By 1958, when Kaunda founded the Zambia African National Congress as a breakaway from Nkumbula's more moderate organisation, it was plain that he commanded the mass of African opinion in Northern Rhodesia. Welensky's protestations that the nationalists were a handful of 'agitators' sounded increasingly thin.

From Northern Rhodesia the infection spread to the other two territories, Southern Rhodesia and Nyasaland. Southern Rhodesia, which had been under firm settler control for half a century, had a relatively weak African nationalist movement; indeed up to the mid-1950s it could be counted as being even more firmly in white hands than South Africa itself. One reason why the white Dominion Party in Southern Rhodesia had opposed federation was the fear of contamination from the 'black north.' Joshua Nkomo, the African nationalist leader, was a moderate, thoughtful man, a Christian, who lacked the driving ambition of the great political pioneer. From 1957 onwards, however, the influence of younger men, fired by the example of Northern Rhodesia, at last got Southern Rhodesian African nationalism alive as a recognisable force. In Nyasaland, too, political development had been slow. This was because of the rural nature of the people and because many of the ablest by long tradition left the colony to seek their fortunes elsewhere. Nyasaland was regarded as a pleasing, truly African country, beautiful although stricken with poverty, educated black men speaking with the Scottish accents they had acquired in the Church of Scotland missions.

But it was backward little Nyasaland, which until the 1960s had virtually no Africans in responsible public office, that set off the chain of events which led to the downfall of the federation.

The leader was Dr. Hastings Banda who had been absent from the country for over 30 years. Born in 1902, he was, by the youthful standards of African nationalist politics, an elderly man. He had qualified in medicine in Tennessee and had practised in Britain and Ghana. Despite his long, self-imposed exile, he had retained a connection with his birthplace and at the outset of the federation had played some part in London in stating Nyasaland's case against it. To the local people he had become a sort of mythical hero, the great and good man who loved them from a distance. Following the example of Northern Rhodesia, Nyasaland nationalism grew during the mid-1950s and in 1958, at the request of the young men, Banda returned home to lead the movement. He had even forgotten how to speak the vernacular and he had to use interpreters at public meetings; but everywhere he drew gigantic crowds of Africans. He appeared as the liberator of the nation. His demand was for political democracy. The movement grew at a speed which astonished and then frightened the administration.

In March 1959, federal and British authorities acted in concert for the last time. A state of emergency was declared, Banda's and Kaunda's organisations were banned and the principal leaders were arrested and detained in the white stronghold of Southern Rhodesia. It was declared that Banda had been organising a plot for the wholesale murder of members of the administration.

These measures attracted world-wide publicity and caused unrest in the House of Commons in London, including some among Conservatives. Welensky did not help by arbitrarily deporting a Labour M.P., John Stonehouse, who during a visit had made speeches telling Africans to hold their heads high in their own country. It was a revelation to discover that words which would be small change in British domestic politics should be regarded in Central Africa as seditious. Moreover, it seemed to be unsatisfactory constitutionally that members of the Westminster parliament, who had the legal duty of legislating for Central Africa, should be liable to be barred from inspecting the territory. Welensky, using professional public relations consultants on a scale not known before in imperial matters, pressed for immediate independence for the federation. Only if it were evident to Africans that the final power lay with Salisbury would they come to accept it. So long as British suzerainty continued the Africans would continue to agitate, appealing to London over the settlers' heads. The net reaction in Britain, though, to the state of emergency and to Welensky's demands was a desire to investigate the facts.

Macmillan sent a commission of inquiry to Nyasaland under a British high court judge, Sir Patrick Devlin. As a Roman Catholic of Irish origin, Devlin was unlikely to have an instinctive sympathy with traditional colonialism. Moreover, he was a man of independence and intelligence on a larger scale than were characteristic of his profession. The very selection of so acute an investigator was evidence of how worried the administration had become; Macmillan must have been really looking for the truth about Central Africa.

The truth, as Devlin found it, turned out to be utterly disastrous. In his report he castigated the Nyasaland authorities. He said Banda's activities were mostly legitimate political propaganda. There had been no murder plot. In a phrase which got into headlines all over the world, the report declared: 'Nyasaland has become, doubtless only temporarily, a police state.' The British Government repudiated the less favourable aspects of the report, securing the support of the House of Commons in doing so; but this was hardly more than a formality. Really the report had bitten deep. The oratory, the imperial dreams, the truths and half-truths which had gone into the federation and into 'partnership' had narrowed down to two words which stuck, 'police state.'

At almost the same moment there arose the affair of Hola Camp in Kenya. This was a detention centre for hard-core Mau Mau prisoners, men who were sullenly determined to keep their oaths to avoid any form of co-operation with the British. In running such camps, the British idea was to 'rehabilitate' Mau Mau men by a combination of severity with the promise of freedom in return for good conduct. It was thought they had been 'brainwashed' by Mau Mau and now should be 'brainwashed' back to the British viewpoint. One aspect of the policy was to make the prisoners work, honest toil being reckoned the sure route for them back to 'civilisation.' At Hola the prisoners stolidly refused to work and the policy was adopted of forcing them to do so. The more obdurate were the prisoners, the angrier the guards became. Then, in February 1959, came a black day on which 11 members of an unco-operative African gang were literally beaten to death. The extent to which African guards were exceeding their duties was open to question but certainly they had been carrying out a policy agreed in high quarters in the Kenya administration. By standards of cruelty prevalent in the 20th century, the beating to death of 11 prisoners, even on one day, was not a major atrocity. But by the standards of British administration it was an exceptional and shocking event. Nor, under the open British system, could the atrocity be concealed; to set against the high talk of civilising the African now stood murder at Hola. It is unlikely that the event had much effect upon world opinion or, even, upon domestic British public opinion. It was, after all, a largely accidental affair caused by ill-management rather than by basic British colonial strategy. Nevertheless it shook the decision-making circles, especially the Macmillan Cabinet and the Conservative backbenchers at Westminster; coming so soon after Devlin with his 'police state' it presented colonialism in a new and unwelcome light. One Conservative, J. Enoch Powell, sat up till the small hours of the morning to launch in the House of Commons an attack on his own government. Powell had originally been an ardent imperialist and, indeed, had entered politics with the specific intention of holding India within the British system. Now he expressed the unanswerable contradiction which lay at the root of British imperialism in its final phase.

'. . . Nor can we ourselves pick and choose where and in what parts of the world we shall use this or that kind of standard. We cannot say, "We will have African standards in Africa, Asian standards in Asia and perhaps British standards here at home." We have not that choice to make. We must be consistent with ourselves everywhere. All Government, all influence of man upon man, rests upon opinion. What we can do in Africa, where we still govern and where we no longer govern, depends upon the opinion which is entertained of the way in which this country acts and the way in which Englishmen act. We cannot, we dare not, in Africa of all places, fall below our own highest standards . . .'

Devlin and Hola, between them, were the last straw in breaking what was left of British imperial morale. This was not immediately evident and it was assumed in Africa that the British general election of the autumn of 1959 would decide the future of the colonial system. If Labour were returned, it would be dismantled; but the Conservatives, if they came back, would continue to propound 'multi-racialism' on the Central African and Kenya models. As an issue before the British electorate it hardly existed but the Kenya settlers in their Muthaiga Club sat up all night to listen to the results; when they saw the Conservatives were leading, they were so joyful that they shouted 'Kenya is saved' and smashed the electric light bulbs.

However, both inside and outside the British territories, the African revolution had already spread far. Nigeria, by settled British policy, was shortly to follow the example of the Gold Coast. United Nations requirements were making the Italians give up Somaliland and this, with British Somaliland added, was due to be independent in the following year, 1960, thus realising the dream of the late 'Mad Mullah.' France under De Gaulle was embarking upon a programme of wholesale independence for her West African colonies. Belgium, in the swiftest change of policy of all, was reducing from 30 years to seven months her timetable for allowing independence for the Congo. In the one year of 1960 Africa was to be transformed from a predominantly colonial continent into predominantly an area of weak but politically sovereign states, with United Nations membership.

Within Britain, too, there had been a silent revolution. Economic pressures were in favour of Britain sacrificing a degree of sovereignty to enter the European Economic Community of six West European countries and the Macmillan government, in its decisive way, was on the point of giving in to those pressures. From the economic and business point of view, the remnants of Empire were now an irrelevancy. Trade with and investment into the underdeveloped parts of the world, so far as it was necessary, could be conducted without the apparatus of political control. What mattered was to get into what was called 'Europe.' The Commonwealth itself had never shown much interest in the colonial territories ruled from Britain and Suez had showed how useless the Commonwealth had become for underpinning Britain's world power.

In January, 1960, Macmillan embarked upon a six weeks' tour of Africa. He was the first British Prime Minister in office ever to see the continent in which his country was the major authority. Moreover, unlike such visitors of the past as King George VI, he met young and ambitious locals jostling for control of their native lands. Towards the end of the tour he reached the bastion of white supremacy, which was celebrating the 50th anniversary of dominion status.

To an audience of white legislators at Cape Town he delivered what in a sense was the greatest speech ever made by a British leader about the British Empire. It outshone anything ever said by Rosebery, Chamberlain, Smuts or Balfour at least in so far as it laid down a definitive, workable and unretractable policy. It was a speech which formally and finally surrendered the British imperial dream.

'. . . Ever since the break-up of the Roman Empire one of the most constant facts of political life in Europe has been the emergence of independent nations. They have come into existence over the centuries in different shapes with different forms of government. But all have been inspired with a keen feeling of nationalism, which has grown as the nations have grown.

'In the twentieth century, and especially since the end of the war, the processes which gave birth to the nation-states of Europe have been repeated all over the world. We have seen the awakening of national consciousness in peoples who have lived for centuries in dependence on some other power.

'Fifteen years ago this movement spread through Asia. Many countries there of different races and civilisations pressed their claims to an independent national life. Today the same thing is happening in Africa. The most striking of all the impressions I have formed since I left London a month ago is of the strength of this African national consciousness. In different places it may take different forms, but it is happening everywhere.

'The wind of change is blowing through the continent.'

# CHAPTER 16

# One with Nineveh and Tyre

DURING the early 1960s, the procedure for giving independence to British colonies slipped into a regular routine. First came one or more constitutional conferences at the former royal residence, Lancaster House. The conferences might last two or three days or two or three months, depending upon the complexity of the politics of the particular colony involved. The agreement reached by the conference was embodied in an Act of the British parliament, passed without a vote and often with a minimum of debate. Then, for the appointed independence day, one of the Queen's close relations, but never the Queen herself, travelled out for the formal ceremony of handing over power. Sometimes the ceremony took place in a specially-built 'independence stadium;' in Kenya the Delamere tradition persisted to the extent of it taking place upon Nairobi racecourse. The capital of the new country was embellished for the occasion, new roads and hotels being constructed, and the people themselves sometimes wore clothes embroidered with portraits of the new national leader. One highlight of the proceedings was an 'independence ball;' in the early period photographs of a British princess dancing with an African potentate were considered newsworthy in British newspapers—and shocking by many South Africans. At midnight on the appointed date came the independence ceremony. Police and soldiers marched up and down, politicians and the retiring British Governor made speeches. A band played 'God Save the Queen' for the last time as the territory's anthem. The union jack, lit by spotlight, fluttered down and, seconds later, to immense cheering, was replaced by the flag of the new country. The band played the new national anthem. Such ceremonies rarely rated more than a 20-second spot on British television news.

After the ceremonies, the new country applied for membership of the United Nations and of the Commonwealth. Between 1959 and 1966, the membership of the former grew from 84 to 121 and of the latter from 10 to 27. In the early years the new countries at first became 'dominions' under the continued theoretical sovereignty of the Queen; then after a year or two they became republics. The process was a confusing one and had little to do with the concept of a dominion, as devised by Balfour. It took research to find out at any given moment exactly how many titles the Queen had—whether or not she was still 'Queen of Kenya' or 'Queen of Sierra Leone'—and the process was less than dignified for the emblem of British sovereignty. As recently as 1937 Stanley Baldwin, as British Prime Minister speaking about the Commonwealth, had insisted upon the indispensibility of the monarchy. 'The Crown. The Crown is the one tangible link we all know; the link which cannot be broken. If it were, which God forbid, would the Commonwealth hold together?' This had been almost a platitude, the small change of people writing and talking about the Commonwealth. In the 1960s, in the rush of constitutional change, the Crown in Africa was just trampled down.

The new atmosphere was exemplified in the withdrawal of South Africa from the Commonwealth in 1961. The 'apartheid' policies of the South African government had, for more than a decade, been repugnant to liberal opinion within Great Britain, and, of course, utterly opposed to the ideas of the newer Asian and African members. For years there had been talk of 'expelling' South Africa from the Commonwealth but there existed no obvious machinery by which this could be done. So long as the Queen of Britain was Queen of South Africa a legal link would remain whether or not the South African Prime Minister attended Commonwealth conferences. Then the South African Nationalists, after a referendum of the white electorate, achieved their old aim of turning South Africa into a republic. Their theory, which from the point of view of their own purposes was a logical one, was that the monarchy was a force which divided rather than united the white minority; with the constitution settled upon a permanent republican basis, British and Boer settlers could work together to defend the fortress. The 'wind of change' speech, as one of its side effects, had helped to unify white South Africans.

Despite the eccentricity of their internal administration, the white South Africans were eager to appear respectable in the world and to play their part in the United Nations. Outside their own territory they had no objection to mixing with people of other races than their own. The pseudo-scientific doctrine of apartheid was a purely domestic matter. In becoming a republic, South Africa lost the automatic membership of the Common-wealth which it had enjoyed as a dominion of the Queen. It was necessary to apply for new membership as a republic and it is a reasonable supposition that Henrik Verwoerd, the South African Prime Minister, expected to get it. He wanted it as a means of maintaining South Africa's international contacts. The British government of Macmillan, announcing that the Commonwealth should be a 'bridge' between countries of different types, supported the South African application. (The 'bridge' theory had replaced that of the Commonwealth as an organic unity; another change was to call the Commonwealth a 'club' instead of the older idea that it was a 'family.') But whether or not South Africa should be readmitted was no longer a matter just for Macmillan and Verwoerd; with Malaya in the lead, the newer Commonwealth countries claimed an equal say. Canada, too, wanted South Africa out. Macmillan had to choose between losing South Africa or losing the Asian and black African Commonwealth; the moment this choice became clear he plumped for maintaining the wider Commonwealth. Verwoerd, rather than be turned down by the Commonwealth Conference, withdrew his application. So the country of Smuts, the man who had so stimulated British dreams of former enemies living happily together in one British Commonwealth of Nations, left the allegiance of the Crown and the Commonwealth. It was a victory at once for the old nationalism of the Boers and the newer nationalisms of Asia and Africa and a defeat for Great Britain.

There were two new members the same year to make up for the departure of South Africa. First came little Cyprus under her new constitution settled by international agreement, Makarios installed as President and the Eoka leader, Grivas (still muttering about Enosis), propelled back to Greece. Then came the biggest of the remaining British possessions, Nigeria with over 40 million population. With Nigerian independence, the Colonial Office lost well over one half of its subject population. The place where Lugard had worked out his 'indirect rule' became a federal state with, formally, an advanced and liberal constitution modelled upon British and Australian procedures. With its 40 million population divided into three antagonistic provinces and the whole riddled with tribal and cultural rivalries, it was doubtful whether Nigeria could survive either as a democracy or as a single country. Within the atmosphere of the 'wind of change' and because of the example of nearby Ghana, the British reckoned they had no alternative but to allow Nigeria to work out its own destiny. Indeed there was no alternative but the impossible one of trying, on a gigantic scale, to repress new but vigorous mass nationalist movements. In the short term the British could congratulate themselves that free Nigeria was less chaotic than the Congo, although civil strife was to come later. Also in 1960 came independence for Somalia, outside the Commonwealth; the new country was predominantly Italian Somaliland. Many thought it regrettable that the British did not prevent future trouble by detaching the Northern Frontier Province of Kenya, largely Somali in population, and adding it to the new republic. Had such an action been sweetened by a more rapid advance of self-government in Kenya, the African politicians in Nairobi might possibly have accepted it. At the time, though, the dream of 'multi-racialism' still had a little substance and the Nairobi Africans had to be conciliated.

With both Ghana and Nigeria independent, it was a matter only for detailed negotiation to release the remaining West African colonies. Sierra Leone, under the brothers Margai, one a doctor and the other a lawyer, became independent in 1961 and little Gambia, with 300,000 population, in 1964.

In East and Central Africa the colonies were less 'prepared' than those in the West for independence. They had fewer educated Africans; the handfuls of graduates they did possess were mostly young men. They had almost no tradition of self-government. Right up to the 'wind of change' speech there had been no Africans in senior public posts. As late as 1963 only eight of the 116 administrative grade officials in Nyasaland were African. On the other hand the demand for independence existed and British policy was now to grant it.

Tanganyika, where there had been no African politics at all until 1954, became independent in 1961 under the 40-year-old Julius Nyerere. Whereas Ghana had had six years of 'internal self-government' before being allowed independence, Tanganyika had only one year in such tutelage. The process was almost as speedy in neighbouring Uganda, which became independent in 1962 with 36-year-old Milton Obote as Prime Minister. A former executive with international building and oil companies, Obote had served only four years in the legislature at the time of independence. For a time he had over him the Kabaka of Buganda as elected President but power rested with Obote. In 1966 Obote, in actions of doubtful legality, ousted the Kabaka by force not only from the presidency but also from the royal authority in Buganda which he had inherited from Mutesa. 'King Freddie' again went on his travels and this time, unlike the time he had challenged the British, it looked as if his exile would be permanent.

The departure of South Africa from the Commonwealth brought to prominence the unsatisfactory position of the three protectorates of Bechuanaland, Basutoland and Swaziland, which had long been administered by the British High Commissioner in South Africa. Their currency, customs and economy generally were bound up with that of South Africa and, indeed, they were hardly more than 'native reserves' for South Africa. For half a century they had been neglected on the increasingly tenuous assumption that eventually they would join South Africa. Now, however, they were transferred to the Colonial Office and launched, abruptly, on a programme aimed at independence. Bechuanaland (under the formerly exiled Seretse Khama) became independent as Botswana in 1966 and Basutoland as Lesotho in the same year; Swaziland followed two years later.

Despite the 'wind of change,' Macmillan in the early 1960s still sought to protect the status of white settlers in Central Africa and Kenya. He had wanted to keep South Africa within the Commonwealth so that 'multi-racial' areas would stand in the middle of the African spectrum instead of on the extreme right. In the 'wind of change' speech itself he had gone out of his way to praise the contribution of white settlers. This policy, however, was now subject to the overriding consideration that come what might, the British now intended to surrender political direction.

The new Colonial Secretary, Iain Macleod, was an ambitious general politician rather than a colonial specialist. He retreated from 'multi-racialism' to the subtly different doctrine of 'non-racialism.' He juggled interest against interest in devising constitutions ever more complicated; the aim in both Northern Rhodesia and Kenya was so to weight the voting procedure as to require white candidates to attract African support and African ones to attract white support. The constitutions were more complicated than anything the Abbe Sieyes had devised after the French Revolution and since they were short-lived there is little point in trying to describe them in detail. The old Marquess of Salisbury called Macleod 'too clever by half.' In result, if not intention, the complicated constitutions were no more than a smoke screen behind which the British attempted to retreat with dignity. The African nationalists had only to push to get their way; whenever a hitch occurred, they just cracked the whip as when Kaunda of Northern Rhodesia hinted in 1961 at 'an uprising . . . which would, by contrast, make Mau Mau a child's picnic.' It was felt that Kaunda was talking in bad taste but he got his way. (Kaunda was delivering a warning rather than a threat.)

Kenya was the first to go. As late as May 1960, Jomo Kenyatta was still held in restriction and the Governor, Sir Patrick Renison, described him in a broadcast as 'the African leader to darkness and death.' However, there was no other leader acceptable to African nationalist opinion. Within a year of that broadcast Kenyatta had been released and within another year (Renison having been removed) he was effectively the head of the government. The Kenya white settlers were indescribably bitter about what they considered to be a betrayal but they lacked leadership and the African nationalists were full of energy and confidence. For a while the British pursued a curious policy of trying to split up the Kenya administration along tribal lines and this led to further constitutional complications. But Kenyatta, restrained and astonishingly unembittered, played his strong hand with skill. In December, 1963, Kenya became independent on the usual one man–one vote basis and the following year converted itself into a republic under Kenyatta's presidency. The statue of Delamere in the centre of Nairobi was replaced by one of Kenyatta—and the whites took to referring to Kenyatta affectionately as 'the old man,' their best protector in an African country.

The Central African Federation posed a more difficult problem in that the settlers actually provided the government and controlled the armed forces. In 1957 the British had specifically pledged themselves not to legislate for Central Africa on any matter within the competence of the federal legislature except at the request of the federal government. However, the British still controlled the territorial governments in Northern Rhodesia and Nyasaland and, to the fury of the federal Prime Minister, Roy Welensky, negotiated new constitutions in those territories which, in effect, handed power to the African nationalists. It was obvious that African nationalist governments would withdraw from the federation as soon as they could. Welensky fought back hard and at one moment appeared to be on the verge of a coup d'état in which he would have seized sovereign power. He claimed that he had been 'betrayed' by the British and, indeed, in the sense that the British had so recently promoted the federation and were now taking measures certain to result in its dismantlement, he was right. It was the British who had changed, not he. In 1962 one of the most skilful and experienced of British politicians, R. A.

Butler, was placed at the head of a new Central Africa Office, in charge of the federation's affairs. Butler, for a moment, thought of trying to remodel the federation to make it an economic rather than a political association but this rapidly proved to be a chimera.

In December, 1962, Butler pronounced the death sentence on the federation by announcing that Nyasaland, with Hastings Banda now in office, would be allowed to secede. The following April he announced that both Northern and Southern Rhodesia could do the same and by the end of the year the federation had ceased to exist. In 1964, Nyasaland became independent under the new name of Malawi and Northern Rhodesia became independent as Zambia.

These events brought a white reaction. In Southern Rhodesia there had always been a substantial body of white opinion, represented by the Dominion Party, which had distrusted the federal idea and had favoured Southern Rhodesia continuing on its own as a white stronghold, with dominion status. (Preferably with the Northern Rhodesian 'copperbelt' tacked on.) Under a new constitution negotiated between London and the federalists in 1961, Southern Rhodesia for the first time acquired African representation in its territorial parliament—15 out of 65 members—and an African franchise based upon educational and economic qualifications which would have made it possible over an unknown number of years (the minimum estimate was ten years) for the Africans to gain control of the country. For the Dominion Party this was beyond the limits of toleration and it campaigned against the new constitution. Then, recruiting such former federalists as the farmer Ian Smith, who had been Welensky's chief whip, the Dominion Party converted itself into the Rhodesia Front, which attracted generous financial support.

The Rhodesia Front fought and won the first election under the new constitution in December, 1962, driving from office the old 'establishment.' (The African nationalists boycotted this election.) The new ministers were mostly amateurs and extremists of no previous experience. They were nicknamed 'the cowboy cabinet.' Their strength rested upon an alliance between the rural farmers, who provided most of the leadership, and the white manual workers in the industries of Salisbury and Bulawayo. The middle class professional and commercial groups, which had previously run the country on lines which, in comparison to those of the Rhodesia Front, were liberal, were squeezed out. The first aim, readily achieved, was to take Southern Rhodesia out of the federation. The black Africans in the north had already fought and won that battle. The next aim was to claim immediate independence on the 1961 constitution, before Whitehall began demanding a large representation for Africans. The Rhodesia Front was determined that the 1961 constitution should mark the limit to African advance and not be, like the constitutions of Kenya and Northern Rhodesia, just a stepping stone towards the realisation of full African aspirations.

Ian Smith, who in 1963 took over the leadership of the government, was successful to the extent of shifting the grounds of dispute away from the liberalisation of the 1961 constitution to the simple one of independence. He was a flat, unimaginative man of a type who could have won power in no system save the peculiarly Rhodesian one; his main talent was a dogged obstinacy. His political ideas were a combination of a muddled Rhodesian 'patriotism' with those of the older-style British Empire. He devised the curious idea that to oppose the Rhodesia Front was to support what he called 'Communism.' Whether he believed this or whether it was just a naïve attempt to enlist United States support is not clear. The little settler-society spun itself into a web of bewildering complexity, Christian bishops and missionaries being denounced as 'Communist' agents; the visitor trying to talk politics in Southern Rhodesia in the early Smith period could feel that it was like trying to read a book in a Turkish bath. Smith himself, with his record as a war hero and his flat reiteration of his determination to maintain 'our standards' was adulated; white women lined up to kiss his photograph.

The British mistake, of course, was ever to have allowed Southern Rhodesia to revert to the unsatisfactory status of 'self-governing colony;' it was a compromise which suited nobody. A minimum of force at an early stage could have constructed a moderate administration of white liberals and African nationalists which, in a referendum, would have undoubtedly commanded the support of the population at large. Alternatively, the British could just have washed their hands of the problem, granted Smith his independence and left others to clear up the mess. It was a misjudgement to suppose that the existing position could continue.

Smith provided at least a temporary resolution of the dilemma in November, 1965, with a 'declaration of independence' that was illegal, probably treasonable and unrecognised internationally. Again, sharp action by the British at the moment of the declaration, when many members of the Civil Service and the armed forces were hesitating about their allegiance, might have removed Smith from power without excessive bloodshed. The new British Labour Government, however, had made no military provision and the Prime Minister, Harold Wilson, had specifically assured the Southern Rhodesians that he would not act against them by force.

At the moment of writing, the outcome of the Rhodesian situation is still unclear. That it should have been allowed to arise was the tragedy of the British abdication in Africa.

Smith's talk of 'Communism' was wide of the mark in relation to African nationalism generally; indeed, applied to African politics, it is an almost meaningless term. In only one area of the former British Empire in Africa did it appear as a discernible force. This was in the little clove island of Zanzibar which was given independence in December, 1963, at the same time as its neighbour Kenya. The Sultan of Zanzibar, supported by the Arab minority of the population, was recognised as sovereign. Within a month revolution broke out among the African section of the population, the Sultan was exiled and various East Germans appeared as advisers to the insurgents. How far the revolution was Communist-inspired is at the moment of writing not clear. The facts are difficult to investigate, the Zanzibar administration having the habit of imprisoning inquisitive visitors and then deporting them. After the revolution Zanzibar joined up with Tanganyika, the union being called 'Tanzania,' but there appear to be limits to the extent to which the writ of President Nyerere runs in his associated island.

Concurrently with the departure from Africa, the British were seeking to divest themselves of the scattered remnants of Empire which existed in the other continents. The theme was to try to combine small scraps of territory into federations which could form viable international units.

The federal idea had been pioneered in the West Indies but it broke down because the representatives of the larger islands were more interested in their own people than in the Caribbean as a whole. The lines of communication of such a big island as Jamaica were more with Great Britain and the United States than with neighbouring islands hundreds of miles away. The break came, indeed, when Jamaica by a referendum in 1961 voted to leave the federation. The following year Jamaica and Trinidad became independent members of the Commonwealth; their populations of 1,600,000 and 800,000 were sufficient, by the new standards, to allow them to rank as sovereign states and members of the United Nations. Barbados, with only 246,000 people, followed in 1966. The smaller islands continued as self-governing colonies until, in 1967, their position was formalised in a new status as 'Associated States,' without full Commonwealth membership or international standing. It meant that Britain continued to conduct their diplomatic affairs, to defend them and to provide economic aid. Otherwise they were self-governing and free to claim full independence whenever they chose. The British, on their side, held the right to terminate the relationship if they disliked the nature of any future regime in them. In one week early in 1967 a British minister, Arthur Bottomley, flew in a six-seater aircraft around St. Kitts, Antigua, Dominica, St. Lucia and Grenada formally to inaugurate the new status. He presented each 'Associated State' with a diamond-shaped silver dish, inscribed to mark the occasion.

Another territory in the same part of the world, British Guiana, presented more delicate problems. In 1953 the actions in power of Cheddi Jagan, reckoned by both the British and the United States to be under Communist influence, had caused the British to suspend the constitution. (The American Central Intelligence Agency helped to foment a semi-political strike aimed at Jagan.) The conundrum was to advance self-government in the territory while keeping Jagan out of power. Fortunately, from the British and American point of view, Jagan had strong opponents in the territory, led by his former associate Forbes Burnham and the complicated racial position in the island (half the population were Indians from India and the remainder consisted of six other groups—African, mixed, Portuguese, Chinese, European and American Indian) gave scope for constitutional juggling. Eventually, on a system of proportional representation, Burnham won an election and in 1966 the territory became independent under the new name of Guyana.

A more immediately successful application of the federal idea was in South-East Asia, a troubled area in which the United States had become heavily involved. The British colonies in Borneo—North Borneo, Brunei and Sarawak—were too small to stand on their own and the idea of simply giving them to Indonesia was, for a variety of reasons, repugnant. So, after referenda of their inhabitants, they were attached on a federal basis to the independent Commonwealth member Malaya under the new name of Malaysia. The failed fortress of Singapore, now controlled

Y

by the Chinese immigrants who formed the majority of the population, was included. Indonesia, claiming that the referenda on which the federation was based were less than satisfactory, attempted to upset the arrangement by force. The British, in cool military operations in which the sad lessons learned during a generation of failure were carefully applied, repulsed the Indonesian onslaught. At the moment of writing, Malaysia appears to have been established. Certainly it is difficult to suppose that the people of the formerly British areas of Borneo could for other than the most theoretical reasons prefer Indonesian administration to Malayan. But what could have been a success in the sunset of Empire was weakened by Singapore which, in 1965, left the Malaysian federation, of which geographically she was an integral part, and set up on her own. Sadly, the British saw her, too, joining the Commonwealth and becoming a sovereign state in membership with the United Nations.

The historic position in the Middle East had been lost even before the 'wind of change' speech. The great garrison which had once squatted on Egypt had moved, emasculated, to Cyprus and thence, further emasculated, to Kenya. Then came the last ditch, Aden. In the early 1960s, Aden was regarded as safe, the place from which the oil could be guarded. The climate was difficult but more and more troops and aircraft were moved there. Air-conditioned quarters, at high cost to the British taxpayer, arose around the extinct volcano; a house just for the naval commander took £23,000. Up the Persian Gulf lay Kuwait and Bahrein and, also, the new discoveries of oil in the Trucial Sheikhdoms. The Sheikh of Abu Dabai at first insisted that he should be paid in gold, which he stored to a value of millions of pounds sterling in his tent. Then his progressive half-brother conducted a coup d'état and took over the money with progressive proposals for erecting schools, hospitals, drainage and roads suitable for motor vehicles. The British accepted any authority which happened to be in charge. At the moment of writing, the Persian Gulf sheikhdoms certainly appear vulnerable to nationalist uprisings.

The intention was to use Aden as a permanent base, the continuing bastion of British power in the Middle East, and political plans were laid accordingly. The main danger, in the early 1960s, was reckoned to be Aden town with its sophisticated, turbulent population infected with Arab nationalism. Accordingly the British decided to federate Aden with the traditionalist Arab sheikhdoms in the desert hinterland, which in the 1930s had been the scene of the final expansion of the British Empire. The Arab sheikhs now supported the British and it was reckoned that they could swamp any opposition in Aden itself. The South Arabian Federation was begun to be formed from 1959 and in 1963 Aden itself acceded, only a minority of the population being allowed to vote. But the Arab nationalists, inspired and financed by Cairo, outmanoeuvred the British by winning over the populations of the sheikhdoms. Armed revolt by the National Liberation Front, on the familiar guerrilla pattern, started in 1963. The British at first did not take it seriously, condemning the N.L.F. leaders as 'a bunch of thugs' but by the mid-1960s the 18,000-strong British garrison, as had happened in so many places before, found its energies being used up just for its own security. A further complication was the appearance of a rival nationalist group, the Front for the Liberation of South Yemen and so the situation became a form of three-sided civil war. With civil war also going on in the neighbouring country of Yemen, the situation was thoroughly uncomfortable and the British began to wonder whether they really needed a base in Aden at all.

The return of the Labour Party to power in London in 1964, with its customary distaste for military expenditure and imperial adventure, clinched the situation. In 1966 the British announced that they intended to withdraw from the South Arabian Federation altogether and this deprived the sheikhs of what remained of their prestige. The following year the federal army went over to the rebels and the British decided to quit as rapidly as possible. They negotiated briefly with the winning rebel group, the National Liberation Front, at Geneva and said they would leave on November 30, 1967. It was a helter-skelter process—no new constitution had been agreed and there were no elections—and the last British forces actually left a day early, a Royal Marine band playing 'Fings Ain't Wot They Used to Be'. The new country called itself The People's Republic of South Yemen and, naturally, did not join the Commonwealth.

The other fortress-colonies of Malta and Gibraltar also presented difficulties.

Malta, the 'George Cross' island, had as always a love–hate relationship with the British. In 1955 a parliamentary commission from London had approved a unique scheme for making Malta an actual part of the United Kingdom, with representation at Westminster. This was a departure from the whole practice of British imperial administration which, after the Irish experience, had been set firmly against the dilution of the imperial parliament with non-British elements. The odd result could have been that in the narrowly-balanced parliament of 1964–66, the Maltese might have been in a position to choose the government of the United Kingdom. The scheme broke down over money, the Maltese insisting that if they were to become part of Britain their welfare services and standard of living ought to be brought up to British levels. There followed a period of chaos, with the Governor resuming direct rule, until in 1961 the island was allowed internal self-government as the 'State of Malta.' Three years later the island became an independent dominion.

Gibraltar represented an almost unique case of a colonial population struggling to remain under the union jack. Although Gibraltar was geographically a part of Spain, the population during 250 years of British rule had become largely non-Spanish. The people liked being British and found the political institutions of Spain distasteful; had it not been for this factor the British might well have ceded the territory back to Spain, which pressed its claims vigorously and, even, conducted a blockade.

At the moment of writing there remain 14 British colonies, most of them very small. In population they total less than one per cent of the old British Empire. The most outlying possessions of all, the Pacific islands, are now the leading responsibility of the shrunken Colonial Office. The policy, as expressed by Lord Caradon, British representative at the United Nations in 1965 is: 'We believe that no nation and no people and no race should be dominated by another. We believe that every nation should be free to shape its own destiny. We believe that colonialism should be ended as rapidly as possible. . . . We believe that in the small and scattered colonial territories which remain we should apply these principles.' This from a man who had governed Cyprus during Eoka is sufficient evidence of the revolution in British thinking. It could have been F. D. Roosevelt speaking. Even paternalism was now outmoded. (Actually Caradon belonged to a radical family background and had combined a career as a professional colonial administrator with a lifelong belief in liberal principles. That such a person could rise to the top in British imperial administration throws a useful sidelight on to the administration and shows one reason why it could not possibly have lasted.) The remaining territories are mostly so small that it is difficult to conceive of them becoming politically sovereign. The more likely line of development is that of the 'Associated State,' as in the West Indies.

Though independence cannot entirely be excluded as a possibility —the Maldives became sovereign, with a United Nations seat, in 1965 with only 97,000 population. Mauritius, which with 750,000 population became independent in 1968, seems a giant in contrast to the Maldives. Could even St. Helena, with 4,600 population, become a sovereign country? A special case is the colony of Hong Kong with its Chinese population disturbed by the occasional efforts of Communist China next door. China could occupy it whenever she wanted to do so but, at the moment of writing in 1968, she appears content with the present position. Hong Kong is convenient as the main point of contact between China and the non-Communist world. The colony's ultimate destiny would seem to be incorporation in China rather than independence.

So far as the end of the British Empire can be set at a definite point of time, it was the afternoon of January 19, 1968, when the Labour Prime Minister, Harold Wilson, announced the final homecoming of the British legions.

His government had already shown a disposition to wind up overseas military commitments. Aden had been abandoned and plans prepared for withdrawing by the mid-1970s the great force, based upon Singapore, which made Britain second only to the United States as a 'western' power in the Far East. During the Malaysian 'confrontation' that force had grown to 100,000 men, with ships and aircraft. Some 48,000 men had already been brought home. Now, for reasons connected with the British domestic economy, it was considered urgently necessary to reduce public expenditure and the remaining overseas garrisons seemed to be an obvious target, even though, ironically, the Americans were now wanting the British to stay. The possibility of instead reducing British forces in Europe was not regarded as realistic.

Wilson announced the withdrawal by 1970 of British forces from the Far East, except for a token garrison in Hong Kong, and, also, the withdrawal of the 8,400 men who in the Persian Gulf formed the remnants of the once mighty Middle East garrison.

Great Britain, for the first time in three centuries, had become a solely European power. It was the united aim of the three main political parties – Labour, Conservatives and Liberals – to secure admission to the European Economic Community, a fresh application having been made by Wilson in 1966.

The importance of the Commonwealth as an institution is easily both exaggerated and minimised. It has come into existence for historical reasons and, as time passes, it is likely to become weaker rather than stronger. Even in such older Commonwealth countries as Canada and Australia the old sentiment is fading and the abolition of the monarchy is capable of becoming a practical political issue. Australia, in changing from British style pounds–shillings–pence currency to a decimal system, rejected the idea of calling the new main unit the 'royal' and chose 'dollar' instead. When two members, India and Pakistan, went to war in 1965 it was the Soviet Union that mediated. With 27 members, the old intimacy has disappeared. Commonwealth conferences no longer take place in 10 Downing Street but in the more formal surroundings of Lancaster House, the delegates behaving as in any other international negotiation. In 1964 a Commonwealth Secretariat under a Canadian, Arnold Smith, was established. This was not entirely a sign of strength for the new body took over functions previously performed by the British Commonwealth Relations Office. What was probably the last Commonwealth political action was the attempt in 1965 and 1966 to handle the Rhodesian question. In this emergency was held the first-ever Commonwealth conference outside London. The place was Lagos, capital of Nigeria; military conspirators obligingly put off a coup d'état until after the Commonwealth visitors had departed. Also the emergency caused Tanzania to break off diplomatic relations with Britain, a fact which in itself showed how tenuous the Commonwealth had become. The Commonwealth could not handle Rhodesia and the matter was handed to the United Nations.

Yet in the meantime the Commonwealth holds a little reality in cultural, educational and economic matters. There is a network of between 30 and 40 specialised Commonwealth organisations, some of which do useful work. They cover a wide field and include such varied bodies as the Commonwealth Society for the Deaf, the Commonwealth Forestry Conference, the Commonwealth Council of Mining and Metallurgical Institutions, and the Commonwealth Air Transport Council. Such groups may become more significant than the Commonwealth Conference itself.

It would be profitless here to go into the jargon of 'neo-colonialism.' The British connection with the former colonies has continued and extended. More British people were working in India in 1966 than there were at the height of the Indian Empire. As in the imperial days, self-interest and idealism go together. It is as much for self-interest as charity that the British give aid to former imperial territories; markets are provided for British goods and the ultimate dangers that would lie in the permanent division of the world into rich and poor are weakened. (Whether the aid is invariably correctly applied is another matter.) Both Asia and Africa are full of vigour but unstable. As the old colonialism fades into a mere historical episode, it will be fascinating to see what emerges.

Why did the British Empire fall?

The superficial reasons are the growth of internal nationalisms, the teachings on elective governments of the British themselves, the development of communications and the domination of the world by such powers as the Soviet Union and the United States which had no sympathy with the imperial spirit. Also it can be clearly traced how the preservation of the British Empire was never the first priority of British policy.

The deeper cause is that the British Empire was an historical accident, a by-product of the first contacts between the vigorous people of Europe and the remainder of the world. The surprising thing is less that the British Empire fell than that it ever arose and could ever have seemed to be stable.

Taking the story as a whole, and admitting many faults, the British can be proud that they once had an empire. Now there is evidence of a new generation shaking itself free from the imperial dream and finding newer and more realistic goals.

# INDEX